Philip Gilbert Hamerton

Wenderholme

A Story of Lancashire and Yorkshire

Philip Gilbert Hamerton

Wenderholme
A Story of Lancashire and Yorkshire

ISBN/EAN: 9783744749404

Printed in Europe, USA, Canada, Australia, Japan

Cover: Foto ©ninafisch / pixelio.de

More available books at **www.hansebooks.com**

WENDERHOLME.

WENDERHOLME.

A STORY OF LANCASHIRE AND YORKSHIRE.

BY

PHILIP GILBERT HAMERTON,

AUTHOR OF "THE INTELLECTUAL LIFE," ETC.

"It takes a deal o' sorts to make a world."
Popular Proverb.

BOSTON:
ROBERTS BROTHERS.
1877.

Cambridge:
Press of John Wilson and Son.

TO AN OLD LADY IN YORKSHIRE.

You remember a time when the country in which this story is placed was quite different from what it is to-day; when the old proprietors lived in their halls undisturbed by modern innovation, and neither enriched by building leases, nor humiliated by the rivalry of mighty manufacturers. You have seen wonderful changes come to pass, — the valleys filled with towns, and the towns connected by railways, and the fields covered with suburban villas. You have seen people become richer and more refined, though perhaps less merry, than they used to be; till the simple, unpretending life of the poorer gentlefolks of the past has become an almost incredible tradition, which few have preserved in their memory.

When this story was first written, some passages of it were read to you, and they reminded you of those strong contrasts in the life of the North of England which are now so rapidly disappearing. WENDERHOLME is therefore associated with you in my mind as one of its first hearers, and I dedicate it to you affectionately.

PREFACE

TO THE AMERICAN EDITION.

———•———

IT happened, some time before this story was originally composed, that the author had a conversation, about the sale of novels, with one of the most eminent publishers of fiction in London.* The result of his experience was, that in the peculiar conditions of the English market short novels did not pay, whilst long ones, of the same quality, were a much safer investment. Having incurred several successive losses on short novels, my friend, the publisher, had made up his mind never to have any thing more to do with them, and strongly recommended me, if I attempted a work of fiction, to go boldly into three volumes at once, and not discourage myself by making an experiment on a smaller scale, which would only make failure a certainty. The reader may easily imagine the effect of such a conversation as this upon an author who, whatever may have been his experience in other departments of literature, had none at all in the publication of novels. The practical consequence of it was, that, when the present story was written, commercial reasons prevailed, as they unhappily so often do prevail, over artistic

---

* This publisher was not a member of the firm of Messrs. W. Blackwood & Sons, who afterwards purchased the copyright of *Wenderholme*, nor was the story ever offered to him ; but his opinion had great influence with the author on account of his large experience.

reasons, and the book was made far longer than, as a work of art, it ought to have been.

The present edition, though greatly abridged, is not by any means, from the author's point of view, a mutilated edition. On the contrary, it rather resembles a building of moderate dimensions, from which excrescences have been removed. The architect has been careful to preserve every thing essential, and equally careful to take away every thing which had been added merely for the sake of size. The work is therefore at the present time much nearer in character to the original conception of the designer than it has ever been before.

Notwithstanding the defect of too great length, and the difficulty which authors often experience in obtaining recognition in a new field, *Wenderholme* was very extensively reviewed in England, and, on the whole, very favorably. Unfortunately, however, for the author's chances of profiting by the suggestions of his critics, it so happened that when any character or incident was selected for condemnation by one writer, that identical character or incident was sure to be praised enthusiastically by another, who spoke with equal authority and decision, in some journal of equal importance. The same contradictions occurred in criticisms by private friends, people of great experience and culture. Some praised the first volume, but did not like the third; whilst others, who certainly knew quite as much about such matters, considered that the book began badly, but improved immensely as it went on, and finished in quite an admirable manner, like a horse that has warmed to his work. These differences of opinion led me to the rather discouraging conclusion that there is nothing like an accepted standard of right and wrong in the criticism of fiction; that the critic praises what interests or amuses him, and condemns what he finds tiresome, with little reference to any governing laws of art. I may observe, however, that the book had an artistic intention, which was the contrast between two classes of society in Lancashire, and that the militia was used as a means of bringing these two classes together. I may here reply to one or two objections which have been made as to the manner in which this plan was carried out.

Most of the local newspapers in the north of England at once recognized the truth of local character in the book; but one Manchester critic, with a patriotism for his native county which is a most respectable sentiment, felt hurt by my descriptions of intemperance, and treated them as a simple calumny, arguing that the best answer to them was the industry of the county, which would not have been compatible with such habits. I have never desired to imply that all Lancashire people were drunkards, but there are certain nooks and corners of the county where drinking habits were prevalent, in the last generation, to a degree which is not exaggerated in this book. Such places did not become prosperous until the energy of the better-conducted inhabitants produced a change in the local customs; and I need hardly say that the hard drinkers themselves were unable to follow business either steadily or long. Downright drunkenness is now happily no longer customary in the middle classes, and in the present day men use stimulants rather to repair temporarily the exhaustion produced by over-work than for any bacchanalian pleasure. In this more modern form of the drinking habit I do not think that Lancashire men go farther than the inhabitants of other very busy counties, or countries, where the strain on human energy is so great that there is a constant temptation to seek help from some kind of stimulating beverage.

The only other objection to the local truth of *Wenderholme* which seems to require notice is that which was advanced in the *Saturday Review*. The critic in that periodical thought it untrue to English character to represent a man in Colonel Stanburne's position as good-natured enough to talk familiarly with his inferiors. Well, if modern literature were a literature of types, and not of persons, such an objection would undoubtedly hold good. The typical Englishman, when he has money and rank, is certainly a very distant and reserved being, except to people of his own condition; but there are exceptions to this rule, — I have known several in real life, — and I preferred to paint an exception, for the simple reason that reserve and pride are the death of human interest. It would be possible enough to introduce a cold and reserved aristocrat in a novel of English life, — such personages have often been delineated with great skill and fidelity, — but I maintain that they do not excite sympathy and interest, and that it would be a mistake in art to place one of them in a central situation, such as that of Colonel Stanburne in this volume. They may be useful in their place, like a lump of ice on a dinner-table.

On the first publication of *Wenderholme*, the author received a number of letters from people who were quite convinced that they had recognized the originals of the characters. The friends and acquaintances of novelists always amuse themselves in this way; and yet it seldom happens, I believe, that there is any thing like a real

Preface to the American Edition.

portrait in a novel. A character is suggested by some real person, but when once the fictitious character exists in the brain of the author, he forgets the source of the original suggestion, and simply reports what the imaginary personage says and does. It is narrated of an eminent painter, famous for the saintly beauty of his virgins, that his only model for them was an old man-servant, and this is a good illustration of the manner in which the imagination operates. Some of my correspondents made guesses which were very wide of the mark. One lady, whom I had never thought about in connection with the novel at all, recognized herself in Mrs. Prigley, confessed her sins, and promised amendment; an illusion scarcely to be regretted, since it may have been productive of moral benefit. A whole township fancied that it recognized Jacob Ogden in a wealthy manufacturer, whose face had not been present to me when I conceived the character. A correspondent recognized Dr. Bardly as the portrait of a surgeon in Lancashire who was never once in my mind's eye during the composition of the novel. The Doctor was really suggested by a Frenchman, quite ignorant of the Lancashire dialect, and even of English. But, of all these guesses, one of the commonest was that Philip Stanburne represented the author himself, probably because he was called Philip. There is no telling what may happen to us before we die; but I hope that the supposed original of Jacob Ogden may preserve his sanity to the end of his earthly pilgrimage, and that the author of this volume may not end his days in a monastery.

P. G. H

CONTENTS.

PART I.

CHAPTER	
I. MANNERS AND CUSTOMS OF SHAYTON	1
II. GRANDMOTHER AND GRANDSON	5
III. AT THE PARSONAGE	16
IV. ISAAC OGDEN BECOMES A BACKSLIDER	29
V. FATHER AND SON	42
VI. LITTLE JACOB IS LOST	52
VII. ISAAC OGDEN'S PUNISHMENT	59
VIII. FROM SOOTYTHORN TO WENDERHOLME	69
IX. THE FUGITIVE	87
X. CHRISTMAS AT MILEND	94
XI. THE COLONEL GOES TO SHAYTON	106
XII. OGDEN'S NEW MILL	119
XIII. STANITHBURN PEEL	130
XIV. AT SOOTYTHORN	136
XV. WITH THE MILITIA	143
XVI. A CASE OF ASSAULT	150
XVII. ISAAC OGDEN AGAIN	155
XVIII. ISAAC'S MOTHER COMES	161
XIX. THE COLONEL AT WHITTLECUP	170
XX. PHILIP STANBURNE IN LOVE	174
XXI. THE WENDERHOLME COACH	179
XXII. COLONEL STANBURNE APOLOGIZES	185

CHAPTER
XXIII. HUSBAND AND WIFE 193
XXIV. THE COLONEL AS A CONSOLER 201
XXV. WENDERHOLME IN FESTIVITY 212
XXVI. MORE FIREWORKS 225
XXVII. THE FIRE 229
XXVIII. FATHER AND DAUGHTER 238
XXIX. PROGRESS OF THE FIRE 241
XXX. UNCLE JACOB'S LOVE AFFAIR 249
XXXI. UNCLE JACOB IS ACCEPTED 252
XXXII. MR. STEDMAN RELENTS 258
XXXIII. THE SADDEST IN THE BOOK 265
XXXIV. JACOB OGDEN FREE AGAIN 273
XXXV. LITTLE JACOB'S EDUCATION 280
XXXVI. A SHORT CORRESPONDENCE 284
XXXVII. AT WENDERHOLME COTTAGE 286
XXXVIII. ARTISTIC INTOXICATION 290
XXXIX. GOOD-BYE TO LITTLE JACOB 301

PART II.

I. AFTER LONG YEARS 303
II. IN THE DINING-ROOM 318
III. IN THE DRAWING-ROOM 322
IV. ALONE 327
V. THE TWO JACOBS 331
VI. THE SALE 336
VII. A FRUGAL SUPPER 340
VIII. AT CHESNUT HILL 345
IX. OGDEN OF WENDERHOLME 354
X. YOUNG JACOB AND EDITH 357

Contents.

CHAPTER

XI.	EDITH'S DECISION	366
XII.	JACOB OGDEN'S TRIUMPH	374
XIII.	THE BLOW-OUT	380
XIV.	MRS. OGDEN'S AUTHORITY	389
XV.	LADY HELENA RETURNS	393
XVI.	THE COLONEL COMES	400
XVII.	A MORNING CALL	404
XVIII.	MONEY ON THE BRAIN	409
XIX.	THE COLONEL AT STANITHBURN	418
XX.	A SIMPLE WEDDING	425
XXI.	THE MONK	431

WENDERHOLME.

PART I.

CHAPTER I.

MANNERS AND CUSTOMS OF SHAYTON.

IT was an immemorial custom in Shayton for families to restrict themselves to a very few Christian names, usually taken from the Old Testament, and these were repeated, generation after generation, from a feeling of respect to parents, very laudable in itself, but not always convenient in its consequences. Thus in the family of the Ogdens, the eldest son was always called Isaac, and the second Jacob, so that if they had had a pedigree, the heralds would almost have been driven to the expedient of putting numbers after these names, — as we say Henry VIII. or Louis XIV. The Isaac Ogden who appears in this history may have been, if collateral Isaacs in other branches were taken into account, perhaps Isaac the fortieth; indeed, the tombstones in Shayton churchyard recorded a number of Isaac Ogdens that was perfectly bewildering. Even the living Isaac Ogdens were numerous enough to puzzle any new-comer; and a postman who had not been accustomed to the place, but was sent there from Rochdale, solemnly declared that "he wished all them Hisaac Hogdens was deead, every one on 'em, nobbut just about five or six, an' then there'd be less bother about t' letters." This wish may seem hard and unchristian, — it may appear, to readers who have had no experience in the delivery of letters, that to desire the death of a fellow-creature merely because he happened to be called Isaac Ogden implied a fearful degree of natural malevolence; but the business of a postman cultivates an eagerness to get rid of letters, whereof the lay mind has no adequate conception; and when a bachelor Isaac Ogden got a letter from an affectionate wife, or an Isaac Ogden, who never owed a penny, received a pressing dun from an impatient and exasperated creditor, these epistles were returned upon the postman's hands, and he became morbidly anxious to get rid of them, or "shut on 'em," as he himself expressed it. Some annoying mistakes of this kind had occurred in reference to *our* Mr. Isaac Ogden at the time when he was engaged to Miss Alice Wheatley, whose first affectionate letter from her father's house at Eatherby had not only miscarried, but actually been opened and read by several Isaac Ogdens in Shayton and its vicinity; for poor Miss Alice, in the flurry of directing her first epistle to her lover, had quite forgotten to put the name of the house where he then lived. This was particularly annoying to Mr. Ogden, who had wished to keep his engagement secret, in order to avoid as long as possible the banter of his friends; and he sware in his wrath that there were far too many Isaac Ogdens in the world, and that, however many sons he had, he would never add to their number. This declaration was regarded by his mother, and by the public opinion of the elder generation generally, as little better than a profession of atheism; and when our little friend Jacob, about whom we shall have much to say, was christened in Shayton church, it was believed that the misguided father would not have the hardihood to maintain his resolution in so sacred a place. He had, however, the courage to resist the name of Isaac, though it was pressed upon him with painful earnestness; but he did not dare to offend tradition so far as to resist that of Jacob also, though the objections to it were in truth equally cogent.

On his retirement to Twistle Farm, an out-of-the-way little

estate up in the hill country near Shayton, Mr. Ogden, who was now a widower, determined, at least for the present, to educate his child himself. And so it was that, at the age of nine, little Jacob was rather less advanced than some other boys of his age. He had not begun Latin yet, but, on the other hand, he read English easily and with avidity, and wrote a very clear and legible hand. His friend Doctor Bardly, the Shayton medical man, who rode up to Twistle Farm very often (for he liked the fresh moorland air, and enjoyed a chat with Mr. Ogden and the child), used to examine little Jacob, and bring him amusing books, so that his young friend had already several shelves in his bedroom which were filled with instructive histories and pleasant tales. The youthful student had felt offended one day at Milend, where his grandmother and his Uncle Jacob lived, when a matronly visitor had asked whether he could read.

"He can read well enough," said his grandmother.

"Well, an' what can he read? can he read i' th' Bible?"

The restriction of Jacob's reading powers to one book offended him. Could he not read all English books at sight, or the newspaper, or any thing? Indeed, few people in Shayton, except the Doctor, read as much as the little boy at Twistle Farm; and when his uncle at Milend discovered one day what an appetite for reading the child had, he was not altogether pleased, and asked whether he could "cast accounts." Finding him rather weak in the elementary practice of arithmetic, Uncle Jacob made him "do sums" whenever he had an opportunity. Arithmetic (or "arethmitic," as Uncle Jacob pronounced it) was at Milend considered a far higher attainment than the profoundest knowledge of literature; and, indeed, if the rank of studies is to be estimated by their influence on the purse, there can be no doubt that the Milend folks were right. Without intending a pun (for this would be a poor one), Uncle Jacob had never found any thing so interesting as interest, and the annual estimate which he made of the increase of his fortune brought home to his mind a more intense sense of the delightfulness of addition than any school-boy ever experienced. But arithmetic, like every other human pursuit, has its painful or unpleasant side, and Uncle Jacob regarded subtraction and division with an indescribable horror and dread. Subtraction, in his vivid though far from poetical imagination, never meant any thing less serious than losses in the cotton trade; and division evoked the alarming picture of a wife and eight children dividing his profits amongst them. Indeed, he never looked upon arithmetic in the abstract, but saw it in the successes of the prosperous and the failures of the unfortunate, — in the accumulations of rich and successful bachelors like himself, and the impoverishment of struggling mortals, for whom there was no increase save in the number of their children. And this concrete conception of arithmetic he endeavored to communicate to little Jacob, who, in consequence of his uncle's teaching, already possessed the theory of getting rich, and was so far advanced in the practice of it that, by keeping the gifts of his kind patrons and friends, he had nearly twenty pounds in the savings bank.

CHAPTER II.

GRANDMOTHER AND GRANDSON.

MRS. OGDEN, at the time when our story commences, was not much above sixty, but had reached an appearance of old age, though a very vigorous old age, which she kept without perceptible alteration for very many years afterward. Her character will develop itself sufficiently in the course of the present narrative to need no description here; but she had some outward peculiarities which it may be well to enumerate.

She is in the kitchen at Milend, making a potato-pie, or at least preparing the paste for one. Whilst she deliberately presses the rolling-pin, and whilst the sheet of paste becomes wider and thinner under the pressure of it as it travels over the soft white surface, we perceive that Mrs. Ogden's arms, which are bare nearly to the elbow, are strong and muscular yet, but not rounded into any form that suggests reminiscences of beauty. There is a squareness and a rigidity in the back and chest, which are evidences rather of strength of body and a resolute character than of grace. The visage, too, can never have been pretty, though it must in earlier life have possessed the attractiveness of health; indeed, although its early bloom is of course by this time altogether lost, there remains a firmness in the fleshy parts of it enough to prove that the possessor is as yet untouched by the insidious advances of decay. The cheeks are prominent, and the jaw is powerful; but although the forehead is high, it suggests no ideas of intellectual development, and seems rather to have grown merely as a fine vegetable-marrow grows, than to have been developed by any exercise of thought. The nose is slightly aquiline in outline, but too large and thick; the lips, on the contrary, are thin and pale, and would be out of harmony with the whole face if the eyes did not so accurately and curiously correspond with them. Those eyes are of an exceedingly light gray, rather inclining to blue, and the mind looks out from them in what, to a superficial observer, might seem a frank and direct way; but a closer analyst of character might not be so readily satisfied with a first impression, and might fancy he detected some shade of possible insincerity or power of dissimulation. The hair seems rather scanty, and is worn close to the face; it is gray, of that peculiar kind which results from a mixture of very fair hairs with perfectly white ones. We can only see a little of it, however, on account of the cap.

Although Mrs. Ogden is hard at work in her kitchen, making a potato-pie, and although it is not yet ten o'clock in the morning, she is dressed in what in any other person would be considered rather an extravagant manner, and in a manner certainly incongruous with her present occupation. It is a theory of hers that she is so exquisitely neat in all she does, that for her there is no danger in wearing any dress she chooses, either in her kitchen or elsewhere; and as she has naturally a love for handsome clothes, and an aversion to changing her dress in the middle of the day, she comes downstairs at five o'clock in the morning as if she had just dressed to receive a small dinner-party. The clothes that she wears just now *have* in fact done duty at past dinner-parties, and are quite magnificent enough for a lady at the head of her table, cutting potato-pies instead of fabricating them, if only they were a little less shabby, and somewhat more in harmony with the prevailing fashion. Her dress is a fine-flowered satin, which a punster would at once acknowledge in a double sense if he saw the farinaceous scatterings which just now adorn it; and her cap is so splendid in ribbons that no writer of the male sex could aspire to describe it adequately. She wears an enormous cameo brooch, and a long gold chain whose fancy links are interrupted or connected by little glittering octagonal bars, like the bright glass bugles in her head-dress. The pattern of her satin is occasionally obscured by spots of grease, notwithstanding Mrs. Ogden's theory that she is too neat and careful to incur any risk of such accidents. One day her son Isaac had ventured to call his mother's attention to these spots, and to express an opinion that it might perhaps be as well to have two servants instead of one, and resign practical kitchen-work; or else that, if she *would* be a servant herself, she ought to dress like one, and not expose her fine things to injury; but Mr. Isaac Ogden received such an answer as gave him no encouragement to renew his remonstrances on a subject so delicate. "My dresses," said Mrs. Ogden, "are paid for out of my own money, and I shall wear them when I like and where I like. If ever my son is applied to to pay my bills for me, he may try to teach me economy, but I'm 'appy to say that I'm not dependent upon him either for what I eat or for what I drink, or for any thing that I put on." The other brother, who lived under the same roof with Mrs. Ogden, and saw her every day, had a closer instinctive feeling of what might and might not be said to her, and would as soon have thought of suggesting any abdication, however temporary, of her splendors, as of suggesting to Queen Victoria that she might manage without the luxuries of her station.

When the potato-pie stood ready for the oven, with an elegant little chimney in the middle and various ornaments of paste upon the crust, Mrs. Ogden made another quantity of paste, and proceeded to the confection of a roly-poly pudding. She was proud of her roly-polies, and, indeed, of every thing she made or did; but her roly-polies were really good, for, as her pride was here more especially concerned, she economized nothing, and was liberal in preserves. She had friends in a warm and fertile corner of Yorkshire who were rich in apricots, and sent every year to Milend several large pots of the most delicious apricot preserve, and she kept this exclusively for roly-polies, and had won thereby a great fame and reputation in Shayton, where apricot-puddings were by no means of everyday occurrence.

The judicious reader may here criticise Mrs. Ogden, or find fault with the author, because she makes potato-pie and a roly-poly on the same day. Was there not rather too much paste for one dinner,—baked paste that roofed over the savory contents of the pie-dish, and boiled paste that enclosed in its ample folds the golden lusciousness of those Yorkshire apricots? Some reflection of this kind may arise in the mind of Jacob Ogden when he comes back from the mill to his dinner. He may possibly think that for to-day the pie might have been advantageously replaced by a beef-steak, but he is too wise not to keep all such reflections within his own breast. No such doubts or perplexities will ever disturb his mother, simply because she is convinced that no man *can* eat too much of *her* pastry. Other people's pastry one might easily get too much of, but that is different.

And there is a special reason for the pudding to-day. Little Jacob is expected at dinner-time, and little Jacob loves pudding, especially apricot roly-poly. His grandmother, not a very affectionate woman by nature, is, nevertheless, dotingly fond of the lad, and always makes a little feast to welcome him and celebrate his coming. On ordinary days they never have any dessert at Milend, but, as soon as dinner is over, Uncle Jacob hastily jumps up and goes to the cupboard where the decanters are kept, pours himself two glasses of port, and swallows them one after the other, standing, after which he is off again to the mill. When little Jacob comes, what a difference! There is a splendid dessert of gingerbread, nuts, apples, and *fruits glacés;* there are stately decanters of port and sherry, with a bottle of sparkling elder-flower wine in the middle, and champagne-glasses to drink it from. There is plenty of real champagne in the cellars, but this home-made vintage is considered better for little Jacob, who feels no other effect from it than an almost irresistible sleepiness. He likes to see the sparkling bubbles rise; and, indeed, few beverages are prettier or pleasanter to the taste than Mrs. Ogden's elder-flower wine. It is as clear as crystal, and sparkles like the most brilliant wit.

But we are anticipating every thing; we have jumped from the very fabrication of the roly-poly to the sparkling of the elder-flower, of that elder-flower which never sparkled at Milend, and should not have done so in this narrative, until the pudding had been fully disposed of. The reader may, however, take that for granted, and feel perfectly satisfied that little Jacob has done his duty to the pudding, as he is now doing it to the nuts and wine. He has a fancy for putting his kernels into the wine-glass, and fishing them out with a spoon, and is so occupied just now, whilst grandmother and Uncle Jacob sit patiently looking on.

"Jerry likes nuts," says little Jacob; "I wonder if he likes wine too."

"It would be a good thing," said Mrs. Ogden, with her slow and distinct pronunciation, — " it would be a good thing if young men would take example by their 'orses, and drink nothing but water."

"Nay, nay, mother," said Uncle Jacob, "you wouldn't wish to see our lad a teetotaller."

"I see no 'arm in bein' a teetotaller, and I see a good deal of 'arm that's brought on with drinking spirits. I wish the lad's father was a teetotaller. But come" (to little Jacob), "you'll 'ave another glass of elder-flower. Well, willn't ye now? Then 'ave a glass of port; it'll do you *no* 'arm."

Mrs. Ogden's admiration for teetotalism was entirely theoretical. She approved of it in the abstract and in the distance, but she could not endure to sit at table with a man who did not take his glass like the rest; the nonconformity to custom irritated her. There was a curate at Shayton who thought it his duty to be a teetotaller in order to give weight to his arguments against the evil habit of the place, and the curate dined occasionally at Milend without relaxing from the rigidity of his rule. Mrs. Ogden was always put out by his empty wine-glass and the pure water in his tumbler, and she let him have no peace; so that for some time past he had declined her invitations, and only dropped in to tea, taking care to escape before spirits and glasses were brought forth from the cupboard, where they lay in wait for him. The reader need therefore be under no apprehensions that little Jacob was likely to be educated in the chilly principles of teetotalism; or at least he may rest assured that, however much its principles might be extolled in his presence, the practice of it would neither be enforced nor even tolerated.

"I say, I wish my son Isaac was a teetotaller. I hear tell of his coming to Shayton time after time without ever so much as looking at Milend. Wasn't your father in the town on Tuesday? I know he was, I was told so by those that saw him; and if he was in the town, what was to hinder him from coming to Milend to his tea? Did he come down by himself, or did you come with him, Jacob?"

"I came with him, grandmother."

"Well, and why didn't you come here, my lad? You know you're always welcome."

"Father had his tea at the Red Lion. Well, it wasn't exactly tea, for he drank ale to it; but I had tea with him, and we'd a lobster."

"I wish he wouldn't do so."

"Why, mother," said Uncle Jacob, "I see no great 'arm in drinking a pint of ale and eating a lobster; and if he didn't come to Milend, most likely he'd somebody to see; very likely one of his tenants belonging to that row of cottages he bought. I wish he hadn't bought 'em; he'll have more bother with 'em than they're worth."

"But what did he do keeping a young boy like little Jacob at the Red Lion? Why couldn't he send him here? The lad knows the way, I reckon." Then to her grandson, — "What time was it when you both went home to Twistle Farm?"

"We didn't go home together, grandmother. Father was in the parlor at the Red Lion, and left me behind the bar, where we had had our tea, till about eight o'clock, when he sent a message that I was to go home by myself. So I went home on Jerry, and father stopped all night at the Red Lion."

"Why, it was after dark, child! and there was no moon!"

"I'm not afraid of being out in the dark, grandmother; I don't believe in ghosts."

"What, hasn't th' child sense enough to be frightened in the dark? If he doesn't believe in ghosts at his age, it's a bad sign; but he's got a father that believes in nothing at all, for he never goes to church; and there's that horrid Dr. Bardly" —

"He isn't horrid, grandmother," replied little Jacob, with much spirit; "he's very jolly, and gives me things, and I love him; he gave me a silver horn."

Now Dr. Bardly's reputation for orthodoxy in Shayton was greatly inferior to his renown as a medical practitioner; but as the inhabitants had both Mr. Prigley and his curate, as well as several Dissenting ministers, to watch over the interests of their souls, they had no objection to allow Mr. Bardly to keep their stomachs in order; at least so far as was compatible with the freest indulgence in good living. His bad name for heterodoxy had been made worse by his favorite studies. He was an anatomist, and therefore was supposed to believe in brains rather than souls; and a geologist, therefore he assigned an unscriptural antiquity to the earth.

"I'm sure it's that Dr. Bardly," said Mrs. Ogden, "that's ruined our Isaac."

"Why, mother, Bardly's one o' th' soberest men in Shayton; and being a doctor beside, he isn't likely to encourage Isaac i' bad 'abits."

"I wish Isaac weren't so fond on him. He sets more store by Dr. Bardly, and by all that he says, than by any one else in the place. He likes him better than Mr. Prigley. I've heard him say so, sittin' at this very table. I wish he liked Mr. Prigley better, and would visit with him a little. He'd get nothing but good at the parsonage; whereas they tell me — and no doubt it's true — that there's many a bad book in Dr. Bardly's library. I think I shall ask Mr. Prigley just to set ceremony on one side, and go and call upon Isaac up at Twistle Farm; no doubt he would be kind enough to do so."

"It would be of no use, mother, except to Prigley's appetite, that might be a bit sharpened with a walk up to Twistle; but supposin' he got there, and found Isaac at 'ome, Isaac 'ud be as civil as civil, and he'd ax Prigley to stop his dinner; and Prigley 'ud no more dare to open his mouth about Isaac's goin's on than our sarvint lass 'ud ventur to tell you as you put too mich salt i' a potato-pie. It's poor folk as parsons talks to; they willn't talk to a chap wi' ten thousand pound till he axes 'em, except in a general way in a pulpit."

"Well, Jacob, if Mr. Prigley were only just to go and renew his acquaintance with our Isaac, it would be so much gained, and it might lead to his amendment."

"Mother, I don't think he needs so much amendment. Isaac's right enough. I believe he's always sober up at Twistle; isn't he, little 'un?"

Little Jacob, thus appealed to, assented, but in rather a doubtful and reserved manner, as if something remained behind which he had not courage to say. His grandmother observed this.

"Now, my lad, tell me the whole truth. It can do your father no 'arm — nothing but good — to let us know all about what he does. Your father is my son, and I've a right to know all about him. I'm very anxious, and 'ave been, ever since I knew that he was goin' again to the Red Lion. I 'oped he'd given that up altogether. You must tell me — I insist upon it."

Little Jacob said nothing, but began to cry.

"Nay, nay, lad," said his uncle, "a great felly like thee should never skrike. Thy grandmother means nout. Mother, you're a bit hard upon th' lad; it isn't fair to force a child to be witness again' its own father." With this Uncle Jacob rose and left the room, for it was time for him to go to the mill; and then Mrs. Ogden rose from her chair, and with the stiff stately walk that was habitual to her, and that she never could lay aside even under strong emotion, approached her grandson, and, bending over him, gave him one kiss on the forehead. This kiss, be it observed, was a very exceptional event. Jacob always kissed his grandmother when he came to Milend; but she was invariably passive, though it was plain that the ceremony was agreeable to her, from a certain softness that spread over her features, and which differed from their habitual expression. So when Jacob felt the old lady's lips upon his forehead, a thrill of tenderness ran through his little heart, and he sobbed harder than ever.

Mrs. Ogden drew a chair close to his, and, putting her hand on his brow so as to turn his face a little upwards that she might look well into it, said, "Come now, little un, tell granny all about it."

What the kiss had begun, the word "granny" fully accomplished. Little Jacob dried his eyes and resolved to tell his sorrows.

"Grandmother," he said, "father is so — so" —

"So *what*, my lad?"

"Well, he beats me, grandmother!"

Now Mrs. Ogden, though she loved Jacob as strongly as her nature permitted, by no means wished to see him entirely exempt from corporal punishment. She knew, on the authority of Scripture, that it was good for children to be beaten, that the rod was a salutary thing; and she at once concluded that little Jacob had been punished for some fault which in her own code would have deserved such punishment, and would have drawn it down upon her own sons when they were of his age. So she was neither astonished nor indignant, and asked, merely by way of continuing the conversation, —

"And when did he beat thee, child?"

If Jacob had been an artful advocate of his own cause, he would have cited one of those instances unhappily too numerous during the last few months, when he had been severely punished on the slightest possible pretexts, or even without any pretext whatever; but as recent events occupy the largest space in our recollection, and as all troubles diminish by a sort of perspective according to the length of time that has happened since their occurrence, Jacob, of course, instanced a beating that he had received that very morning, and of which certain portions of his bodily frame, by their uncommon stiffness and soreness, still kept up the most lively remembrance.

"He beat me this morning, grandmother."

"And what for?"

"Because I spilt some ink on my new trowsers that I'd put on to come to Milend."

"Well, then, my lad, all I can say is that you deserved it, and should take better care. Do you think that your father is to buy good trowsers for you to spill ink upon them the very first time you put them on? You'll soon come to ruin at that rate. Little boys should learn to take care of their things; your Uncle Jacob was as kerfle* as possible of his things; indeed he was the kerflest boy I ever saw in all my

* Careful.

life, and I wish you could take after him. It's a very great thing is kerfleness. There's people as thinks that when they've worn * their money upon a thing, it's no use lookin' after it, and mindin' it, because the money's all worn and gone, and so they pay no heed to their things when once they've got them. And what's the consequence? They find that they have to be renewed, that new ones must be bought when the old ones ought to have been quite good yet; and so they spend and spend, when they might spare and have every thing just as decent, if they could only learn a little kerfleness."

After this lecture, Mrs. Ogden slowly rose from her seat and proceeded to put the decanters into a triangular cupboard that occupied a corner of the room. In due course of time the apples, the gingerbread, and the nuts alike disappeared in its capacious recesses, and were hidden from little Jacob's eyes by folding-doors of dark mahogany, polished till they resembled mirrors, and reflected the window with its glimpse of dull gray sky. After this Mrs. Ogden went into the kitchen to look after some household affairs, and her grandson went to the stable to see Jerry, and to make the acquaintance of some puppies which had recently come into the world, but were as yet too blind to have formed any opinion of its beauties.

* Spent.

CHAPTER III.

AT THE PARSONAGE.

MRS. OGDEN'S desire to bring about a renewal of the acquaintance between her son Isaac and Mr. Prigley was not an unwise one, even if considered independently of his religious interests. Mr. Prigley, though by no means a man of first-rate culture or capacity, was still the only gentleman in Shayton, — the only man in the place who resolutely kept himself up to the standard of the outer world, and refused to adopt the local dialect and manners. No doubt the Doctor was in a certain special sense a gentleman, and much more than a gentleman, — he was a man of high attainment, and had an excellent heart. But, so far from desiring to rise above the outward ideal of the locality, he took a perverse pleasure in remaining a little below it. His language was a shade more provincial than that of the neighboring manufacturers, and his manners somewhat more rugged and abrupt than theirs. Perhaps he secretly enjoyed the contrast between the commonplace exterior which he affected, and the elaborate intellectual culture which he knew himself to possess. He resembled the house he lived in, which was, as to its exterior, so perfectly commonplace that every one would pass it without notice, yet which contained greater intellectual riches, and more abundant material for reflection, than all the other houses in Shayton put together. Therefore, if I say that Mr. Prigley was the only gentleman in the place, I mean externally, — in language and manner.

The living of Shayton was a very meagre one, and Mr.

Prigley had great difficulty in keeping himself above water; but there is more satisfaction in struggling with the difficulties of open and avowed poverty than in maintaining deceitful appearances, and Mr. Prigley had long since ceased to think about appearances at all. It had happened some time ago that the carpets showed grievous signs of wear, and in fact were so full of holes as to be positively dangerous. They had been patched and mended over and over again, and an ingenious seamstress employed by Mrs. Prigley, and much valued by her, had darned them with variously colored wools in continuation of the original patterns, so that (unless on close inspection) the repairs were not very evident. Now, however, both Mrs. Prigley and the seamstress, notwithstanding all their ingenuity and skill, had reluctantly come to the conclusion that to repair the carpets in their present advanced stage of decay it would be necessary to darn nothing less than the whole area of them, and Mrs. Prigley declared that she would rather manufacture new ones with her knitting-needles. But if buying carpets was out of the question, so it was not less out of the question for Mrs. Prigley to fabricate objects of luxury, since her whole time was taken up by matters of pressing necessity; indeed, the poor lady could only just keep up with the ceaseless accumulations of things that wanted mending; and whenever she was unwell for a day or two, and unable to work, there rose such a heap of them as made her very heart sink. In this perplexity about the carpets, nature was left to take her course, and the carpets were abandoned to their fate, but still left upon the floors; for how were they ever to be replaced? By a most unfortunate coincidence, Mr. Prigley discovered about the same time that his shirts, though apparently very sound and handsome shirts indeed, had become deplorably weak in the tissue; for if, in dressing himself in a hurry, his hand did not just happen to hit the orifice of the sleeve, it passed through the fabric of the shirt itself, and that with so little difficulty that he was scarcely aware of any impediment; whilst if once the hem were severed, the immediate consequence was a rent more than a foot long. Poor Mrs. Prigley had mended these patiently for a while; but one day, after marvelling how it happened that her husband had become so violent in his treatment of his linen, she tried the strength of it herself, and, to use her own expressive phrase, "it came in two like a sheet of wet paper." It was characteristic of the Prigleys that they determined to renew the linen at once, and to abandon carpets for ever.

Shayton is not in France, and to do without carpets in Shayton amounts to a confession of what, in the middle class, is looked upon as a pitiable destitution. Mr. Prigley did not care much about this; but his wife was more sensitive to public opinion, and, long after that heroic resolution had been taken, hesitated to put it in execution. Day after day the ragged remnants remained upon the floor, and still did Mrs. Prigley procrastinate.

Whilst things were in this condition at the parsonage, the conversation took place at Milend which we have narrated in the preceding chapter; and as soon as Mrs. Ogden had seen things straight in the kitchen, she "bethought her," as she would have herself expressed it, that it might be a step towards intercourse between Isaac Ogden and the clergyman if she could make little Jacob take a fancy to the parsonage. There was a little boy there nearly his own age, and as Jacob was far too much isolated, the acquaintance would be equally desirable for him. The idea was by no means new to her; indeed, she had long been anxious to find suitable playmates for her grandson, a matter of which Isaac did not sufficiently perceive the importance; and she had often intended to take steps in this direction, but had been constantly deterred by the feelings of dislike to Mr. Prigley, which both her sons did not hesitate to express. What had Mr. Prigley done to them that they should never be able to speak of him without a shade of very perceptible aversion or contempt? They had no definite accusation to make against him; they did not attempt to justify their antipathy, but the antipathy did not disguise itself. In an agricultural district the relations between the parson and the squire are often cordial; in a manufacturing district the relations between the parson and the mill-owners are usually less intimate, and have more the character of accidental neighborship than of natural alliance.

The intercourse between Milend and the parsonage had been so infrequent that Mrs. Prigley was quite astonished when Betty, the maid-of-all-work, announced Mrs. Ogden as she pushed open the door of the sitting-room. But she was much more astonished when Mrs. Ogden, instead of quietly advancing in her somewhat stiff and formal manner, fell forward on the floor with outstretched arms and a shriek. Mrs. Prigley shrieked too, little Jacob tried manfully to lift up his grandmother, and poor Betty, not knowing what to say under circumstances so unexpected, but vaguely feeling that she was likely to incur blame, and might possibly (though in some manner not yet clear to her) deserve it, begged Mrs. Ogden's pardon. Mr. Prigley was busy writing a sermon in his study, and being suddenly interrupted in the midst of what seemed to him an uncommonly eloquent passage on the spread of infidelity, rushed to the scene of the accident in a state of great mental confusion, which for some seconds prevented him from recognizing Mrs. Ogden, or Mrs. Ogden's bonnet, for the lady's face was not visible to him as he stood amazed in the doorway. "Bless me!" thought Mr. Prigley, "here's a woman in a fit!" And then came a dim and somewhat unchristian feeling that women liable to fits need not just come and have them in the parlor at the parsonage. "It's Mrs. Ogden, love," said Mrs. Prigley; "and, oh dear, I *am* so sorry!"

By the united efforts of the parson and his wife, joined to those of Betty and little Jacob, Mrs. Ogden was placed upon the sofa, and Mr. Prigley went to fetch some brandy from the dining-room. On his way to the door, the cause of the accident became apparent to him in the shape of a yawning rent in the carpet, which was dragged up in great folds and creases several inches high. He had no time to do justice to the subject now, and so refrained from making any observation; but he fully resolved that, whether Mrs. Prigley liked it or not, all ragged old carpets should disappear from the parsonage as soon as Mrs. Ogden could be got out of it. When Mrs. Prigley saw the hole in her turn, she was overwhelmed with a sense of culpability, and felt herself to be little better than a murderess.

"Betty, run and fetch Dr. Bardly as fast as ever you can."

"Please let *me* go," said little Jacob; "I can run faster than she can."

The parson had a professional disapproval of Dr. Bardly because he would not come to church, and especially, perhaps, because on the very rare occasions when he *did* present himself there, he always contrived to be called out in time to escape the sermon; but he enjoyed the Doctor's company more than he would have been willing to confess, and had warmly seconded Mrs. Prigley's proposal that, since Mrs. Ogden, in consequence of her accident, was supposed to need the restoration of "tea and something to it," the Doctor should stay tea also. The arrival of Isaac and Jacob gave a new turn to the matter, and promised an addition to the small tea-party already organized.

It was rather stiff and awkward just at first for Isaac and Jacob when they found themselves actually in the parson's house, and forced to stop there to tea out of filial attention to their mother; but it is wonderful how soon Mr. Prigley contrived to get them over these difficulties. He resolved to take advantage of his opportunity, and warm up an acquaintance that might be of eminent service in certain secret projects of his. Shayton church was a dreary old building of the latest and most debased Tudor architecture; and, though it sheltered the inhabitants well enough in their comfortable old pews, it seemed to Mr. Prigley a base and degraded sort of edifice, unfit for the celebration of public worship. He therefore nourished schemes of reform; and when he had nothing particular to do, especially during the singing of the hymns, he could not help looking up at the flat ceiling and down along the pew-partitioned floor, and thinking what might be done with the old building,—how it would look, for instance, if those octagon pillars that supported those hateful longitudinal beams were crowned with beautiful Gothic arches supporting a lofty clerestory above; and how the organ, instead of standing just over the communion-table, and preventing the possibility of a creditable east window, might be removed to the west end, to the inconvenience, it is true, of all the richest people in the township, who held pews in a gallery at that end of the church, but to the general advancement of correct and orthodox principles. Once the organ removed, a magnificent east window might gleam gorgeously over the renovated altar, and Shayton church might become worthy of its incumbent.

And now, as he saw, by unhoped-for good-luck, these three rich Ogdens in his own parlor, it became Mr. Prigley's earnest wish to keep them there as long as possible, and cultivate their acquaintance, and see whether there was not some vulnerable place in those hard practical minds of theirs. As for the Doctor, he scarcely hoped to get any money out of *him;* he had preached at him over and over again, and, though the Doctor only laughed and took care to keep out of the way of these sermons, it was scarcely to be expected that he should render good for evil,—money for hard language. Nobody in Shayton precisely knew what the Doctor's opinions were; but when Mr. Prigley was writing his most energetic onslaughts on the infidel, it is certain that the type in the parson's mind had the Doctor's portly body and plain Socratic face.

Mrs. Prigley had rather hesitated about asking the man to stay tea at the parsonage, for her husband freely expressed his opinion of him in privacy, and when in a theological frame of mind spoke of him with much the same aversion that Mrs. Prigley herself felt for rats and toads and spiders. And as she looked upon the Doctor's face, it seemed to her at first the face of the typical "bad man," in whose existence she firmly believed. The human race, at the parsonage, was divided into sheep and goats, and Dr. Bardly was amongst the goats. Was he not evidently a goat? Had not nature herself stamped his badness on his visage! His very way of laughing had something suspicious about it; he seemed always to be thinking more than he chose to express. What was he thinking? There seemed to be something doubtful and wrong even about his very whiskers, but Mrs. Prigley could not define it, neither can we. On the contrary, they were respectable and very commonplace gray whiskers, shaped like mutton-chops, and no doubt they would have seemed only natural to Mrs. Prigley, if they had been more frequently seen in Shayton church.

It was a very pleasant-looking tea-table altogether. Mrs. Prigley, who was a Miss Stanburne of Byfield, a branch of the Stanburnes of Wenderholme, possessed a little ancestral plate, a remnant, after much subdivision, of the magnificence of her ancestors. She had a tea-pot and a coffee-pot, and a very quaint and curious cream-jug; she also possessed a pair of silver candlesticks, of a later date, representing Corinthian columns, and the candles stood in round holes in their graceful acanthus-leaved capitals. Many clergymen can display articles of contemporary manufacture bearing the most flattering inscriptions, but Mr. Prigley had never received any testimonials, and, so long as he remained in Shayton, was not in the least likely to enrich his table with silver of that kind. Mrs. Prigley, whilst apparently listening with respectful attention to Mrs. Ogden's account of a sick cow of hers (in which Mrs. Ogden seemed to consider that she herself, and not the suffering animal, was the proper object of sympathy), had in fact been debating in her own mind whether she ought to display her plate on a mere chance occasion like the present; but the common metal tea-pot was bulged and shabby, and the thistle in electro-plate, which had once decorated its lid, had long since been lost by one of the children, who had fancied it as a plaything. The two brass candlesticks were scarcely more presentable; indeed, one of them would no longer stand upright, and Mrs. Prigley had neglected to have it repaired, as one candle sufficed in ordinary times; and when her husband wrote at night, he used a tin bed-candlestick resembling a frying-pan, with a tin column, *not* of the Corinthian order, sticking up in the middle of it, and awkwardly preventing those culinary services to which the utensil seemed naturally destined. As these things were not presentable before company, Mrs. Prigley decided to bring forth her silver, but in justice to her it is necessary to say that she would have preferred something between the two, as more fitted to the occasion. For similar reasons was displayed a set of old china, of whose value the owner herself was ignorant; and so indeed would have been the present writer, if he had not recognized Mrs. Prigley's old cups and saucers in Jacquemart's 'Histoire de la Porcelaine.'

The splendor of Mrs. Prigley's tea-table struck Mrs. Ogden with a degree of surprise which she had not art enough to conceal, for the manners and customs of Shayton had never inculcated any kind of reticence as essential to the ideal of good-breeding. The guests had scarcely taken their places round this brilliant and festive board when Mrs. Ogden said, —

"You've got some very *'andsome* silver, Mrs. Prigley. I'd no idea you'd got such 'andsome silver. Those candlesticks are taller than any we've got at Milend."

A slight shade of annoyance passed across the countenance of the hostess as she answered, "It came from Wenderholme;

there's not much of it except what is on the table; there were six of us to divide it amongst."

"Those are the Stanburne arms on the tea-pot," said the Doctor; "I've hoftens noticed them at Wendrum 'all. They have them all up and down. Young Stanburne's very fond of his coat-of-arms, but he's a right to be proud of it, for it's a very old one. He's quite a near relation of yours, isn't he, Mrs. Prigley?"

"My father and his grandfather were brothers, but there was a coolness between them on account of a small estate in Yorkshire, which each thought he'd a right to, and they had a lawsuit. My father lost it, and never went to Wenderholme again; and they never came from Wenderholme to Byfield. When my Uncle Reginald died, my father was not even asked to the funeral, but they sent him gloves and a hatband."

"Have you ever been at Wenderholme, Mrs. Prigley?" said Isaac.

"Never! I've often thought I should like to see it, just once; it's said to be a beautiful place, and I should like to see the house my poor father was born in."

"Why, it's quite close to Shayton, a great deal nearer than anybody would think. It isn't much more than twelve or fourteen miles off, and my house at Twistle is within nine miles of Wenderholme, if you go across the moor. There is not a single building of any kind between. But it's thirty miles to Wenderholme by the turnpike. You have to go through Sootythorn."

"It's a very nice estate," said Uncle Jacob; and, to do him justice, he was an excellent judge of estates, and possessed a great fund of information concerning all the desirable properties in the neighborhood, for he made it his business to acquire this sort of knowledge beforehand, in case such properties should fall into the market. So that when Uncle Jacob said an estate was "very nice," you may be sure it was so.

"There are about two thousand acres of good land at Wendrum," he continued, "all in a ring-fence, and a very large moor behind the house, with the best shooting anywhere in the whole country. Our moors join up to Mr. Stanburne's, and, if the whole were put together, it would be a grand shooting."

"That is," said Mr. Prigley, rather maliciously, "if Mr. Stanburne were to buy your moor, I suppose. Perhaps he might feel inclined to do so if you wished to sell."

Mrs. Ogden could not endure to hear of selling property, even in the most remote and hypothetical manner. Her back was generally as straight as a stone wall, but it became, if possible, straighter and stiffer, as, with a slight toss of the head, she spoke as follows :—

"We don't use selling property, Mr. Prigley; we're not sellers, we are buyers."

These words were uttered slowly, deliberately, and with the utmost distinctness, so that it was not possible for any one present to misunderstand the lady's intention. She evidently considered buying to be the nobler function of the two, as implying increase, and selling to be a comparatively degrading operation, — a confession of poverty and embarrassment. This feeling was very strong, not only in Shayton, but for many miles round it, and instances frequently occurred of owners who clung to certain properties against their pecuniary interest, from a dread of it being said of them that they had sold land. There are countries where this prejudice has no existence, and where a rich man sells land without hesitation when he sees a more desirable investment for his money; but in Shayton a man was married to his estate or his estates (for in this matter polygamy was allowed); and though the law, after a certain tedious and expensive process, technically called conveyancing, permitted divorce, public opinion did *not* permit it.

Mr. Prigley restored the harmony of the evening by admitting that the people who sold land were generally the old landowners, and those who bought it were usually in trade,— not a very novel or profound observation, but it soothed the wounded pride of Mrs. Ogden, and at the same time flattered a shade of jealousy of the old aristocracy which coexisted with much genuine sympathy and respect.

"But we shouldn't say Mister Stanburne now," observed the Doctor; "he's Colonel Stanburne."

"Do militia officers keep their titles when not on duty?" asked Mr. Isaac.

"Colonels always do," said the Doctor, "but captains don't, in a general way, though there are some places where it is the custom to call 'em captain all the year round. I suppose Mr. Isaac here will be Captain Ogden some of these days."

"I was not aware you intended to join the militia, Mr. Isaac," said the clergyman. "I am very glad to hear it. It will be a pleasant change for you. Since you left business, you must often be at a loss for occupation."

"I've had plenty to do until a year or two since in getting Twistle Farm into order. It's a wild place, but I've improved it a good deal, and it amused me. I sometimes wish it were all to be done over again. A man is never so happy as when he's very busy about carrying out his own plans."

"You made a fine pond there, didn't you?" said Mr. Prigley, who always had a hankering after this pond, and was resolved to improve his opportunity.

"Yes, I need a small sheet of water. It is of use to me nearly the whole year round. I swim in it in summer, I skate on it in winter, and in the spring and autumn I can sail about on it in a little boat, though there is not much room for tacking, and the pond is too much in a hollow to have any regular wind."

"Ah! when the aquatic passion exists in any strong form," said Mr. Prigley, "it will have its exercise, even though on a small scale. One of the great privations to me in Shayton is that I never get any swimming."

"My pond is very much at your service," said Mr. Isaac, politely. "I am sorry that it is so far off, but one cannot send it down to Shayton in a cart, as one might send a shower-bath."

Mrs. Ogden was much pleased to see her scheme realizing itself so naturally, without any ingerence of her own, and only regretted that it was not the height of summer, in order that Mr. Prigley might set off for Twistle Farm the very next morning. However enthusiastic he might be about swimming, he could scarcely be expected to explore the too cool recesses of the Twistle pond in the month of November, — at least for purposes of enjoyment; and Mrs. Ogden was not Papist enough to encourage the good man in any thing approaching to a mortification of the flesh.

Little Jacob had been admitted to the ceremony of tea, and had been a model of good behavior, being "seen and not heard," which in Shayton comprised the whole code of etiquette for youth when in the presence of its seniors and superiors. Luckily for our young friend, he sat between the Doctor and the hostess, who took such good care of him that by the time the feast was over he was aware, by certain feelings of tightness and distension in a particular region, that the necessities of nature were more than satisfied, although, like Vitellius, he had still quite appetite enough for another equally copious repast if only he had known where to put it. If Sancho Panza had had an equally indulgent physician at his side, one of the best scenes in Don Quixote could never have been written, for Dr. Bardly never hindered his little neighbor, but, on the other hand, actually encouraged him to do his utmost, and mentally amused himself by enumerating the pieces of tea-cake and buttered toast, and the helpings to crab and potted meat, and the large spoonfuls of raspberry-jam, which our hero silently absorbed. The Doctor, perhaps, acted faithfully by little Jacob, for if nature had not intended boys of his age to acomplish prodigies in eating, she would surely never have endowed them with such vast desires ; and little Jacob suffered no worse results from his present excesses than the uncomfortable tightness already alluded to, which, as his vigorous digestion operated, soon gave place to sensations of comparative elasticity and relief.

The parson's children had not been admitted to witness and partake of the splendor of the festival, but had had their own tea — or rather, if the truth must be told, their meal of porridge and milk — in a nursery upstairs. They had been accustomed to tea in the evening, but of late the oatmeal-porridge which had always been their breakfast had been repeated at tea-time also, as the Prigleys found themselves compelled to measures of still stricter economy. People must be fond of oatmeal-porridge to eat it with pleasure seven hundred times a-year ; and whenever a change *did* come, the children at the parsonage relished it with a keenness of gastronomic enjoyment which the most refined epicure might envy, and which he probably never experienced. There were five little Prigleys, and it is a curious fact that the parson's children were the only ones in the whole parish that did not bear Biblical names. All the other households in Shayton sought their names in the Old Testament, and had a special predilection for the most ancient and patriarchal ones ; but the parson's boys were called Henry and William and Richard, and his girls Edith and Constance — not one of which names are to be found anywhere in Holy Scripture, either in the Old Testament or the New.

CHAPTER IV.

ISAAC OGDEN BECOMES A BACKSLIDER.

ABOUT a month later in the year, when December reigned in all its dreariness over Shayton, and the wild moors were sprinkled with a thin scattering of snow, little Jacob began to be very miserable.

His grandmother had gone to stay a fortnight with some old friends of hers beyond Manchester, and his father had declared that for the next two Sundays he should remain at Twistle, and not "go bothering his uncle at Milend." Mr. Prigley had walked up to the farm, and kindly offered to receive little Jacob at the parsonage during Mrs. Ogden's absence; but Mr. Isaac had declined the proposal rather curtly, and, as Mr. Prigley thought, in a manner that did not sufficiently acknowledge the kindness of his intention. Indeed, the clergyman had not been quite satisfied with his reception; for although Mr. Isaac had shown him the pond, and given him something to eat, there had been, Mr. Prigley thought, symptoms of secret annoyance or suppressed irritation. Little Jacob's loneliness was rendered still more complete by the continued absence of his friend the Doctor, who, in consequence of a disease then very prevalent in the neighborhood, found his whole time absorbed by pressing professional duties, so that the claims of friendship, and even the anxious interest which he took in Mr. Isaac's moral and physical condition, had for the time to be considered in abeyance. We have already observed that Mr. Jacob Ogden of Milend never came to Twistle Farm at all, so that his absence was a matter of course; and as he was not in the habit of writing any letters except about business, there was an entire cessation of intercourse with Milend.

It had been a part of Mr. Isaac's plan of reformation not to keep spirits of any kind at the farm, but he had quite enough ale and wine to get drunk upon in case his resolution gave way. He had received such a lecture from the Doctor after that evening at the parsonage as had thoroughly frightened him. He had been told, with the most serious air that a doctor knows how to assume, that his nervous system was already shattered, that his stomach was fast becoming worthless, and that, if he continued his present habits, his life would terminate in eighteen months. Communications of this kind are never agreeable, but they are especially difficult to bear with equanimity when the object of them has lost much of the combative and recuperative powers which belong to a mind in health; and the Doctor's terrible sermon produced in Mr. Isaac *not* a manly strength of purpose that subdues and surmounts evil, and passes victoriously beyond it, but an abject terror of its consequences, and especially a nervous dread of the Red Lion. He would enter that place no more, he was firmly resolved upon *that*. He would stay quietly at Twistle Farm and occupy himself, — he would try to read, — he had often regretted that business and pleasure had together prevented him from cultivating his mind by reading, and now that the opportunity was come, he would seize it and make the most of it. He would qualify himself to direct little Jacob's studies, at least so far as English literature went. As for Latin, the little he ever knew had been forgotten many years ago, but he might learn enough to judge of his boy's progress, and perhaps help him a little. He knew no modern language, and had not even that pretension to read French which is so common in England, and which is more injurious to the character of the nation than perfect ignorance, whilst it is equally unprofitable to its intellect. If Mr. Isaac were an ignorant man, he had at least the great advantage of clearly knowing that he was so, but it might not even yet be too late to improve himself. Had he not perfect leisure? could he not study six hours a day, if he were so minded? This would be better than destroying himself in eighteen months in the parlor at the Red Lion.

There were not many books at Twistle, but there *were* books. Mr. Isaac differed from his brother Jacob, and from the other men in Shayton, in having long felt a hankering after various kinds of knowledge, though he had never possessed the leisure or the resolution to acquire it. There was a bookseller's shop in St. Ann's Square, in Manchester, which he used to pass when he was in the cotton business on his way from the exchange to a certain oyster-shop where it was his custom to refresh himself; and he had been occasionally tempted to make purchases, — amongst the rest, the works of Charles Dickens and Sir Walter Scott, and the 'Encyclopædia Britannica.' He had also bought Macaulay's 'History of England,' and subscribed to a library edition of the British poets in forty volumes, and a biographical work containing lives of eminent Englishmen, scarcely less voluminous. These, with several minor purchases, constituted the whole collection, — which, though not extensive, had hitherto much more than sufficed for the moderate wants of its possessor. He had read all the works of Dickens, having been enticed thereto by the pleasant merriment in 'Pickwick;' but the Waverley Novels had proved less attractive, and the forty volumes of British poets reposed uncut upon the shelf which they adorned. Even Macaulay's History, though certainly not less readable than any novel, had not yet been honored with a first perusal; and, as Mr. Ogden kept his books in a bookcase with glass doors, the copy was still technically a new one.

He resolved now that all these books should be *read*, all except perhaps the 'Encyclopædia Britannica;' for Mr. Ogden was not then aware of the fact, which a successful man has recently communicated to his species, that a steady reading of that work according to its alphabetical arrangement *may* be a road to fortune, though it must be admitted to be an arduous one. He would begin with Macaulay's History; and he *did* begin one evening in the parlor at Twistle Farm after Sarah had removed the tea-things. He took down the first volume, and began to cut the leaves; then he read a page or two, but, in spite of the lucid and engaging style of the historian, he felt a difficulty in fixing his attention, — the difficulty common to all who are not accustomed to reading, and which in Mr. Ogden's case was perhaps augmented by the peculiar condition of his nervous system. So he read the page over again, but could not compel his mind to follow the ideas of the author: it *would* wander to matters of everyday interest and habit, and then there came an unutterable sense of blankness and dulness, and a craving — yes, an all but irresistible craving — for the stimulus of drink. There could be no harm in drinking a glass of wine, — everybody, even ladies, might do that, — and he had always allowed himself wine at Twistle Farm. He would see whether there was any in the decanters. What! not a drop? No port in the port decanter, and in the sherry decanter nothing but a shallow stratum of liquid which would not fill a glass, and was not worth drinking. He would go and fill both decanters himself: there ought always to be wine ready in case any one should come. Mr. Prigley might walk up any day, or the Doctor might come, and he always liked a glass or two of port.

There was a nice little cellar at Twistle Farm, for no inhabitant of Shayton ever neglects that when he builds himself a new house; and Mr. Ogden had wine in it to the value of three hundred pounds. Some friends of his near Manchester, who came to see him in the shooting season and help him to kill his grouse, were connoisseurs in port, and he had been careful to "lay down" a quantity of the finest he could get. He was less delicate in the gratification of his own palate, and contented himself with a compound of no particular vintage, which had the advantage of being exceedingly strong, and therefore allowed a sort of disguised dram-drinking. It need therefore excite little surprise in the mind of the reader to be informed that, when Mr. Isaac had drunk a few glasses of this port of his, the nervous system began to feel more comfortable, and at the same time tempted him to a still warmer appreciation of the qualities of the beverage. His mind was clearer and brighter, and he read Macaulay with a sort of interest, which, perhaps, is as much as most authors may hope for or expect; that is, his mind kept up a sort of double action, following the words of the historian, and even grasping the meaning of his sentences, and feeling their literary power, whilst at the same time it ran upon many subjects of personal concern which could not be altogether excluded or suppressed. Mr. Ogden was not very delicate in any of his tastes; but it seemed to him, nevertheless, that clay tobacco-pipes consorted better with gin-and-water than with the juice of the grape; and he took from a cupboard in the corner a large box of full-flavored havannas, which, like the expensive port in the cellar, he kept for the gratification of his friends.

Now, although the first five or six glasses had indeed done no more than give a beneficial stimulus to Mr. Ogden's brain, it is not to be inferred, as Mr. Ogden himself appeared to infer, that the continuation of the process would be equally salutary. He went on, however, reading and sipping, at the rate of about a glass to a page, smoking at the same time those full-flavored havannas, till after eleven at night. Little Jacob and the servants had long since gone to bed; both decanters had been on the table all the evening, and both had been in equal requisition, for Mr. Ogden had been varying his pleasures by drinking port and sherry alternately,

At last the eloquence of Macaulay became no longer intelligible, for though his sentences had no doubt been constructed originally in a perfectly workmanlike manner, they now seemed quite out of order, and no longer capable of holding together. Mr. Ogden put the book down and tried to read the Manchester paper, but the makers of articles and the penny-a-liners did not seem to have succeeded better than Macaulay, for their sentences were equally disjointed. The reader rose from his chair in some discouragement and looked at his watch, and put his slippers on, and began to think about going to bed, but the worst of it was he felt so thirsty that he must have something to drink. The decanters were empty, and wine would not quench thirst; a glass of beer might, perhaps — but how much better and more efficacious would be a tall glass of brandy-and-soda-water! Alas! he had no brandy, neither had he any soda-water, at least he thought not, but he would go down into the cellar and see. He took a candle very deliberately, and walked down the cellar-steps with a steady tread, never staggering or swerving in the least. "Am I drunk?" he thought; "no, it is impossible that I should be drunk, I walk so well and so steadily. I'm not afraid of walking down these stone steps, and yet if I were to fall I might hit my forehead against their sharp edges, sharp edges — yes, they have very sharp edges; they are very new steps, cut by masons; and so are these walls new — good ashlar stones; and that arched roof — that arch is well made: there isn't a better cellar in Shayton."

There was no soda-water, but there were bottles whose round, swollen knobs of corks were covered with silvery foil, that glittered as Mr. Ogden's candle approached them. The glitter caught his eye, and he pulled one of the bottles out. It wasn't exactly soda-water, but it would fizz; and just now Mr. Ogden had a morbid, passionate longing for something that would "fizz," as he expressed it in his muttered soliloquy. So he marched upstairs with his prize, in that stately and

CHAP. IV. *Isaac Ogden becomes a Backslider.* 35

deliberate manner which marks his particular stage of intoxication.

"It's good slekk!"* said Mr. Ogden, as he swallowed a tumblerful of the sparkling wine, "and it *can* do me no harm — it's only a lady's wine." He held it up between his eye and the candle, and thought that really it looked very nice and pretty. How the little bubbles kept rising and sparkling! how very clear and transparent it was! Then he sat down in his large arm-chair, and thought he might as well have another cigar. He had smoked a good many already, perhaps it would be better not; and whilst his mind was resolving not to smoke another, his fingers were fumbling in the box, and making a sort of pretence at selection. At last, for some reason as mysterious as that which decides the famous donkey between two equidistant haystacks, the fingers came to a decision, and the cigar, after the point had been duly amputated with a penknife, was inserted between the teeth. After this the will made no further attempt at resistance, and the hand poured out champagne into the tumbler, and carried the tumbler to the lips, with unconscious and instinctive regularity.

Mr. Isaac was now drunk, but it was not yet proved to him that he was drunk. His expedition to the cellar had been perfectly successful; he had walked in the most unexceptionable manner, and even descended those dangerous stone steps. He looked at his watch — it was half-past twelve; he read the hour upon the dial, though not just at first, and he replaced the watch in his fob. He would go to bed — it was time to go to bed; and the force of habits acquired at the Red Lion, where he usually went to bed drunk at midnight, aided him in this resolution. But when he stood upon his legs this project did not seem quite so easy of realization as it

* Slake; it is good slake — it slakes thirst well. The expression was actually used by a carter, to whom a gentleman gave champagne in order to ask his opinion of the beverage.

had done when viewed in theory from the arm-chair. "Go to bed!" said Mr. Isaac; "but how are we to manage it?"

There were two candles burning on the table. He blew one of them out, and took the other in his hand. He took up the volume of Macaulay, with an idea that it ought to be put somewhere, but his mind did not successfully apply itself to the solution of this difficulty, and he laid the book down again with an air of slight disappointment, and a certain sense of failure. He staggered towards the doorway, steadied himself with an effort, and made a shot at it with triumphant success, for he found himself now in the little entrance-hall. The staircase was a narrow one, and closed by a door, and the door of the cellar was next to it. Instead of taking the door that led up to his bedroom, Mr. Ogden took that of the cellar, descended a step or two, discovered his mistake, and, in the attempt to turn round, fell backwards heavily down the stone stair, and lay at last on the cold pavement, motionless, and in total darkness.

He might have remained there all night, but there was a sharp little Scotch terrier dog that belonged to little Jacob, and was domiciled in a snug kennel in the kitchen. The watchful animal had been perfectly aware that Mr. Ogden was crossing the entrance on his way to his bedroom, but if Feo made any reflections on the subject they were probably confined to wonder that the master of the house should go to bed so unusually late. When, however, the heavy *thud* of Mr. Ogden's body on the staircase and the loud, sharp clatter of the falling candlestick came simultaneously to her ears, Feo quitted her lair at a bound, and, guided by her sure scent, was down in the dark cellar in an instant. A less intelligent dog than Feorach (for that was her Gaelic name in the far Highlands where she was born) would have known that something was wrong, and that the cold floor of the cellar was not a suitable bed for a gentleman; and no sooner had Feorach ascertained the state of affairs than she rushed to the upper regions.

CHAP. IV. *Isaac Ogden becomes a Backslider.*

Feorach went to the door of little Jacob's chamber, and there set up such a barking and scratching as awoke even *him* from the sound sleep of childhood. Old Sarah came into the passage with a lighted candle, where Jim joined her, rubbing his eyes, still heavy with interrupted sleep. "There's summat wrong," said old Sarah; "I'm feared there's summat wrong."

"Stop you here," said Jim, "I'll wake master: he's gotten loaded pistols in his room. If it's thieves, it willn't do to feight 'em wi' talk and a tallow candle."

Jim knocked at his master's door, and, having waited in vain a second or two for an answer, determined to open it. There was no one in the room, and the bed had not been slept upon.

"Hod thy din, dog," said Jim to Feorach; and then, with a grave, pale face, said, "It isn't thieves; it's summat 'at's happened to our master."

Now Lancashire people of the class to which Jim and Sarah belonged never, or hardly ever, use the verb *to die*, but in the place of it employ the periphrase of something happening; and, as he chanced to use this expression now, the idea conveyed to Sarah's mind was the idea of death, and she believed that Jim had seen a corpse in the room. He perceived this, and drew her away, whispering, "He isn't there: you stop wi' little Jacob." So the man took the candle, and left Sarah in the dark with the child, both trembling and wondering.

Feorach led Jim down into the cellar, and he saw the dark inert mass at the bottom of the steps. A chill shudder seized him as he recognized the white, inanimate face. One of Mr. Ogden's hands lay upon the floor; Jim ventured to touch it, and found it deadly cold. A little blood oozed from the back of the head, and had matted the abundant brown hair. Perhaps the hand may have been cold simply from contact with the stone flag, but Jim did not reflect about this, and concluded that Mr. Ogden was dead. He went hastily back to old Sarah. "Master Jacob," he said, "you must go to bed."

"No, I won't go to bed, Jim!"

"My lad," said old Sarah, "just come into your room, and I'll light you a candle." So she lighted a candle, and then left the child, and Jim quietly locked the door upon him. The lock was well oiled, and Jacob did not know that he was a prisoner.

"Now what is 't?" said old Sarah, in a whisper.

"Master's deead: he's fallen down th' cellar-steps and killed hisself."

Old Sarah had been fully prepared for some terrible communication of this kind, and did not utter a syllable. She simply followed the man, and between them they lifted Mr. Ogden, and carried him, not without difficulty, up the cellar-steps. Sarah carried the head, and Jim the legs and feet, and old Sarah's bed-gown was stained with a broad patch of blood.

It is one of the most serious inconveniences attending a residence in the country that on occasions of emergency it is not possible to procure prompt medical help; and Twistle Farm was one of those places where this inconvenience is felt to the uttermost. When they had got Mr. Ogden on the bed, Jim said, "I mun go an' fetch Dr. Bardly, though I reckon it's o' no use;" and he left Sarah alone with the body.

The poor woman anticipated nothing but a dreary watch of several hours by the side of a corpse, and went and dressed herself, and lighted a fire in Mr. Ogden's room. Old Sarah was not by any means a woman of a pusillanimous disposition; but it may be doubted whether, if she had had any choice in the matter, a solitary watch of this kind would have been exactly to her taste. However, when the fire was burning briskly, she drew a rocking-chair up to it,

CHAP. IV. *Isaac Ogden becomes a Backslider.*

and, in order to keep up her courage through the remainder of the night, fetched a certain physic-bottle from the kitchen, and her heavy lead tobacco-pot, for like many old women about Shayton she enjoyed the solace of a pipe. She did not attempt to lay out the body, being under the impression that the coroner might be angry with her for having done so when the inquest came to be held.

The physic-bottle was full of rum, and Sarah made herself a glass of grog, and lighted her pipe, and looked into the fire. She had drawn the curtains all round Mr. Ogden's bed; ample curtains of pale-brown damask, with an elaborate looped valance, from whose deep festoons hung multitudes of little pendants of turned wood covered with flossy silk. The movement communicated to these pendants by the act of drawing the curtains lasted a very long time, and Sarah was startled more than once when on looking round from her arm-chair she saw them swinging and knocking against each other still. As soon as the first shock of alarm was past, the softer emotions claimed their turn, and the old woman began to cry, repeating to herself incessantly, "And quite yoong too, quite yoong, quite a yoong man!"

Suddenly she was aware of a movement in the room. Was it the little dog? No; Feorach had elected to stay with his young master, and both little Jacob and his dog were fast asleep in another room. She ventured to look at the great awful curtained bed. The multitudinous pendants had not ceased to swing and vibrate, and yet it was now a long time since Sarah had touched the curtains. She wished they would give up and be still; but whilst she was looking at them and thinking this, a little sharp shock ran round the whole valance, and the pendants rattled against each other with the low dull sound which was all that their muffling of silk permitted; a low sound, but an audible one,—audible especially to ears in high excitement; a stronger shock, a visible agitation, not only of the tremulous pendants, but even of the heavy curtain-folds themselves. Then they open, and Mr. Ogden's pale face appears.

"Well, Sarah, I hope you 've made yourself comfortable, you damned old rum-drinking thief! D'ye think I can't smell rum? Give me that bottle."

Sarah was much too agitated to say or do any thing whatever. She had risen from her chair, and stood looking at the bed in speechless amazement. Mr. Ogden got up, and walked towards the fire with an unsteady pace. Then he possessed himself of the rum-bottle, and, putting it to his lips, began to swallow the contents. This brought Sarah to herself.

"Nay, nay, master: you said as you wouldn't drink no sperrits at Twistle Farm upo' no 'count."

But the rum had been tasted, and the resolution broken. It had been broken before as to the intention and meaning of it, and was now broken even as to the letter. Isaac Ogden had got drunk at Twistle Farm; and now he was drinking spirits there, not even diluting them with water.

After emptying old Sarah's bottle, which fortunately did not contain enough to endanger, for the present, his existence, Mr. Ogden staggered back to his bed, and fell into a drunken sleep, which lasted until Dr. Bardly's arrival. The Doctor found the wound at the back of the head exceedingly slight; there was abrasure of the skin and a swelling, but nothing more. The blood had ceased to flow soon after the accident; and there would be no worse results from it than the temporary insensibility, from which the patient had already recovered. The most serious results of what had passed were likely, for the present, to be rather moral than physical. Dr. Bardly greatly dreaded the moral depression which must result from the breaking down of the only resolution which stood between his friend and an utter abandonment to his propensity. Twistle Farm would no longer be a refuge for him against the demon, for the demon had been admitted, had crossed the threshold, had taken possession.

CHAP. IV. *Isaac Ogden becomes a Backslider.*

Mr. Ogden was not in a condition to be advised, for he was not yet sober, and, if he had been, the Doctor felt that advice was not likely to be of any use: he had given enough of it already. The parson might try, if he liked, but it seemed to the Doctor that the case had now become one of those incurable cases which yield neither to the desire of self-preservation nor to the fear of hell; and that if the warnings of science were disregarded by a man intelligent enough to appreciate the certainty of the data on which they were founded, those of religion were not likely to have better success.

CHAPTER V.

FATHER AND SON.

MR. OGDEN came downstairs in the middle of the day, and ordered breakfast and dinner in one meal. He asked especially for Sarah's small-beer, and drank two or three large glasses of it. He did not eat much, and used an unusual quantity of pepper. He was extremely taciturn, contrarily to his ordinary habit, for he commonly talked very freely with old Sarah whilst she served him. When his repast was finished, he expressed a wish to see little Jacob.

"Good morning, papa! I hope you are better. Sarah says you were poorly last night when Feorach barked so."

"Oh, she says I was poorly, does she? Then she lies: I wasn't poorly,—I was drunk. I want you to read to me."

"Must I read in that book Mr. Prigley gave me when he came?"

"Read what you please."

So little Jacob opened for the first time a certain volume which will be recognized by every reader when he begins:—

"'The way was long, the wind was cold,
The minstrel was infirm and old.'"

"That would be difficult," said Mr. Ogden.

"What, papa?"

"I say, it would be difficult."

Little Jacob felt rather frightened. He did not understand in what the supposed difficulty consisted, and yet felt that he was expected to understand it. He did not dare to ask a second time for enlightenment on the point, so he stood quite still and said nothing. His father waited a minute in perfect silence, and then burst out, —

"Why, you little confounded blockhead, I mean that it would be difficult for a man to be infirm and bold at the same time! Infirm people are timid, commonly."

"Please, papa, it doesn't say infirm and bold — it says infirm and old — see, papa;" and little Jacob pointed with his finger to the place.

"Then you read damned badly, for you read it 'bold,' and it's 'old.' I expect you to read better than that — you read badly, damned badly."

"Please, papa, I read it 'old' the first time, and not 'bold.'"

"Then you mean to say I cannot trust my own ears, you little impertinent monkey. I say you read it 'bold,' and I heard you."

An elder person would have perceived that Mr. Ogden was ill, and humored him; and a child of a more yielding disposition would have submitted to the injustice, and acquiesced. But little Jacob had an instinctive hatred of injustice, and his whole nature rose in revolt. He had also made up his mind never to tell lies — less perhaps from principle than from a feeling that it was cowardly. The present was an occasion which roused these feelings in all their energy. He was required to utter a falsehood, and submit to an injustice.

"No, papa, I said 'old.' I didn't say 'bold' at all. It was you that heard wrong."

Mr. Ogden became white with anger. "Oh, *I* was mistaken, was I? Do you mean to say that I am deaf?"

"No, papa."

"Well, then, if I'm not deaf I have been lying. I am a liar, am I?"

The state of extreme nervous depression, in combination with irritability, under which Mr. Ogden's system was laboring that day, made him a dangerous man to contradict, and not by any means a pleasant antagonist in argument. But he was not altogether lost; he still kept some control over himself, in proof of which may be mentioned the fact that he simply dismissed little Jacob without even a box on the ear. "He deserves a good thrashing," said Mr. Ogden; "but if I were to begin with him I should nearly kill him, the little impudent scoundrel!"

The afternoon was exceedingly dull and disagreeable to Mr. Ogden. He walked out into his fields and round the pond. He had made a small footpath for his walks, which, after leaving the front-door first, went all round the pond, and then up to the rocks that overlooked the little valley, and from which he enjoyed a very extensive view. There were several springs in the little hollow, but before Mr. Ogden's settlement they had contented themselves with creating those patches of that emerald grass, set in dark heather, which are so preciously beautiful in the scenery of the moors. At each of these springs Mr. Ogden had made a circular stone-basin, with a water-duct to his pond, and it was his fancy to visit these basins rather frequently to see that they were kept clean and in order. He did so this afternoon, from habit, and by the time he had finished his round it was nearly dark.

He was intensely miserable. Twistle Farm had been sweet and dear to him because he had jealously guarded the purity of the associations that belonged to it. Neither in the house nor in the little undulating fields that he had made was there a single object to remind him of his weakness and his sin, and therefore the place had been a refuge and a sanctuary. It could never again be for him what it had been; this last lamentable failure had broken down the moral defences of his home, and invaded it and contaminated it for ever. Whatever the future might bring, the event of the past night was irrevocable; he had besotted himself with drink; he had brought the mire of the outer world into his pure dwelling, and defiled it. Isaac Ogden felt this the more painfully that he had little of the support of religion, and few of the consolations and encouragements of philosophy. A religious mind would have acknowledged its weakness and repented of its sin, yet in the depths of its humiliation hoped still for strength from above, and looked and prayed for ultimate deliverance and peace. A philosophic mind would have reflected that moral effort is not to be abandoned for a single relapse, or even for many relapses, and would have addressed itself only the more earnestly to the task of self-reformation that the need for effort had made itself so strikingly apparent. But Mr. Ogden had neither the faith which throws itself on the support of Heaven, nor the faculty of judging of his own actions with the impartiality of the independent intellect. He was simply a man of the world, so far as such a place as Shayton could develop a man of the world, and had neither religious faith nor intellectual culture. Therefore his misery was the greater for the density of the darkness in which he had stumbled and fallen. What he needed was light of some sort; either the beautiful old lamp of faith, with its wealth of elaborate imagery, or the plainer but still bright and serviceable gas-light of modern thought and science. Mr. Prigley possessed the one, and the Doctor gave his best labor to the maintenance of the other; but Mr. Ogden was unfortunate in not being able to profit by the help which either of these friends would have so willingly afforded.

No one except Dr. Bardly had suspected the deplorable fact that Mr. Ogden was no longer in a state of mental sanity. The little incident just narrated, in which he had mistaken one word for another, and insisted, with irritation, that the error did not lie with him, had been a common one during the last few weeks, whenever little Jacob read to him. If our little friend had communicated his sorrows to the Doctor, this fact would have been a very valuable one as evidence of his father's condition; but he never mentioned it to any one except his grandmother and old Sarah, who both inferred that the child had read inaccurately, and saw no reason to suspect the justice of Mr. Ogden's criticism. The truth was, that by a confusion very common in certain forms of brain-disease, a sound often suggested to Mr. Ogden some other sound resembling it, or of which it formed a part, and the mere suggestion became to him quite as much a fact as if he had heard it with his bodily ears. Thus, as we have seen, the word "old" had suggested "bold;" and when, as in that instance, the imagined word did not fit in very naturally with the sense of the passage, Mr. Ogden attributed the fault to little Jacob's supposed inaccuracy in reading. Indeed he had now a settled conviction that his son was unpardonably careless, and no sooner did the child open his book to read, than his father became morbidly expectant of some absurd mistake, which, of course, never failed to arrive, and to give occasion for the bitterest reproaches.

On his return to the house Mr. Ogden desired his son's attendance, and requested him to resume his reading. Little Jacob took up his book again, and this time, as it happened, Mr. Ogden heard the second line correctly, and expressed his satisfaction. But in the very next couplet —

"His withered cheek and tresses gray
Seemed to have known a better day" —

Mr. Ogden found means to imagine another error. "It seems to me curious," said he, "that Scott should have described the minstrel as having a 'withered cheek and tresses gay;' there could be little gayety about him, I should imagine."

"Please, papa, it isn't gay, but gray."

"Then why the devil do you read so incorrectly? I have always to be scolding you for making these absurd mistakes!"

If little Jacob had had an older head on his shoulders he would have acquiesced, and tried to get done with the reading as soon as possible, so as to make his escape. But it was repugnant to him to admit that he had made a blunder of which he was innocent, and he answered, —

Father and Son.

"But, papa, I read it right — I said *gray;* I didn't say *gay.*"

Mr. Ogden made a violent effort to control himself, and said, with the sort of calm that comes of the intensest emotion, —

"Then you mean to say I am deaf."

Little Jacob had really been thinking that his father might be deaf, and admitted as much.

"Fetch me my riding-whip."

Little Jacob brought the whip, expecting an immediate application of it, but Mr. Ogden, still keeping a strong control over himself, merely took the whip in his hands, and began to play with it, and look at its silver top, which he rubbed a little with his pocket-handkerchief. Then he took a candle in his right hand, and brought the flame quite close to the silver ornament, examining it with singular minuteness, so as apparently to have entirely ceased to pay attention to his son's reading, or even to hear the sound of his voice.

"Is this my whip?"

"Yes, papa."

"Well, then, I am either blind or I have lost my memory. My whip was precisely like this, except for one thing — my initials were engraved upon it, and I can see no initials here."

Little Jacob began to feel very nervous. A month before the present crisis he had taken his father's whip to ride with, and lost it on the moor, after dark, where he and Jim had sought for it long and vainly. Little Jacob had since consulted a certain saddler in Shayton, a friend of his, as to the possibility of procuring a whip of the same pattern as the lost one, and it had fortunately happened that this saddler had received two precisely alike, of which Mr. Isaac Ogden had bought one, whilst the other remained unsold. There was thus no difficulty in replacing the whip so as to deceive Mr. Ogden into the belief that it had never been lost, or rather so as to prevent any thought or suspicion from presenting itself to his mind. When the master of a house has given proofs of a tyrannical disposition, or of an uncontrollable and unreasonable temper, a system of concealment naturally becomes habitual in his household, and the most innocent actions are hidden from him as if they were crimes. Some trifling incident reveals to him how sedulously he is kept in ignorance of the little occurrences which make up the existence of his dependants, and then he is vexed to find himself isolated and cut off from their confidence and sympathy.

Mr. Ogden continued. "This is *not* my whip; it is a whip of the same pattern, that some people have been buying to take me in. Fetch me my own whip—the one with my initials."

Little Jacob thought the opportunity for escaping from the room too good to be thrown away, and vanished. Mr. Ogden waited quietly at first, but, after ten minutes had escaped, became impatient, and rang the bell violently. Old Sarah presented herself.

"Send my son here."

On his reappearance, little Jacob was in that miserable state of apprehension in which the most truthful child will lie if it is in the least bullied or tormented, and in which indeed it is not possible to extract pure truth from its lips without great delicacy and tenderness.

"Have you brought my whip?"

"Please, papa," said little Jacob, who began to get very red in the face, as he always did when he told a downright fib — "please, papa, that's your whip." There was a mental reservation here, slightly Jesuitical; for the boy had reflected, during his brief absence, that since he had given that whip to Mr. Ogden, it now, of course, might strictly be said to belong to him.

"What has become of my whip with I. O. upon it?"

"It's that whip, papa; only you — you told Jim to clean the silver top, and — and perhaps he rubbed the letters off."

"You damned little lying sneaking scoundrel, this whip is

perfectly new; but it will not be new long, for I will lay it about you till it isn't worth twopence."

The sharp switching strokes fell fast on poor little Jacob. Some of them caught him on the hands, and a tremendous one came with stinging effect across his lips and cheek; but it was not the first time he had endured an infliction of this sort, and he had learned the art of presenting his body so as to shield the more sensitive or least protected places. On former occasions Mr. Ogden's anger had always cooled after a score or two of lashes, but this time it rose and rose with an ever-increasing violence. Little Jacob began to find his powers of endurance exhausted, and, with the nimble ingenuity of his years, made use of different articles of furniture as temporary barriers against his enemy. For some time he managed to keep the table between Mr. Ogden and himself, but his father's arm was long, and reached far, and the child received some smarting cuts about the face and neck, so then he tried the chairs. Mr. Ogden, who was by this time a furious madman, shivered his whip to pieces against the furniture, and then, throwing it with a curse into the fire, looked about him for some other means of chastisement. Now there hung a mighty old hunting-whip in a sort of trophy with other memorials of the chase, and he took this down in triumph. The long knotted lash swung heavily as he poised it, and there was a steel hammer at the end of the stick, considered as of possible utility in replacing lost nails in the shoes of hunters.

A great terror seized little Jacob, a terror of that utterly hopeless and boundless and unreasoning kind that will sometimes take possession of the nervous system of a child — a terror such as the mature man does not feel even before imminent and violent death, and which he can only conceive or imagine by a reference to the dim reminiscences of his infancy. The strong man standing there · menacing, armed with a whip like a flail, his eyes glaring with the new and baleful light of madness, became transfigured in the child's imagination to something supernatural. How tall he seemed, how mighty, how utterly irresistible! When a Persian travels alone in some wide stony desert, and sees a column of dust rise like smoke out of the plain and advance rapidly towards him, and believes that out of the column one of the malignant genii will lift his colossal height, and roll his voice of thunder, and wield his sword of flame, all that that Persian dreads in the utmost wildness of his credulous Oriental imagination this child felt as a present and visible fact. The Power before him, in the full might and height of manhood, in the fury of madness, lashing out the great thong to right and left till it cracked like pistol-shots — with glaring eyes, and foaming lips out of which poured curses and blasphemies — was this a paternal image, was it civilized, was it human? The aspect of it paralyzed the child, till a sharp intolerable pain came with its fierce stimulus, and he leaped out from behind his barricade and rushed towards the door.

The lad had thick fair hair in a thousand natural curls. He felt a merciless grip in it, and his forehead was drawn violently backwards. Well for him that he struggled and writhed! for the steel hammer was aimed at him now, and the blows from it crashed on the furniture as the aim was continually missed.

The man-servant was out in the farm-buildings, and old Sarah had been washing in an out-house. She came in first, and heard a bitter cry. Many a time her heart had bled for the child, and now she could endure it no longer. She burst into the room, she seized Ogden's wrist and drove her nails into it till the pain made him let the child go. She had left both doors open. In an instant little Jacob was out of the house.

Old Sarah was a strong woman, but her strength was feebleness to Ogden's. He disengaged himself quite easily, and at every place where his fingers touched her there was a mark on her body for days. The child heard curses following him as he flew over the smooth grass. The farm was bounded by a six-foot wall. The curses came nearer and nearer; the wall loomed black and high. "I have him now," cried Ogden, as he saw the lad struggling to get over the wall.

Little Jacob felt himself seized by the foot. An infinite terror stimulated him, and he wrenched it violently. A sting of anguish crossed his shoulders where the heavy whip-lash fell, — a shoe remained in Ogden's hand.

CHAPTER VI.

LITTLE JACOB IS LOST.

OGDEN flung the shoe down with an imprecation, and the whip after it. He then climbed the wall and tried to run, but the ground here was rough moorland, and he fell repeatedly. He saw no trace of little Jacob. He made his way back to the house, sullen and savage, and besmeared with earth and mud.

"Give me a lantern, damn you," he said to old Sarah, "and look sharp!"

Old Sarah took down a common candle-lantern, and purposely selected one with a hole in it. She also chose the shortest of her candle-ends. Ogden did not notice these particulars in his impatience, and went out again. Just then Jim came in.

"Well," said old Sarah, "what d' ye think master's done? He 's licked little Jacob while * he 's wenly† kilt him, but t' little un 's reight enough now. He 'll never catch him."

"What! has little Jacob run away?"

"Ay, that he has; and he *can* run, can little Jacob; and he knows all th' places about. I 've no fears on him. Master 's gone after him wi' a lantern wi' a hoile in it, and auve a hinch o' cannle. It 's like catchin' a bird wi' a pinch o' salt."

"Little un 's safe enough, I 'se warrant him."

"We mun just stop quite ‡ till th' ould un 's i' bedd, and then we 'll go and seech § little Jacob."

In a quarter of an hour Ogden came back again. His

* Till. † Almost. ‡ Quiet. § Seek.

light had gone out, and he threw the lantern down on the kitchen-floor without a word, and shut himself up in his sitting-room.

The furniture was in great disorder. The chairs were all overturned, the mahogany table bore deep indentations from the blows of the hammer. Some pieces of old china that had ornamented the chimney-piece lay scattered on the hearth. He lifted up a chair and sat upon it. The disorder was rather pleasing to him than otherwise; he felt a bitter satisfaction in the harmony between it and the state of his own mind. A large fragment of broken china lay close to his foot. It belonged to a basin, which, having been broken only into three or four pieces, was still repairable. Ogden put it under his heel and crushed it to powder, feeling a sort of grim satisfaction in making repair out of the question.

He sat in perfect inaction for about a quarter of an hour, and then rang the bell. "Bring me hot water, and, stop — put these things in their places, will you?"

Old Sarah restored some order in the room, removed the broken china, and brought the hot water.

"Now, bring me a bottle of rum."

"Please, Mestur Ogden, you've got no rum in the house."

"No, but you have."

"Please, sir, I've got very little. I think it's nearly all done."

"D'ye think I want to rob you? I'll pay ye for 't, damn you!"

"Mestur Ogden, you don't use drinkin' sperrits at Twistle Farm."

Ogden gave a violent blow on the table with his fist, and shouted, "Bring me a bottle of rum, a bottle of rum! D'ye think you're to have all the rum in the world to yourself, you drunken old witch?"

There was that in his look which cowed Sarah, and she reflected that he might be less dangerous if he were drunk. So she brought the rum.

Ogden was pouring himself a great dose into a tumbler, when a sudden hesitation possessed him, and he flung the bottle from him into the fireplace. There was a shivering crash, and then a vast sheet of intolerable flame. The intense heat drove Ogden from the hearth. He seized the candle, and went upstairs into his bedroom.

Sarah and Jim waited to see whether he would come down again, but he remained in his room, and they heard the boards creak as he walked from wall to wall. This continued an hour. At last old Sarah said, —

"I cannot bide no longer. Let's go and seech th' childt;" and she lighted two lanterns, which, doubtless, were in better condition, and better provided with candles, than the one she had lent to Mr. Ogden.

They went into the stable and cowhouse (or *mistle* as it was called in that country), and called in the softest and most winning tones their voices knew how to assume. "Little Jacob, little Jacob, come, my lad, come; it's nobbut old Sarah an' Jim. Mestur's i' bedd."

They went amongst the hay with their lanterns, in spite of the risk of setting it on fire, but he was not there. He was not to be found in any of the out-buildings. Suddenly an idea struck Jim.

"If we'd nobbut his bit of a dog, who'd find him, sure enough."

But Feorach had disappeared. Feorach was with her young master.

They began to be rather alarmed, for it was very cold, and intensely dark. The lad was certainly not on the premises. They set off along the path that led to the rocks. They examined every nook and cranny of the huge masses of sandstone, and their lanterns produced the most unaccustomed effects, bringing out the rough projections of the rock against the unfathomable black sky, and casting enormous shadows from one rock to another. Wherever their feet could tread they went, missing nothing; but the lad was not amongst the rocks. It began to be clear to them that he could not even be in a place of such shelter as that. He must be out on the open moor.

"We mun go and tell Mestur," said Jim. "If he's feared about th' childt, he willn't be mad at him."

So they returned straight to the house, and went to Mr. Ogden's room. He had gone to bed, but was not asleep. If he thought about little Jacob at all, his reflections were probably not of an alarming kind. The child would come back, of course.

"Please, sir," said Jim, "Master Jacob isn't come back, and we can't find him."

"He'll come back," said Ogden.

"Please, sir, I'm rather feared about him," said Jim; "it's nearly two hours sin' he left the house, and it's uncommon cold. We've been seekin' him all up and down, old Sarah and me, and he's nowhere about th' premises, and he isn't about th' rocks neither."

Mr. Ogden began to feel rather alarmed. The paroxysm of his irritation was over by this time, and he had become rational again; indeed his mind was clearer, and, in a certain sense, calmer, than it had been for two or three days. For the last half-hour he had been suffering only from great prostration, and a feeling of dulness and vacancy, which this new anxiety effectually removed. Notwithstanding the violence of his recent treatment of his son — a violence which had frequently broken out during several months, and which had culminated in the scene described in the last chapter, when it had reached the pitch of temporary insanity — he really had the deepest possible affection for his child, and this paternal feeling was more powerful than he himself had ever consciously known or acknowledged. When once the idea was realized that little Jacob might be suffering physically from the cold, and mentally from a dread of his father, which the events of the night only too fully justified, Mr. Ogden began to feel the tenderest care and anxiety. "I'll be down with you in a moment," he said. "See that the lanterns are in good order. Have the dogs ready to go with us — they may be of some use."

He came downstairs with a serious but quite reasonable expression on his face. He spoke quite gently to old Sarah, and said, with a half-smile, "You needn't give me a lantern with a hole in it this time;" and then he added, "I wasted all that rum you gave me."

"It 'ud 'ave been worst wasted if you'd swallowed it, Mestur."

"It would — it would; but we may need a little for the lad if we find him — very cold, you know. Give a little to Jim, if you have any; and take a railway rug, or a blanket from my bed, to wrap him in if he should need it."

The dogs were in the kitchen now — a large mastiff and a couple of pointers. Mr. Ogden took down a little cloak that belonged to Jacob, and made the dogs smell at it. Then he seemed to be looking about for something else.

"Are ye seekin' something, Mr. Ogden?"

"I want something to make a noise with, Sarah." She fetched the little silver horn that had been the Doctor's last present to his young friend. "That's it," said Mr. Ogden; "he'll know the sound of that when he hears it."

The little party set out towards the moor. Mr. Ogden led it to the place where Jacob had crossed the wall; and as Jim was looking about with his lantern he called out, "Why, master, here's one of his shoes, and — summat else."

The "summat else" was the great whip.

Mr. Ogden took the shoe up, and the whip. They were within a few yards of the pond, and he went down to the edge of it. A slight splash was heard, and he came back without the whip. The weight of the steel hammer had sunk it, and hidden it from his eyes for ever. He carried the little shoe in his right hand.

Little Jacob is Lost.

When they had crossed the wall, Mr. Ogden bent down and put the shoe on the ground, and called the dogs. The pointers understood him at once, and went rapidly on the scent, whilst the little party followed them as fast as they could.

It led out upon the open moor. When they were nearly a mile from the house, Mr. Ogden told Sarah to go back and make a fire in little Jacob's room, and warm his bed. The two men then went forward in silence.

It was bitterly cold, and the wind began to rise, whistling over the wild moor. It was now eleven o'clock; Mr. Ogden looked at his watch. Suddenly the dogs came to a standstill; they had reached the edge of a long sinuous bog with a surface of treacherous green, and little black pools of peat-water and mud. Mr. Ogden knew the bog perfectly, as he knew every spot on the whole moor that he was accustomed to shoot over, and he became terribly anxious. "We must mark this spot," he said; but neither he nor Jim carried a stick, and there was no wood for miles round. The only resource was to make a little cairn of stones.

When this was finished, Mr. Ogden stood looking at the bog a few minutes, measuring its breadth with his eye. He concluded that it was impossible for a child to leap over it even at the narrowest place, and suggested that little Jacob must have skirted it. But in which direction — to the right hand or the left? The dogs gave no indication; they were off the scent. Mr. Ogden followed the edge of the bog to the right, and after walking half a mile, turned the extremity of it, and came again on the other side till he was opposite the cairn he had made. The dogs found no fresh scent; they were perfectly useless. "Make a noise," said Mr. Ogden to Jim; "make a noise with that horn."

Jim blew a loud blast. There came no answering cry. The wind whistled over the heather, and a startled grouse whirred past on her rapid wings.

An idea was forcing its way into Mr. Ogden's mind — a hateful, horrible, inadmissible idea — that the foul black pit before him might be the grave of his only son. How ascertain it? They had not the necessary implements; and what would be the use of digging in that flowing, and yielding, and unfathomable black mud? He could not endure the place, or the intolerable supposition that it suggested, and went wildly on, in perfect silence, with compressed lips and beating heart, stumbling over the rough land.

Old Sarah warmed the little bed, and made a bright fire in Jacob's room. When Ogden came back, he went there at once, and found the old woman holding a small night-gown to the fire. His face told her enough. His dress was covered with snow.

"Th' dogs is 'appen mistaken," she said; "little Jacob might be at Milend by this time."

Mr. Ogden sent Jim down to Shayton on horse-back, and returned to the moor alone. They met again at the farm at three o'clock in the morning. Neither of them had any news of the child. Jim had roused the household at Milend, and awakened everybody both at the parsonage and the Doctor's. He had given the alarm, and he had done the same at the scattered cottages and farm-houses between Twistle Farm and Shayton. If Jacob were seen anywhere, news would be at once sent to his father. Dr. Bardly was not at home; he had left about noon for Sootythorn on militia business, and expected to go on to Wenderholme with Colonel Stanburne, where he intended to pass the night.

CHAPTER VII.

ISAAC OGDEN'S PUNISHMENT.

DURING what remained of the night, it is unnecessary to add that nobody at Twistle Farm had rest. The search was continually renewed in various directions, and always with the same negative result. Mr. Ogden began to lose hope, and was more and more confirmed in his supposition that his son must have perished in the bog. Jim returned to Shayton, where he arrived about half-past four in the morning. When the hands assembled at Ogden's mill, Mr. Jacob told them that the factory would be closed that day, but that he would pay them their full wages; and he should feel grateful to any of the men who would help him in the search for his little nephew, who had unfortunately disappeared from Twistle on the preceding evening, and had not been since heard of. He added, that a reward of a hundred pounds would be given to any one who would bring him news of the child. Soon after daylight, handbills were posted in every street in Shayton offering the same reward. Mr. Jacob returned to Milend from the factory, and prepared to set out for Twistle.

The sun rose in clear frosty air, and the moors were covered with snow. Large groups began to arrive at the farm about eight o'clock, and at nine the hill was dotted with searchers in every direction. It was suggested to Mr. Ogden by a policeman that if he had any intention of having the pond dragged, it would be well that it should be done at once, as there was already a thin coat of ice upon it, and it would probably freeze during the whole of the day and following night, so that delay would entail great additional labor in the breaking of the ice. An apparatus was sent up from Shayton for this purpose. Mr. Ogden did not superintend this operation, but sat alone in his parlor waiting to hear the result. There was a tap at the door, and the policeman entered.

"We 've found nothing in the pond, Mr. Isaac, except —"

"Except what?"

"Only this whip, sir, that must belong to you;" and he produced the whip with the steel hammer. "It may be an important hindication, sir, if it could be ascertained whether your little boy had been playin' with it yesterday evenin'. You don't remember seein' him with it, do you, sir?"

Mr. Ogden groaned, and covered his face with his hands. Then his whole frame shook convulsively. Old Sarah came in.

"I was just askin' Mr. Ogden whether he knew if the little boy had been playin' with this 'ere whip yesterday — we 've found it in the pond; and as I was just sayin', it might be a useful hindication."

Old Sarah looked at the whip, which lay wet upon the table. "I seed that whip yistady, but I dunnot think our little lad played wi' it. He didn't use playin' wi' that whip. That there whip belongs to his father, an' it's him as makes use on it, and non little Jacob."

Mr. Ogden removed his hands from his face, and said, "The whip proves nothing. I threw it into the pond yesterday myself."

The policeman looked much astonished. "It's a fine good whip, sir, to throw away."

"Well, take it, then, if you admire it. I'll make ye a present of it."

"I 've no use for it, sir."

"Then, I reckon," said old Sarah, "as you 'aven't got a little lad about nine year old; such whips as that is considhered useful for thrashin' little lads about nine year old."

CHAP. VII. *Isaac Ogden's Punishment.* 61

Mr. Ogden could bear this no longer, and said he would go down to the pond. When he had left the room, old Sarah took up the whip and hung it in its old place, over the silver spurs. The policeman lingered. Old Sarah relieved her mind by recounting what had passed on the preceding evening. " I am some and glad* as you brought him that there whip. Th' sight of it is like pins and needles in 'is een. You 've punished 'im with it far worse than if you 'd laid it ovver his shoulthers."

Mr. Ogden gave orders that every one who wanted any thing to eat should be freely supplied in the kitchen. One of old Sarah's great accomplishments was the baking of oatcake, and as the bread in the house was soon eaten up, old Sarah heated her oven, and baked two or three hundred oatcakes. When once the mixture is prepared, and the oven heated, a skilful performer bakes these cakes with surprising rapidity, and old Sarah was proud of her skill. If any thing could have relieved her anxiety about little Jacob, it would have been this beloved occupation — but not even the pleasure of seeing the thin fluid mixture spread over the heated sheet of iron, and of tossing the cake dexterously at the proper time, could relieve the good heart of its heavy care. Even the very occupation itself had saddening associations, for when old Sarah pursued it, little Jacob had usually been a highly interested spectator, though often very much in the way. She had scolded him many a time for his " plaguiness ; " but, alas! what would she have given to be plagued by that small tormentor now!

The fall of snow had been heavy enough to fill up the smaller inequalities of the ground, and the hills had that aspect of exquisite smoothness and purity which would be degraded by any comparison. Under happier circumstances, the clear atmosphere and brilliant landscape would have been

---

* " Some and glad " is a common Lancashire expression, meaning " considerably glad."

in the highest degree exhilarating; but I suppose nobody at Twistle felt that exhilaration now. On the contrary, there seemed to be something chilling and pitiless in that cold splendor and brightness. No one could look on the vast sweep of silent snow without feeling that *somewhere* under its equal and unrevealing surface lay the body of a beloved child.

The grave-faced seekers ranged the moors all day, after a regular system devised by Mr. Jacob Ogden. The circle of their search became wider and wider, like the circles from a splash in water. In this way, before nightfall, above thirty square miles had been thoroughly explored. At last, after a day that seemed longer than the longest days of summer, the sun went down, and one by one the stars came out. The heavens were full of their glittering when the scattered bands of seekers met together again at the farm.

The fire was still kept alive in little Jacob's room. The little night-gown still hung before it. Old Sarah changed the hot water in the bed-warmer regularly every hour. Alas! alas! was there any need of these comforts now? Do corpses care to have their shrouds warmed, or to have hot-water bottles at their icy feet?

Mr. Ogden, who had controlled himself with wonderful success so long as the sun shone, began to show unequivocal signs of agitation after nightfall. He had headed a party on the moor, and came back with a sinking heart. He had no hope left. The child must certainly have died in the cold. He went into little Jacob's bedroom and walked about alone for a few minutes, pacing from the door to the window, and looking out on the cold white hills, the monotony of which was relieved only by the masses of black rock that rose out of them here and there. The fire had burnt very briskly, and it seemed to Mr. Ogden that the little night-gown was rather too near. As he drew back the chair he gazed a minute at the bit of linen; his chest heaved with violent emotion, and then there came a great and terrible agony. He sat down on the low iron bed, his strong frame shook and quivered, and with painful gasps flowed the bitter tears of his vain repentance. He looked at the smooth little pillow, untouched during a whole night, and thought of the dear head that had pressed it, and might never press it more. Where was it resting now? Was the frozen snow on the fair cheek and open brow, or — oh horror, still more horrible! — had he been buried alive in the black and treacherous pit, and were the dear locks defiled with the mud of the bog, and the bright eyes filled with its slimy darkness for ever? Surely he had not descended into *that* grave; they had done what they could to sound the place, and had found nothing but earth, soft and yielding — no fragment of dress had come up or their boat-hooks. It was more endurable to imagine the child asleep under the snow. When the thaw came they would find him, and bring him to his own chamber, and lay him again on his own bed, at least for one last night, till the coffin came up from Shayton.

How good the child had been! how brutally Ogden felt that he had used him! Little Jacob had been as forgiving as a dog, and as ready to respond to the slightest mark of kindness. He had been the light of the lonely house with his innocent prattle and gayety. Ogden had frightened him into silence lately, and driven him into the kitchen, where he had many a time heard him laughing with old Sarah and Jim, and been unreasonably angry with him for it. Ogden began to see these things in a different light. "I used him so badly," he thought, "that it was only natural he should shun and avoid me." And then he felt and knew how much sweet and pure companionship he had missed. He had not half enjoyed the blessing he had possessed. He ought to have made himself young again for the child's sake. Would it have done him any harm to teach little Jacob cricket, and play at ball with him, or at nine-pins? The boy's life had been terribly lonely, and his father had done nothing to dissipate or mitigate its loneliness. And then there came a bitter sense that he had really loved the child with an immense affection, but that the coldness and roughness and brutality of his outward behavior had hidden this affection from his son. In this, however, Mr. Ogden had not been quite so much to blame as in the agony of his repentance he himself believed. His self-accusation, like all sincere and genuine self-accusation, had a touch of exaggeration in it. The wrong that he had done was attributable quite as much to the temper of the place he lived in as to any peculiar evil in himself as an individual man. He had spoiled his temper by drinking, but every male in Shayton did the same; he had been externally hard and unsympathetic, but the inhabitants of Shayton carried to an excess the English contempt for the betrayal of the softer emotions. In all that Ogden had done, in the whole tenor of his life and conversation, he had merely obeyed the great human instinct of conformity. Had he lived anywhere else — had he even lived at Sootythorn — he would have been a different man. Such as he was, he was the product of the soil, like the hard pears and sour apples that grew in the dismal garden at Milend.

He had been sitting more than an hour on the bed, when he heard a knock at the door. It was old Sarah, who announced the arrival of Mr. Prigley and Mrs. Ogden. Mr. Prigley had been to fetch her from the place where she was visiting, and endeavored to offer such comfort to her during the journey as his heart and profession suggested. As on their arrival at Milend there had been no news of a favorable or even hopeful kind, Mrs. Ogden was anxious to proceed to Twistle immediately, and Mr. Prigley had kindly accompanied her.

The reader may have inferred from previous pages of this history, that although Mr. Prigley may have been a blameless and earnest divine, he was not exactly the man best fitted to influence such a nature as that of Isaac Ogden. He had

Isaac Ogden's Punishment.

little understanding either of its weakness or its strength—of its weakness before certain forms of temptation, or its strength in acknowledging unwelcome and terrible facts. After Mrs. Ogden had simply said, "Well, Isaac, there's no news of him yet," the clergyman tried to put a cheerful light on the subject by expressing the hope that the boy was safe in some farmhouse. Mr. Ogden answered that every farmhouse within several miles had been called at, and that Twistle Farm was the last of the farms on the moor side. It was most unlikely, in his opinion, that the child could have resisted the cold so long, especially as he had no provisions of any kind, and was not even sufficiently clothed to go out; and as he had certainly not called at any house within seven or eight miles of Twistle, Mr. Ogden could only conclude that he must have perished on the moor, and that the thick fall of snow was all that had prevented the discovery of his body.

Mrs. Ogden sat down and began to cry very bitterly. The sorrow of a person like Mrs. Ogden is at the same time quite frank in its expression, and perfectly monotonous. Her regrets expressed themselves adequately in three words, and the repetition of them made her litany of grief—"Poor little lad!" and then a great burst of weeping; and then "Poor little lad!" again, perpetually.

The clergyman attempted to "improve" the occasion in the professional sense. "The Lord hath given," he said, "and the Lord hath taken away;" then he paused, and added, "blessed be the name of the Lord." But this brought no solace to Ogden's mind. "It was not the Lord that took the lad away," he answered; "it was his father that drove him away."

The great agony came over him again, and he flung himself on his breast upon the sofa and buried his face in the cushions. Then his mother rose and came slowly to his side, and knelt down by him. Precious maternal feelings, that had been, as it were, forgotten in her heart for more than twenty years, like jewels that are worn no more, shone forth once more from her swimming eyes. "Isaac, lad," she said, with a voice that sounded in his ears like a far-off recollection of childhood,—"Isaac, lad, it were none o' thee as did it,—it were drink. Thou wouldn't have hurt a hair of his head." And she kissed him.

It was a weary night at Twistle. Nobody had any hope left, but they felt bound to continue the search, and relays of men came up from Shayton for the purpose. They were divided into little parties of six or eight, and Mr. Jacob directed their movements. Each group returned to the house after exploring the ground allotted to it, and Mr. Ogden feverishly awaited its arrival. The ever-recurring answer, the sad shake of the head, the disappointed looks, sank into the heart of the bereaved father. About two in the morning he got a little sleep, and awoke in half an hour somewhat stronger and calmer.

It is unnecessary to pursue the detail of these sufferings. The days passed, but brought no news. Dr. Bardly came back from Wenderholme, and seemed less affected than would have been expected by those who knew his love and friendship for little Jacob. He paid, however, especial attention to Mr. Isaac, whom he invited to stay with him for a few weeks, and who bore his sorrow with a manly fortitude. The Doctor drank his habitual tumbler of brandy-and-water every evening before going to bed, and the first evening, by way of hospitality, had offered the same refreshment to his guest. Mr. Ogden declined simply, and the offer was not renewed. For the first week he smoked a great deal, and drank large quantities of soda-water, but did not touch any intoxicating liquor. He persevered in this abstinence, and declared his firm resolve to continue it as a visible sign of his repentance, and of his respect to the memory of his boy. He was very gentle and pleasant, and talked freely with the Doctor about ordinary subjects; but, for a man whose vigor and energy had manifested themselves in some abruptness and rudeness in the common intercourse of life, this new gentleness was a marked sign of sadness. When the Doctor's servant, Martha, came in unexpectedly and found Mr. Ogden alone, she often observed that he had shed tears; but he seemed cheerful when spoken to, and his grief was quiet and undemonstrative.

The search for the child was still actively pursued, and his mysterious disappearance became a subject of absorbing interest in the neighborhood. The local newspapers were full of it, and there appeared a very terrible article in the 'Sootythorn Gazette' on Mr. Ogden's cruelty to his child. The writer was an inhabitant of Shayton, who had had the misfortune to have Mr. Jacob Ogden for his creditor, and had been pursued with great rigor by that gentleman. He got the necessary data from the policeman who had brought the whip back from the pond, and wrote such a description of it as made the flesh of the Sootythorn people creep upon their bones, and their cheeks redden with indignation. The Doctor happened to be out of the house when this newspaper arrived, and Mr. Isaac opened it and read the article. The facts stated in it were true and undeniable, and the victim quailed under his punishment. If he had ventured into Sootythorn, he would have been mobbed and pelted, or perhaps lynched. He was scarcely safe even in Shayton; and when he walked from the Doctor's to Milend, the factory operatives asked him where his whip was, and the children pretended to be frightened, and ran out of his way. A still worse punishment was the singular gravity of the faces that he met — a gravity that did not mean sympathy but censure. The 'Sootythorn Gazette' demanded that he should be punished — that an example should be made of him, and so on. The writer had his wish, without the intervention of the law.

After a few weeks the mystery was decided to be insoluble, and dismissed from the columns of the newspapers. Even the ingenious professional detectives admitted that they were at fault, and could hold out no hopes of a discovery. Mr. Ogden had with difficulty been induced to remain at the Doctor's during the prosecution of these inquiries ; but Dr. Bardly had represented to him that he ought to have a fixed address in case news should arrive, and that he need not be wholly inactive, but might ride considerable distances in various directions, which indeed he did, but without result.

Mrs. Ogden remained at Milend, but whether from the strength of her nature, or some degree of insensibility, she did not appear to suffer greatly from her bereavement, and pursued her usual household avocations with her accustomed regularity. Mr. Jacob went to his factory, and was absorbed in the details of business. No one put on mourning, for the child was still considered as possibly alive, and perhaps his relations shrank from so decided an avowal of their abandonment of hope. The one exception to this rule was old Sarah at Twistle, who clad herself in a decent black dress that she had by her. "If t' little un's deead," she said, " it's nobbut reight to put mysel' i' black for him ; and if he isn't I 'm so sore in my heart ovver him 'at I 'm fit to wear nought else."

CHAPTER VIII.

FROM SOOTYTHORN TO WENDERHOLME.

THE next scene of our story is in the Thorn Hotel at the prosperous manufacturing town of Sootythorn, a place superior to Shayton in size and civilization and selected by the authorities as the head-quarters of Colonel Stanburne's regiment of militia.

Dr. Bardly arrived at the Thorn the morning after Isaac Ogden's relapse, having driven all the way from Shayton, through scenery which would have been comparable to any thing in England, if the valleys had not been spoiled by cotton-mills, rows of ugly cottages, and dismal-looking coal-pits.

"Colonel Stanburne's expecting you, Doctor," said Mr. Garley, the landlord of the Thorn: "he's in the front sitting-room."

The Colonel was sitting by himself, with the 'Times' and a little black pipe.

"Good morning, Dr. Bardly! you've a nice little piece of work before you. There are a lot of fellows here to be examined as to their physical constitution — fellows, you know, who aspire to the honor of serving in the twentieth regiment of Royal Lancashire Militia."

"Perhaps I'd better begin with the hofficers," said the Doctor.

The Colonel looked alarmed, or affected to be so. "My dear Doctor, there's not the least necessity for examining officers — it isn't customary, it isn't legal; officers are always perfect, both physically and morally."

A theory of this kind came well enough from Colonel Stanburne. He was six feet high, and the picture of health. He brought forth the fruits of good living, not, as Mr. Garley did, in a bloated and rubicund face and protuberant corporation, but in that admirable balance of the whole human organism which proves the regular and equal performance of all its functions. Dr. Bardly was a good judge of a man, and he had the same pleasure in looking at the Colonel that a fox-hunter feels in contemplating a fine horse. Beyond this, he liked Colonel Stanburne's society, not precisely, perhaps, for intellectual reasons — for, intellectually, there was little or nothing in common between the two men — but because he found in it a sort of mental refreshment, very pleasant to him after the society at Shayton. The Colonel was a different being — he lived in a different world from the world of the Ogdens and their friends; and it amused and interested the Doctor to see how this strange and rather admirable creature would conduct itself under the conditions of its present existence. The Doctor, as the reader must already feel perfectly assured, had not the weakness of snobbishness or parasitism in any form whatever; and if he liked to go to Wenderholme with the Colonel, it was not because there was an earl's daughter there, and the sacred odor of aristocracy about the place, but rather because he had a genuine pleasure in the society of his friend, whether amongst the splendors of Wenderholme, or in the parlor of the inn at Sootythorn.

The Colonel, too, on his part, liked the Doctor, though he laughed at him, and mimicked him to Lady Helena. The mimicry was not, however, very successful, for the Doctor's Lancashire dialect was too perfect and too pure for any mere ultramontane (that is, creature living beyond the hills that guarded the Shayton valley) to imitate with any approximation to success. If the Colonel, however, notwithstanding all his study and effort, could not succeed in imitating the Doctor's happy selection of expressions and purity of style,

CHAP. VIII. *From Sootythorn to Wenderholme.*

he could at any rate give him a nickname — so he called him Hoftens, not to his face, but to Lady Helena at home, and to the adjutant, and to one or two other people who knew him, and the nickname became popular; and, after a while, the officers called Dr. Bardly Hoftens to his face, which he took with perfect good-nature. The first time that this occurred, the Doctor (such was the delicacy of his ear) believed he detected something unusual in the way an impudent ensign pronounced the word *often*, and asked what he meant, on which the adjutant interposed, and said, — "Don't mind his impudence, Doctor; he's mimicking you." "Well," said the Doctor, simply, "I wasn't aware that there was hany thing peculiar in my pronunciation of the word, but people *hoftens* are unaware of their own defects." But we anticipate.

They lunched at the Thorn with the adjutant, a fair-haired and delicate-looking little gentleman of exceedingly mild and quiet manners, whose acquaintance the Doctor had made very recently. Captain Eureton had retired a year or two before from the regular army, and was now living in the neighborhood of Sootythorn with his old mother whom he loved with his whole heart. He had never married, and now there was little probability of his ever marrying. The people of Sootythorn would have set him down as a milk-sop if he had not seen a good deal of active service in India and at the Cape; but a soldier who has been baptized in the fire of the battle-field has always that fact in his favor, and has little need to give himself airs of boldness in order to impose upon the imagination of civilians.

"I believe, Dr. Bardly," said Eureton, "that we are going to have an officer from your neighborhood, a Mr. Ogden. His name has been put down for a lieutenant's commission."

"Yes, he's a neighbor of mine," answered the Doctor, rather curtly.

"You should have brought him with you, Doctor," said Colonel Stanburne, "that we might make his acquaintance.

I've never seen him, you know, and he gets his commission on your recommendation. I should like, as far as possible, to know the officers personally before we meet for our first training. What sort of a fellow is Mr. Ogden? Tell us all about him."

The Doctor felt slightly embarrassed, and showed it in his manner. Any true description of Isaac Ogden, as he was just then, must necessarily seem very unfavorable. Dr. Bardly had been to Twistle that very morning before daylight, and had found Mr. Ogden suffering from the effects of that fall down the cellar-steps in a state of drunkenness. The Doctor had that day abandoned all hope of reclaiming Isaac Ogden, and saving him from the fate that awaited him.

"I've nothing good to tell of Mr. Ogden, Colonel Stanburne. I wish I hadn't recommended him to you. He's an irreclaimable drunkard!"

"Well, if you'd known it you wouldn't have recommended him, of course. You found it out since, I suppose. You must try and persuade him to resign. Tell him there'll be some awfully hard work, especially for lieutenants."

"I knew that he drank occasionally, but I believed that it was because he had nobody to talk to except a drunken set at the Red Lion at Shayton. I thought that if he came into the regiment it would do him good, by bringing him into more society. Shayton's a terrible place for drinking. There's a great difference between Shayton and Sootythorn."

"What sort of a man is he in other respects?" asked the Colonel.

"He's right enough for every thing else. He's a good-looking fellow, tall, and well-built; and he used to be pleasant and good-tempered, but now his nervous system must be shattered, and I would not answer for him."

"If you still think he would have sufficient control over himself to keep sober for a month we might try him, and see whether we cannot do him some good. Perhaps, as you thought, it's only want of society that drives him to amuse himself by drinking. Upon my word, I think I should take to drinking myself if I lived all the year round in such a place as Sootythorn — and I suppose Shayton's no better."

Captain Eureton, who was simple and even abstemious in his way of living, and whose appetite had not been sharpened, like that of the Doctor, by a long drive in the morning, finished his lunch in about ten minutes, and excused himself on the plea that he had an appointment with a joiner about the orderly-room, which had formerly been an infant-school of some Dissenting persuasion, and therefore required remodelling as to its interior fittings. We shall see more of him in due time, but for the present must leave him to the tranquil happiness of devising desks and pigeon-holes in company with an intelligent workman, than which few occupations can be more delightful.

" Perhaps, unless you've something to detain you in Sootythorn, Doctor, we should do well to leave here as early as possible. It's a long drive to Wenderholme — twenty miles, you know; and I always make a point of giving the horses a rest at Rigton."

As the Doctor had nothing to do in Sootythorn, the Colonel ordered his equipage. When he drove alone, he always preferred a tandem, but when Lady Helena accompanied him, he took his seat in a submissive matrimonial manner in the family carriage. As Wenderholme was so far from Sootythorn, the Colonel kept two pairs of horses; and one pair was generally at Wenderholme and the other in Mr. Garley's stables, where the Colonel had a groom of his own permanently. The only inconvenience of this arrangement was that the same horses had to do duty in the tandem and the carriage; but they did it on the whole fairly well, and the Colonel contented himself with the carriage-horses, so far as driving was concerned.

The Doctor drove his own gig with the degree of skill

which results from the practice of many years; but he had never undertaken the government of a tandem, and felt, perhaps, a slight shade of anxiety when John Stanburne took the reins, and they set off at full trot through the streets of Sootythorn. A manufacturing town, in that particular stage of its development, is one of the most awkward of all possible places to drive in — the same street varies so much in breadth that you never can tell whether there will be room enough to pass when you get round the corner; and there are alarming noises of many kinds — the roar of a cotton-mill in the street itself, or the wonderfully loud hum of a foundry, or the incessant clattering hammer-strokes of a boiler-making establishment — which excite and bewilder a nervous horse, till, if manageable at all, he is manageable only with the utmost delicacy and care. As Colonel Stanburne seemed to have quite enough to do to soothe and restrain his leader, the Doctor said nothing till they got clear of the last street; but once out on the broad turnpike, or "Yorkshire Road," the Colonel gave his team more freedom, and himself relaxed from the rigid accuracy of seat he had hitherto maintained. He then turned to the Doctor, and began to talk.

"I say, Doctor, why don't you drive a tandem? You — you *ought* to drive a tandem. 'Pon my word you ought, seriously, now."

The Doctor laughed. He didn't see the necessity or the duty of driving a tandem, and so begged to have these points explained to him.

"Well, because, don't you see, when you've only got one horse in your dog-cart, or gig, or whatever two-wheeled vehicle you may possess, you've no fun, don't you see?"

The Doctor didn't see, or did not seem to see.

"I mean," proceeded the Colonel, explanatorily, "that you haven't that degree of anxiety which is necessary to give a zest to existence. Now, when you've a leader who is almost perfectly free, and over whom you can only exercise a control of — the most gentle and persuasive kind, you're always slightly anxious, and sometimes you're *very* anxious. For instance, last time we drove back from Sootythorn it was pitch dark, — wasn't it, Fyser?"

Here Colonel Stanburne turned to his groom, who was sitting behind; and Fyser, as might be expected, muttered something confirmatory of his master's statement.

"It was pitch dark; and, by George! the candles in the lamps were too short to last us; and that confounded Fyser forgot to provide himself with fresh ones before he left Sootythorn, and — didn't you, Fyser?"

Fyser confessed his negligence.

"And so, when the lamps were out, it was pitch dark; so dark that I couldn't tell the road from the ditch — upon my word, I couldn't; and I couldn't see the leader a bit, I could only feel him with the reins. So I said to Fyser, 'Get over to the front seat, and then crouch down as low as you can, so as to bring the horses' heads up against the sky, and tell me if you can see them.' So Fyser crouched down as I told him; and when I asked him if he saw any thing, he said he *did* think he saw the leader's ears. Well, damn it, then, if you *do* see 'em, I said, keep your eye on 'em."

"And were you going fast?" asked the Doctor.

"Why, of *course* we were. We were trotting at the rate of, I should say, about nine miles an hour; but after a while, Fyser, by hard looking, began to see rather more distinctly — so distinctly that he clearly made out the difference between the horses' heads and the hedges; and he kept calling out 'right, sir,' 'left, sir,' 'all right, sir,' and so he kept me straight. If he'd been a sailor he'd have said 'starboard' and 'port;' but Fyser isn't a sailor."

"And did you get safe to Wenderholme?"

"Of *course* we did. Fyser and I *always* get safe to Wenderholme."

"I shouldn't recommend you to try that experiment hoftens."

"Well, but you see the advantage of driving tandem. If you've only one horse you know where he is, however dark it is — he's in the shafts, of course, and you know where to find him: but when you've got a leader you never exactly know where he is, unless you can see him."

The Doctor didn't see the advantage.

The reader will have gathered from this specimen of Colonel Stanburne's conversation that he was a pleasant and lively companion; but if he is rather hasty in forming his opinion of people on a first acquaintance, he may also infer that the Colonel was a man of somewhat frivolous character and very moderate intellectual powers. He certainly was not a genius; but he conveyed the impression of being less intelligent and less capable of serious thought than nature had made him. His predominant characteristic was simple good-nature, and he possessed also, notwithstanding a sort of swagger in his manner, an unusual share of genuine intellectual humility, that made him contented to pass for a less able and less informed man than he really was. The Doctor's perception of character was too acute to allow him to judge Colonel Stanburne on the strength of a superficial acquaintance, and he clearly perceived that his friend was in the habit of wearing, as it were, his lighter nature outside. Some ponderous Philistines in Sootythorn, who had been brought into occasional contact with the Colonel, and who confounded gravity of manner with mental capacity, had settled it amongst themselves that he had no brains; but as the most intelligent of quadrupeds is at the same time the most lively, the most playful, the most good-natured, and the most affectionate, — so amongst human beings it does not always follow that a man is empty because he is lively and amusing, and seems merry and careless, and says and does some foolish things.

An hour later they reached Rigton, a little dull village quite out of the manufacturing district, and where it was the Colonel's custom to bait. The remainder of the drive was in summer exceedingly beautiful ; but as it passed through a rich agricultural country, whose beauty depended chiefly on luxuriant vegetation, the present time of the year was not favorable to it. All this region had a great reputation for beauty amongst the inhabitants of the manufacturing towns, and no doubt fully deserved it ; but it is probable that their faculties of appreciation were greatly sharpened by the stimulus of contrast. To get fairly clear of factory-smoke, to be in the peaceful quiet country, and see no buildings but picturesque farms, was a definite happiness to many an inhabitant of Sootythorn. There were fine bits of scenery in the manufacturing district itself — picturesque glens and gorges, deep ravines with hidden rivulets, and stretches of purple moorland ; but all this scenery lacked one quality — *amenity.* Now the scenery from Rigton to Wenderholme had this quality in a very high degree indeed, and it was instantly felt by every one who came from the manufacturing district, though not so perceptible by travellers from the south of England. The Sootythorn people felt a soothing influence on the nervous system when they drove through this beautiful land ; their minds relaxed and were relieved of pressing cares, and they here fell into a state very rare indeed with them — a state of semi-poetical reverie.

The reader is already aware that Wenderholme is situated on the opposite side of the hills which separate Shayton from this favored region, and close to the foot of them. Great alterations have been made in the house since the date at which our story begins, and therefore we will not describe it as it exists at present, but as it existed when the Colonel drove up the avenue with the Doctor at his side, and the faithful Fyser jumped up behind after opening the modest green gate. A large rambling house, begun in the reign of Queen Elizabeth, but grievously modernized under that of King George the Third, it formed three sides of a quadrangle, and, as is usual in that arrangement of a mansion, had a great hall in the middle, and the principal reception rooms on each side on the ground floor. The house was three stories high, and there were great numbers of bedrooms. An arched porch in the centre, preceded by a flight of steps, gave entrance at once to the hall; and over the porch was a projection of the same breadth, continued up to the roof, and terminated in a narrow gable. This had been originally the centre of enrichment, and there had been some good sculpture and curious windows that went all round the projection, and carried it entirely upon their mullions; but the modernizer had been at work and inserted simple sash-windows, which produced a deplorable effect. The same owner, John Stanburne's grandfather, had ruthlessly carried out that piece of Vandalism over the whole front of the mansion, and, except what architects call a string-course (which was still traceable here and there), had effaced every feature that gave expression to the original design of the Elizabethan builder.

The entrance-hall was a fine room fifty feet long, and as high as two of the ordinary stories in the mansion. It had, no doubt, been a splendid specimen of the Elizabethan hall; but the modernizer had been hard at work here also, and had put himself to heavy expense in order to give it the aspect of a thoroughly modern interior. The wainscot which had once adorned the walls, and which had been remarkable for its rich and fanciful carving, the vast and imaginative tapestries, the heraldic blazonries in the flaming oriels, the gallery for the musicians on twisted pillars of sculptured chestnut, — all these glories had been ruthlessly swept away. The tapestries had been used as carpets, and worn out; the wainscot had been made into kitchen cupboards, and painted lead-color; and the magnificent windows had been thrown down on the floor of a garret, where they had been trodden under foot and crushed into a thousand fragments: and in place of these things, which the narrow taste of the eighteenth century had condemned as barbarous, and destroyed without either hesitation or regret, it had substituted — what? — absolute emptiness

CHAP. VIII. *From Sootythorn to Wenderholme.*

and negation; for the heraldic oriels, sash-windows of the commonest glass; for the tapestry and carving, a bare wall of yellow-washed plaster; for the carved beams of the roof, a blank area of whitewash.

The Doctor found Lady Helena in the drawing-room; a little woman, who sometimes looked very pretty, and sometimes exceedingly plain, according to the condition of her health and temper, the state of the weather, and a hundred things beside. Hence there were the most various and contradictory opinions about her; the only approach to unanimity being amongst certain elderly ladies who had formed the project of being mother-in-law to John Stanburne, and failed in that design. The Doctor was not much accustomed to ladyships — they did not come often in his way; indeed, if the truth must be told, Lady Helena was the only specimen of the kind he had ever enjoyed the opportunity of studying, and he had been rather surprised, on one or two preceding visits to Wenderholme, to find that she behaved so nicely. But there are ladyships and ladyships, and the Doctor had been fortunate in the example which chance had thrown in his way. For instance, if he had known Lady Eleanor Griffin, who lived about ten miles from Wenderholme, and came there occasionally to spend the day, the Doctor would have formed quite a different opinion of ladyships in general, so much do our impressions of whole classes depend upon the individual members of them who are personally known to us.

Lady Helena asked the Doctor a good many questions about Shayton, which it is quite unnecessary to report here, because the answers to them would convey no information to the reader which he does not already possess. Her ladyship inquired very minutely about the clergyman there, and whether the Doctor "liked" him. Now the verb "to like," when applied to a clergyman, is used in a special sense. Everybody knows that to like a clergyman and to like gooseberry-pie are very different things; for nobody in England eats clergyman, though the natives of New Zealand are said to appreciate cold roast missionary. But there is yet another distinction — there is a distinction between liking a clergyman and liking a layman. If you say you like a clergyman, it is understood that it gives you a peculiar pleasure to hear him preach, and that you experience feelings of gratification when he reads prayers. And in this sense could Dr. Bardly say that he liked the reverend incumbent of his parish? certainly not; so he seemed to hesitate a little — and if he said "yes" he said it as if he meant *no*, or a sort of vague, neutral answer, neither negative nor affirmative.

"I mean," said Lady Helena, "do you like him as a preacher?"

"Upon my word, it's so long since I heard him preach that I cannot give an opinion."

"Oh! I thought you attended his church. There are other churches in Shayton, I suppose."

"No, there's only one," said the imprudent and impolitic Doctor.

Lady Helena began to think he was some sort of a Dissenter. She had heard of Dissenters — she knew that such people existed — but she had never been brought into contact with one, and it made her feel rather queer. She felt strongly tempted to ask what place of worship this man *did* attend, since by his own confession he never went to his parish church; but curiosity, and the natural female tendency to be an inquisitor, were kept in check by politeness, and also, perhaps, a little restrained by the perfectly fearless aspect of the Doctor's face. If he had seemed in the least alarmed or apologetic, her ladyship would probably have assumed the functions of the inquisitor at once; but he looked so cool, and so very capable of a prolonged and vigorous resistance, that Lady Helena retired. When she began to talk about Mrs. Prigley, the Doctor knew that she was already in full retreat.

CHAP. VIII. *From Sootythorn to Wenderholme.*

A little relieved, perhaps (for it is always disagreeable to quarrel with one's hostess, even though one has no occasion to be afraid of her), the Doctor gladly told Lady Helena all about Mrs. Prigley, and even narrated the anecdote about the hole in the carpet, and its consequences to Mrs. Ogden, which put Lady Helena into good humor, for nothing is more amusing to rich people than the ludicrous consequences of a certain kind of poverty. The sense of a pleasant contrast, all in their own favor, is delightful to them; and when the Doctor had told this anecdote, Lady Helena became agreeably aware that she had carpets, and that her carpets had no holes in them — two facts of which use and custom had made her wholly unconscious. Her eye wandered with pleasure over the broad soft surface of dark pomegranate color, with its large white and red flowers and its nondescript ornaments of imitated gold, and the ground seemed richer, and the flowers seemed whiter and redder, because poor Mrs. Prigley's carpets were in a condition so lamentably different.

"Mrs. Prigley's a relation of yours, Lady Helena, — rather a near relation, — perhaps you are not aware of it?"

Lady Helena looked, and was, very much surprised. "A relation of *mine*, Dr. Bardly! you must be mistaken. I believe I know the names of all my relations!"

"I mean a relation of your husband — of Colonel Stanburne. Mrs. Prigley was a Miss Stanburne of Byfield, and her father was brother to Colonel Stanburne's father, and was born in this house."

"That's quite a near relationship indeed," said Lady Helena; "I wonder I never heard of it. John never spoke to me about Mrs. Prigley."

"There was a quarrel between Colonel Stanburne's father and his uncle, and there has been no intercourse between their families since. I daresay the Colonel does not even know how many cousins he had on that side, or what marriages they made." On this the Colonel came in.

"John, dear, Dr. Bardly has just told me that we have some cousins at Shayton that I knew nothing about. It's the clergyman and his wife, and their name is Prig — Prig" —

"Prigley," suggested the Doctor.

"Yes, Prigley; isn't it curious, John? did you know about them?"

"Not very accurately. I knew one of my cousins had married a clergyman somewhere in that neighborhood, but was not aware that he was the incumbent of Shayton. I don't know my cousins at all. There was a lawsuit between their father and mine, and the two branches have never eaten salt together since. I haven't the least ill-will to any of them, but there's an awkwardness in making a first step — one never can tell how it may be received. What do you say, Doctor? How would Mrs. Prig — Prigley and her husband receive me if I were to go and call upon them?"

"They'd give you cake and wine."

"Would they really, now? Then I'll go and call upon them. I like cake and wine — always liked cake and wine."

The conversation about the Prigleys did not end here. The Doctor was well aware that it would be agreeable to Mrs. Prigley to visit at Wenderholme, and be received there as a relation; and he also knew that the good-nature of the Colonel and Lady Helena might be relied upon to make such intercourse perfectly safe and pleasant. So he made the most of the opportunity, and that so successfully, that by the time dinner was announced both John Stanburne and his wife had promised to drive over some day to Shaytón from Sootythorn, and lunch with the Doctor, and call at the parsonage before leaving.

Colonel Stanburne's conversation was not always very profound, but his dinners were never dull, for he *would* talk, and make other people talk too. He solemnly warned the Doctor not to allow himself to be entrapped into giving gratuitous medical advice to Lady Helena. "She thinks

CHAP. VIII. *From Sootythorn to Wenderholme.* 83

she's got fifteen diseases, she does, upon my word; and she's a sort of notion that because you're the regimental doctor, she has a claim on you for gratuitous counsel and assistance. Now I consider that I *have* such a claim — if a private has it, surely a colonel has it too — and when we come up for our first training I shall expect you to look at my tongue, and feel my pulse, and physic me as a militiaman, at her Majesty's expense. But it is by no means so clear to me that my wife has any right to gratuitous doctoring, and mind she doesn't extort it from you. She's a regular screw, my wife is; and she loses no opportunity of obtaining benefits for nothing." Then he rattled on with a hundred anecdotes about ladies and doctors, in which there was just enough truth to give a pretext for his audacious exaggerations.

When they returned to the drawing-room, the Colonel made Lady Helena sing; and she sang well. The Doctor, like many inhabitants of Shayton, had a very good ear, and greatly enjoyed music. Lady Helena had seldom found so attentive a listener; he sought old favorites of his in her collection of songs, and begged her to sing them one after another. It seemed as if he never would be tired of listening. Her ladyship felt pleased and flattered, and sang with wonderful energy and feeling. The Doctor, though in his innocence he thought only of the pure pleasure her music gave him, could have chosen no better means of ingratiating himself in her favor; and if there had not, unhappily, been that dark and dubious question about church attendance, which made her ladyship look upon him as a sort of Dissenter, or worse, the Doctor would that night have entered into relations of quite frank and cordial friendship with Lady Helena. English ladies are very kind and forgiving on many points. A man may be notoriously immoral, or a gambler, or a drinker, yet if he be well off they will kindly ignore and pass over these little defects; but the unpardonable sin is failure in church attendance, and they will not pass over *that.*

Lady Helena, in her character of inquisitor, had discovered this symptom of heresy, and would have been delighted to find a moral screw of some kind by which the culpable Doctor might be driven churchwards. If the law had permitted it, I have no doubt that she would have applied material screws, and pinched the Doctor's thumbs, or roasted him gently before a slow fire, or at least sent him to church between two policemen with staves; but as these means were beyond her power, she must wait until the moral screw could be found. A good practical means, which she had resorted to in several instances with poor people, had been to deprive them of their means of subsistence; and all men and women whom her ladyship's little arm could reach knew that they must go to church or leave their situations; so they attended with a regularity which, though exemplary in the eyes of men, could scarcely, one would think (considering the motive), be acceptable to Heaven. But Lady Helena acted in this less from a desire to please God than from the instinct of domination, which, in her character of spiritual ruler, naturally exercised itself on this point. It seldom happens that the master of a house is the spiritual ruler of it; he is the temporal power, not the spiritual. Colonel Stanburne felt and knew that he had no spiritual power.

This matter of the Doctor's laxness as a church-goer had been rankling in Lady Helena's mind all the time she had been singing, and when she closed the piano she was ready for an attack. If the Doctor had been shivering blanketless in a bivouac, and she had had the power of giving him a blanket or withholding it, she would have offered it on condition he promised to go to church, and she would have withheld it if he had refused compliance. But the Doctor had blankets of his own, and so could not be touched through a deprivation of blanket. She might, however, deprive the old woman he had recommended, and at the same time give the Doctor a lesson, indirectly.

"I forgot to ask you, Dr. Bardly, whether the old woman you recommended for a blanket was a churchwoman, and regular in her attendance."

"Two questions very easily answered," replied that audacious and unhesitating Doctor; "she is a Wesleyan Methodist, and irregular in her attendance."

"Then I'm — very sorry — Dr. Bardly, but I cannot give her a blanket, as I had promised. I can only give them to our — own people, you know ; and I make it essential that they should be *good* church-people — I mean, very regular church-people."

"Very well ; I'll give her a blanket myself."

The opportunity was not to be neglected, and her ladyship fired her gun. She had the less hesitation in doing so, that it seemed monstrously presumptuous in a medical man to give blankets at all! What right had he to usurp the especial prerogative of great ladies? And then to give a blanket to this very woman whom, for good reasons, her ladyship had condemned to a state of blanketlessness!

"I quite understand," she said, with much severity of tone, "that Dr. Bardly, who never attends public worship himself, should have a fellow-feeling with those who are equally negligent."

It is a hard task to fight a woman in the presence of her husband, who is at the same time one's friend. The Doctor *thought*, " Would the woman have me offer premiums on hypocrisy as she does?" but he did not say so, because there was poor John Stanburne at the other end of the hearth-rug in a state of much uncomfortableness. So the Doctor said nothing at all, and the silence became perfectly distressing. Lady Helena had a way of her own out of the difficulty. Though it was an hour earlier than the usual time for prayers, she rang the bell and ordered all the servants in. When they were kneeling, each before his chair, her ladyship read the prayers herself, and accentuated with a certain severity a paragraph in which she thanked God that she was not as unbelievers, who were destined to perish everlastingly. It was a satisfaction to Lady Helena to have the Doctor there down upon his knees, with no means of escape from the expression of spiritual superiority.

CHAPTER IX.

THE FUGITIVE.

"I SAY, Doctor," said John Stanburne, when her ladyship was fairly out of hearing, and half-way in her ascent of the great staircase — "I say, Doctor, I hope you don't mind what Helena says about you not being — you know some women are so — indeed I do believe all women are so. They seem laudably anxious to keep us all in the right path, but perhaps they 're just a little *too* anxious."

The Doctor said he believed Lady Helena meant to do right, but — and then he hesitated.

"But you don't see the sense of bribing poor people into sham piety with blankets."

"Well, no, I don't."

"Neither do I, Doctor. There's a Roman Catholic family about three miles off, and the lady there gives premiums on going to mass, and still higher premiums on confession. She has won a great many converts; and there's a strong antagonism between her and Helena — a most expensive warfare it is too, I assure you, this warfare for souls. However, it's an ill wind that blows nobody good, and the poor profit by it, which is a consolation, only it makes them sneaks — it makes them sneaks and hypocrites. Doctor, come into my study, will you, and let's have a weed?"

The "study," as John Stanburne called it, was a coscy little room, with oak wainscot that his grandfather had painted white. It contained a small bookcase, and the bookcase contained a good many novels, some books of poetry, a treatise on dog-breaking, a treatise on driving, and a treatise on fishing. The novels were very well selected, and so was the poetry; and John Stanburne had read all these books, many of them over and over again. Such literary education as he possessed had been mainly got out of that bookcase; and though he had no claim to erudition, a man's head might be worse furnished than with such furniture as that. There was a splendid library at Wenderholme — a big room lined with the backs of books as the other rooms were lined with paper or wainscot; and when Stanburne wanted to know something he went there, and disturbed his ponderous histories and encyclopædias; but he *used* the little bookcase more than the big library. He could not read either Latin or Greek. Few men can read Latin and Greek, and of the few who can, still fewer do read them; but his French was very much above the usual average of English French — that is, he spoke fluently, and would no doubt have spoken correctly if only he could have mastered the conjugations and genders, and imitated the peculiar Gallic sounds.

The society of ladies is always charming, but it must be admitted that there is an hour especially dear to the male sex, and which does not owe its delightfulness to their presence. It is the hour of retirement into the smoking-room. When the lady of the house has a tendency to make the weight of her authority felt (and this will sometimes happen), the male members of her family and their guests feel a schoolboyish sense of relief in escaping from it; but even when she is very genial and pleasant, and when everybody enjoys the light of her countenance, it must also be confessed that the timely withdrawal of that light, like the hour of sunset, hath a certain sweetness of its own.

"My wife's always very good about letting me sit here, and smoke and talk as long as I like with my friends, after she's gone to bed," said Colonel Stanburne. "You smile because I seem to value a sort of goodness that seems only natural, but that's on account of your old-bachelorish ignorance of womankind. There are married men who no more dare sit an hour with a cigar when their wives are gone to bed than they dare play billiards on Sunday. Now, for instance, I was staying this autumn with a friend of mine in another county, and about ten o'clock his wife went to bed. He and I wanted to talk over a great many things. We had been old schoolfellows, and we had travelled together when we were both bachelors, and we knew lots of men that his wife knew nothing about, and each of us wanted to hear all the news that the other had to tell; so he just ventured, the first night I was there, to ask me into his private study and offer me a cigar. Well, we had scarcely had time to light when his wife's maid knocks at the door and says, 'Please, sir, Missis wishes to see you;' so he promised to go, and began to look uncomfortable, and in five minutes the girl came again, and she came three times in a quarter of an hour. After that came the lady herself, quite angry, and ordered her husband to bed, just as if he had been a little boy; and though he seemed cool, and didn't stir from his chair, it was evident that he was afraid of her, and he solemnly promised to go in five minutes. At the expiration of the five minutes in she bursts again (she had been waiting in the passage — perhaps she may have been listening at the door), and held out her watch without one word. The husband got up like a sheep, and said 'Goodnight, John,' and she led him away just like that; and I sat and smoked by myself, thinking what a pitiable spectacle it was. Now my wife is not like that; she will have her way about her blankets, but she's reasonable in other respects."

They sat very happily for two hours, talking about the regiment that was to be. Suddenly, about midnight, a large watch-dog that inhabited a kennel on that side of the house began to bark furiously, and there was a cry, as of some woman or child in distress. The Colonel jumped out of his chair, and threw the window open. The two men listened attentively, but it was too dark to see any thing. At length Colonel Stanburne said, "Let us go out and look about a little — that was a human cry, wasn't it?" So he lighted a lantern, and they went.

There was a thick wood behind the house of Wenderholme, and this wood filled a narrow ravine, in the bottom of which was a little stream, and by the stream a pathway that led up to the open moor. This moor continued without interruption over a range of lofty hills, or, to speak more strictly, over a sort of plateau or table-land, till it terminated at the enclosed pasture-lands near Shayton. John Stanburne and the Doctor walked first along this pathway. The watch-dog's kennel was close to the path, at a little green wooden gate, where it entered the garden.

The dog, hearing his master's step, came out of his kennel, much excited with the hope of a temporary release from the irksomeness of his captivity; but his master only caressed and spoke to him a little, and passed on. Then he began to talk to the Doctor. The sound of his voice reached the ears of a third person, who came out of the wood, and began to follow them on the path.

The Doctor became aware that they were followed, and they stopped. The Colonel turned his lantern, and the light of it fell full upon the intruder.

"Why, it's a mere child," said the Colonel. "But what on earth's the matter with the Doctor?"

Certainly that eccentric Doctor *did* behave in a most remarkable manner. He snatched the lantern from the Colonel's hand without one word of apology, and having cast its beams on the child's face, threw it down on the ground, and seized the vagrant in his arms. "The Doctor's mad," thought the Colonel, as he picked up the lantern.

"Why, *it's little Jacob!*" cried Dr. Bardly.

But this conveyed nothing to the mind of the Colonel. What did he know about little Jacob?

The Fugitive.

Meanwhile the lad was telling his tale to his friend. Father had beaten him so, and he'd run away. "Please, Doctor, don't send me back again." The child's feet were bare, and icy cold, and covered with blood. His clothes were wet up to the waist. His little dog was with him.

"It's a little boy that's a most particular friend of mine," said the Doctor; "and he's been very ill-used. We must take care of him. I must beg a night's lodging for him in the house."

They took him into the Colonel's study, before the glowing fire. "Now, what's to be done?" said the Colonel. "It's lucky you're a doctor."

"Let us undress him and warm him first. We can do every thing ourselves. There is a most urgent reason why no domestic should be informed of his being here. His existence here must be kept secret."

The Colonel went to his dressing-room and brought towels. Then he set some water on the fire in a kettle. The Doctor took the wet things off, and examined the poor little lacerated feet. He rubbed little Jacob all over with the towels most energetically. The Colonel, whose activity was admirable to witness, fetched a tub from somewhere, and they made arrangements for a warm bath.

"One person must be told about this," said Dr. Bardly, "and that's Lady Helena. Go and tell her now. Ask her to get up and come here, and warn her not to rouse any of the servants."

Her ladyship made her appearance in a few minutes in a dressing-gown. "Lady Helena," said the Doctor, "you're wanted as a nurse. This child requires great care for the next twenty-four hours, and you must do every thing for him with your own hands. Is there a place in the house where he can be lodged out of the way of the servants?"

Lady Helena had no boys of her own. She had had one little girl at the beginning of her married life, who had lived, and was now at Wenderholme, comfortably sleeping in the prettiest of little beds, in a large and healthy nursery in the left wing of the building. She had had two little boys since, but *they* were both sleeping in Wenderholme churchyard. When she saw little Jacob in his tub, the tears came into her eyes, and she was ready to be his nurse as long as ever he might have need of her.

"I'll tell you all about him, Lady Helena, when we've put him to bed."

Little Jacob sat in his tub looking at the kind, strange lady, and feeling himself in a state of unrealizable bliss. "You must be very tired and very hungry, my poor child," she said. Little Jacob said he was very hungry, but he didn't feel tired now. He had felt tired in the wood, but he didn't feel tired now in the tub.

The boy being fairly put to bed, female curiosity could not wait till the next day, and she sought out the Doctor, who was still with the Colonel in his study. "I beg to be excused, gentlemen," she said, "for intruding in this room in an unauthorized manner, but I want to know all about that little boy."

The Doctor told his history very minutely, and the history of his father. Then he added, "I believe the only possible chance of saving his father from killing himself with drinking is to leave him for some time under the impression that the boy, having been driven away by his cruelty, has died from exposure on the moor. This may give him a horror of drinking, and may effect a permanent cure. There is another thing to be considered, the child's own safety. If we send him back to his father, I will not answer for his life. The father is already in a state of hirritability bordering on insanity — in fact he is partially insane; and if the child is put under his power before there has been time to work a thorough cure, it is likely that he will beat him frequently and severely — he may even kill him in some paroxysm of rage. If Isaac Ogden knew that the child were here, and claimed him to-morrow, I believe it would be your duty not to give him up, and

I should urge his uncle to institute legal proceedings to deprive the father of the guardianship. A man in Isaac Ogden's state is not fit to have a child in his power. He has beaten him very terribly already, — his body is all bruises ; and now if we send him back, he will beat him again for having run away."

These reasons certainly had great weight, but both the Colonel and Lady Helena foresaw much difficulty in keeping the child at Wenderholme without his presence there becoming immediately known. His disappearance would make a noise, not only at Shayton, but at Sootythorn, and everywhere in the neighborhood. The relations of the child were in easy circumstances, and a heavy reward would probably be offered, which the servants at Wenderholme Hall could scarcely be expected to resist, still less the villagers in the neighboring hamlet. It would be necessary to find some very solitary person, living in great obscurity, to whose care little Jacob might be safely confided — at any rate, for a few days. Lady Helena suggested two old women who lived together in a sort of almshouse of hers on the estate, but the Colonel said they were too fond of gossip, and received too many visitors, to be trusted. At last the Doctor's countenance suddenly brightened, and he said that he knew where to hide little Jacob, but where that was he positively refused to tell. All he asked for was, that the child should be kept a close prisoner in the Colonel's sanctum for the next twenty-four hours, and that the Colonel would lend him a horse and gig — *not* a tandem.

CHAPTER X.

CHRISTMAS AT MILEND.

IT is quite unnecessary to inform the reader where Dr. Bardly had determined to hide little Jacob. His resolution being decidedly taken, the Colonel and he waited till the next night at half-past twelve, and then, without the help of a single servant, they harnessed a fast-trotting mare to a roomy dogcart. Little Jacob and Feorach were put where the dogs were kept on shooting expeditions. And both fell asleep together. It was six o'clock in the morning when the Doctor arrived at his destination.

Mr. Isaac Ogden, whose wretchedness the reader pities perhaps as much as the Doctor did, continued his researches for some weeks in a discouraged and desultory way, but little Jacob was perfectly well hidden. Mrs. Ogden had been admitted into the secret by the Doctor, and approved of his policy of concealment. Under pretext of a journey to Manchester with Dr. Bardly, to consult an eminent physician there, she absented herself two days from Milend and went to visit her grandson. The truth was also known to Jacob Ogden, senior, who supported his mother's resolution, which would certainly have broken down without him. It pained her to see her son Isaac in the misery of a bereavement which he supposed to be eternal. The Doctor took a physiological view of the case, and argued that time was a necessary condition of success. "We aren't sure of having saved him yet," said the Doctor: "we must persevere till his constitution has got past the point of craving for strong drink altogether."

Matters remained in this state until Christmas Eve. Periodical festivals are highly agreeable institutions for happy people, who have the springs of merriment within them, ready to gush forth on any pretext, or on the strength of simple permission to gush forth; but it is difficult for a man oppressed by a persistent weight of sorrow to throw it off because the almanac has brought itself to a certain date, and it is precisely at the times of general festivity that such a man feels his burden heaviest. It may be observed also, that as a man, or a society of men, approaches the stage of maturity and reflection, the events of life appear more and more to acquire the power of coloring the whole of existence; so that the faculty of being merry at appointed times, and its converse, the faculty of weeping at appointed times, both give place to a continual but quiet sadness, from which we never really escape, even for an hour, though we may still be capable of a manly fortitude, and retain a certain elasticity, or the appearance of it. In a word, our happiness and misery are no longer alternative and acute, but coexist in a chronic form, so that it has ceased to be natural for men to wear sackcloth and heap ashes on their heads, and sit in the dust in their wretchedness; and it has also ceased to be natural for them to crown themselves with flowers, and anoint themselves with the oil of gladness, and clothe themselves in the radiance of purple and cloth-of-gold. No hour of life is quite miserable enough or hopeless enough for the sackcloth and the ashes — no hour of life is brilliant enough for the glorious vesture and the flowery coronal.

A year before, Isaac Ogden would have welcomed the Christmas festivities as a legitimate occasion for indulgence in his favorite vice, without much meditation (and in this perhaps he may have resembled some other very regular observers of the festival) on the history of the Founder of Christianity. But as it was no longer his desire to celebrate either this or any other festival of the Church by exposing himself to a temptation which, for him, was the strongest and most dangerous of all temptations — and as the idea of a purely spiritual celebration was an idea so utterly foreign to the whole tenor of his thoughts and habits as never even to suggest itself to him — he had felt strongly disposed to shun Christmas altogether, — that is, to escape from the outward and visible Christmas to some place where the days might pass as merely natural days, undistinguished by any sign of national or ecclesiastical commemoration. He had determined, therefore, to go back to Twistle Farm, from which it seemed to him that he had been too long absent, and had announced this intention to the Doctor. But when the Doctor repeated it to Mrs. Ogden, she would not hear of any such violation of the customs and traditions of the family. Her sons had always spent Christmas Eve together; and so long as she lived, she was firmly resolved that they always should. The pertinacity with which a determined woman will uphold a custom that she cherishes is simply irresistible — that is, unless the rebel makes up his mind to incur her perpetual enmity; and Isaac Ogden was less than ever in a condition of mind either to brave the hostility of his mother or wound her tenderer feelings. So it came to pass that on Christmas Eve he went to Milend to tea.

Now on the tea-table there were some little cakes, and Mrs. Ogden, who had not the remotest notion of the sort of delicacy that avoids a subject because it may be painful to somebody present, and who always simply gave utterance to her thoughts as they came to her, observed that these little cakes were of her own making, and actually added, "They're such as I used makin' for little Jacob — he was so fond on 'em."

Isaac Ogden's feelings were not very sensitive, and he could bear a great deal; but he could not bear this. He set down his cup of tea untasted, gazed for a few seconds at the plateful of little cakes, and left the room.

The Doctor was there, but he said nothing. Jacob Ogden did not feel under any obligation to be so reticent. "Mother," he said, "I think you needn't have mentioned little Jacob — our Isaac cannot bear it; he knows no other but what th' little un's dead, and he's as sore as sore."

This want of delicacy in Mrs. Ogden arose from an all but total lack of imagination. She could sympathize with others if she suffered along with them — an expression which might be criticised as tautological, but the reader will understand what is meant by it. If Mrs. Ogden had had the toothache, she would have sympathized with the sufferings of another person similarly afflicted so long as her own pangs lasted; but if a drop of creosote or other powerful remedy proved efficacious in her own case, and released her from the torturing pain, she would have looked upon her fellow-sufferer as pusillanimous, if after that she continued to exhibit the outward signs of torment. Therefore, as she herself knew that little Jacob was safe it was now incomprehensible by her that his father should not feel equally at ease about him, though, as a matter of fact, she was perfectly well aware that he supposed the child to be irrecoverably lost. Mrs. Ogden, therefore, received her son Jacob's rebuke with unfeigned surprise. She had said nothing to hurt Isaac that she knew of — she "had only said that little Jacob used being fond o' them cakes, and it was quite true."

Isaac did not return to the little party, and they began to wonder what had become of him. After waiting some time in silence, Mrs. Ogden left her place at the tea-tray, and went to a little sitting-room adjoining — a room the men were more accustomed to than any other in the house, and where indeed they did every thing but eat and sleep. Mr. Ogden had gone there from habit, as his mother expected, and there she found him sitting in a large rocking-chair, and gazing abstractedly into the fire. The chair rocked regularly but gently, and its occupant seemed wholly unconscious —

not only of its motion, but of every other material circumstance that surrounded him.

Mrs. Ogden laid her hand upon his shoulder, and said, "Isaac, willn't ye come to your tea? we're all waiting for you."

The spell was broken, and Ogden suddenly started to his feet. "Give me my hat," he said, "and let me go to my own house. I'm not fit to keep Christmas this year. How is a man to care about tea and cakes when he's murdered his own son? I'm best by myself; let me go up to Twistle Farm. D'ye expect me to sing songs at supper, and drink rum-punch?"

"There'll be no songs, and you needn't drink unless you like, but just come and sit with us, my lad — you always used spendin' Christmas Eve at Milend, and Christmas Day too."

"It signifies nought what I used doin'. Isaac Ogden isn't same as he used to be. He'd have done better, I reckon, if he'd altered a month or two sooner. There'd have been a little lad here then to make Christmas merry for us all."

"Well, Isaac, I'm very sorry for little Jacob; but it cannot be helped now, you know, and it's no use frettin' so much over it."

"Mother," said Isaac Ogden, sternly, "it seems to me that *you're* not likely to spoil your health by frettin' over my little lad. You take it very easy it seems to me, and my brother takes it easy too, and so does Dr. Bardly — but then Dr. Bardly was nothing akin to him. Folk says that grandmothers care more for chilther than their own parents does; but you go on more like a stepmother nor a grandmother."

This was hard for Mrs. Ogden to bear, and she was strongly tempted to reveal the truth, but she forebore and remained silent. Ogden resumed, —

"I cannot tell how you could find in your heart to bake them little cakes when th' child isn't here to eat 'em."

The effort to restrain herself was now almost too much for

Mrs. Ogden, since it was the fact that she had baked the said little cakes, or others exactly like them, and prepared various other dainties, for the especial enjoyment of Master Jacob, who at that very minute was regaling himself therewith in the privacy of his hiding-place. Still she kept silent.

After another pause, a great paroxysm of passionate regret seized Ogden — one of those paroxysms to which he was subject at intervals, but which in the presence of witnesses he had hitherto been able to contend against or postpone. "Oh, my little lad!" he cried aloud, "oh, my little innocent lad, that I drove away from me to perish! I'd give all I'm worth to see thee again, little 'un!" He suddenly stopped, and as the tears ran down his cheeks, he looked out of the window into the black night. "If I did but know," he said, slowly, and with inexpressible sadness — "mother, mother, if I did but know where his bits o' bones are lying!"

It was not possible to witness this misery any longer. All Dr. Bardly's solemn injunctions, all dread of a possible relapse into the terrible habit, were forgotten. The mother had borne bitter reproaches, but she could not bear this agony of grief. "Isaac," she said, "Isaac, my son, listen to me: thy little lad is alive — he's alive and he's well, Isaac."

Ogden did not seem to realize or understand this communication. At last he said, "I know what you mean, mother, and I believe it. He's alive in heaven, and he can ail nothing, and want nothing, there."

"I hope he'll go there when he's an old man, but a good while after we go there ourselves, Isaac."

A great change spread over Ogden's face, and he began to tremble from head to foot. He laid his hand on his mother's arm with a grasp of iron. His eyes dilated, the room swam round him, his heart suspended its action, and in a low hissing whisper, he said, "Mother, have they found him?"

"Yes — and he's both safe and well."

Ogden rushed out of the house, and paced the garden-walk

hurriedly from end to end. The intensity of his excitement produced a commotion in the brain that needed the counter-stimulus of violent physical movement. It seemed as if the roof of his skull must be lifted off, and for a few minutes there was a great crisis of the whole nervous system, to which probably his former habits may have more especially exposed him. When this was over, he came back into the house, feeling unusually weak, but incredibly calm and happy. Mrs. Ogden had told the Doctor and Mr. Jacob what had passed, and the Doctor without hesitation set off at once for his own house, where he ordered his gig, and drove away rapidly on the Sootythorn road.

"Mother," said Isaac, when he came in, "give me a cup of tea, will you?"

"A glass of brandy would do you more good."

"Nay, mother, we've had enough of brandy, it will not do to begin again now."

He sat down in evident exhaustion and drank the tea slowly, looking rather vacantly before him. Then he laid his head back upon the chair and closed his eyes. The lips moved, and two or three tears ran slowly down the cheeks. At last he started suddenly, and, looking sharply round him, said, "Where is he, where is he, mother? where is little Jacob, my little lad, my lad, my lad?"

"Be quiet, Isaac—try to compose yourself a little; Dr. Bardly's gone to fetch him. He'll be with us very soon."

Mr. Ogden remained quietly seated for some minutes without speaking, and then, as his mind began to clear after the shock of the great emotion it had passed through, he asked who had found his boy, and where they had found him, and when.

These questions were, of course, somewhat embarrassing to his mother, and she would probably have sheltered herself behind some clumsy invention, but her son Jacob interposed.

"The fact is, Isaac, the loss of your little 'un seemed to be doin' you such a power o' good 'at it seemed a pity to spoil it by tellin' you. And it's my opinion as mother's let th' cat out o' th' bag three week too soon as it is."

"Do you mean to tell me," said Isaac, "that you knew the child was found, and hid him from his own father?"

"Isaac, Isaac, you mun forgive us," said the mother; "we did it for your good."

"Partly for his good, mother," interposed Jacob, "but still more for th' sake o' that child. What made him run away from Twistle Farm, Isaac Ogden? answer me that."

Isaac remained silent.

"Do you fancy, brother Isaac, that any consideration for your feelin's was to hinder us from doin' our duty by that little lad? What sort of a father is it as drives away a child like that with a horsewhip? Thou was no more fit to be trusted with him nor a wolf wi' a little white lamb. If he'd been brought back to thee two days after, it 'ud a' been as much as his life was worth. And I'll tell thee what, Isaac Ogden, if ever it comes to my ears as you take to horse-whippin' him again, I'll go to law wi' you and get the guardianship of him into safer hands. There'd be little difficulty about that as it is. I've taken my measures — my witnesses are ready — I've consulted lawyers; and I tell you candidly, I mean to act at once if I see the least necessity for it. Little Jacob was miserable for many a week before you drove him out o' th' house, an' if we'd only known, you would never have had the chance."

"Nay, Jacob," interposed Mrs. Ogden, "you're a bit too hard on Isaac; he's the child's own father, and he had a right to punish him within reason."

"Father! father!" cried Jacob, scornfully; "there isn't a man in Shayton as isn't more of a father to our little un than Isaac has been for many a month past. There isn't a man in Shayton but what would have been kinder to a nice little lad like that than he has been. What signifies havin' begotten a child, if fatherin' it is to stop there?"

At last Isaac Ogden lifted up his face and spoke.

"Brother Jacob, you have said nothing but what is right and true, and you have all acted right both by me and him. But let us start fresh. I've turned over a new leaf; I'm not such as I used to be. I mean to be different, and to do different, and I will be a good father to that child. So help me God!"

He held out his hand, and Jacob took it and shook it heartily. The two brothers looked in each other's face, and there was more of brotherly affection in their look than there had ever been since the dissolution of their partnership in the cotton business, which had taken place some years before. Mrs. Ogden saw this with inexpressible pleasure. "That's right, lads — that's right, lads; God bless you! God bless both on you!"

The customs of Shayton were mighty, especially the custom of drinking a glass of port-wine on every imaginable occasion. If a Shayton man felt sorry, he needed a glass of port-wine to enable him to support his grief; but if he felt glad, there arose at once such a feeling of true sympathy between his heart and that joyous generous fluid, that it needed some great material impediment to keep them asunder, and such an impediment was not to be found in any well-to-do Shayton household, where decanters were always charged, and glasses ever accessible. So it was inevitable that on an occasion so auspicious as this Mr. Jacob Ogden should drink a glass — or, more probably, two glasses — of port; and his mother, who did not object to the same refreshment, bore him company.

"Now Isaac, lad, let's drink a glass to mother's good health."

Mr. Ogden had not made any positive vow of teetotalism, and though there might be some danger in allowing himself to experience afresh, however slightly, the seductive stimulus of alcohol, whole centuries of tradition, the irresistible power

Christmas at Milend.

of prevalent custom, and the deep pleasure he felt in the new sense of brotherly fellowship, made his soul yearn to the wine.

"Here's mother's good health. Your good health, mother," he said, and drank. Jacob repeated the words, and drank also, and thus in a common act of filial respect and affection did these brothers confirm and celebrate their perfect reconciliation.

Isaac now began to show symptoms of uneasiness and restlessness. He walked to the front door, and listened eagerly for wheels. "How fidgety he is, th' old lad!" said Jacob; "it's no use frettin' an' fidgetin' like that; come and sit thee down a bit, an' be quiet."

"How long will he be, mother?"

Before Mrs. Ogden could reply, Isaac's excited ear detected the Doctor's gig. He was out in the garden immediately, and passed bareheaded through the gate out upon the public road. Two gig-lamps came along from the direction of Sootythorn. He could not see who was in the gig, but something told him that little Jacob was there, and his heart beat more quickly than usual.

Perhaps our little friend might have behaved himself somewhat too timidly on this occasion, but the Doctor had talked to him on the road. He had explained to him, quite frankly, that Mr. Ogden's harshness had been wholly due to the irritable state of his nervous system, and that he would not be harsh any more, because he had given up drinking. He had especially urged upon little Jacob that he must not seem afraid of his father; and as our hero was of a bold disposition, and had plenty of assurance, he was fully prepared to follow the Doctor's advice.

Isaac Ogden hails the gig; it stops, and little Jacob is in his arms.

"Please, papa, I wish you a merry Christmas and a happy New Year!"

Little Jacob's pony was sent for, and the next morning his

father and he rode together up to Twistle Farm. Until the man came for the pony, old Sarah had not the faintest hope that little Jacob was in existence, and the shock had nearly been too much for her. The messenger had simply said, "I'm comed for little Jacob* tit." "And who wants it?" Sarah said; for it seemed to her a desecration for any one else to mount that almost sacred animal. "Why, little Jacob wants it hissel, to be sure." And this (with some subsequent explanations of the most laconic description) was his way of breaking the matter delicately to old Sarah.

The old woman had never spent an afternoon, even the afternoon of Christmas Day, so pleasantly as she spent that. How she did toil and bustle about? The one drawback to her happiness was that she did not possess a Christmas cake; but she set to work and made tea-cakes, and put such a quantity of currants in them that they were almost as good as a Christmas cake. She lighted a fire in the parlor, and another in little Jacob's room; and she took out the little night-gown that she had cried over many a time, and, strange to say, she cried over it this time too. And she arranged the small bed so nicely, that it looked quite inviting, with its white counterpane, and clean sheets, and bright brass knobs, and pretty light iron work painted blue. When all was ready, it occurred to her that since it was Christmas time she would even attempt a little decoration; and as there were some evergreens at Twistle Farm, and some red berries, she went and gathered thereof, and attempted the adornment of the house — somewhat clumsily and inartistically, it must be confessed, yet not without giving it an air of festivity and rejoicing. She had proceeded thus far, and could not "bethink her" of any thing else that needed to be done, when, suddenly casting her eye on her own costume, she perceived that it was of the deepest black; for, being persuaded that the dear child was dead, she had so clothed herself out of respect for

* The possessive is omitted in the genuine Lancashire dialect.

his memory. She held her sombre skirt out with both her hands as if to push it away from her, and exclaimed aloud, "I'll be shut o' *thee*, onyhow, and sharply too;" and she hurried upstairs to change it for the brightest garment in her possession, which was of sky-blue, spotted all over with yellow primroses. She also put on a cap of striking and elaborate magnificence, which the present writer does not attempt to describe, only because such an attempt would incur the certainty of failure.

That cap had hardly been assumed and adjusted when it was utterly crushed and destroyed in a most inconsiderate manner. A sound of hoofs had reached old Sarah's ears, and in a minute afterwards the cap was ruined in Master Jacob's passionate embraces. You may do almost any thing you like to a good-tempered old woman, so long as you do not touch her cap; and it is an undeniable proof of the strength of old Sarah's affection, and of the earnestness of her rejoicing, that she not only made no remonstrance in defence of her head-dress, but was actually unaware of the irreparable injury which had been inflicted upon it.

CHAPTER XI.

THE COLONEL GOES TO SHAYTON.

THE next time the Doctor met Colonel Stanburne at Sootythorn, he gave such a good account of Mr. Isaac Ogden, that the Colonel, who took a strong interest in little Jacob, expressed the hope that Mr. Ogden would still join the regiment; though in the time of his grief and tribulation he had resigned his commission, or, to speak more accurately — for the commission had not yet been formally made out and delivered to him — he had withdrawn his name as a candidate for one. The Colonel, in his friendly way, declared that the Doctor was not a hospitable character. "I ask you to Wenderholme every time I see you, and you come and stay sometimes, though not half often enough, but you never ask me to your house; and, by Jove! if I want to be invited at all, I must invite myself." The Doctor, who liked John Stanburne better and better the more he knew of him, still retained the very erroneous notion that a certain state and style were essential to his happiness; and, notwithstanding many broad hints that he had dropped at different times on the subject, still hung back from asking him to a house where, though comfort reigned supreme, there was not the slightest pretension to gentility. The old middle-class manner of living still lingered in many well-to do houses in Shayton, and the Doctor faithfully adhered to it. Every thing about him was perfectly clean and decent, but he had not marched with the times; and whilst the attorneys and cotton-spinners in Sootythorn and elsewhere had the chairs of their dining-rooms covered with morocco leather, and their drawing-rooms filled with all manner of glittering fragilities, and Brussels carpets with pretty little tasteful patterns, and silver forks, and napkins, and a hundred other visible proofs of the advance of refinement, the worthy Doctor had not kept up with them at all, but lagged behind by the space of about thirty years. He had no drawing-room; the chairs of his parlor were of an ugly and awkward pattern, and their seats were covered with horsehair; the carpet was cheap and coarse, with a monstrous pattern that no artistic person would have tolerated for a single day; and though the Doctor possessed a silver punch-ladle and teapot, and plenty of silver spoons of every description, all the forks in the house were of steel! Indeed, the Doctor's knives and forks, which had belonged to his mother, or perhaps even to his grandmother, were quite a curiosity in their way. They had horn handles, of an odd indescribable conformation, supposed to adapt itself to the hollow of the hand, but which, from some misconception of human anatomy on the part of the too ingenious artificer, seemed always intended for the hand of somebody else. These handles were stained of such a brilliant green, that, in the slang of artists, they "killed" every green herb on the plate of him who made use of them. The forks had spring guards, to prevent the practitioner from cutting his left hand with the knife that he held in his right; and the knife had a strange round projection at what should have been the point, about the size of a shilling, which (horrible to relate!) had been originally designed to convey gravy and small fragments of viands, not prehensible by means of the two-pronged fork, into the human mouth! In addition to these strange relics of a bygone civilization the Doctor possessed two large rocking-chairs, of the same color as the handles of his knives. The Doctor loved a rocking-chair, in which he did but share a taste universally prevalent in Shayton, and defensible on the profoundest philosophical grounds. The human creature loves repose, but a thousand causes may hinder the perfect enjoyment of it, and torment him into restlessness at the very time when he most longs for rest. He may sit down after the business of the day, and some mental or bodily uneasiness may make the quiet of the massive easy-chair intolerable to him. The easy-chair does not sympathize with him, does not respond to the fidgety condition of his nervous system; and yet he tries to sit down in it and enjoy it, for, though fidgety, he is also weary, and needs the comfort of repose. Now, the rocking-chair — that admirable old Lancashire institution — and the rocking-chair alone, responds to both these needs. If you are fidgety, you rock; if not, you don't. If highly excited, you rock boldly back, even to the extremity of danger; if pleasantly and moderately stimulated, you lull yourself with a gentle motion, like the motion that little waves give to a pleasure boat. It is true that the bolder and more emphatic manner of rocking has become impossible in these latter days, for the few upholsterers who preserve the tradition of the rocking-chair at all make it in such a highly genteel manner, that the rockers are diminished to the smallest possible arc; but the Doctor troubled himself little concerning these achievements of fashionable upholstery, and regarded his old rocking-chairs with perfect satisfaction and complacency — in which, without desiring to offend against the decisions of the fashionable world, we cannot help thinking that he was right.

A large green rocking-chair, with bold high rockers and a soft cushion like a small feather-bed, a long clay pipe quite clean and new, a bright copper spittoon, and a jug of strong ale, — these things, with the necessary concomitants of a briskly burning fire and an unlimited supply of tobacco, formed the ideal of human luxury and beatitude to a generation now nearly extinct, but of which the Doctor still preserved the antique traditions. In substance often identical, but in outwardly visible means and appliances differing in every detail, the pleasures of one generation seem quaint and even ridiculous in comparison with the same pleasures as pursued by its successor. Colonel Stanburne smoked a pipe, but it was a short meerschaum, mounted in silver; and he also used a knife and fork, and used them skilfully and energetically, but they were not like the Doctor's grandmother's knives and forks.

And yet, when the Colonel came to Shayton, he managed to eat a very hearty dinner at one P.M. with the above-named antiquated instruments. After the celery and cheese, Dr. Bardly took one of the rocking-chairs, and made the Colonel sit down in the other; and Martha brought a fresh bottle of uncommonly fine old port, which she decanted on a table in the corner that did duty as a sideboard. When they had done full justice to this, the Doctor ordered hot water; and Martha, accustomed to this laconic command, brought also certain other fluids which were hot in quite a different sense. She also brought a sheaf of clay tobacco-pipes, about two feet six inches long, and in a state of the whitest virginity — emblems of purity! emblems, alas! at the same time, of all that is most fragile and most ephemeral!

"Nay, Martha," said the Doctor, "we don't want them clay pipes to-day. Colonel Stanburne isn't used to 'em, I reckon. Bring that box of cigars that I bought the other day in Manchester."

The Colonel, however, would smoke a clay pipe, and he tried to rock as the Doctor did, and soon, by the effect of that curious sympathy which exists between rocking-chairs (or their occupants), the two kept time together like musicians in a duet, and clouds of the densest smoke arose from the two long tobacco-pipes.

It had been announced to the inhabitants of the parsonage that the representative of the house of Stanburne intended to call there that afternoon; and though it would be an exaggeration to state that the preparations for his reception were on a scale of magnificence, it is not an exaggeration to describe them as in every respect worthy of Mrs. Prigley's skill as a manager, and her husband's ingenuity and taste. New carpets they could *not* buy, so it was no use thinking about them; and though Mrs. Prigley had indulged the hope that Mrs. Ogden's attention would be drawn to the state of her carpets by that accident with which the reader is already acquainted, so as to lead, it might be, to some act of generosity on her part, this result had not followed, and indeed had never suggested itself to Mrs. Ogden, who had merely resolved to look well to her feet whenever she ventured into the parlor at the parsonage, as on dangerous and treacherous ground. Under these circumstances Mrs. Prigley gradually sank into that condition of mind which accepts as inevitable even the outward and visible signs of impecuniosity; and though an English lady must indeed be brought low before she will consent to see the boards of her floors in a condition of absolute nakedness, poor Mrs. Prigley had come down to this at last; and she submitted without a murmur when her husband expressed his desire that "that old rag" on the floor of the drawing-room might be removed out of his sight. When the deal boards were carpetless, Mrs. Prigley was proceeding with a sigh to replace the furniture thereon; but her husband desired that it might be lodged elsewhere for a few days, during which space of time he kept the door of the drawing-room locked, and spent two or three hours there every day in the most mysterious seclusion, to the neglect of his parochial duties. Mrs. Prigley in vain endeavored to discover the nature of his occupation there. She tried to look through the key-hole, but a flap of paper had been adapted to it on the inside to defeat her feminine curiosity; she went into the garden and attempted to look in at the window, but the blind was down, and as it was somewhat too narrow, slips of paper had been pasted on the glass down each side so as to make the interstice no longer available. The reverend master of the house endeavored to appear as frank and communicative as usual, by talking volubly on all sorts of subjects except the mystery of the drawing-room ; but Mrs. Prigley did not consider it consistent with her self-respect to appear to take any interest in his discourse, and during all these days she preserved, along with an extreme gentleness of manner, the air of a person borne down by secret grief. An invisible line of separation had grown up between the two ; and though both were perfectly courteous and polite, each felt that the days of mutual confidence were over. There was a difference, however, in their respective positions ; for the parson felt tranquil in the assurance that the cloud would pass away, whereas his wife had no such assurance, and the future was dark before her. It is true, that, notwithstanding the outward serenity of her demeanor, Mrs. Prigley was sustained by the inward fires of wrath, which enable an injured woman to endure almost any extremity of mental misery and distress.

We have seen that the Shayton parson had that peculiar form of eccentricity which consists in the love of the Beautiful. He had great projects for Shayton Church, which as yet lay hidden in the privacy of his own breast ; and he had also projects for the parsonage, of which the realization, to the eye of reason and common-sense, would have appeared too remote to be entertained for an instant. But the enthusiasm for the Beautiful does not wait to be authorized by the Philistines, — if it *did*, it would wait till the end of all things ; and Mr. Prigley, poor as he was, determined to have such a degree of beauty in his habitation as might be consistent with his poverty. Without being an artist, or any thing approaching to an artist, he had practised the drawing of the simpler decorative forms, and was really able to combine them very agreeably. He could also lay a flat tint with a brush quite neatly, though he could not manage a gradation. When it had been finally decided that carpets could no longer be afforded, Mr. Prigley saw that the opportunity had come for the exercise of his talents ; but he was far too wise a man to confide to his wife projects so entirely outside the orbit of her ideas. He had attempted, in former days, to inoculate her mind with the tastes that belong to culture, but he had been met by a degree of impenetrability which proved to him that the renewal of such attempts, instead of adding to his domestic happiness by creating closer community of ideas, might be positively detrimental to it, by proving too plainly the impossibility of such a community. Mrs. Prigley, like many good women of her class, was totally and absolutely devoid of culture of any kind. She managed her house admirably, and with a wonderful thrift and wisdom; she was an excellent wife in a certain sense, though more from duty than any great strength of affection; but beyond this and the Church Service, and three or four French phrases which she did not know how to pronounce, her mind was in such a state of darkness and ignorance as to astonish even her husband from time to time, though he had plenty of opportunities for observing it.

But what *was* he doing in the drawing-room? He was doing things unheard of in the Shayton valley. In the days of his youth and extravagance he had bought a valuable book on Etruscan design; and though, as we have said elsewhere, his taste and culture, though developed up to a certain point, were yet by no means perfect or absolutely reliable, still he could not but feel the singular simplicity and grace of that ancient art, and he determined that the decoration of his drawing-room should be Etruscan. On the wide area of the floor he drew a noble old design, and stained it clearly in black and red; and, when it was dry, rubbed linseed-oil all over it to fix it. The effect was magnificent! the artist was delighted with his performance! but on turning his eye from the perfect unity of the floor, with its centre and broad border, to the old paper on the walls, which was covered with a representation of a brown angler fishing in a green river, with a blue hill behind him, and an equally blue church-steeple, and a cow who had eaten so much grass that it had not only fattened her but colored her with its own greenness — and when the parson counted the number of copies of this interesting landscape that adorned his walls, and saw that they numbered sixscore and upwards — then he felt that he had too much of it, and boldly resolved to abolish it. He looked at all the wall-papers in the shop at Shayton, but the endurable ones were beyond his means, and the cheap ones were not endurable — so he purchased a quantity of common brown parcel-paper, of which he took care to choose the most agreeable tint; and he furtively covered his walls with *that*, conveying the paper, a few sheets at a time, under his topcoat. When the last angler had disappeared, the parson began to feel highly excited at the idea of decorating all that fresh and inviting surface. He would have a frieze — yes, he would certainly have a frieze; and he set to work, and copied long Etruscan processions. Then the walls must be divided into compartments, and each compartment must have its chosen design, and the planning and the execution of this absorbed Mr. Prigley so much, that for three weeks he did not write a single new sermon, and, I am sorry to say, scarcely visited a single parishioner except in cases of pressing necessity. As the days were so short, he took to working by candle-light; and when once he had discovered that it was possible to get on in this way, he worked till two o'clock in the morning. He made himself a cap-candlestick, and with this crest of light on the top of his head, and the fire of enthusiasm inside it, forgot the flying hours.

The work was finished at last. It was not perfect; a good critic might have detected many an inaccuracy of line, and some incongruousness in the juxtaposition of designs, which, though all antique and Etruscan, were often of dissimilar epochs. But, on the whole, the result justified the proud satisfaction of the workman. The room would be henceforth marked with the sign of culture and of taste: it was a little Temple of the Muse in the midst of a barbarian world.

But what would Mrs. Prigley say? The parson knew that he had done a bold deed, and he rather trembled at the consequence. "My love," he said, one morning at breakfast-time, "I've finished what I was doing in the drawing-room, and you can put the furniture back when you like; but I should not wish to have any thing hung upon the walls — they are sufficiently decorated as it is. The pictures" (by which Mr. Prigley meant sundry worthless little lithographs and prints) — "the pictures may be hung in one of the bed-rooms wherever you like."

Mrs. Prigley remained perfectly silent, and her husband did not venture to ask her to accompany him into the scene of his artistic exploits. He felt that in case she did not approve what he had done, the situation might become embarrassing. So, immediately after breakfast, he walked forth into the parish, and said that he should probably dine with Mr. Jacob Ogden, who (by his mother's command) had kindly invited him to do so whenever he happened to pass Milend about one o'clock in the day. And in this way the parson managed to keep out of the house till tea-time. It was not that Mr. Prigley dreaded any criticism, for to criticise, one must have an opinion. Mrs. Prigley on these matters had not an opinion. All that Mr. Prigley dreaded was the anger of the offended spouse — of the spouse whom he had not even gone through the formality of seeming to consult.

He was punished, but not as he had expected to be punished. Mrs. Prigley said nothing to him on the subject; but when they went into the drawing-room together at night, she affected not to perceive that he had done any thing whatever there. Not only did she not speak about these changes, but, though Mr. Prigley watched her eyes during the whole evening to see whether they would rest upon his handiwork, they never seemed to perceive it, even for an instant. She played the part she had resolved upon with marvellous persistence and self-control. She seemed precisely as she had always been: — sulky? not in the least; there was not the slightest trace of sulkiness, or any thing approaching to sulkiness in her manner — the Etruscan designs were simply invisible for her, that was all.

They were not so invisible for the Colonel when he came to pay his visit at the parsonage, and, in his innocence, he complimented Mrs. Prigley on her truly classical taste. He had not the least notion that the floor was carpetless because the Prigleys could not afford a carpet — the degree of poverty which could not afford a carpet not being conceivable by him as a possible attribute of one of his relations or friends. He believed that this beautiful Etruscan design was preferred by Mrs. Prigley to a carpet — to the best of carpets — on high æsthetic grounds. Ah! if he could have read her heart, and seen therein all the shame and vexation that glowed like hidden volcanic fires! All these classical decorations seemed to the simple lady a miserable substitute for the dear old carpet with its alternate yellow flourish and brown lozenge; and she regretted the familiar fisherman whose image used to greet her wherever her eyes might rest. But she felt a deeper shame than belongs to being visibly poor or visibly ridiculous. The room looked poor she knew, and in her opinion it looked ridiculous also; but there was something worse than that, and harder far to bear. How shall I reveal this bitter grief and shame — how find words to express the horror I feel for the man who was its unpardonable cause! Carried away by his enthusiasm for a profane and heathen art, Mr. Prigley had actually introduced, in the frieze and elsewhere, several figures which — well, were divested of all drapery whatever! "And he a clergyman, too!" thought Mrs. Prigley. True, they were simply outlined; and the conception of the original designer had been marvellously elegant and pure, chastened to the last degree by long devotion to the ideal; but there they were, these shameless nymphs and muses, on the wall of a Christian clergyman!

John Stanburne, who had travelled a good deal, and who had often stayed in houses where there were both statues and pictures, saw nothing here but the evidence of cultivated taste. "What *will* he think of us?" said Mrs. Prigley to herself; and she believed that his compliments were merely a kind way of trying to make her feel less uncomfortable. She thought him very nice, and he chattered as pleasantly as he possibly could, so that the Doctor, who had come with him, had no social duty to perform, and spent his time in studying the Etruscan decorations. Colonel Stanburne apologized for Lady Helena, who had intended to come with him; but her little girl was suffering from an attack of fever — not a dangerous fever, he hoped, though violent.

The Doctor, who had not before heard of this, was surprised; but as he did not visit Wenderholme professionally (for Wenderholme Hall was, medically speaking, under the authority of the surgeon at Rigton, whose jealousy was already awakened by our Doctor's intimacy with the Colonel), he reflected that it was no business of his. The fact was, that little Miss Stanburne was in the enjoyment of the most perfect health, but her mother thought it more prudent to let the Colonel go to Shayton by himself in the first instance, so as to be able to regulate her future policy according to his report. Mr. Prigley came in before the visitor had exhausted the subject of the fever, which he described with an accuracy that took in these two very experienced people, for he described from memory — his daughter having suffered from such an attack about six months earlier than the very recent date the Colonel found it convenient to assign to it.

It was, of course, a great satisfaction to the Prigleys that the head of the Stanburnes should thus voluntarily renew a connection which, so far as personal intercourse was concerned, was believed to have been permanently severed. It was not simply because the Colonel was a man of high standing in the county that they were glad to become acquainted with him — there were certain clannish and romantic sentiments which now found a satisfaction long denied to them. Mrs. Prigley felt, in a minor degree, what a Highland gentlewoman still feels for the chief of her clan; and she was disposed to offer a sort of loyalty to the Colonel as the head of her house, which was very different from the common respect for wealth and position in general. The Stanburnes had never taken any conspicuous part in the great events of English history, but the successive representatives of the family had at least been present in many historical scenes, in conflicts civil and military, on the field, on the quarter-deck of the war-ship, in stormy Parliamentary struggles; and the present chief of the name, for other descendants of the family, inherited in an especial sense a place in the national life of England. Not that Mrs. Prigley had any definite notions even about the history of her own family; the sentiment of birth is quite independent of historical knowledge, and many a good gentlewoman in these realms is in a general way proud of belonging to an old family, without caring to inquire very minutely into the history of it, just as she may be proud of her coat-of-arms without knowing any thing about heraldry.

The Colonel, in a very kind and graceful manner, expressed his regret that such near relations should have been separated for so long by an unfortunate dispute between their fathers. "I believe," he said, "that your side has most to forgive, since my father won the lawsuit, but surely we ought not to perpetuate ill-feeling, generation after generation." Mr. Prigley said that no ill-feeling remained; but that though he had often wished to see Wenderholme and its owner, he knew that, as a rule, poor relations were liked best at a distance, and that not having hitherto had the pleasure of knowing Colonel Stanburne, he must be held excusable for having supposed him to be like the rest of the world. John Stanburne was not quite satisfied with this somewhat formal and dignified assurance, and was resolved to establish a more intimate footing before he left the parsonage. He exerted himself to talk about ecclesiastical matters and church architecture, and when Mr. Prigley offered to show him the church, accompanied him thither with great apparent interest and satisfaction. The Doctor had patients to visit, and went his own way.

CHAPTER XII.

OGDEN'S NEW MILL.

OUR Jacob, or big Jacob, or Jacob at Milend, as he now began to be called in the Ogden family, to distinguish him from his nephew and homonym, had arrived at that point in the career of every successful cotton-spinner when a feeling of great embarrassment arises as to the comparative wisdom of purchasing an estate or "laying down a new mill." When his brother Isaac retired from the concern with ten thousand pounds, Jacob had not precisely cheated him, perhaps, but he had made a bargain which, considered prospectively, was highly favorable to his own interest; and since he had been alone, the profits from the mill had been so considerable that his savings had rapidly accumulated, and he was now troubled with a very heavy balance at his bankers, and in various investments, which, to a man accustomed to receive the large interest of successful cotton-spinning, seemed little better than letting money lie idle. Mrs. Ogden had three hundred a-year from five or six very small farms of her own, which she had inherited from her mother, and this amply sufficed for the entire expenses of the little household at Milend. Jacob spent about a hundred and fifty pounds a-year on himself personally, of which two-thirds were absorbed in shooting,—the only amusement he cared about. His tailor's bill was incredibly small, for he had the excuse, when in Shayton, of being constantly about the mill, and it was natural that he should wear old fustian and corduroy there; and as for his journeys to Manchester, it was his custom on these occasions to wear the suit which had been the Sunday suit of the preceding year. His mother knitted all his stockings for him, and made his shirts, these being her usual occupations in an evening. His travelling expenses were confined to the weekly journeys to Manchester, and as these were always on business, they were charged to the concern. If Jacob Ogden had not been fond of shooting, his personal expenses, beyond food and lodging (which were provided for him by his mother), would not have exceeded fifty pounds a-year; and it is a proof of the great firmness of his character in money matters that, although by nature passionately fond of sport, he resolutely kept the cost of it within the hundred. His annual outlay upon literature was within twenty shillings; not that it is to be supposed that he spent so large a sum as one pound sterling in a regular manner upon books, but he had been tempted by a second-hand copy of Baine's 'History of Lancashire,' which, being much the worse for wear, had been marked by the bookseller at five pounds, and Jacob Ogden, by hard bargaining, had got it for four pounds nine shillings and ninepence. After this extravagance he resolved to spend no more "foolish money," as he called it, and for several years made no addition to his library, except a book on dog-breeding, and a small treatise on the preservation of game, which he rightly entered amongst his expenses as a sportsman. We are far from desiring to imply that Jacob Ogden is in this respect to be considered a representative example of the present generation of cotton-manufacturers, many of whom are highly educated men, but he may be fairly taken as a specimen of that generation which founded the colossal fortunes that excite the wonder, and sometimes, perhaps, awaken the envy, of the learned. When nature produces a creature for some especial purpose, she does not burden it with wants and desires that would scatter its force and impair its efficiency. The industrial epoch had to be inaugurated, the manufacturing districts had to be created — and to do this a body of men were needed who should be fresh springs of pure energy, and reservoirs of all but illimitable capital ; men who should act with the certainty and steadiness of natural instincts which have never been impaired by the hesitations of culture and philosophy — men who were less nearly related to university professors than to the ant, and the beaver, and the bee. And if any cultivated and intellectual reader, in the thoughtful retirement of his library, feels himself superior to Jacob Ogden, the illiterate cotton-spinner, he may be reminded that he is not on all points Ogden's superior. We are all but tools in the hands of God ; and as in the mind of a writer great delicacy and flexibility are necessary qualities for the work he is appointed to do, so in the mind of a great captain of industry the most valuable qualities may be the very opposite of these. Have we the energy, the directness, the singleness of purpose, the unflinching steadiness in the dullest possible labor, that mark the typical industrial chief? We know that we have not ; we know that these qualities are not compatible with the tranquillity of the studious temperament and the meditative life. And if the Ogdens cannot be men of letters, neither can the men of letters be Ogdens.

It is admitted, then, that Jacob Ogden was utterly and irreclaimably illiterate. He really never read a book in his life, except, perhaps, that book on dog-breaking. Whenever he tried to read, it was a task and a labor to him ; and as literature is not of the least use in the cotton trade, the energy of his indomitable will had never been brought to bear upon the mastery of a book. And yet you could not meet him without feeling that he was very intelligent — that he possessed a kind of intelligence cultivated by the closest observation of the men and things within the narrow circle of his life. Has it never occurred to the reader how wonderfully the most illiterate people often impress us with a sense of their intelligence — how men and women who never learned the alphabet have its light on their countenance and in their eyes? In Ogden's face there were clear signs of that, and of other qualities also. And there was a keenness in the glance quite different from the penetration of the thinker or the artist — a keenness which always comes from excessively close and minute attention to money matters, and from the passionate love of money, and which no other passion or occupation ever produces.

In all that related to money Jacob Ogden acted with the pitiless regularity of the irresistible forces of nature. As the sea which feeds the fisherman will drown him without remorse — as the air which we all breathe will bury us under heaps of ruin — so this man, though his capital enabled a multitude to live, would take the bed from under a sick debtor, and, rather than lose an imperceptible atom of his fortune, inflict the utmost extremity of misery. Even Hanby, his attorney, who was by no means tender-hearted, had been staggered at times by his pitilessness, and had ventured upon a feeble remonstrance. On these occasions a shade of sternness was added to the keenness of Ogden's face, and he repeated a terrible maxim, which, with one or two others, guided his life: "If a man means to be rich, he must have no fine feelings;" and then he would add, "*I* mean to be rich."

Perhaps he would have had fine feelings on a Sunday, for on Sundays he was religious, and went to church, where he heard a good deal about being merciful and forgiving which on week-days he would have attributed to the influence of the sentiments which he despised. But Ogden was far too judicious an economist of human activities to be ignorant of the great art of self-adaptation to the duties and purposes of the hour; and as a prudent lawyer who has a taste for music will take care that it shall not interfere with his professional work, so Jacob Ogden, who really had rather a taste for

Ogden's New Mill.

religion, and liked to sit in church with gloved hands and a clean face, had no notion of allowing the beautiful sentiments which he heard there to paralyze his action on a week-day. Every Sunday he prayed repeatedly that God would forgive him his debts or trespasses as he forgave his debtors or those that trespassed against him; but that was no reason why he should not, from Monday morning to Saturday night inclusively, compel everybody to pay what he owed, and distress him for it if necessary. After all, he acted so simply and instinctively that one can hardly blame him very severely. The truest definition of him would be, an incarnate natural force. The forces of wealth, which are as much natural forces as those of fire and frost, had incarnated themselves in him. His sympathy with money was so complete, he had so entirely subjected his mind to it, so thoroughly made himself its pupil and its mouth-piece, that it is less accurate to say that he *had* money than that he *was* money. Jacob Ogden was a certain sum of money whose unique idea was its own increase, and which acted in obedience to the laws of wealth as infallibly as a planet acts in obedience to the cosmic forces.

It is only natural that a man so endowed and so situated should grow rich. In all respects circumstances were favorable to him. He had robust health and indefatigable energy. His position in a little place like Shayton, where habits of spending had not yet penetrated, was also greatly in his favor, because it sheltered him in undisturbed obscurity. No man who is born to wealth, and has lived from his infancy in the upper class, will confine his expenditure during the best years of manhood to the pittance which sufficed for Ogden. It was an advantage to him, also, that his mind should be empty, because he needed all the room in it for the endless details concerning his property and his trade. No fact of this nature, however minute, escaped him. His knowledge of the present state of all that belonged to him was so clear and accurate, and his foresight as to probable changes so sure, that he anticipated every thing, and neutralized every cause of loss before it had time to develop itself.

That a man whose daily existence proved the fewness of his wants should have an eager desire for money, may appear one of the inconsistencies of human nature; but in the case of Jacob Ogden, and in thousands of cases similar to his, there is no real inconsistency. He did not desire money in order to live luxuriously; he desired it because the mere possession of it brought increased personal consideration, and gave him weight and importance in the little community he lived in. And when a man relies on wealth *alone* for his position — when he is, obviously, not a gentleman — he needs a great quantity of it. Another reason why Jacob Ogden never felt that he had enough was because the men with whom he habitually compared himself, and whom he wished to distance in the race, did not themselves remain stationary, but enriched themselves so fast that it needed all Jacob Ogden's genius for money-getting to keep up with them; for men of talent in every order compare themselves with their equals and rivals, and not with the herd of the incapable. It was his custom to go to Manchester in the same railway carriage with four or five men of business, who talked of nothing but investments, and it would have made Jacob Ogden miserable not to be able to take a share in these conversations on terms of perfect equality.

"I'm sure," thought Mrs. Ogden, "that our Jacob's got something on his mind. He sits and thinks a deal more than he used doin'. He's 'appen * fallen in love, an' doesn't like to tell me about it, because it's same as tellin' me to leave Milend."

Mrs. Ogden was confirmed in her suspicions that very evening by the fact that "our Jacob" shut himself up in the little sitting-room with a builder. "If it's to build himself a new

* Perhaps.

'ouse and leave me at Milend, I willn't stop; and if it's to build me a new 'ouse, I shall never live there. I shall go an' live i' th' Cream-pot."

The idea of Mrs. Ogden living in a cream-pot may appear to some readers almost as mythical as the story of that other and much more famous old lady who lived in a shoe; but although a cream-pot would not be a bad place to live in if one were a mouse, and the rich fluid not dangerously deep, it is not to be supposed that Mrs. Ogden entertained such a project in an obvious and literal sense. Her intentions were rational, but they need a word of explanation. She possessed a small farm called the Cream-pot; and of all her small farms this was her best beloved. Therefore had she resolved, years and years before, that when Jacob married she would go to the Cream-pot, and dwell there for the days that might remain to her.

She waited till the builder had gone, and then went into the little room. Jacob was busy examining a plan. "I wish you wouldn't trouble yourself about that buildin', Jacob," said Mrs. Ogden; "there needs no buildin', for as soon as ever you get wed I shall go to th' Cream-pot."

Her son looked up from his plan with an air of the utmost astonishment. Mrs. Ogden continued, —

"I think you might have told me about it a little sooner. I don't even know her name, not positively, though I may guess it, perhaps. There's no doubt about one thing — you'll have time enough to repent in. As they make their bed, so they must lie."

"What the devil," said Jacob, thinking aloud and *very* loudly, — "what the devil is th' ould woman drivin' at?"

"Nay, if I'm to be sworn at, I've been too long i' this 'ouse already."

And Mrs. Ogden, with that stately step which distinguished her, made slowly for the door.

In cases where the lady of a house acts in a manner which

is altogether absurd, the male or males, whose comfort is in a great degree dependent upon her good temper, have a much better chance of restoring it than when she is but moderately unreasonable. They are put upon their guard; they are quite safe from that most fatal of errors, an attempt to bring the lady round by those too direct arguments which are suggested by masculine frankness; they are warned that judicious management is necessary. Thus, although Jacob Ogden, in the first shock of his astonishment, had not replied to his mother in a manner precisely calculated to soothe her, he at once perceived his error, and saw that she must be brought round. In politer spheres, where people beg pardon of each other for the most trifling and even imaginary offences, the duty of begging pardon is so constantly practised that (like all well-practised duties) it is extremely easy. But it was impossible for Jacob Ogden, who had never begged pardon in his life.

"I say, mother, stop a bit. You've gotten a bit o' brass o' your own, an' I'm layin' down a new mill, and I shall want o' th'* brass I can lay my hands on. I willn't borrow none, out of this 'ouse, not even of my brother Isaac; but if you could lend me about four thousand pound, I could give a better finish to th' new shed."

"Why, Jacob, you never told me as you were layin' down a new mill."

"No, but I should a' done if you'd a' waited a bit. I never right made up my mind about it while last night."

It was not Jacob Ogden's custom to be confidential with his mother about money matters, and she on her part had been too proud to seek a confidence that was never offered; but many little signs had of late led her to the conclusion that Jacob was in a period of unusual prosperity. He had bought one or two small estates for three or four thousand pounds

---

* All the. In Lancashire the word *all* is abbreviated, as in Scotland, to a', but pronounced *o*.

each, and then had suddenly declared that he would lay out no more money in "potterin' bits o' property like them, but keep it while he'd a good lump for summat o' some use." The decision about the new mill proved to Mrs. Ogden that the "lump" in question was already accumulated.

"Jacob," she said, "how much do you reckon to put into th' new mill?"

"Why, 'appen about forty thousand; an' if you'll lend me four, that'll be forty-four."

This was a larger sum than Mrs. Ogden had hoped; but she showed no sign of rejoicing beyond a quiet smile.

"And where do you think of buildin' it?"

"Well, mother, if you don't mind sellin' me Little Mouse Field, it's the best mill-site in all Shayton. There's that water-course so handy; and it'll increase the valley* of our land round about it."

Mrs. Ogden was perfectly soothed by this time. Jacob wanted to borrow four thousand pounds of her. She had coal under her little farms, of which the accumulated produce had reached rather more than that amount; and she promised the loan with a facetious hope that the borrower would be able to give her good security. As to Little Mouse Field, he was quite welcome to it, and she begged him to accept it as a present.

"Nay, mother; you shouldn't give me no presents bout † givin' summat to our Isaac. But I reckon it's all one; for all as I have, or shall have, 'll go to little Jacob."

"Eh, how you talk, lad! Why, you'll get wed an' have chilther of your own. You're young enough, an' well off beside."

"There's no need for me to get wed, mother, so long as th' old woman lasts, an' who'll last a long while yet, I reckon. There's none o' these young ladies as is kerfle enough to do for a man like me as has been accustomed to see his house

* Value.　　　　　　　　　　　　† Without.

well managed. Why, they cannot neither make a shirt nor a puddin'."

These disparaging remarks concerning the "Girl of the Period" filled (as they were designed to fill) Mrs. Ogden's mind with tranquillity and satisfaction. To complete her good-humor, Jacob unrolled the plans and elevation of his new mill. The plans were most extensive, but the elevation did not strike the spectator by its height; for as the site was not costly, Jacob Ogden had adopted a system then becoming prevalent in the smaller towns of the manufacturing districts, where land was comparatively cheap — the system of erecting mills rather as sheds than on the old five-storied model. His new mill was simply a field walled in and roofed over, with a tall engine house and an enormous chimney at one end. People of æsthetic tastes would see nothing lovely in the long straight lines of roofs and rows of monotonously identical windows which displayed themselves on the designs drawn by Ogden's architect; but to Ogden's eyes there was a beauty here greater than that of the finest cathedral he had ever beheld. He was not an imaginative person; but he had quite enough imagination to realize the vista of the vast interior, the roar of the innumerable wheels, the incessant activity of the living makers of his wealth. He saw himself standing in the noble engine-room, and watching the unhurried see-saw of the colossal beams; the rise and fall of the pistons, thicker than the spear of Goliath, and brighter than columns of silver; the revolution of the enormous fly-wheel; the exquisite truth of motion; the steadiness of man's great creature, that never knows fatigue. That engine-room should be the finest in all Shayton. It should have a plaster cornice round its ceiling, and a great moulded ornament in the middle of it; the gas-lights should be in handsome ground-glass globes; and about the casings of the cylinders there should be a luxury of mahogany and brass.

"But, Jacob," said his mother, when she had duly adjusted

her spectacles, and gradually mastered the main features of the plan, "it seems to me as you've put th' mill all o' one side, and th' engine nobbut half-fills th' engine-house."

Ogden had never heard of Taymouth Castle and the old Earl of Breadalbane, who, when somebody asked him why he built his house at the extremity of his estate, instead of in the middle of it, answered that he intended to "brizz yint."* But, like the ambitious Earl, Ogden was one of those who "brizz yint."

"Why, mother," he said, "this 'ere's nobbut half the new mill. What can you do with forty-five thousand?"

* Push beyond.

CHAPTER XIII.

STANITHBURN PEEL.

"HELENA!" said Colonel Stanburne one morning when he came down to breakfast, "I've determined on a bold stroke. I'm going to take the tandem this morning to Stanithburn Peel, to see young Philip Stanburne and get him to accept a captaincy in the new regiment."

Her ladyship did not see why this should be called a bold stroke, so she asked if the road were particularly dangerous to drive upon, and suggested that, if it were, one horse would be safer than two.

"That's not it. The sort of courage wanted on the present occasion, my dear Helena, is moral courage and not physical courage, don't you see? Did you never hear the history of the Stanburnes of Stanithburn? Surely female ignorance does not go so far as to leave you uninformed about such a distinguished family as ours?"

"I know the history of its present representative, or at least as much of it as he chooses to tell me."

"Error added to ignorance! I am not the representative of the family. We of Wenderholme are only a younger branch. The real representative is Philip Stanburne, of Stanithburn Peel."

"I scarcely ever heard of him before. I had some vague notion that such a person existed. Why does he never come here?"

"It's a long story, but you will find it all in the county histories. In Henry the Eighth's time Sir Philip Stanburne was a rebel and got beheaded, some people say hanged, for treason, so his estates were confiscated. Wenderholme and Stanithburn Tower were given back to the family in the next generation, but the elder branch had only Stanithburn, which is a much smaller estate than this. Since then they married heiresses, but always regularly spent their fortunes, and,now young Philip Stanburne has nothing but the tower with a small estate of bad land which brings him in four or five hundred a-year."

"Not much certainly; but why does he never come here?"

"My father used to say that there had been no intercourse between Stanithburn and Wenderholme for three hundred years. Most likely the separation was a religious quarrel, to begin with. The elder branch always remained strictly Roman Catholic; but the Wenderholme branch was more prudent, and turned Protestant in Queen Elizabeth's time."

"All this is quite a romantic story, but those county histories are so full of archæology that one does not venture to look into them. Would it not be better to write to Mr. Philip Stanburne? There is no knowing how he may receive you."

The Colonel thought it better to go personally. "I'm not clever, Helena, at persuading people with a pen; but I can generally talk them round, when I have a chance of seeing them myself."

The distance from Wenderholme to Stanithburn Peel was exactly twenty-five miles; but the Colonel liked a long drive, and the tandem was soon on its way through the narrow but well-kept lanes that traversed the stretch of fertile country which separated the two houses. The Colonel lunched and baited his horses at a little inn not often visited by such a stylish equipage, and it was nearly three o'clock in the afternoon when he began to enter the hilly country near the Peel.

The roads here were not so good as those in the plain, and instead of being divided from the fields by hedges they passed between gray stone walls. The scenery became more and more desolate as the horses advanced. There was little sylvan beauty left in it except that of the alders near a rapid stream in the valley, and the hills showed the bare limestone in many places through a scanty covering of grass. At length a turn of the road brought the Colonel in sight of the Tower or Peel of Stanithburn itself, an edifice which had little pretension to architectural beauty, and lacked altogether that easily achieved sublimity which in so many Continental buildings of a similar character is due to the overhanging of *machicoulis* and *tourelles*. It possessed, however, the distinguishing feature of a battlement, which, still in perfect preservation, entirely surrounded the leads of the flat roof. Beyond this the old Tower retained no warlike character, but resembled an ordinary modern house, with an additional story on the top of it. There were, alas! some modern sash-windows, which went far to destroy the character of the edifice; yet whatever injury the Philistinism of the eighteenth century might have inflicted upon the building itself, it had not been able to destroy the romantic beauty of its site. The hill that separates Shayton from Wenderholme *is* of sandstone; and though behind Twistle Farm and elsewhere there are groups of rocks of more or less picturesque interest, they are not comparable to the far grander limestone region about the Tower of Stanithburn. The Tower itself is situated on a bleak eminence, half surrounded by a curve of the stream already mentioned; but a mile below the Tower the stream passes through a ravine of immense depth, and in a series of cascades reaches the level of the plain below. Above Stanithburn Peel, on the other hand, the stream comes from a region of unimaginable desolation — where the fantastic forms of the pale stone lift themselves, rain-worn, like a council of rude colossi, and no sound is heard but the wind and the stream, and the wild cry of the plover.

A very simple gateway led from the public to a private road, which climbed the hill till it ended in a sort of farm-yard between the Peel and its outbuildings. When the Colonel arrived here, he was received by a farm-servant, who showed the way to the stable, and said that his master was out fishing. By following the stream, the Colonel would be sure to find him.

John Stanburne set off on foot, not without some secret apprehension. "Perhaps Helena was right," he thought; "perhaps I ought to have written. They say he is a strange, eccentric sort of fellow, and there is no telling how he may receive me."

Philip Stanburne, of the Peel, was in fact reputed to be morbid and misanthropic, with as much justice as there usually is in such reports. After his father's death he had been left alone with his mother, and the few years that he lived in this way with her had been the sweetest and happiest of his life. When he lost her, his existence became one of almost absolute solitude, broken only by a weekly visit to a great house ten miles from Stanithburn, where a chaplain was kept, and he could hear mass — or by the occasional visits of the doctor, and one or two by no means intimate neighbors. In country places a difference of religion is a great impediment to intercourse; and though people thought it quite right that Philip Stanburne should be a Catholic, they never could get over a feeling of what they called "queerness" in the presence of a man who believed in transubstantiation, and said prayers to the Virgin Mary. Like many other recluses, he was credited with a dislike to society far different from his real feeling, and much less creditable to his good sense. Habit had made solitude endurable to him, and there was something agreeable, no doubt, in the sense of his independence, but there was not the slightest taint of misanthropy in his whole nature. He naturally shrank from the society of Sootythorn because it was so strongly Protestant; and there were no families of his own creed in his immediate neighborhood. His way of living was too simple for the entertainment of guests. Having no profession by which money might be earned, he was reduced to mere economy, which got him a reputation for being stingy and unsociable.

The Colonel walked a mile along the stream without perceiving anybody, but at length he saw Philip Stanburne, very much occupied with his fly-book, and accompanied only by a dog, which began to bark vigorously as soon as he perceived the presence of a stranger. A quarter of an hour afterwards the two new acquaintances were talking easily enough, and the recluse of the Tower began to feel inclined to join the militia, though he had asked for time to consider.

"I have heard," said the Colonel, "that the name which your house still keeps, and from which our own name comes, is due to some stone in your stream — stone in the burn, or stane i' th' burn, and so to Stanithburn and Stanburne. Is there any particular stone here likely to give a ground for the theory, or is it only a tradition?"

"I have no doubt," said Philip Stanburne, "of the accuracy of tradition in this instance. Come and look at the stone itself."

He turned aside from the direct path to the Tower, and they came again to the brink of the stream, which had here worn for itself two channels deep in the limestone. Between these channels rose an islanded rock about thirty feet above the present level of the water. A fragment of ruined building was discernible on its narrow summit.

As the two men looked together on the stone from which their race had taken its name centuries ago, both fell under the influence of that mysterious sentiment, so different from the pride of station or the vanity of precedence, which binds us to the past. Neither of them spoke, but it is not an exaggeration to say that both felt their relationship then. Had not the time been when Stanburne of the Peel and Stanburne of Wenderholme were brothers? A fraternal feeling began to unite these two by subtle, invisible threads.

CHAPTER XIV.

AT SOOTYTHORN.

NOT many days after the little events narrated in the preceding chapter, Mr. Philip Stanburne awoke in a small bedroom on the second floor of the Thorn Inn, or Thorn Hotel, at Sootythorn. It was a disagreeable, stuffy little room; and an extensive four-poster covered fully one-half the area of the floor. There was the usual wash-hand stand, and close to the wash-hand stand a chair, and on the chair the undress uniform of a militia officer. Philip Stanburne lay in the extensive four-poster, and contemplated the military equipment, of which the most brilliant portions were the crimson sash, and the bright, newly gilded hilt of a handsome sword. As it was only the undress uniform, there was nothing particularly striking in the dress itself, which consisted of a plain dark-blue frock-coat, and black trowsers with narrow red seam. Nevertheless, Captain Stanburne felt no great inclination to invest his person with what looked very like a disguise. His instincts were by no means military; and the idea of marching through the streets of Sootythorn with a drawn sword in his hand had little attraction for him.

When he drew up his blind, the view from the window was unpleasantly different from the view that refreshed his eye every morning at Stanithburn Peel. The Thorn Inn was higher than most of the houses in Sootythorn, and Philip Stanburne had a view over the roofs. Very smoky they all were, and still smokier were the immense chimney-stalks of the cotton-mills. "One, two, three, four," began Philip, aloud, as he counted the great chimneys, and he did not stop till he had counted up to twenty-nine. The Thorn Inn was just in the middle of the town, and there were as many on the other side — a consideration which occurred to Philip Stanburne's reflective mind, as it sometimes occurs to very philosophical people to think about the stars that are under our feet, on the other side of the world.

"What a dirty place it is!" thought Philip Stanburne. "I wish I had never come into the militia. Fancy me staying a month in such a smoky hole as this! I wish I were back at the Peel. And just the nicest month in the year, too!" However, there he was, and it was too late to go back. He had to present himself at the orderly-room at half-past nine, and it was already a quarter to nine.

On entering the coffee-room of the hotel he found half-a-dozen gentlemen disguised like himself in military apparel, and engaged in the business of breakfast. He did not know one of them. He knew few people, especially amongst the Protestant gentry; and he literally knew nobody of the middle class in Sootythorn except Mr. Garley the innkeeper, and one or two tradesmen.

Philip had no sooner entered the coffee-room than Mr. Garley made his appearance with that air of confidence which distinguished him. Mr. Garley was not Philip Stanburne's equal in a social point of view, but he was immensely his superior in *aplomb* and knowledge of the world. Thus, whilst Captain Stanburne felt slightly nervous in the presence of the gentlemen in uniform, and disguised his nervousness under an appearance of lofty reserve, Mr. Garley, though little accustomed to the sight of military men, or of gentlemen wearing the appearance of military men, was no more embarrassed than in the presence of his old friends the commercials. "Good morning, Captain Stanburne," said

Mr. Garley; "good morning to *you*, sir; 'ope you slep well; 'ope you was suited with your room."

Philip muttered something about its being "rather small."

"Well, sir, it *is* rather small, as you say, sir. I could have wished to have given you a better, but you see, sir, I kep the best room in the 'ouse for the Curnle; and then there was the majors, and his lordship here, Captain Lord Henry Ughtred, had bespoke a good room more than six weeks ago; so you see, sir, I wasn't quite free to serve you quite so well as I could have wished. Sorry wè can't content *all* gentlemen, sir. What will you take to breakfast, Captain Stanburne? Would you like a boiled hegg, new-laid, or a little fried 'am, or shall I cut you some cold meat; there's four kinds of cold meat on the sideboard, besides a cold beefsteak-pie?"

As he finished his sentence, Mr. Garley drew a chair out, the seat of which had been under the table, and, with a mixture of servility and patronage (servility because he was temporarily acting the part of a waiter, patronage because he still knew himself to be Mr. Garley of the Thorn Hotel), he invited Philip Stanburne to sit down. The other gentlemen at the table had not been engaged in a very animated conversation, and they suspended it by mutual consent to have a good stare at the new-comer. For it so happened that these men were the swell clique, which had for its head Captain Lord Henry Ughtred, and for its vice-captain the Honorable Fortunatus Brabazon; and the swell clique had determined in its own corporate mind that it would have as little to do with the snobs of Sootythorn as might be. It was apprehensive of a great influx of the snob element into the regiment. There was a belief or suspicion in the clique that there existed cads even amongst the captains; and as the officers had not yet met together, a feeling of great circumspection predominated amongst the members of the clique. Philip Stanburne ventured to observe that it was a fine morning; but although his next neighbor admitted that fact, he at once allowed the conversation to drop. Mr. Garley had given Philip his first cup of tea; but, in his temporary absence, Philip asked a distinguished member of the swell clique for a second. The liquid was not refused, yet there was something in the manner of giving it which might have turned the hottest cup of tea in Lancashire to a lump of solid ice. At length Lord Henry Ughtred, having for a length of time fixed his calm blue eyes on Philip (they were pretty blue eyes, and he had nice curly hair, and a general look of an overgrown Cupid), said, —

"Pray excuse me; did I not hear Mr. Garley say that your name was Stanburne?"

"Yes, my name is Stanburne."

"Are you Colonel Stanburne's brother, may I ask?"

"No; the Colonel has no brothers."

"Ah, true, true; I had forgotten. Of *course*, I knew Stanburne had no brothers. Indeed, he told me he'd no relations — or something of the kind. You're not a relation of his, I presume; you don't belong to his family, do you?"

Philip Stanburne, in these matters, had very much of the feeling of a Highland chief. He was the representative of the Stanburnes, and the Colonel was head of a younger branch only. So when he was asked in this way whether he belonged to the Colonel's family, he at once answered "no," seeing that the Colonel belonged to *his* family, not he to the Colonel's. He was irritated, too, by the tone of his questioner; and, besides, such a relationship as the very distant one between himself and Colonel Stanburne was rather a matter for poetical sentiment than for the prose of the outer world.

Mr. Garley only made matters worse by putting his word in. "Beg pardon, Captn Stanburne, but I've always 'eard say that your family was a younger branch of the Wendrum family."

"Then you were misinformed, for it isn't."

"Perhaps it isn't just clearly traced out, sir," said Mr. Garley, intending to make himself agreeable; "but all the old people says so. If I was you, sir, I'd have it properly traced out. Mr. Higgin, the spinner here, got his pedigree traced out quite beautiful. It's really a very 'andsome pedigree, coats of arms and all. Nobody would have thought Mr. Higgin 'ad such a pedigree; but there's nothin' like tracin' and studyin', and 'untin' it all hup."

Philip Stanburne was well aware that his position as chief of his house was very little known, and that he was popularly supposed to descend from some poor cadet of Wenderholme; but it was disagreeable to be reminded of the popular belief about him in this direct way, and in the hearing of witnesses before whom he felt little disposed to abate one jot of his legitimate pretensions. However, pride kept him silent, even after Mr. Garley's ill-contrived speech, and he sought a diversion in looking at his watch. This made the others look at their watches also; and as it was already twenty-five minutes after nine, they all set off for the orderly-room, the swell clique keeping together, and Philip Stanburne following about twenty yards in the rear.

The streets of Sootythorn were seldom very animated at ten o'clock in the morning, except on a market-day; and though there was a great deal of excitement amongst the population of the town on the subject of the militia, that population was safely housed in the fifty-seven factories of Sootythorn, and an officer might pass through the streets in comparative comfort, free from the remarks which would be likely to assail him when the factories loosed. With the exception of two or three urchins who ran by Philip's side, and stared at him till one of them fell over a wheelbarrow, nothing occurred to disturb him. As the orderly-room was very near, Captain Stanburne thought he had time to buy a pocket-book at the bookseller's shop, and entered it for that purpose.

Whilst occupied with the choice of his pocket-book he heard a soft voice close to him.

"Papa wishes to know if you have got Mr. Blunting's Sermons on Popery."

"No, Miss Stedman, we haven't a copy left, but we can order one for Mr. Stedman if he wishes it. Perhaps it would be well to order it at once, as there has been a great demand for the book, and it is likely to be out of print very soon, unless the new edition is out in time to keep up the supply. Four editions are exhausted already, and the book has only been out a month or two. We are writing to London to-day; shall we order the book for you, Miss Stedman?"

The lady hesitated a little, and then said, "Papa seemed to want it very much — yes, you can order it, please."

There was something very agreeable to Philip Stanburne's ear in what he had heard, and something that grated upon it harshly. The tone of the girl's voice was singularly sweet. It came to him as comes a pure unexpected perfume. It was amongst sounds what the perfume of violets is amongst odors, and he longed to hear it again. What had grated upon him was the word "Popery;" he could not endure to hear his religion called "Popery." Still, it was only the title of some Protestant book the girl had mentioned, and she was not responsible for it — she could not give the book any other title than its own. Philip Stanburne was examining a quantity of morocco contrivances (highly ingenious, most of them) in a glass case in the middle of the shop, and he turned round to look at the young lady, but she had her back to him. She was now choosing some note-paper on the counter. Her dress was extremely simple — white muslin, with a little sprig; and she wore a plain straw bonnet — for in those days women *did* wear bonnets. It was evident that she was not a fashionable young lady, for her whole dress showed a timid lagging behind the fashion.

When she had completed her little purchases Miss Stedman left the shop, and Captain Stanburne was disappointed, for she had given him no opportunity of seeing her face; but just as he was leaving she came back in some haste, and they met rather suddenly in the doorway. "I beg your pardon," said the Captain, making way for her—and then he got a look at her face. The look must have been agreeable to him, for when he saw a little glove lying on the mat in the doorway, he picked it up rather eagerly and presented it to the fair owner. "Is this your glove, Miss—Miss Stedman?"

Now Miss Stedman had never in her life been spoken to by a gentleman in military uniform, with a sword by his side, and the fact added to her confusion. It was odd, too, to hear him call her Miss Stedman, but it was not disagreeable, for he said it very nicely. There is an art of pronouncing names so as to turn the commonest of them into titles of honor; and if Philip had said "your ladyship," he could not have said it more respectfully. So she thanked him for the glove with the warmth which comes of embarrassment, and she blushed, and he bowed, and they saw no more of each other —that day.

It was a poor little glove—a poor little cheap thread glove ; but all the finest and softest kids that lay in their perfumed boxes in the well-stocked shops of Sootythorn,—all the pale gray kids and pale yellow kids which the young shopmen so strongly recommended as "suitable for the present season," —were forgotten in a month, whereas Alice Stedman's glove was remembered for years and years.

CHAPTER XV.

WITH THE MILITIA.

THE officers met at the orderly-room, after which they all went to the parade-ground at once ; the field-officers and the Adjutant on horseback, the rest on foot.

Philip Stanburne followed the others. He knew nobody except the Colonel and the Adjutant, who had just said "Good morning" to him in the orderly-room ; but they had trotted on in advance, so he was left to his own meditations. It was natural that in passing the bookseller's shop he should think of Miss Stedman, and he felt an absurd desire to go into the shop again and buy another pocket-book, as if by acting the scene over again he could cause the principal personage to reappear. "I don't think she's pretty," said Philip to himself — "at least, not really pretty ; but she's a sweet girl. There's a simplicity about her that is very charming. Who would have thought that there was anything so nice in Sootythorn?" Just as he was thinking this, Philip Stanburne passed close to one of the blackest mills in the place — an old mill, — that is, a mill about thirty years old, for mills, like horses, age rapidly ; and through the open windows there came a mixture of bad smells on the hot foul air, and a deafening roar of machinery, and above the roar of machinery a shrill clear woman's voice singing. The voice must have been one of great power, for it predominated over all the noises in the place ; and it either was really a very sweet one or its harshness was lost in the noises, whilst it rose above them purified. Philip stopped to listen, and as he stopped, two other officers came up behind him. The footpath was narrow, and as soon as he perceived that he impeded the circulation, Philip went on.

"That's one o' th' oudest mills i' Sootythorn," said one of the officers behind Captain Stanburne; "it's thirty year oud, if it's a day."

The broad Lancashire accent surprised Captain Stanburne, and attracted his attention. Could it be possible that there were officers in the regiment who spoke no better than that? Evidently this way of speaking was not confined to an individual officer, for the speaker's companion answered in the same tone,—

"Why, that's John Stedman's mill, isn't it?"

"John Stedman? John Stedman? it cannot be t' same as was foreman to my father toward thirty year sin'?"

When Philip Stanburne heard the name of Stedman, he listened attentively. The first speaker answered, "Yes, but it is — it's t' same man."

"Well, an' how is he? he must be well off. Has he any chilther?"

"Just one dorter, a nice quiet lass, 'appen eighteen year old."

"So she's the daughter of a cotton-spinner," thought Philip, "and a Protestant cotton-spinner, most likely a bigot. Indeed, who ever heard of a Catholic cotton-spinner? I never did. I believe there aren't any. But what queer fellows these are to be in the militia; they talk just like factory lads." Then, from a curiosity to see more of these extraordinary officers, and partly, no doubt, from a desire to cultivate the acquaintance of a man who evidently knew something about Miss Stedman, Philip left the causeway, and allowed the officers to come up with him.

"I beg your pardon," he said; "no doubt you are going to the parade-ground. Will you show me the way? I was following some officers who were in sight a minute or two since, but they turned a corner whilst I was not looking at them, and I have lost my guides."

To Captain Stanburne's surprise he was answered in very good English, with no more indication of the Lancashire accent than a clearly vibrated *r*, and a certain hardness in the other consonants, which gave a masculine vigor to the language, not by any means disagreeable. The aspirate, however, was too frequently omitted or misplaced.

"We are going straight to the parade-ground ourselves, so if you come with us you cannot go wrong." There was a short silence, and the same speaker continued, "The Colonel said we were to consider ourselves introduced. I know who you are — you're Captain Stanburne of Stanithburn Peel; and now I'll tell you who we are, both of us: I'm the Doctor — my name's Bardly. I don't look like a doctor, do I? Perhaps you are thinking that I don't look very like an officer either, though I'm dressed up as one. Well, perhaps I don't. This man here is called Isaac Ogden, and he lives at Twistle Farm, on a hill-top near Shayton, when he's at home."

This queer introduction, which was accompanied by the oddest changes of expression in the Doctor's face, and by a perpetual twinkle of humor in his gray eye, amused Philip Stanburne, and put him into a more genial frame of mind than his experience of the swell clique at breakfast-time. Isaac Ogden asked Stanburne what company he had got, and on being told that it was number six, informed him that he himself was only a lieutenant.

"He's lieutenant in the grenadier company," said the Doctor, "and on Sunday morning we shall see him like a butterfly with a pair of silver wings.* He's only a chrysalis to-day; his wings haven't budded yet. He's very likely put 'em on in private — most of them put on their full uniform in private,

---

* For the information of some readers, it may be well to explain that the epaulettes of flank companies, which were of a peculiar shape, used to be called wings.

as soon as ever it comes from the tailor's. It's necessary to try it on, you know — it *might* not fit. The epaulettes would fit, though; but they generally take their epaulettes out of the tin box and put them on, to see how they look in the glass."

"Well, Doctor," said Stanburne, "I suppose you are describing from personal experience. When your own epaulettes came, you looked at yourself in the glass, I suppose."

Here an indescribably comic look irradiated Dr. Bardly's face. "You don't imagine that *I* have laid out any money on epaulettes and such gear? The tailor tried to make me buy a full uniform, of course, but it didn't answer with me. What do I want with a red coat, and dangling silver fringes over my shoulders? I've committed one piece of tomfoolery, and that's enough — I've bought this sword; but a sword might just possibly be of use for a thief. There was a man in Shayton who had an old volunteer sword always by his bedside, and one night he put six inches of it into a burglar; so you see a sword *may* be of use, but what can you do with a bit of silver fringe?"

"But I don't see how you are to do without a full uniform. How will you manage on field days, and how will you go to church on Sundays?"

"Get leave of absence on all such occasions," said the Doctor; "so long as I haven't a full uniform I have a good excuse." The fact was, that the Doctor's aversion to full dress came quite as much from a dislike to public ceremonies as from an objection to scarlet and silver in themselves. He had a youthful assistant in the regiment who was perfectly willing to represent the medical profession in all imaginable splendor, and who had already passed three evenings in full uniform, surrounded by his brothers and sisters, and a group of admiring friends.

The day was a tiresome idle day for everybody except the Adjutant, who shouted till his throat was sore, and the ser-

geants, on whom fell the real work of the companies. After
lunch, the important matter of billets had to be gone into,
and it was discovered that it was impossible to lodge all the
men in Sootythorn. One company, at least, must seek accommodation elsewhere. The junior captain must therefore
submit, for this training, to be banished from the mess, and
sent to eat his solitary beefsteak in some outlandish village,
or, still worse, in some filthy and uncouth little manufacturing
town. His appetite, it is true, might so far benefit by the
long marches to and from the parade-ground that the beefsteak might be eaten with the best of sauces; but the ordinary exercises of the regiment would have been sufficient
to procure that, and the great efforts of Mr. Garley at the
Thorn might have been relied upon for satisfying it. So the
junior captain was ordered to take his men to Whittlecup, a
dirty little town, of about six thousand inhabitants, four miles
distant from Sootythorn; and the junior captain was Philip
Stanburne.

Behold him, therefore, marching at the head of his rabble,
for the men as yet had neither uniforms nor military bearing,
on the dusty turnpike road! The afternoon had been uncommonly hot for the season of the year; and a military
uniform, closely buttoned across the breast, and padded with
cotton wool, is by no means the costume most suitable for
the summer heats. There were so few lieutenants in the
regiment (there was not one ensign) that a junior captain
could not hope for a subaltern, and all the work of the
company fell upon Philip Stanburne and his old sergeant. It
was not easy to keep any thing like order amongst the men.
They quarrelled and fought during the march; and it became
necessary to arrange them so as to keep enemies at a distance
from each other. Still, by the time they reached the pre-
cincts of Whittlecup several of the men were adorned with
black eyes; and as a few had been knocked down and
tumbled in the dust by their comrades, the company presented

rather the appearance of a rabble after a riot than of soldiers in her Majesty's service. Philip Stanburne's uniform was white with dust; but as the dust that alighted on his face was wetted by perspiration, it did not there remain a light-colored powder, but became a thick coat of dark paste. Indeed, to tell the truth, the owner of Stanithburn had never been so dirty in his life.

Now there was a river at the entrance to Whittlecup, and over the river a bridge; and on the bridge, or in advance of it (for the factories had just loosed), there stood a crowd of about three thousand operatives awaiting the arrival of the militia-men.

The Lancashire operative is not accustomed to restrain the expression of his opinions from motives of delicacy, and any consideration for your feelings which he may have when isolated diminishes with the number of his companions. Three factory lads may content themselves with exchanging sarcastic remarks on your personal appearance when you are out of hearing, thirty will make them in your presence, three hundred will jeer you loudly; and from three thousand, if once you are unlucky enough to attract their attention, there will come such volleys of derision as nobody but a philosopher could bear with equanimity.

Not only was the road lined on both sides with workpeople, but they blocked it up in front, and made way for the militia-men so slowly, that there was ample time for Philip Stanburne to hear every observation that was directed against him. Amidst the roars of laughter which the appearance of the men gave rise to, a thousand special commentaries might be distinguished.

"Them chaps sowdiers! Why, there's nobbut one sowdier i' th' lot as I can see on."

"Where is he? I can see noan at o'."

"Cannot ta see th' felly wi' th' red jacket?"

"Eh, what a mucky lot!"

"They'll be right uns for fightin',.for there's four on 'em 'as gotten black een to start wi'."

"Where's their guns?"

"They willn't trust 'em wi' guns. They'd be shootin' one another."

"There's one chap wi' a soourd."

"Why, that's th' officer."

"Eh, captain!" screamed a factory girl in Philip's ear, "I could like to gi' thee a kiss, but thou's getten sich a mucky face!"

"I wouldn't kiss him for foive shillin'," observed another.

"Eh, but I would!" said a third; "he's a nice young felly. I'll kiss him to-neet when he's washed hissel!"

CHAPTER XVI.

A CASE OF ASSAULT.

THE officers' mess was rather a good thing for Mr. Garley. He charged five shillings a-head for dinner without wine; and although both the Colonel and the large majority of his officers were temperate men, a good deal of profit may be got out of the ordinary vinous and spirituous consumption of a set of English gentlemen in harder exercise than usual, and more than usually disposed to be convivial. Even the cigars were no inconsiderable item of profit for Mr. Garley, who had laid in a stock large enough and various enough for a tobacconist.

A dense cloud of smoke filled the card-room, and through it might be discerned a number of officers in red shelljackets reposing after the labors of the day, and wisely absolving nature from other efforts, in order that she might give her exclusive care to the digestion of that substantial repast which had lately been concluded in the mess-room. There was a party of whist-players in a corner, and the rattle of billiard-balls came through an open door.

Captain Eureton's servant came in and said that there was an innkeeper from Whittlecup who desired to speak to the Adjutant. The Captain left the card-room, and the officers scarcely noticed his departure, but when he came back their attention was drawn to him by an exclamation of the Colonel's. "Why, Eureton, what's the matter now? how grave you look!"

The Adjutant came to the hearth-rug where John Stanburne was standing, and said, "Is not Captain Stanburne a relation of yours, Colonel?"

"Cousin about nine times removed. But what's the matter? He's not ill, I hope."

"Very ill, very ill indeed," said Eureton, with an expression which implied that he had not yet told the whole truth. "There's no near relation or friend of Captain Stanburne in the regiment, is there, Colonel?"

"None whatever; out with it, Eureton — you're making me very anxious;" and the Colonel nervously pottered with the end of a new cigar.

"The truth is, gentlemen," said Eureton, addressing himself to the room, for every one was listening intently, "a great crime has been committed this evening. Captain Stanburne has been murdered — or if it's not a case of murder it's a case of manslaughter. He has been killed, it appears, whilst visiting a billet, by a man in his company."

The Colonel rang the bell violently. Fyser appeared — he was at the door, expecting to be called for.

"Harness the tandem immediately."

"The tandem is at the door, sir, or will be by the time you get downstairs. I knew you would be wantin' it as soon as I 'eard the bad news."

The Doctor was in the billiard-room, trying to make a cannon, to the infinite diversion of his more skilful brother officers. His muscular but not graceful figure was stretched over the table, and his scarlet shell-jacket, whose seams were strained nearly to bursting by his attitude, contrasted powerfully with the green cloth as the strong gas-light fell upon him. Just as he was going to make the great stroke a strong hand was laid upon his arm.

"Now then, Isaac Ogden, you've spoiled a splendid stroke. I don't hoftens get such a chance."

"You're wanted for summat else, Doctor. Come, look sharp; the Colonel's waiting for you."

In common with many members of his profession, Dr. Bardly had a dislike to be called in a hurried and peremptory manner, and a disposition, when so called, to take his time. He had so often been pressed unnecessarily that he had acquired a general conviction that cases could wait — and he made them wait, more or less. In this instance, however, Isaac Ogden insisted on a departure from the Doctor's usual customs, and threw his gray military cloak over his shoulders, and set his cap on his head, and led him to the street-door, where he found the tandem, the Colonel in his place with the Adjutant, Fyser already mounted behind, and the leader dancing with impatience.

The bright lamps flashed swiftly through the dingy streets of Sootythorn, and soon their light fell on the blossoming hedges in the country. Colonel Stanburne had been too much occupied with his horses whilst they were in the streets; but now on the broad open road he had more leisure to talk, and he was the first to break silence.

"You don't know any further details, do you, Eureton?"

"Nothing beyond what I told you. The innkeeper who brought the news was the one Captain Stanburne was billeted with, and he quitted Whittlecup immediately after the event. He appears quite certain that Captain Stanburne is dead. The body was brought to the inn before the man left, and he was present at the examination of it by a doctor who had been hastily sent for."

"Beg pardon, sir," said Fyser from behind, "I asked the innkeeper some questions myself. It appears that Captain Stanburne was wounded in the head, sir, and his skull was broken. It was done with a deal board that a Hirish militiaman tore up out of a floor. There was two Hirish that was quarrellin' and fightin', and the Captain put 'em both into a hempty room which was totally without furnitur', and where they'd nothink but straw to lie upon; and he kep 'em there under confinement, and set a guard at the door. And then

A Case of Assault.

these two drunken Hirish fights wi' their fists — but fists isn't bloody enough for Hirish, so they starts tearin' up the boards o' the floor, and the guard at the door tried to interfere between 'em, but, not havin' no arms, could do very little ; and the Captain was sent for, and as soon as hever one o' these Hirish sees him he says, ' Here's our bloody Captain,' and he aims a most tremenjious stroke at him with his deal board, and it happened most unfortunate that it hit the Captain with the rusty nail in it."

"I wonder it never occurred to him to separate the Irishmen," observed Eureton, in a lower tone, to the Colonel. "He ought not to have confined them together."

"Strictly speaking, he ought not to have placed them in confinement at all at Whittlecup, but sent them at once under escort to headquarters."

"What's this that we are meeting?" said the Adjutant. "I hear men marching."

The Colonel drew up his horses, and the regular footfall of soldiers became audible, and gradually grew louder. "They march uncommonly well, Eureton, for militia-men who have had no training ; I cannot understand it."

"There were half-a-dozen old soldiers in Captain Stanburne's company, and I suppose the sergeant has selected them as a guard for the prisoners."

The night was cloudy and dark, and the lamps of the Colonel's vehicle were so very splendid and brilliant that they made the darkness beyond their range blacker and more impenetrable than ever. As the soldiers came nearer, the Colonel stopped his horses and waited. Suddenly out of the darkness came a corporal and four men with two prisoners. The Colonel shouted, "Halt!"

"Have you any news of Captain Stanburne?"

"He's not quite dead, sir, or was not when we left."

The tall wheels rolled along the road, and in a quarter of

an hour the leader had to make his way through a little crowd of people in front of the Blue Bell.

The Doctor was the first in the house, and was led at once to young Stanburne's room. The Whittlecup surgeon was there already. No professional men are so ticklish on professional etiquette as surgeons are, but in this instance there could be little difficulty of that kind. "You are the surgeon to the regiment, I believe," said the Whittlecup doctor; "you will find this a very serious case. I simply took charge of it in your absence."

The patient was not dead, but he was perfectly insensible. He breathed faintly, and every few minutes there was a rattling in the throat, resembling that which precedes immediate dissolution. The two doctors examined the wound together. The skull had been fractured by the blow, and there was a gash produced by the nail in the board. The face was extremely pale, and so altered as to be scarcely recognizable. The innkeeper's wife, Mrs. Simpson, was moistening the pale lips with brandy.

When the Colonel and Captain Eureton had seen the patient, they had a talk with Dr. Bardly in another room. The Doctor's opinion was that there were chances of recovery, but not very strong chances. Though Philip Stanburne had enjoyed tolerably regular health in consequence of his temperate and simple way of living, he had by no means a robust constitution, and it was possible — it was even probable — that he would succumb; but he *might* pull through. Dr. Bardly proposed to resign the case entirely to the Whittlecup doctor, as it would require constant attention, and the surgeon ought to be on the spot.

CHAPTER XVII.

ISAAC OGDEN AGAIN.

AS the lieutenant of the Grenadier Company, Mr. Isaac Ogden was appointed to do captain's work at Whittlecup in the place of Philip Stanburne.

For many weeks Mr. Ogden had displayed a strength of resolution that astonished his most intimate friends. Without meanly taking refuge in the practice of total abstinence, he had kept strictly within the bounds of what in Shayton is considered moderation.

The customs of the mess at Sootythorn were not likely to place him in the power of his old enemy again; for although the officers were not severely abstinent, their utmost conviviality scarcely extended beyond the daily habits of the very soberest of Shaytonians.

Viewing the matter, therefore, from the standpoint of his personal experience, Dr. Bardly looked upon Ogden as now the most temperate of men. It is true that as a militia officer he could not follow a new rule of his about not entering inns, for the business of the regiment required him to visit a dozen inns every day, and to eat and sleep in one for a month together; and it is obvious that the other good rule about not drinking spirits at Twistle Farm could not be very advantageous to him just now, seeing that, although it was always in force, it was practically efficacious only during his residence under his own roof. It seems a pity that he did not legislate for himself anew, so as to meet his altered circumstances; but the labors of regimental duty appeared so onerous that extraordinary stimulation seemed necessary to meet this extraordinary fatigue, and it would have appeared imprudent to confine himself within rigidly fixed limits which necessity might compel him to transgress. So in point of fact Mr. Ogden was a free agent again.

Whilst Philip Stanburne had remained at the Blue Bell, Lieutenant Ogden had been in all respects a model of good behavior. He had watched by Philip's bedside in the evenings, sometimes far into the night, and the utmost extent of his conviviality had been a glass of grog with the Whittlecup doctor. But the day Philip Stanburne was removed, Lieutenant Ogden, after having dined and inspected his billets, began to feel the weight of his loneliness, and he felt it none the less for being accustomed to loneliness at the Farm. Captain Stanburne's illness, and the regular evening talk with the Whittlecup doctor, had hitherto given an interest to Isaac Ogden's life at the Blue Bell, and this interest had been suddenly removed. Something must be found to supply its place; it became necessary to cultivate the acquaintance of somebody in the parlor.

It is needless to trouble the reader with details about the men of Whittlecup whom Mr. Ogden found there, because they have no connection with the progress of this history. But he found somebody else too, namely, Jeremiah Smethurst, a true Shaytonian, and one of the brightest ornaments of the little society that met at the Red Lion. When Jerry saw his old friend Isaac Ogden, whom he had missed for many weeks, his greeting was so very cordial, so expressive of good-fellowship, that it was not possible to negative his proposition that they should "take a glass together."

Now the keeper of the Blue Bell Inn knew Jerry Smethurst. He knew that Jerry drank more than half a bottle of brandy every night before he went to bed, and without giving Mr. Ogden credit for equal powers, he had heard that he came from Shayton, which is a good recommendation to a vendor of spirituous liquors. He therefore, instead of bringing a glass of brandy for each of the Shayton gentlemen, uncorked a fresh bottle and placed it between them, remarking that they might take what they pleased — that there was 'ot warter on the 'arth, for the kettle was just bylin, an' there was shugger in the shugger-basin.

The reader foresees the consequences. After two or three glasses with his old friend, Isaac Ogden fell under the dominion of the old Shayton associations. Jerry Smethurst talked the dear old Shayton talk, such as Isaac Ogden had not heard in perfection for many a day. For men like the Doctor and Jacob Ogden were, by reason of their extreme temperance, isolated beings — beings cut off from the heartiest and most genial society of the place — and Isaac had been an isolated being also since he had kept out of the Red Lion and the White Hart.

> "Why should a man desire in any way
> To vary from the kindly race of men?"

That abandonment of the Red Lion had been a moral gain — a moral victory — but an intellectual loss. Was such a fellow as Parson Prigley any compensation for Jerry Smethurst? And there were half-a-dozen at the Red Lion as good as Jerry. He was short of stature — so short, that when he sat in a rocking-chair he had a difficulty in giving the proper impetus with his toes; and he had a great round belly, and a face which, if not equally great and round, seemed so by reason of all the light and warmth that radiated from it. It was enough to cure anybody of hypochondria to look at Jerry Smethurst's face. I have seen the moon look rather like it sometimes, rising warm and mellow on a summer's night; but though anybody may see that the moon has a nose and eyes, she certainly lacks expression. It was pleasant to Isaac Ogden to see the friendly old visage before him once again. Genial and kind thoughts rose in his mind. Tennyson had not yet written "Tithonus," and if he had, no Shaytonian

would have read it — but the thoughts in Ogden's mind were
these : —

> "Why should a man desire in any way
> To vary from the kindly race of men,
> Or pass beyond the goal of ordinance,
> Where all should pause, as is most meet for all?"

The "goal of ordinance," at Shayton, being death from *delirium tremens*.

Mr. Smethurst would have been much surprised if anybody had told him that he was inducing Ogden to drink more than was good for him. It seemed so natural to drink a bottle of brandy! And Jerry, too, in his way, was a temperate man — a man capable of self-control — a man who had made a resolution and kept it for many years. Jerry's resolution had been never to drink more than one bottle of spirits in an evening; and, as he said sometimes, it was "all howin' to that as he enjy'd sich gud 'ealth." Therefore, when Mr. Simpson had placed the bottle between them, Mr. Smethurst made a little mental calculation. He was strong in mental arithmetic. "I've 'ad three glasses afore Hogden coom, so when I've powered him out three glasses, the remainder 'll be my 'lowance." Therefore, when Isaac had mixed his third tumbler, Jerry Smethurst rang the bell.

"Another bottle o' brandy."

Mr. Simpson stood aghast at this demand, and his eyes naturally reverted to the bottle upon the table. "You've not finished that yet, gentlemen," he ventured to observe.

"What's left in it is my 'lowance," said Mr. Smethurst. "Mr. Hogden shalln't 'ave none on 't."

"Well, that *is* a whimmy gent," said Mr. Simpson to himself — but he fetched another bottle.

They made a regular Red Lion evening of it, those two. A little before midnight Mr. Smethurst rose and said Good night. He had finished his bottle, and his law of temperance, always so faithfully observed, forbade him one drop more. The reader probably expects that Mr. Smethurst was intoxicated; but his genial nature was only yet more genial. He lighted his bed-candle with perfect steadiness, shook Ogden's hand affectionately, and mounted the stair step by step. When he got into his bedroom he undressed himself in a methodical manner, laid his clothes neatly on a chair, wound his watch up, and when he had assumed his white cotton night-cap, looked at himself in the glass. He put his tongue out, and held the candle close to it. The result of the examination was satisfactory, and he proceeded to pull down the corners of his eyes. This he did every night. The bugbear of his life was dread of a coming fit, and he fancied he might thus detect the premonitory symptoms.

Meanwhile Mr. Ogden, left by himself, took up the "Sootythorn Gazette," and when Mr. Simpson entered he found him reading, apparently. "Beg pardon, sir," said Mr. Simpson, "but it's the rule to turn the gas out at twelve, and it's a few minutes past. I'll light you your bed-candle, sir, -and you can sit up a bit later if you like. You'll find your way to your room."

Ogden was too far gone to have any power of controlling himself now. The type danced before his eyes, the sentences ran into one another, and the sense of the phrases was a mystery to him. He kept drinking mechanically; and when at length he attempted to reach the door, the candlestick slipped from his hand, and the light was instantly extinguished.

A man who is quite drunk cannot find the door of a dark room — he cannot even walk in the dark; his only chance of walking in broad daylight is to fix his eye steadily on some object, and when it loses its hold of that, to fasten it upon some other, and so on. Ogden stumbled against the furniture and fell. The deep insensibility of advanced drunkenness supervened, and he lay all night upon the floor. The servant-girl found him there the next morning when she came to clean the room.

He could not go to Sootythorn that day, and the true reason for his absence soon became known to Dr. Bardly, who asked leave to drive over to Shayton to see a patient of his own. He drove directly to Milend.

"Well, Mrs. Ogden," said the Doctor, "I've come wi' bad news for you this time. Your Isaac's made a beast of himself once more. He lay all night last night dead drunk upo' th' parlor-floor o' th' Blue Bell Inn i' Whittlecup."

"Why — you don't say so, Dr. Bardly! Now, really, this *is* provokin', and 'im as was quite reformed, as one may say. I could like to whip him — I could."

"Well, I wish you'd just go to Whittlecup and take care of him while he stops there. If he'd nobbut stopped at Sootythorn I could have minded him a bit mysen, but there's nout like his mother for managin' him."

Little Jacob was staying at Milend during his father's military career, and so Mrs. Ogden objected — "But what's to become o' th' childt?"

"Take him with ye — take him with ye. It'll do him a power o' good, and it'll amuse him rarely. He'll see the chaps with their red jackets, and his father with a sword, and a fine scarlet coat on Sundays, and he'll be as fain as fain."

So it was immediately decided that Mrs. Ogden and little Jacob should leave for Whittlecup as soon as they possibly could. A fly was sent for, and Mrs. Ogden hastily filled two large wooden boxes, which were her portmanteaus. Little Jacob was at the parsonage with the youthful Prigleys, and had to be sent for. Mrs. Ogden took the decanters from the corner cupboard, and drank two glasses of port to sustain her in the hurry of the occasion. "Well, who would have thought," she said to herself, as she ate a piece of cake — "who would have thought that I should go and stop at Whittlecup? I wonder how soon Mary Ridge will have finished my new black satin."

CHAPTER XVIII.

ISAAC'S MOTHER COMES.

MRS. OGDEN and her grandson reached Sootythorn rather late that evening — namely, about eight o'clock; and as it happened that she knew an old maid there — one Miss Mellor — whose feelings would have been wounded if Mrs. Ogden had passed through Sootythorn without calling upon her, she took the opportunity of doing so whilst the horse was baited at the inn. The driver took the fly straight to the Thorn; and when Mr. Garley saw a lady and a little boy emerge therefrom he concluded that they intended to stay at his house, and came with his apologies for want of room. "But we can let you 'ave a nice parlor, mum, to take your tea, and I can find you good bedrooms in the town."

Mrs. Ogden declined these obliging propositions, in the hope that Miss Mellor would offer her a night's lodging. It was not that she loved Miss Mellor so much as to desire to stay longer under her roof than was necessary to keep her in a good temper, but she had made sundry reflections on the road. "If I stop at th' Thorn they'll charge me 'appen 'alf-a-crown for my bedroom, and Jane Mellor 'ad a nice spare bedroom formerly. It really is no use throwin' money away on inn-keepers. And then there's our tea; they'll make me pay eighteenpence or two shillin' for 't at Garley's, and very likely charge full as much for little Jacob. It's quite enough to 'ave to pay seven shillin' for th' horse and fly." And in any case there would be time to get on to Whittlecup after the horse had had his feed.

But Miss Mellor, who had not been to Shayton or heard direct news of Shayton for several years, was so delighted to see Mrs. Ogden that she would not hear of her going forward that night. "It's lucky I 'appened to be at 'ome," said Miss Mellor, "for I'm often out of an evening." It was lucky, certainly, for little Jacob, who got a much better tea than he would have done at the Thorn Inn, with quantities of sweet things greatly to his taste. Little Jacob was convinced that there was nobody in the world so kind and generous as his grandmother, yet he conceived an affection for Miss Mellor also before the close of the evening.

"The devil take the people," said Isaac Ogden, when he got back from Sootythorn to the Blue Bell, and had gone as usual to his bedroom there — "the devil take the people, they've hidden all my things!"

Just then came a gentle knock at the door, and the servant-maid entered. "Please, sir, your mother's come, and she says you aren't to sleep here any more, sir; and she's fetched your things to lodgings that she's took over Mr. Wood's, the shoemaker's."

It is at all times vexatious and humiliating to the independent spirit of a man to be disposed of by female authority, but it is most especially so when the authority is one's mamma. A grown-up man will submit to his mother on most points if he is worth any thing, but the best of sons does not quite like to see his submission absolutely taken for granted. In this case there was an aggravation in the look of the servant-girl. Notwithstanding the respectful modesty of her tone, there was just a twinkle of satire in her eye. It was plain that she was inwardly laughing at the Lieutenant. "Damn it!" he said, "this house is good enough for me; I don't want to leave it." Yet he *did* leave, nevertheless.

The next day was Sunday, and it was a satisfaction to Mrs. Ogden to think that Isaac would be professionally compelled to attend public worship. Little Jacob was one of the crowd of spectators who gathered round the company when it was mustered for church-parade. He was proud of his resplendent papa — a papa all scarlet and silver; and it was a matter of peculiar anxiety with him that they should sit in the same pew. Mr. Ogden gratified him in this respect, and the child felt himself the most important young personage in Whittlecup. A steady attention to the service is not commonly characteristic of little boys; and on this occasion little Jacob's eye was so continually caught by the glitter of his father's gold sword-knot and the silver embroidery on his sleeve, that he followed the clergyman much less regularly than usual.

The neighborhood of Whittlecup was not aristocratic, but there were one or two manufacturing families of rather a superior description. One of these families, the Anisons, were at church not far from the pew which the Ogdens occupied. They lived at a house near Whittlecup called Arkwright Lodge, in a comfortable manner, with most of those refinements of civilization which are to be met with in the houses of rich professional men in London. Mr. Anison, indeed, was a manufacturer of the new school, whilst Jacob Ogden belonged to the old one. Men of the Anison class sometimes make large fortunes, but they more frequently content themselves with a moderate independence and a sufficient provision for their families. Money does not seem to them an end in itself, but they value the comforts and refinements which it procures and which cannot be had without it. Jacob Ogden, on the other hand, did not care a fig for comforts and refinements, and had no domestic objects: his only purpose was the inward satisfaction and the outward glory of being rich. Mr. Anison worked in moderation, spent a good deal, saved something, and kept a very hospitable house, where everybody who had the slightest imaginable claim upon his kindness was always heartily welcome.

After Philip Stanburne's accident he had been immediately moved to Arkwright Lodge, in compliance with the surgeon's advice and Mr. Anison's urgent request. Here he had rapidly passed into a state of agreeable convalescence, and found the house so pleasant that the prospect of a perfect recovery, and consequent departure, was not very attractive to him now.

When the service in Whittlecup church was over, Joseph Anison went straight to Mr. Ogden's pew and reminded him that he had promised to dine that day at Arkwright Lodge. When they got out of the church, Isaac presented his mother to Mr. Anison, and to Mrs. Anison also, who joined them in the midst of that ceremony. This was followed by a polite little speech from Mrs. Anison (she was an adept in polite little speeches), to the effect that, as Mr. Ogden had kindly promised to eat a dinner and pay his first call at the Lodge at the same time, his duties in the militia having prevented him from calling during the week, perhaps they might hope that Mrs. Ogden would allow them to call upon her at once at her lodgings, and then would she come with her son to the Lodge to spend the afternoon? So when the militia-men were disbanded, the Anisons accompanied the Ogdens to the lodging over Mr. Wood's, the shoemaker.

It was a very fine May morning, and they had all come on foot. There are families in Sootythorn (perhaps also there may be families out of Sootythorn) who, though living within a very short distance of their parish church, go thither always in their carriages — on the same principle which causes the Prince of Wales to go from Marlborough House to St James's Palace in a state-coach — namely, for the maintenance of their dignity. But though the Anisons' carriage was an institution sufficiently recent to have still some of the charms of novelty, they dispensed with it as much as possible on Sundays.

The young ladies had gone slowly forwards towards the

Lodge with the clergyman, who had a standing invitation to dine there whenever he came to Whittlecup. Mrs. Ogden's great regret in going to dine at the Lodge was for the dinner she left behind her, and she did not hesitate to express it. "It seems quite a pity," she said, "to leave them ducks and green peas — they were such fine ducks, and we're all of us very fond o' ducks, 'specially when we've green peas to 'em." After this little speech, she paused regretfully, as if meditating on the delightfulness of the ducks, and then she added, more cheerfully, " But what —ducks are very good cold, and they'll do very well for supper to-morrow night, when our Isaac comes back from Sootythorn."

The dinner at the Lodge was good enough to compensate even for the one left untasted at the shoemaker's, and nobody did better justice to it than the Rev. Abel Blunting. A man may well be hungry who has preached vehemently for seventy minutes, and eaten nothing since seven in the morning, which was Mr. Blunting's habitual breakfast-hour. He was a very agreeable guest, and worth his salt. He had a vein of rich humor approaching to joviality, yet he drank only water. On this matter of teetotalism he was by no means fanatical, but he said simply that in his office of minister it was useful to his work amongst the poor. Mrs. Ogden sat next to him at table, and was perfectly delighted with him. The Rev. Abel perceived at once what manner of woman she was, and talked to her accordingly. When he found out that she came from Shayton, he said that he had a great respect for Shayton, it was such a sound Protestant community — there was not a single Papist in the place — Popery had no hold *there*. Unfortunately, when Mr. Blunting made this observation, there happened to be a lull in the talk, and it was audible to everybody, including Philip Stanburne, who was well enough to sit at table. Poor Mrs. Anison began to feel very uncomfortable, but as Mr. Blunting sat next to her, she whispered to him that they had a Roman Catholic at table.

This communication not having been loud enough to be heard by Mrs. Ogden, who, never having sat down with a Roman Catholic in her life, was incapable of imagining such a contingency, that lady replied,—

"Shayton folk believe i' th' Bible."

"And may I ask," said Philip, very loudly and resolutely from the other end of the table, "what Catholics believe in?"

"Why, they believe i' th' Koran."

The hearers — and everybody present had heard Mrs. Ogden distinctly — could not credit their ears. Each thought that he must be mistaken — that by some wholly unaccountable magic he had heard the word "Koran" when it had been pronounced by no mortal lips. Nobody laughed — nobody even smiled. There is a degree of astonishment which stuns the sense of humor. Every one held his breath when Mr. Blunting spoke.

"No, ma'am," he said, respectfully, "you are somewhat mistaken. You appear to have confounded the Papal and the Mohammedan religions."

What Mrs. Ogden's answer may have been does not matter very much, for Mr. and Mrs. Anison both saw the necessity for an immediate diversion, and talked about something else in the most determined manner. On reflection, Philip Stanburne thought his Church quite sufficiently avenged already. "As I believe in the Koran," he said to Miss Anison, "I may marry four wives. What an advantage that will be!"

"You horrible man!"

"Why am I a horrible man? Why are you so ungracious to me? The Sultan and the Viceroy of Egypt are like me — they believe in the Koran — and they act upon their belief as I intend to do. Yet a Christian queen has been gracious to them. She did not tell them they were horrible men. Why should you not be gracious to me in the same way?

When I have married my four wives, you will come and visit me, won't you, in my palace on the Bosphorus? Black slaves shall bring you coffee in a little jewelled cup, and your lips shall touch the amber mouth-piece of a diamonded chibouque."

"But then your four wives will all be Orientals, and I shall not be able to talk to them."

The Misses Anison were not the only young ladies at the table. Philip Stanburne had a neighbor on his left hand who interested him even more than the brilliant girl on his right. This was Miss Alice Stedman, whom he had seen in the bookseller's shop at Sootythorn.

"And if you believe in the Koran," said Miss Stedman, "you ought to show it by refusing to drink wine."

"Ah, then, I renounce Mohammed, that I may have the pleasure of drinking wine with you, Miss Stedman!" This was said with perfect grace, and in the little ceremony which followed, the young gentleman contrived to express so much respect and admiration for his fair neighbor, that Mrs. Anison took note of it. "Mr. Stanburne is in love with Alice," she said to herself.

"Would you renounce your religion for love?" asked Madge Anison, in a low tone.

Philip felt a sudden sensation, as if a doctor had just probed him. Garibaldi felt the corresponding physical pain when Nélaton found the bullet.

He turned slowly and looked at Madge. There was a strange expression about her lips, and the perennial merriment had faded from her face. "Are you speaking seriously, Miss Anison, I wonder?"

The talk was noisy enough all round the table to isolate the two completely. Even Miss Stedman was listening to her loud-voiced neighbor, the Lieutenant. Madge Anison looked straight at Philip, and said, "Yes, I *am* speaking seriously."

"I believe I should not, now. But nobody knows what he may do when he is in love."

"You *are* in love."

This time the room whirled, and the voices sounded like the murmur of a distant sea. In an instant Philip Stanburne passed from one state of life to another state of life. A crisis, which changed the whole future of four persons there present, occurred in the world of his consciousness. His imagination rioted in wild day-dreams; but one picture rose before him with irresistible vividness — a picture of Alice kneeling with him under a canopy, before the high altar at St. Agatha's.

A slight pressure on his left arm recalled him to the actual world. The ladies were all leaving their seats, and Madge had kindly reminded him where he was.

"A sad place for drinking is Shayton," observed Mr. Blunting, as he poured himself a glass of pure water. "I wonder if one could do any good there?"

"They're past curing, mostly, are Shayton folk," answered John Stedman. "Are not they, Mr. Ogden?"

"There's one here that is, I'm afraid," answered Isaac, with much humility.

Mr. Blunting inquired, with sympathy in his tone, whether Mr. Ogden had himself fallen under temptation. When Isaac confessed his backslidings of the past week, the reverend gentleman requested permission to see him in private. Isaac had a dislike to clergymen in general, and in matters of religion rather shared the latitudinarian views of his friend Dr. Bardly; but he was in a state of profound moral discouragement, and ready to be grateful to any one who held out prospects of effectual help. So it ended by his accepting an invitation to take tea at the parsonage at Sootythorn.

"If you take tea with Mr. Blunting," said Joseph Anison, "you must mind he doesn't inoculate you with his own sort of intemperance, if he cures you of your little excesses. He drinks tea enough in a year to float a canal-boat. It's a terribly bad habit. In my opinion it's far worse than drinking brandy. The worst of it is that it makes men like gossip just as women do. Stick to your brandy-bottle, Mr. Ogden, like a man, and let Mr. Blunting empty his big tea-pot!"

CHAPTER XIX.

THE COLONEL AT WHITTLECUP.

WHILST the gentlemen were still in the dining-room, Mr. Blunting saw a horse pass the window — a riderless, yet harnessed horse — followed by another horse in an unaccustomed manner; and then came a lofty vehicle, drawn by the latter animal. I have described this equipage as it appeared to Mr. Blunting; but the experienced reader will perceive that it was a tandem, and by the association of ideas will expect to see Fyser and the Colonel.

Colonel Stanburne came into the dining-room, and soon made himself at home there. He had never happened to meet Joseph Anison or Mr. Stedman, but he knew the incumbent of Sootythorn slightly, and the other two men were his own officers, though he had as yet seen very little of either of them. The Stanburnes of Wenderholme held a position in all that part of the country so far above that to which their mere wealth would have entitled them (for there were manufacturers far richer than the Colonel), that Joseph Anison felt it an honor that the head of that family should have entered his gates. "He's only calling on young Stanburne," thought Joseph Anison; "he isn't calling upon us."

"I came to thank you and Mrs. Anison," said the Colonel, "for having so kindly taken care of our young friend here. He seems to be getting on uncommonly well; and no wonder, when he's in such good quarters."

"Captain Stanburne is gaining strength, I am glad to say,"

replied the master of the house. "He rather alarmed us when he came here, he seemed so weak; but he has come round wonderfully."

"I am very much better, certainly," said the patient himself.

The commanding officer hoped he would be fit for duty again at an early date, but Captain Stanburne declared that he did not feel strong enough yet to be equal to the march and the drill; that he was subject to frequent sensations of giddiness, which would make him most uncomfortable, if not useless, on the parade-ground; and that, in a word, he was best for the present where he was. This declaration was accompanied by due expressions of regret for the way in which he abused the kind hospitality of the Anisons — expressions which, of course, drew forth from the good host a cordial renewal of his lease.

"And what have you done with the Irishman who nearly killed him?" asked Mr. Anison of the Colonel. "I've heard nothing about him. If you'd had him shot, we should have heard of it."

"It was a perplexing case. If you consider the man a soldier, the punishment is most severe — in fact it is death, even if he did not mean to kill. But we hardly could consider him a soldier — he had had no military experience — a raw Irish laborer, who had never worn a uniform. I have been unwilling to bring the man before a court-martial. He is in prison still."

"He has been punished enough," said Philip. "Pray consider him simply as having been drunk. Irishmen are always combative when they are drunk. It was not a deliberate attack upon me as his officer. The man was temporarily out of his senses, and struck blindly about him."

It having been settled that the Irishman was to be pardoned on the intercession of Captain Stanburne, the Colonel begged to be presented to Mrs. Anison. "He had not much time," he said, looking at his watch; "he had to be back in

Sootythorn in time for mess, and he was anxious to pay his respects to the lady of the house."

So they all went into the drawing-room. After the introductory bows, the Colonel perceived our friend, little Jacob (who had retreated with the ladies); but as he had not quite finished his little speech to Mrs. Anison about her successful nursing, he did not as yet take any direct notice of him. When the duties of politeness had been fully performed, the Colonel beckoned for little Jacob, and when he came to him, laid both hands on his shoulders.

"And so you're here, too, are you, young man? I thought you were at Shayton with your grandmamma."

Lieutenant Ogden came up at this instant to excuse himself. "My mother only came to Whittlecup yesterday, Colonel, and she brought my little boy with her." Mrs. Ogden approached the group.

"I'm little Jacob's grandmother," she said, "and I'm mother to this great lad here" (pointing to the Lieutenant), "and it's as much as ever I can do to take care of him. What did you send him by himself to Whittlecup for? You should have known better nor that; sending a drunkard like him to stop by hisself in a public-house. If he's a backslider now, it's 'long o' them as turned him into temptation, same as a cow into a clover-field. I wish he'd never come into th' malicious (militia) — I do so."

The Colonel was little accustomed to be spoken to with that unrestrained frankness which characterizes the inhabitants of Shayton, and felt a temporary embarrassment under Mrs. Ogden's onslaught. "Well, Mrs. Ogden, let us hope that Mr. Isaac will be safe now under your protection."

"Safe? Ay, he is safe now, I reckon, when he's getten his mother to take care of him; and there's more on ye as wants your mothers to take care on ye, by all accounts."

"Mother," said the Lieutenant, "you shouldn't talk so to

the Colonel. You should bear in mind how he kept little Jacob at Wenderholme Hall."

Mrs. Ogden was pacified immediately, and held out her hand. "I thank you for that," she said, "you were very kind to th' childt; and I 've been doin' a piece of needlework ever since for your wife, but it willn't be finished while Christmas."

"Mother, you shouldn't say 'your wife'—you should say 'her ladyship,'" observed the Lieutenant, in a low tone.

"My wife will be greatly obliged to you, Mrs. Ogden. I hope you will make her acquaintance before you leave the regiment; for I may say that you belong to the regiment now, since you have come to be Lieutenant Ogden's commanding officer."

Mrs. Anison had been first an astonished and then an amused auditor of this colloquy, but she ended it by offering Mrs. Ogden a cup of tea. Then the Colonel began to talk to Mrs. Anison. He had that hearty and frank enjoyment of the society of ladies which is not only perfectly compatible with morality, but especially belongs to it as one of its best attributes and privileges. Good women liked the Colonel, and the Colonel liked good women; he liked them none the less when they were handsome, as Mrs. Anison was, and when they could talk well and easily, as she did. Some women are distinguished by nature; and though Mrs. Anison had seen little of the great world, and the Colonel had seen a good deal of it, the difference of experience did not place a perceptible barrier between them. The time seemed to have passed rapidly for both when the visitor took his leave.

CHAPTER XX.

PHILIP STANBURNE IN LOVE.

IF any rational and worldly-minded adviser had said to Philip Stanburne a month before, "Why don't you look out for some well-to-do cotton-spinner's daughter in Sootythorn? you might pick up a good fortune, that would mend the Stanithburn property, and you might find a nice well-educated girl, who would do you quite as much credit as if she belonged to one of the old families"—if any counsel of this kind had been offered to Philip Stanburne then, before he saw Alice Stedman, he would have rejected it at once as being altogether inadmissible. *He*, the representative of the house of Stanburne, connect himself with a family of cotton-spinners! He, the dutiful son of the Church, ally himself with a member of one of those heretical sects who insult her in her affliction! Our general views of things may, however, be very decided, and admit, nevertheless, of exception in favor of persons who are known to us. To hate Protestants in general—to despise the commercial classes as a body—is one thing; but to hate and despise a gentle maiden, whose voice sounds sweetly in our ears, is quite another thing.

"She's as perfect a lady as any I ever saw," thought Philip, as she walked before him in the garden at Arkwright Lodge. A closer social critic might have answered, that although Alice Stedman was a very admirable and good young woman, absolutely free from the least taint of vulgarity, she lacked the style and "go" of a young lady of the world. Her deficiency in this respect may, however, have gone far to produce the charm which attracted Philip. Alice had not the *aplomb* of a fine lady, nor the brilliance of a clever woman; but nature had given her a stamp of genuineness which is sometimes effaced by the attrition of society.

"It's wrong of me to have taken possession of you, Captain Stanburne," said Margaret Anison; "I see you are longing to be with Alice Stedman — you would be a great deal happier with her;" and, without consulting him further, she called her sister, adding, "I beg pardon, Lissy, but I want to say something to Sarah."

Of course, as Miss Anison had some private communication to make to her sister, Philip and Alice had nothing to do but *s'éloigner*. The young gentleman offered his arm, which was accepted, and they went on down a deviously winding walk. Alice looked round, and seeing nobody, said, "Hadn't we better wait, or go back a little? we have been walking faster than they have." Philip did as he was bid, not precisely knowing or caring which way he went. But the young ladies were not there.

"I think," he said at last, "we should do better to go in our first direction, as they will expect us to do. Very likely Miss Anison may have taken her sister to the house, to show her something, and they will meet us in the garden again, if we go in the direction they calculate upon." So they turned round and walked down the winding path again.

"You often come to this place, I believe," said Philip. "The Anisons are old friends of yours, are they not, Miss Stedman?"

"Oh yes; I come to stay here very often. The Anisons are very kind to me."

"They are kind to me also, Miss Stedman, and yet I have no claim of old-acquaintance. A fortnight since I did not even know their name, and yet it seems to me now as if I had known them for years. *You* are rather an older acquaintance, Miss Stedman. I had the pleasure of seeing you at Sootythorn before I came to Whittlecup."

Alice looked up at her companion rather archly, and said, "You mean in the bookseller's shop?"

"Yes, when you came to buy a book of sermons. Shall I tell you what book you ordered? I remember the name perfectly. It was 'Blunting's Sermons on Popery.'"

"So you were listening, were you?"

"I wasn't listening when I heard your voice for the first time, but I listened very attentively afterwards. My attention was attracted by the title of the book. You know that I am a Catholic, Miss Stedman?"

"Yes," said Alice, very briefly, and in a tone which seemed to endeavor not to imply disapprobation.

"And perhaps you know that Catholics don't quite like to hear their religion called 'Popery.' So I was a little irritated; but then I reflected that as the title of the book was so, you could not order it by another name than the name upon its titlepage." Here there was a pause, as Alice did not speak. Philip resumed, —

"Do you live *in* Sootythorn, Miss Stedman?"

"Not far out of the town. Indeed our house is surrounded by buildings now. It used to be quite in the country."

"I — I should like to call upon Mr. Stedman very much when I am quite well again."

For some seconds there was no answer. Then Alice said in a low tone, almost inaudible, "I should be very glad to see you again."

A heavy and rapid step on the gravel behind them abruptly ended this interesting conversation.

It was not Madge Anison's step. They stopped and looked round. The Reverend Abel Blunting confronted them.

If poor Alice had not had that miserable habit of blushing, the reverend gentleman would have perceived nothing beyond the simple fact that the young lady was walking in a garden with Mr. Philip Stanburne. But Alice's face was suffused with crimson, and the knowledge that it was so made her so uncomfortable that she blushed more than ever. In spite of his manhood, there was a slightly heightened color on Philip's cheek also, but a good deal of this may be attributed to vexation at what he was disposed to consider an ill-timed and unwarrantable intrusion.

"Good morning, Miss Alice! I hope you are quite well: and you, sir, I wish you good morning; I hope I see you well."

Philip bowed, a little stiffly, and Alice proceeded to make hasty inquiries about her papa. Did Mr. Blunting know if her papa had changed his intentions?

Mr. Blunting was always very polite, the defect in his manners (betraying that he was not quite a gentleman) being that they were only too deferential. He had a fatherly affection for Alice Stedman, whose spiritual guide he had been from her infancy, and it was certainly the very first time in her life that she had seen him without feelings of unmingled satisfaction.

"I have come to fetch you myself, Miss Alice. I met your papa in Sootythorn this morning as I was leaving in my gig, and he asked if I were coming to Whittlecup. So he requested me to offer you the vacant seat, Miss Alice, which I now do with great pleasure." Here Mr. Blunting made a sort of a bow. There was an unctuousness in his courtesy that irritated Philip, but perhaps Philip envied him his place in the gig.

"Are we going to leave immediately, then?" inquired Miss Stedman, in a tone which did not imply the most perfect satisfaction with these arrangements.

"Mrs. Anison has been so kind as to invite me to dine, and I have accepted." Mr. Blunting was too honest to say that Miss Alice ought to dine before her drive. He accepted avowedly in his own interest. He had a large body to nourish, he had to supply energies for an enormous amount of work, and the dinners at the Sootythorn parsonage were not always very succulent. He therefore thought it not wrong to accept effective aid in his labors when it offered itself in the shape of hospitality.

At dessert the clergyman found an opportunity of conveying, not too directly, a little hint or lesson which he felt it his duty to convey, and which had been tormenting him since the meeting in the garden. The conversation, which at Whittlecup, as elsewhere, very generally ran upon people known to the speakers, had turned to a case of separation between a neighboring country gentleman and his wife, who were, or had been, of different religions.

"Marriages of that kind," said Mr. Blunting, "between people of different religions, seldom turn out happily, and it is a great imprudence to contract them."

Mrs. Anison expressed a hearty concurrence in this view, but certain young persons present believed that, however just Mr. Blunting's observation might be, considered generally, there must be exceptions to a rule so discouraging.

CHAPTER XXI.

THE WENDERHOLME COACH.

THE distance from Wenderholme to Sootythorn was rather inconveniently great, being about twenty miles; and as there was no railway in that direction, the Colonel determined to set up a four-in-hand, which he facetiously entitled "The Wenderholme Coach." The immediate purpose of the Wenderholme coach was to enable the officers to enjoy more frequently the hospitalities of the Hall; but it may be admitted that John Stanburne had a natural gift for driving, and also a cultivated taste for that amusement, which may have had their influence in deciding him to add this item to his establishment. He had driven his tandem so long now, that, though it was still very agreeable to him, it no longer offered any excitement; but his experience of a four-in-hand was much more limited, and it therefore presented many of the allurements of novelty. Nothing is more agreeable than a perfect harmony between our duties towards others and our private tastes and predilections. It was clearly a duty to offer hospitality to the officers; and the hospitality would be so much more graceful if Wenderholme were brought nearer to Sootythorn by a capacious conveyance travelling at high speed, and with the style befitting a company of officers and gentlemen. At the same time, when John Stanburne imagined the charms of driving a four-in-hand, his fingers tingled with anticipations of their delight in holding "the ribbons." Like all men of a perfectly healthy nature, he still retained a great deal of the boy (alas for him whose boyhood is at an end for ever!), and he was still capable of joyously anticipating a new pleasure. The *idea* of the four-in-hand was not new to him. He had long secretly aspired to its realization, but then Lady Helena (who had not the sacred fire) was not likely to see the thing quite in the same light. John Stanburne had never precisely consulted her upon the subject — he had never even gone so far as to say that he should like a four-in-hand if he could afford it; but he had expatiated on the delights of driving other people's teams, and his enthusiasm had met with no answering warmth in Helena's unresponsive breast. She had known for years that her husband had a hankering after a four-in-hand, and had discouraged it in her own way — namely, by steadily avoiding the least expression (even of simple politeness) which might be construed into approbation. In this negative way, without once speaking openly about the matter, she had clearly conveyed to the Colonel's mind her opinion thereupon. The reader, no doubt, approves her ladyship's wisdom and economy. But Lady Helena was not on all points wise and economical. Her qualities of this order shone most conspicuously with reference to pleasures which she did not personally appreciate. It is with sins of extravagance as with most other sins — we compound for those which we're inclined to by condemning those that we've no mind to. On the other hand, it may most reasonably be argued, in favor of her ladyship and other good women who criticise their husbands' expenditure on this excellent old principle, that if they not only encouraged the outlay which procures them the things they like, but also outlay for things they are indifferent about, the general household expenditure would be ruinously augmented.

The Colonel's manner of proceeding about the four-in-hand was characteristic of a husband in his peculiar position. He knew by experience the strength of the *fait accompli*. He wrote privily to a knowing friend of his who was spending the pleasant month of May amidst the joys of the London season, to purchase for him at once the commodious vehicle destined to become afterwards famous as the Wenderholme coach. He wrote for it on that Monday evening when Alice Stedman returned from her interrupted visit to Whittlecup; and as it was sent down on a truck attached to a passenger train, it arrived at the Sootythorn station within forty-eight hours of the writing of the letter, and was brought to the Thorn Inn by two of Mr. Garley's hacks. The officers turned out to look at it after mess, and as it was known to have been selected by a man of high repute in the sporting world, its merits were unanimously allowed. There was a complete set of silver-mounted harness for four horses in the boot, carefully wrapped up in three sorts of paper; and London celerity had even found time to emblazon the Stanburne arms on the panels. It is true that they were exceedingly simple, like the arms of most old families, and the painter had omitted to impale them with the bearings of her ladyship — an accident which might also be considered ominous under the circumstances, since it seemed to imply that in this extravagance of the Colonel's his wife had no part nor lot.

As the mess was just over when the coach entered Mr. Garley's yard, the Colonel, with the boyish impulsiveness which he did not attempt to conceal, said, "Let's have a drive in the Wenderholme coach! Where shall we go to? Let's go and look up Lieutenant Ogden at Whittlecup, and see what he's doing!" So the two tandem horses and two of Mr. Garley's hacks were clothed in the splendors of the new harness, and attached to the great vehicle, whilst a dozen officers mounted to the lofty outside places. They wore the mess costume (red shell-jacket, &c.), and looked something like a lot of scarlet geraniums on the top of a horticulturist's van.

Just as they were starting, and as the Colonel was beginning to feel his reins properly, a youthful lieutenant who possessed a cornet-à-piston, and had privily carried it with him as he climbed to his place behind, filled the streets of Sootythorn with triumphant trumpet-notes. The sound caused many of the inhabitants to come to their windows, and amongst others Miss Mellor and her friend, Mrs. Ogden, who had been drinking tea with her that evening. "Why," said Miss Mellor, "it's a new coach!" "And it's boun' to'rd Whittlecup, I declare," added Mrs. Ogden. She had already put her things on, intending to walk back to Whittlecup with little Jacob in the cool of the evening, for it was quite contrary to Mrs. Ogden's character (at once courageous and economical) to hire a fly for so short a distance as four miles. But when she saw the coach, it occurred to her that here was a golden mean betwixt the extravagance of fly-hiring and the fatigues of pedestrianism; so she clapped little Jacob's cap on his head (in a manner unsatisfactory to that young gentleman, for nobody can put a boy's cap on to suit him except himself), and dragged him out at the front door, hardly taking time to say good night to the worthy lady by whom she had just been so hospitably entertained.

When the Colonel saw Mrs. Ogden making signs with her parasol, he recognized her at once, and good-naturedly drew up his horses that she might get inside. Fyser got down to open the door, and the following conversation, which was clearly overheard by several of the officers, and partially by the Colonel himself, took place between Fyser and Mrs. Ogden.

"Is this Whittlecup coach?"

"Yes, mum."

"Is there room inside for me and this 'ere little lad?"

"Plenty of room, mum. Step in, please; the horses is waitin'."

"Stop a bit. What's the fare as far as Whittlecup?"

"One shilling, mum," said Fyser, who ventured thus far, from his knowledge of the Colonel's indulgent disposition when a joke was in the wind.

CHAP. XXI.   *The Wenderholme Coach.*

"The childt 'll be half-price?" said Mrs. Ogden, mixing the affirmative with the interrogative.

"Very well, mum," said Fyser, and shut the door on Mrs. Ogden and little Jacob.

The Colonel, since the box-seat was on the other side of the vehicle, had not heard the whole of this colloquy; and when it was reported to him amidst roars of laughter, he looked rather graver than was expected. "It's a good joke, gentlemen," he said, "but there is one little matter I must explain to you. Our inside passenger is the mother of one of our brother officers, Lieutenant Ogden, who is commanding number six company at Whittlecup, and the little boy with her is his son; so please be very careful never to allude to this little incident in his presence, you understand."

Meanwhile Mrs. Ogden found the Whittlecup coach comfortable in a supreme degree. "They've rare good coaches about Sootythorn," she said to little Jacob; "this is as soft as soft — it's same as sittin' on a feather-bedd." A few minutes later she continued: "Th' outside passengers is mostly soldiers * by what I can see. They're 'appen some o' your father's men as are boun' back to Whittlecup."

In less than half an hour the Colonel drew up in the market-place at Whittlecup, at the sign of the Blue Bell. He handed the reins to his neighbor on the box, and descended with great alacrity. Fyser had just opened the door when the Colonel arrived in time to help Mrs. Ogden politely as she got out.

"It's eighteenpence," she said, and handed him the money. The Colonel had thrown his gray cloak over his shell-jacket, and, to a person with Mrs. Ogden's habits of observation, or non-observation, looked sufficiently like a

---

* The reader who cares to attain the perfection of Mrs. Ogden's pronunciation will please to bear in mind that she pronounced the *d* well in "soldiers" (thus, sol-di-ers), and did not replace it with a *g*, according to the barbarous usage of the polite world.

coachman. He thought it best to take the money, to prevent an explanation in the presence of so many witnesses. So he politely touched his cap, and thanked her. It being already dusk, she did not recognize him. Suddenly the love of a joke prevailed over other considerations, and the Colonel, imitating the cabman's gesture, contemplated the three sixpences in his open hand by the light of the lamp, and said, "Is there nothing for the coachman, mum?" The lamplight fell upon his features, and Mrs. Ogden recognized him at once; so did little Jacob. Her way of taking the discovery marked her characteristic self-possession. She blundered into no apologies; but, fixing her stony gray eyes full on the Colonel's face, she said, "I think you want no sixpences; Stanburnes o' Wendrum Hall doesn't use wantin' sixpences. Give me my eighteenpence back." Then, suddenly changing her resolution, she said, "Nay, I willn't have them three sixpences back again; it's worth eighteenpence to be able to tell folk that Colonel Stanburne of Wenderholme Hall took money for lettin' an old lady ride in his carriage." She said this with real dignity, and taking little Jacob by the hand, moved off with a steady step towards her lodging over the shoemaker's shop.

CHAPTER XXII.

COLONEL STANBURŇE APOLOGIZES.

THE next day Lieutenant Ogden appeared not on the parade-ground at Sootythorn. Captain Stanburne commanded his own company for the first time since his accident (his cure having been wonderfully advanced by the departure of Miss Stedman from Arkwright Lodge); and during one of the short intervals of repose which break the tedium of drill, he went to pay his respects to the Colonel, who was engaged in conversation with the Adjutant on a bit of elevated ground, whilst Fyser promenaded his war-horse to and fro.

Colonel Stanburne, who was ignorant of the cause to which he owed the rapid recovery of his young friend, heartily congratulated him, and then said, "But where is Ogden? what's Ogden doing? Why didn't he come to the parade-ground to join the grenadier company again? Is he taking a day's holiday with those pretty girls at Arkwright Lodge?"

"Mr. Ogden begs to be excused from attending drill to-day. I have a note from him." And Captain Stanburne handed the letter to the Colonel.

As soon as John Stanburne had read the letter he looked very grave, or rather very much put out, and made an ejaculation. The ejaculation was "Damn it!" Then he folded the letter again, and put it in his pocket-book.

"Have you had any conversation with Mr. Ogden on the subject of this letter?" Captain Stanburne knew nothing about it.

The Colonel made a signal for Fyser, and mounted his horse. Fyser mounted another, and followed his master. The senior Major was telling humorous anecdotes to a group of captains, and the Colonel went straight to him at a canter. He told him to command the regiment in his absence, entering into some details about what was to be done — details which puzzled the Major exceedingly, for he knew nothing whatever about battalion drill, or any drill, though in some former state of existence he had been an ornamental officer in the Guards. This done, the Colonel galloped off the field.

The letter which had caused this sudden departure was as follows: —

"SIR, — As you have thought fit to play a practical joke upon my mother, I send in my resignation.

"Your obedient servant,   ISAAC OGDEN."

There was no hesitation about the Colonel's movements; he rode straight to Whittlecup as fast as his horse could carry him. He went first to the Blue Bell, where he found a guide to Mrs. Ogden's lodging over the shoemaker's shop. In answer to his inquiries, the shoemaker's wife admitted that all her lodgers were at home, but — but — in short, they were "getting their breakfast." The Colonel said his business was urgent — that he must see the Lieutenant, and Mrs. Ogden too — so Mrs. Wood guided him up the narrow stairs.

We may confess for John Stanburne that he had not much of that courage which rejoices in verbal encounters, or if he had, it was of that kind which dares to do what the man is constitutionally most afraid to do. The reader may remember an anecdote of another English officer, who, as he went into battle, betrayed the external signs of fear, and in reply to a young subaltern, who had the impudence to taunt him, said, "Yes, I *am* afraid, and if you were as much afraid as I am, you would run away." Yet, by the strength of his will, he conducted himself like a true soldier. And there is that other

Chap. XXII. *Colonel Stanburne apologizes.*

stirring anecdote about a French commander, who, when his body trembled at the opening of a battle, thus apostrophized it: "Tu trembles, vile carcasse! tu tremblerais bien plus si tu savais où je vais te mener!" If these men were cowards, John Stanburne was a coward too, for he mortally dreaded this encounter with the Ogdens; but if they were not cowards (having will enough to neutralize that defect of nature), neither was John Stanburne.

Lieutenant Ogden rose from his seat, and bowed rather stiffly as the Colonel entered. Mrs. Ogden made a just perceptible inclination of the head, and conveyed to her mouth a spoonful of boiled egg, which she had just dipped in the salt.

"I beg pardon," said the Colonel, "for intruding upon you during breakfast time, but—but I was anxious"— The moment of hesitation which followed was at once taken advantage of by Mrs. Ogden.

"And is that all you've come to beg pardon for?"

This thrust put the Colonel more on his defence than a pleasanter reception would have done. He had intended to offer nothing but a very polite apology; but as there seemed to be a disposition on the part of the enemy to extort concessions so as to deprive them of the grace of being voluntary, he withdrew into his own retrenchments.

"I came to ask Mr. Ogden for an explanation about his letter of this morning."

"I should think you need no explanations, Colonel Stanburne. You know what passed yesterday evening."

"He knows that well enough," said Mrs. Ogden.

"I should be glad if Lieutenant Ogden would tell me in detail what he thinks that he has to complain of."

"Leaftenant! Leaftenant! nay, there's no more leaftenantin', I reckon. This is Isaac Ogden—plain Isaac Ogden— an' nout elz. He's given up playin' at soldiers. He's a cotton-spinner, or he were one, nobbut his brother an' him quarrelled; and I wish they hadn't done, many a time I do—for our Jacob's as much as ever he can manage, now as he's buildin' a new mill; an' if he gets wed—and there's Hiram Ratcliff's dorther"— Mrs. Ogden might have gone very far into family matters if her son had not perceived (or imagined that he perceived) something like a smile on Colonel Stanburne's face. In point of fact, the Colonel did not precisely smile; but there was a general relaxation of the muscles of his physiognomy from their first expression of severity, betraying an inward tendency to humor.

"Well, sir," broke in Ogden, "I'll tell you what you did, if you want me. It seems that you've set up a new carriage, a four-in-hand, which looks very like a mail coach, and you drove this vehicle yesterday through the streets of Sootythorn, and you saw my mother on the footpath, and you made a signal to her with your whip, as coachmen do, and you allowed her to get inside under the impression that it was a public conveyance, so that you might make a laughing-stock of her with the officers. And"—

"Pardon me," said the Colonel, "it was not"—

"You've asked me to tell you why I sent in my resignation, and I'm telling you. If you stop me, I shalln't begin it over again. Let me say my say, Colonel Stanburne; you may explain it away afterwards at your leisure, if you can. When you got into Whittlecup, and stopped at the Blue Bell, you took my mother's money—and not only that, but you asked for a gratuity for yourself, as driver, to make her ridiculous in the eyes of your friends on the vehicle. I suppose, though your joke may have been a very good one, that you will be able to understand why it is not very pleasing to me, and why I don't choose to remain under you in the militia."

"If the thing had occurred as you have told it"— the Colonel began, but was instantly interrupted by Mrs. Ogden.

"Do you mean to say I didn't tell him right what happened? If anybody knows what happened, I do."

"Let the Colonel say what he has to say, mother; don't you stop him. I've said my say, and it's his turn now."

The Colonel told the facts as the reader knows them. "He had made no sign to Mrs. Ogden," he said, "in the street at Sootythorn, but she had made a sign with her parasol, which he had interpreted as a request for a place. He had been ignorant that Fyser had kept up her illusion about the vehicle being a public one until after the fact; and so far from encouraging the merriment of the officers, had put a stop to it by telling them who Mrs. Ogden was, particularly requesting that the incident might not be made a subject of pleasantry, lest it should reach Mr. Ogden's ears. On arriving in Whittlecup, he had taken her money, but with the express purpose of saving her the pain of an explanation. He had intended Mrs. Ogden to remain ignorant — happily ignorant — of her little mistake."

"Pardon me," said Isaac Ogden; "this might have been equally well accomplished without asking my mother for a coachman's gratuity. *That* was done to make a fool of her, evidently; and no doubt you laughed about it with your friends as you drove back to Sootythorn."

"Here is the only point on which I feel that I owe an apology to Mrs. Ogden, and I very willingly make it. In every thing else I did what lay in my power to save her from ridicule, but on this point I confess that I did wrong. I couldn't help it. I was carried away by a foolish fancy for acting the coachman out and out. The temptation was too strong for me, you know. I thought I had taken the money cleverly, in the proper professional manner, and I was tempted to ask for a gratuity. I acknowledge that I went too far. Mrs. Ogden, I am very sorry for this."

Mrs. Ogden had been gradually softening during the Colonel's explanation, and when it came to its close she turned to him and said, "We've been rather too hard upon you, I think." Such an expression as this from Mrs. Ogden was equivalent to a profuse apology. The Lieutenant added a conciliatory little speech of his own: "I think my mother may accept your explanation. I am willing to accept it myself." This was not very cordial, but at any rate it was an expression of satisfaction.

Little Jacob had hitherto been a silent and unobserved auditor of this conversation, but it now occurred to the Colonel that he might be of considerable use. "Mrs. Ogden," he said, "will you allow me to transfer your eighteen-pence to this young gentleman's pocket?" Mrs. Ogden consented, and it will be believed that little Jacob on his part had no objection. Then the Colonel drew little Jacob towards him, and began to ask him questions — "What would he like to be?" Little Jacob said he would like to be a coachman, as the Colonel was, and drive four horses. The Colonel promised him a long drive on the coach.

"And may I drive the horses?"

"Well, we shall see about that. Yes, you shall drive them a little some day." Then turning towards Mrs. Ogden, he continued, —

"Lady Helena is not at Wenderholme just now, unfortunately; she is gone to town to her father's for a few days, so that I am a bachelor at present, and cannot invite ladies; but if it would please little Jacob to ride on the coach with me, I should be very glad if you would let him. I am going to drive to Wenderholme this evening as soon as our afternoon drill is finished, and shall return to-morrow morning. About half-a-dozen officers are going to dine with me. Ogden, you'll dine with me too, won't you? Do — there's a good fellow; and pray let us forget this unlucky bit of unpleasantness. Don't come full fig — come in a shell-jacket."

"Well, but you know, Colonel Stanburne, I've resigned my commission, and so how can I come in a red jacket?"

This was said with an agreeable expression of countenance, intended to imply that the resignation was no longer to be

Chap. XXII. *Colonel Stanburne apologizes.*

taken seriously. The Colonel laughed. "Nonsense," he said; "you don't talk about resigning? It isn't a time for resigning when there's such a capital chance of promotion. Most likely you'll be a captain next training, for there's a certain old major who finds battalion drill a mystery beyond the utmost range of his intellect, and I don't think he'll stop very long with us, and when he leaves us there'll be a general rise, and the senior lieutenant, you know, will be a captain."

Mrs. Ogden's countenance began to shine with pride at these hints of promotion. After all, he would be somebody at Shayton, would Captain Ogden, for she was fully determined that when once he should be in possession of the title, it should not perish for want of use.

When the Colonel rose to take his leave, Mrs. Ogden said, "Nay, nay, you shalln't go away without drinking a glass of wine. There's both port and sherry in the cupboard; and if you'd like something to eat — you must be quite hungry after your ride. Why, you've 'appen never got your breakfast?"

The Colonel confessed that he had not breakfasted. He had come away from early drill just before his usual breakfast-hour.

"Eh, well, I wish I'd known sooner; indeed I do. The coffee's quite cold, and there's nothing worse than cold coffee; but Mr. Wood 'll very soon make some fresh." Colonel Stanburne was really hungry, and ate his breakfast in a manner which gave the greatest satisfaction to Mrs. Ogden. The more he ate the more he rose in her esteem, and at length she could no longer restrain her feelings of approval, and said, "You *can* eat your breakfast; it does me good to watch ye. There's many a young man as cannot eat half as much as you do. There's our Isaac here that's only a very poor breakfast-eater. I tell him so many a time."

Indeed she *did* tell him so many a time — namely, about

fifteen times whenever they breakfasted together. When the Colonel had done eating, he looked at his watch and said it was time to go. "Well, I'm very sorry you're goin' so soon — indeed I am," said Mrs. Ogden, who, when he ceased to eat, felt that her own pleasure was at an end. But you *must* drink a glass of wine. It isn't bought at the Blue Bell at Whittlecup — it comes from Shayton." She said this with a calm assurance that it settled the question of the wine's merits, just as if Shayton had been the centre of a famous wine-district. Returning to the subject of breakfast-eating, she repeated, "Eh, I do wish our Isaac could eat his breakfast same as you do, but he's spoiled his stomach wi' drinking." Then addressing her son: "Isaac, I put two glasses with the decanter — why don't you fill your glass?"

"I've given up drinking."

"Do you mean to say as you're teetotal?"

"Yes, I do, mother; I'm teetotal now."

Mrs. Ogden's face assumed an expression of extreme astonishment and displeasure. "Well," she said, "Isaac Ogden, you're the first teetotal as has been in our family!" and she looked at him in scorn. Then she resumed: "If I'd known what was to come of your meeting that teetotal clergyman — for it's him that's done it — I'd have prevented it if I could. Turned teetotal! turned teetotal! Well, Isaac, I never could have believed this of any son of mine!"

CHAPTER XXIII.

HUSBAND AND WIFE.

WHEN Lady Helena came back from London, she found the Wenderholme coach already in full activity. It ran from Sootythorn to Wenderholme twice a week regularly with many passengers, who, so far from contributing to its maintenance, did but yet further exhaust the pocket of its proprietor. It happened precisely that on the day of her ladyship's return the Colonel had one of his frequent dinner-parties at the Hall — parties composed almost exclusively of militia officers, and already known in the regiment as the "Wenderholme mess." The Colonel had thought it prudent to prepare Lady Helena for his new acquisition by mentioning it in a letter, so that she experienced no shock of surprise when the four-in-hand came swinging heavily round the drive in front of the house, announcing itself with loud blasts from Ensign Featherby's cornet-à-piston. They had such numbers of spare bed-rooms at Wenderholme that these hospitalities caused no perceptible inconvenience, except that of getting up very early the next morning, which chiefly affected the guests themselves, who had to be in time for early drill. On this point the Colonel was inexorable, so that the Wenderholme mess was much more popular on Saturday than on Thursday evening, as the officers stayed at Wenderholme till after luncheon, going to the village church in the morning with the people at the Hall, and returning to Sootythorn in the course of the afternoon, so as to be in time for mess. It happened that the day of Lady Helena's return was a Saturday, and the Colonel thought, " She said nothing about the coach to-night, but I'm in for it to-morrow morning." However, when Sunday morning came, beautiful with full spring sunshine, her ladyship's countenance appeared equally cloudless. Encouraged by these favorable appearances, John Stanburne observed, a little before church-time, —

" I say, Helena, you haven't seen the Wenderholme coach. Come and look at it ; *do* come, Helena — that's a good gell It's in the coach-house."

But her ladyship replied that she had seen the coach the evening before from the drawing-room window, when it arrived from Sootythorn.

"Well, but you can't have seen it properly, you know. You can't have looked inside it. Come and look inside it, and see what comfortable accommodation we've got for inside passengers. Inside passengers don't often present themselves, though, and 'yet there's no difference in the fare. You'll be an inside passenger yourself — won't you, now, Helena?"

Her ladyship was clearly aware that this coaxing was intended to extract from her an official recognition of the new institution, and she was resolutely determined to withhold it. So she looked at her watch, and observed that it was nearly church-time, and that she must go at once and put her things on.

As they walked to church, she said to one of the officers, "We always walk to church from the Hall, even in rainy weather."

" Helena's a capital walker," said the Colonel.

" It is fortunate for ladies to be good walkers," replied her ladyship, " when they have no carriage-horses."

Here was a stab ; and the worst of it was, that it might clearly be proved to be deserved. The Colonel had suggested in his letter to Lady Helena that she would do well to come by way of Manchester to Sootythorn, instead of going by Bradford to a little country station ten miles on the Yorkshire side of Wenderholme. Her ladyship had not replied to this communication, but had written the day before her return to the housekeeper at Wenderholme, ordering her carriage, as usual, to the Yorkshire station. The carriage had not come; the housekeeper had only been able to send the pony carriage, a tiny basket that Lady Helena drove herself, with seats for two persons, no place for luggage, and a black pony a little bigger than a Newfoundland dog. Lady Helena had driven herself from the station; there had been a smart shower, and, notwithstanding a thin gray cloak, which was supposed to be waterproof, she had been wet through. The Colonel had taken possession of all the carriage-horses for his four-in-hand, and they were at Sootythorn. Her ladyship would continue to be equally carriageless, since the Colonel would take his whole team back with him, unless he sent back the horses from Sootythorn on the day following. These things occupied John Stanburne's mind when he should have been attending to the service. They had always kept four carriage-horses since their marriage, but never more than four; and though one of the two pairs had been often kept at Sootythorn, when circumstances required them to go there frequently, still her ladyship had never been left carriageless without being previously consulted upon the subject, and then only for twenty-four hours at the longest. The idea of setting up a four-in-hand with only two pairs of horses, one of which was in almost daily requisition for a lady's carriage, would indeed have been ridiculous if John Stanburne had quite seriously entertained it; but, though admitting vaguely the probable necessity of an increase, he had not yet recognized that necessity in a clear and definite way. It came to his mind, however, on that Sunday morning with much distinctness. "Well, hang it!" he thought, as he settled down in his corner at the beginning of the sermon, "I have as much right to spend my own money as Helena has. Every journey she makes to town costs more than a horse. I spend nothing on myself—really nothing whatever. Look at my tailor's bill! I positively *haven't* any tailor's bill. Helena spends more on dress in a month than I do in a year. And then her jeweller's bill! She spends hundreds of pounds on jewellery, and I never spend one penny. Every time she goes to a Drawing-room she has all her old jewels pulled to pieces and set afresh, and it costs nobody knows what—it does. I'll have my four-in-hand properly horsed with horses of my own, by George! and none of those confounded Sootythorn hacks any more; and Helena shall keep her carriage-horses all to herself, and drive about all day long if she likes. Of course I can't take her carriage-horses—she's right there."

On her own part, her ladyship was steadily resolved not to be deprived of any of those belongings which naturally appertained to a person of her rank and consideration; and there had existed in her mind for several years a feeling of jealous watchfulness, which scrutinized at the same time John Stanburne's projects of economy and his projects of expense. It had happened several times within the experience of this couple that the husband had taken little fits of parsimony, during which he attacked the expenditure he least cared for, but which, by an unfortunate fatality, always seemed to his wife to be most reasonable and necessary. It might perhaps have been more favorable to his tranquillity to ally himself with some country girl acclimatized to the dulness of a thoroughly provincial existence, and satisfied with the position of mistress of Wenderholme Hall, who would have let him spend his money in his own way, and would never have dragged him beyond the circle of his tastes and inclinations. He hated London, especially during the season; and though he enjoyed the society of people whom he really knew something about, he disliked being in a crowd. Lady Helena, on the other hand, was fond of society, and even of the spectacle of the court. John Stanburne had regularly accompanied his wife on these annual

visits to the metropolis until this year, when the militia
afforded an excellent pretext for staying in the country; but
every year he had given evidence of an increasing disposition
to evade the performance of his duties; and it had come to
this at last, that Lady Helena was obliged to go about with
the Adisham family, since John Stanburne could not be
made to go to parties any more. He grumbled, too, a good
deal about the costliness of these London expeditions, and
sometimes talked of suppressing them altogether. There
was another annual expedition that he disliked very much,
namely, a winter expedition to Brighton; and it had come to
pass that a coolness had sprung up between John Stanburne
and the Adisham family (who went to Brighton every year),
because his indisposition to meet them there had been somewhat too openly manifested. His old mother was the confidant
of these rebellious sentiments. She lived in a picturesque
cottage situated in Wenderholme Park, which served as a
residence for dowagers. She came very regularly to Wenderholme church, and sat there in a small pew of her own,
which bore the same relation to the big family pew that the
cottage bore to the Hall. John Stanburne had objected
very strongly to his mother's removal to the cottage, and he
had also objected to the separate pew, but his mother maintained the utility of both institutions. She said it was good
for an old woman, who found some difficulty in fixing her
attention steadily, not to be disturbed in her devotions by
the presence of too many strangers in the same pew; and
as there would often be company at the Hall, she would
stick to her own seat. So she sat there as usual on this
particular Sunday, looking very nice in her light summer
dress. The Colonel's little daughter, Edith, had slipped
into her grandmamma's pew, as she often did, when they
were walking up the aisle. She had been staying at the
cottage during her mother's absence, as was her custom when
Lady Helena went to London; and it had cost her, as usual,

a little pang to leave the old lady by herself again. Besides, she felt that it would be pleasanter to sit with her grandmother than with all those strange militia officers. She would have felt, in the family pew, as a very young sapling may be supposed to feel when it is surrounded by overpoweringly big trees — sufficiently protected, no doubt, but more than sufficiently overshadowed.

Amongst the officers in the Wenderholme pew was Lieutenant Ogden, and by his side a young gentleman whose presence has not hitherto been mentioned, namely, little Jacob. Little Jacob's curious eyes wandered over the quaint old church during the sermon, and they fixed frequently upon the strange hatchments and marble monuments in the chapel of the Stanburnes. He had never seen such things before in his life (for there were no old families at Shayton), and he marvelled greatly thereat. Advancing, however, from the known to the unknown, he remembered the royal arms which decorated the front of the organ gallery in Shayton church, and finding a similar ornament at Wenderholme, proceeded to the inference that the hatchments were something of the same kind, in which he was not far wrong. Gradually his eyes fell upon Mrs. Stanburne's pew, and rested there. A vague new feeling crept into his being; Edith Stanburne seemed very nice, he thought. It was pleasant to look upon her face.

Here the more rigid of my readers may exclaim, "Surely he is not going to make little Jacob fall in love at *that* age!" Well, not as you would fall in love, respected reader, if that good or evil fortune were to happen to you; but a child like little Jacob is perfectly capable of falling in love in his own way. The loves of children bear about the same proportion to the great passion which rules the destiny of men, that their contests in fisticuffs do to the bloody work of the bayonet; but as we may many of us remember having given Bob or Tom an ugly-looking black eye, or perchance remember having received one from Tom or Bob, so also there may linger amongst the recollections of our infancy some vision of a sweet little child-face that seemed to us brighter than any other face in the whole world. In this way did Edith Stanburne take possession of Master Jacob's honest little heart, and become the object of his silent, and tender, and timid, and exceedingly respectful adoration. He intensely felt the distance between himself and the heiress of Wenderholme Hall, and so he admired her as some young officer about a court may admire some beautiful princess whom it is his dangerous privilege to see. Children are affected by the externals of ancient wealth to a degree which the mature mind, dwelling amongst figures, is scarcely capable of realizing; and the difference between Wenderholme and Twistle Farm, or Wenderholme and Milend, seemed to little Jacob's imagination an utterly impassable abyss. But there was steam in Ogden's mill, and there was a leak in John Stanburne's purse, and the slow months and years were gradually bringing about great changes.

Little Jacob's adventure on the moor, and his fortunate arrival at the Hall, had given him a peculiar footing there. Colonel Stanburne had taken a marked fancy to the lad; and Lady Helena — who, as the reader may perhaps remember, had lost two little boys in their infancy — was always associating him with her tenderest regrets and recollections, so that there was a sad kindness in her ways with him that drew him very strongly towards her. Isaac Ogden spoke the Lancashire dialect as thoroughly, when it suited him, as any cotton-spinner in the county; but he could also speak, when he chose, a sort of English which differed from aristocratic English by greater hardness and body, rather than by any want of correctness, and he had always strictly forbidden little Jacob to speak the Lancashire dialect in his presence. The lad spoke Lancashire all the more energetically for this prohibition when his father was not within hearing; but the severity of the paternal law had at least given him an equal facility in English, and he kept the two languages safely in separate boxes in his cranium. It is unnecessary to say that at Wenderholme Hall the box which contained the Lancashire dialect was shut up with lock and key, and nothing but the purest English was produced, so that her ladyship thought that the little boy "spoke very nicely — with a northern accent, of course, but it was not disagreeable."

When they came out of church Lady Helena said to Lieutenant Ogden, "Of course you will bring your little boy here on Thursday for the presentation of colors;" and then, whilst Mr. Ogden was expressing his acknowledgments, she interrupted him: "Why not let him remain with us till then? We will try to amuse him, and make him learn his lessons." Mr. Ogden said he would have been very glad, but — in short, his mother was staying at Sootythorn, and might wish to keep her little grandson with her. Colonel Stanburne came up just then, and her ladyship's answer was no doubt partially intended for his ear. "Let me keep little Jacob till to-morrow at any rate. I have several people to see in Sootythorn, and must go there to-morrow. I scarcely know how I am to get there, though, for I have no carriage-horses."

CHAPTER XXIV.

THE COLONEL AS A CONSOLER.

"I SAY, Doctor," said Colonel Stanburne to Dr. Bardly, the day before the presentation of colors, "I wish you'd look to Philip Stanburne a little. He doesn't seem to me to be going on satisfactorily at all. I'm afraid that accident at Whittlecup has touched his brain — he's so absent. He commanded his company very fairly a short time back, and he took an interest in drill, but now, upon my word, he gets worse and worse. To-day he made the most absurd mistakes; and one time he marched his company right off, and, by George! I thought he was going to take them straight at the hedge; and I believe he would have done so if the Adjutant hadn't galloped after him. Eureton rowed him so, that it brought him to his senses. I never saw such a youth. He doesn't seem to be properly awake. I'm sure he's ill. He eats nothing. I noticed him at mess last night. He didn't eat enough to keep a baby alive. I don't believe he sleeps properly at nights. His face is quite haggard. One might imagine he'd got something on his conscience. If you can't do him any good, I'll see the Catholic priest, and beg him to set his mind at ease. I'm quite anxious about him, really."

The Doctor smiled. "It's my opinion," he said, "that the young gentleman has a malady that neither you nor I can cure. Some young woman may cure it, but we can't. The lad's fallen in love."

"Why, Doctor, you don't believe that young fellows make themselves ill about such little matters as that, do you? Men are ill in that way in novels, but never in real life. I was desperately spoony myself before I married Helena, and it wasn't Helena I was spoony about either, and the girl jilted me to marry a marquis; and I think she did quite right, for I'd rather she ran away with the marquis before she was my wife than after, you know. But it didn't spoil me a single meal —it didn't make me sleep a wink the less. In fact I felt immensely relieved after an hour or two; for there's nothing like being a bachelor, Doctor — it's so jolly being a bachelor; no man in his senses can be sad and melancholy because he's got to remain a bachelor."

The Doctor heartily agreed with this opinion, but observed that men in love were *not* men in their senses. "Indeed they're not, Doctor — indeed they're not; but, I say, have you any idea about who the girl is in this business of Philip's? It isn't that pretty Miss Anison, is it?"

Now the Doctor had seen Captain Stanburne coming out of Mr. Stedman's mill one day when he went there to get the manufacturer's present address, and, coupling this incident with his leave of absence, had arrived at a conclusion of his own. But he was not quite sure where young Stanburne had been during his leave of absence.

"Why, he was down in Derbyshire," said the Colonel. "He told me he didn't feel quite well, and wanted a day or two for rest in the country. He said he was going to fish. I don't like giving leaves of absence — we're here only for twenty-eight days; but in his case, you know, after that accident " —

"Oh, he went down to Derbyshire, did he? Then I know for certain who the girl is. It's Alice Stedman. Her father is down there, fishing."

"And who's she?"

"Why, you met her at Whittlecup, at Joseph Anison's.

CHAP. XXIV. *The Colonel as a Consoler.*

She's a quiet bit of a lass, and a nice-looking lass, too. He might do worse."

"I say," said the Colonel, "tell me now, Doctor, has she got any tin?"

"She's safe to have thirty thousand if she's a penny; but it'll most likely be a good bit more." Then the Doctor continued, "But there's no blood in that family. Her father began as a working man in Shayton. It wouldn't be much of a match for a Stanburne. It would not be doing like you, Colonel, when you married an earl's daughter."

"Hang earls' daughters!" said the Colonel, energetically; and then, recollecting himself, he added, "Not all of 'em, you know, Doctor — I don't want all of 'em to be hanged. But this young woman — I suppose she hasn't been presented at Court, and doesn't want to be — and doesn't go to London every season, and has no swell relations." The Doctor gave full assurances on all these points. "Then I'll tell you what it is, Doctor; if this young fellow's fretting about the girl, we'll do all we can to help him. He'd be more prudent still if he remained a bachelor; but it seems a rational sort of a marriage to make. She ain't got an uncle that's a baronet — eh, Doctor?"

"There's no danger of that."

"That's right, that's right; because, look you here, Doctor — it's a foolish thing to marry an earl's daughter, or a marquis's, or a duke's; but the foolishest thing of all is to marry a baronet's niece. A baronet's niece is the proudest woman in the whole world, and she's always talking about her uncle. A young friend of mine married a baronet's niece, and she gave him no rest till, by good luck, one day *his* uncle was created a baronet, and then he met her on equal terms. It's the only way out of it: you *must* under those circumstances get your uncle made a baronet. And if you don't happen to have such a thing as an uncle, what then? What can cheer the hopelessness of your miserable position?"

After this conversation with the Doctor, the Colonel had another with Philip Stanburne himself. "Captain Stanburne," he said, gravely, in an interval of afternoon drill, "I consider you wanting in the duties of hospitality. I ask you to the Sootythorn mess, and you never ask me to the Whittlecup mess. I am reduced to ask myself. I beg to inform you that I shall dine at the Whittlecup mess this evening."

"I should be very happy, but — but I'm afraid you'll have a bad dinner. There's nothing but a beefsteak."

"Permit me to observe," continued the Colonel, in the same grave tone, "that there's a most important distinction to be drawn between bad dinners and simple dinners. Some of the very worst dinners I ever sat down to have been elaborate, expensive affairs, where the ambition of the cook exceeded his artistic skill; and some of the best and pleasantest have been simple and plain, and all the better because they were within the cook's capacity. That's my theory about dining, and every day's experience confirms it. For instance, between you and me, it seems to me highly probable that your Whittlecup mess is better than ours at headquarters, for Mr. Garley *rather* goes beyond what nature and education have qualified him for. His joints are good, but his side-dishes are detestable, and his sweets dangerous. So let us have the beefsteak to-night; there'll be enough for both of us, I suppose. And, I say," added the Colonel, "don't ask anybody to meet me. I want to have a quiet hour or two with you."

When drill was over, Fyser appeared on the field with a led horse for the Captain, and the two Stanburnes rode off together in advance of the company, which for once was left to the old sergeant's care. The dinner turned out to be a beefsteak, as had been promised, and there was a pudding and some cheese. The Colonel seemed to enjoy it very much, and ate very heartily, and declared that every thing was excellent, and talked at random about all sorts of subjects.

CHAP. XXIV.   *The Colonel as a Consoler.*   205

They had the inn parlor all to themselves; and when dinner was over, and coffee had been served, and Mr. Simpson, the innkeeper (who had waited), had retired into other regions, the Colonel lighted a cigar, and plunged *in medias res.*

"I know what you went down into Derbyshire for. You didn't go to fish; you went to ask Mr. Stedman to let you marry his daughter, Miss Alice Stedman."

For the first time since he had known him, Philip Stanburne was angry with the Colonel. His face flushed at once, and he asked, in a tone which was any thing but conciliatory, —

"Do you keep spies in your regiment, Colonel Stanburne?"

"Bardly saw you accidentally just as you were coming out of Mr. Stedman's counting-house, and between us we have made a guess at the object of your visit to Derbyshire."

"You are very kind to interest yourself so much in my affairs."

"Try not to be angry with me. What if I *do* take an interest in your affairs? It isn't wrong, is it? I take an interest in all that concerns you, because I wish to do what I can to be of use to you."

"You are very kind."

"You are angry with me yet; but if I had plagued you with questions about your little excursion, would it not have been more impertinent and more irritating? I thought it best to let you see that I know all about it."

"It was unnecessary to speak upon that subject until I had informed you about it."

"My dear fellow, look here. It is not in the nature of things that you *would* tell me. You have been rejected either by the father or the daughter, and you are going to make yourself ill about it; you are ill already — you are pale, and you never eat any thing, and your face is as melancholy as a face well can be. Be a good fellow, and take me into your confidence, and we will see if we cannot put you out of your misery."

"That is a phrase commonly used by people who kill diseased or wounded animals. You are becoming alarming. You will let me live, I hope, such as I am."

The Colonel perceived that Philip was coming round a little. He waited a minute, and then went on.

"She's a very nice girl. I met her at Mr. Anison's here. I would rather you married her than one of those pretty Miss Anisons. She seems a quiet sensible young lady, who will stay at home with her husband, and not always be wanting to go off to London, and Brighton, and the Lord knows where."

Philip had had a suspicion that the Colonel was going to remonstrate with him for making a plebeian alliance, but that began to be dispelled. To induce him to express an opinion on that point, Philip said, —

"Her father is not a gentleman, you know."

"I know who he is — a very well-to-do cotton manufacturer; and a very intelligent, well-informed man, I'm told. A gentleman! pray what *is* a gentleman?"

"A difficult question to answer in words; but we all know what we mean by the word when we use it."

"Well, yes; but is it quite necessary to a man to be a gentleman at all? Upon my word, I very often think that in our line of life we are foolishly rigid on that point. I have met very clever and distinguished men — men of science, and artists, and even authors — who didn't seem quite to answer to our notions of what a gentleman is; and I know scores of fellows who are useless and idle, and vicious too, and given up to nothing but amusement — and not always the most innocent amusement either — and yet all who know society would recognize them as gentlemen at once. Now, between ourselves, you and I answer to what is called a gentleman, and your proposed father-in-law, Mr. Stedman, you say doesn't; but it's highly probable that he is superior to either of us, and a deal more useful to mankind. He spins cotton, and he studies botany and geology. I wish I could spin cotton, or increase my income in any honest way, and I wish I had some pursuit. I tried once or twice: I tried botany myself, but I had no perseverance; and I tried to write a book, but I found my abilities weren't good enough for that; so I turned my talents to tandem-driving, and now I've set up a four-in-hand. By the by, my new team's coming to-morrow from London — a friend of mine there has purchased it for me."

There was a shade of dissatisfaction on John Stanburne's face as he concluded this little speech about himself. He did not seem to anticipate the arrival of the new team with pleasure unalloyed. The price, perhaps, may have been somewhat heavy — somewhat beyond his means. That London friend of his was a sporting character, with an ardent appreciation of horse-flesh in the abstract, and an elevated ideal. When he purchased for friends, which he was sometimes commissioned to do, he became truly a servant of the Ideal, and sought out only such realities as a servant of the Ideal might contemplate with feelings of satisfaction. These realities were always very costly — they always considerably exceeded the pecuniary limits which had been assigned to him. This was his only fault; he purchased well, and none of the purchase-money, either directly or indirectly, found its way into his own pocket.

The Colonel did not dwell, as he might have been expected to do, upon the subject of the horses — he returned almost immediately to that of matrimonial alliances.

"It's not very difficult to make a guess at the cause of Mr. Stedman's opposition. Bardly tells me he's a most tremendous Protestant, earnest to a degree, and you, my dear fellow, happen to be a Catholic. You'll have to let yourself be converted, I'm afraid, if you really want the girl."

"A man cannot change his faith, when he has one, because it is his interest to do so. I would rather you did not talk about that subject — at least, in that strain. You know my views; you know that nothing would induce me to profess any other views."

"Bardly tells me he doesn't think Stedman will give in, so long as you remain a Catholic."

"Very well."

"Yes, it may be very well — it may be better than marrying. It's a very good thing, no doubt, to marry a good wife, but I'm not sure that the condition of a bachelor isn't really better than that of the most fortunate husband in the world. You see, Philip (excuse me calling you by your Christian name; I wish you'd call me John), you see a married man either cares about his wife or he doesn't. If he doesn't care about her, what's the use of being married to her? If, on the other hand, he *does* care about her, then his happiness becomes entirely dependent upon her humors. Some women — who are very good women in other respects — are liable to long fits of the sulks. You omit some little attention which they think is their due; you omit it in pure innocence, because your mind is very much occupied with other matters, and then the lady attributes it to all sorts of imaginary motives — it is a plan of yours to insult her, and so on. Or, if she attributes it to carelessness, then your carelessness is itself such a tremendous crime that she isn't quite certain whether you ought ever to be forgiven for it or not; and she hesitates about forgiving you for a fortnight or three weeks, and then she decides that you shall be forgiven, and taken into her grace and favor once more. But by the time this has been repeated twenty or thirty times, a fellow gets rather weary of it, you know. It's my belief that women are divided into two classes — the sulky ones and the scolds. Some of 'em do their sulking in a way that clearly shows it's done consciously, and intentionally, and artistically, as a Frenchwoman arranges her ribbons. The great object is to show you that the lady holds herself in perfect command — that she is mistress of her own manner in every thing; and this makes her manner all the more aggravating; because, if she is so perfectly mistress of it, why doesn't she make it rather pleasanter?"

"It's rather a gloomy picture that you have been painting, Colonel, but every lover will believe that there is *one* exception to it."

"Of course he will. You believe Miss Alice Stedman is the exception; only, if you can't get her, don't fret about her. She seems a very admirable young lady, and I should be glad if you married her; because, if you don't, the chances are that you will marry somebody else not quite so suitable. But if I could be quite sure that you would remain a bachelor, and take a rational view of the immense advantages of bachelorhood, I shouldn't much regret Mr. Stedman's obduracy on your account."

These views of the Colonel's were due, no doubt, to his present position with Lady Helena. The causes which were gradually dividing them had been slowly operating for several years, but the effects which resulted from them were now much more visible than they had ever previously been. First they had walked together on one path, then the path had been divided into two by an all but invisible separation — still they had walked together. But now the two paths were diverging so widely that the eye began to measure the space between them, and as it measured the space widened. It is as when two trains leave some great railway station side by side. For a time they are on the same railroad, but after a while you begin to perceive that the distance from your own train to the other is gradually widening; and on looking down to the ground, which seems to flow like a swift stream, you see a streak of green between the two diverging ways, and it deepens to a chasm between two embankments; and after that they are separated by spaces ever widening — spaces of field and river and wood — till the steam of the other engine has vanished on the far horizon.

John Stanburne's offers of assistance were very sincere,

but what, in a practical way, could he do? He could not make Mr. Stedman come round by asking him to Wenderholme. There were plenty of people at Sootythorn who would have done any thing to be asked to Wenderholme, but Mr. Stedman was not one of them. Him the blandishments of aristocracy seduced not; and there was something in his looks, even when you met him merely by accident for an hour, as the Colonel had met him at Arkwright Lodge, which told you very plainly how obdurate he would be where his convictions were concerned, and how perfectly inaccessible to the most artful and delicate coaxing. So the Colonel's good offices were for the present very likely to be confined to a general willingness to do something when the opportunity should present itself.

The day fixed for the ceremony of presentation of colors was now rapidly approaching, and the invitations had all been sent out. It was the Colonel's especial desire that this should take place at Wenderholme, and the whole regiment was to arrive there the evening before, after a regular military march from Sootythorn. The Colonel had invited as many guests of his own as the house could hold; and, in addition to these, many of the Sootythorn people, and one family from Whittlecup, were asked to spend the day at Wenderholme Hall, and be witnesses of the ceremony. The Whittlecup family, as the reader has guessed already, was that from Arkwright Lodge; and it happened that whilst the Colonel was talking with Philip Stanburne about his matrimonial prospects, Mr. Joseph Anison came to the Blue Bell to call upon his young friend.

Philip and the Colonel were both looking out of the window when he came, and before he entered the room, the Colonel found time to say, "Take Anison into your confidence — he'll be your best man, he knows Stedman so well. Let me tell him all about it, will you? Do, now, let me." Philip consented, somewhat reluctantly, and Mr. An-

CHAP. XXIV. *The Colonel as a Consoler.*

ison had not been in the room a quarter of an hour before the Colonel had put him in possession of the whole matter. Mr. Anison's face did not convey very much encouragement. "John Stedman is very inflexible," he said, "where his religious convictions are in any way concerned, and he is very strongly Protestant. I will do what I can with him. I don't see why he should make such a very determined opposition to the match — it would be a very good match for his daughter — but he is a sort of man that positively enjoys sacrificing his interests and desires to his views of duty. If I've any advice to offer, it will be to leave him to himself for a while, and especially not to do any thing to conciliate him. His daughter *may* bring him round in her own way; she's a clever girl, though she's a quiet one — and she can manage him better than anybody else."

When Mr. Anison got back to Arkwright Lodge, he had a talk with Mrs. Anison about Philip's prospects. "*I* shouldn't have objected to him as a son-in-law," said the husband; "he'll be reasonable enough, and let his wife go to her own church."

"I wish he'd taken a fancy to Madge," said Mrs. Anison.

"Have you any particular reason for wishing so? Do you suspect any thing in Madge herself? Do you think she cares for him?"

Mrs. Anison looked grave, and, after a moment's hesitation, said, "I'm afraid there *is* something. I'm afraid she *does* think about him more than she ought to do. She is more irritable and excitable than she used to be, and there is a look of care and anxiety on her face which is quite painful sometimes. And yet I fancy that when Alice was here she rather encouraged young Stanburne to propose to Alice. She did it, no doubt, from anxiety to know how far he would go in that direction, and now he's gone farther than she wished."

CHAPTER XXV.

WENDERHOLME IN FESTIVITY.

AT length the eve of the great day arrived on which the Twentieth Royal Lancashire was to possess its colors — those colors which (according to the phrase so long established by the usage of speech-making subalterns) it was prepared to dye with all its blood — yes, to the very last drop thereof.

Lady Helena had had a terribly busy time during the whole week. Arrangements for this ceremony had been the subject of anxious planning for months before; and during her last stay in London her ladyship had been very active in seeing tradesmen accustomed to create those temporary splendors and accommodations which are necessary when great numbers of people are to be entertained. Mr. Benjamin Edgington had sent down so many tents and marquees that the park of Wenderholme presented the appearance of a rather extensive camp. The house itself contained even more than the amount of accommodation commonly found in houses of its class, but every chamber had its destined occupant. A great luncheon was to be given in the largest of the marquees, and the whole regiment was to be entertained for a night and a day.

The weather, fortunately, was most propitious, the only objection to it being the heat, and the consequent dust on the roads. Once fairly out of Sootythorn, the Colonel gave permission to march at ease, and the men opened their jackets and took their stiff collars off, and began to sing and talk

Wenderholme in Festivity.

very merrily. They halted, too, occasionally, by the banks of clear streams, and scattered themselves on the grass, drinking a great deal of water, there being fortunately nothing stronger within reach. At the half-way house, however, the Colonel gave every man a pint of ale, and drank one himself, as he sat on horseback.

It was after sunset when they reached Wenderholme, and the men marched into the park — not at ease, as they had marched along the road, but in fairly good military order. Lady Helena and a group of visitors stood by the side of the avenue, at the point where they turned off towards the camp. A quarter of an hour afterwards the whole regiment was at supper in the tents, except the officers, who dined at the Hall, with the Colonel's other guests, in full uniform. The dining-room presented a more splendid and animated appearance than it had ever presented since the days of John Stanburne's grandfather, who kept a pack of hounds, and received his scarlet-coated companions at his table. And even the merry fox-hunters of yore glittered not as glittered all these majors and captains and lieutenants. Their full uniforms were still as fresh as when they came from the tailor's. They had not been soiled in the dust of reviews, for the regiment had never been reviewed. The silver of the epaulettes was as brilliant as the brilliant old plate that covered the Colonel's hospitable board, and the scarlet was as intense as that of the freshest flower with which the table was decorated. It was more than a dinner — it was a stately and magnificent banquet. The Stanburnes, like many old families in England, had for generations been buyers of silver plate, and there was enough of the solid metal in the house to set up a hundred showy houses with electro. Rarely did it come forth from the strong safes where it reposed, eating up in its unprofitable idleness the interest of a fortune. But now it glittered once again under the innumerable lights, a heterogeneous, a somewhat barbarous, medley of magnificence.

Lady Helena, without being personally self-indulgent — without caring particularly about eating delicately or being softly clad — had a natural taste for splendor, which may often be independent both of vanity and the love of ease. Human pomp suited her as the pomp of nature suits the mind of the artist and the poet; instead of paralyzing or oppressing her, it only made her feel the more perfectly at home. John Stanburne had known beforehand that his clever wife would order the festivities well, and he had felt no anxiety about her management in any way, but he had not quite counted upon this charming gayety and ease. There are ladies who, upon occasions of this kind, show that they feel the weight of their responsibility, and bring a trouble-clouded visage to the feast. They cannot really converse, because they cannot really listen. They hear your words, perhaps, but do not receive their meaning, being distracted by importunate cares. Nothing kills conversation like an absent and preoccupied hostess; nothing animates it like her genial and intelligent participation. Surely, John Stanburne, you may be proud of Helena to-night! What would your festival have been without her?

He recognizes her superiorities, and admires them; but he would like to be delivered from the little inconveniences which attend them. That clear-headed little woman has rather too much of the habit and the faculty of criticism, and John Stanburne would rather be believed in than criticised. Like many other husbands, he would piously uphold that antique religion of the household which sets up the husband as the deity thereof — a king who can do no wrong. If these had been his views from the beginning — if he had wanted simple unreasoning submission to his judgment, and unquestioning acceptance of his actions — what a mistake he made in choosing a woman like Lady Helena! He who marries a woman of keen sight cannot himself expect to be screened from its keenness. And this woman was so fearless — shall we say so proud? — that she disdained the artifices of what

might have been a pardonable hypocrisy. She made John
Stanburne feel that he was living in a glass case, — nay,
more, that she saw through his clothes — through his skin —
into his viscera — into his brain. You must love a woman
very much indeed to bear this perpetual scrutiny, or she must
love you very much to make it not altogether intolerable.
The Colonel had a reasonable grievance in this, that in the
presence of his wife he found no moral rest. But her criticisms were invariably just. For example, in that last cause
of irritation between them — that about the horses — Lady
Helena had been clearly in the right. It was, to say the
least, a want of good management on the Colonel's part to
have all the carriage-horses at Sootythorn on the day of her
arrival. And so it always was. She never made any observation on his conduct except when such an observation was
perfectly justified — perfectly called for, if you will ; but then,
on the other hand, she never omitted to make an observation
when it *was* called for. It would have been more graceful —
it would certainly have been more prudent — to let things
pass sometimes without taking them up in that way. She
might have let John Stanburne rest more quietly in his own
house, I think ; she might have forgiven his little faults more
readily, more freely, more generously than she did. The
reader perhaps wonders whether she loved him. Yes, she
was greatly attached to him. She loved him a great deal
better than some women love their husbands who give them
perfect peace, and yet she contrived to make him feel an irksomeness in the tie that bound him. Perhaps, with all her
perspicacity, she did not quite thoroughly comprehend — did
not quite adequately appreciate — his simple, and frank, and
honorable nature, his manly kindness of heart, his willingness
to do all that could fairly be required of him, and the sincerity with which he would have regretted all his little failures
in conjugal etiquette, if only he might have been left to find
them out for himself, and repent of them alone.

The digression has been long, but the banquet we were describing was long enough to permit us to absent ourselves from the spectacle for a while, and still find, on returning to it, all the guests seated in their places, and all the lights burning, though the candles may be half an inch shorter. Amongst the guests are several personages to whom we have not yet had the honor of being introduced, and some good people, not personages, whom we know already, but have lost sight of for a long time. There are two belted earls — namely, the Earl of Adisham, Lady Helena's august papa; and the Earl Brabazon, who is papa to Captain Brabazon of the Sootythorn mess. There are two neighboring baronets, and five or six country squires from distant manor-houses, some of which are not less considerable than Wenderholme itself, whilst the rent-rolls which maintain them are longer. Then there is a military commander, with gray whiskers and one eye, and an ugly old sword-cut across the cheek. He is in full uniform, with three medals and perfect ladders of clasps — the ladders by which he has climbed to his present distinguished position. He wears also the insignia of the Bath, of which he is Grand Cross.

But of all these personages, the most distinguished in point of rank must certainly be the little thin gentleman who is sitting by Lady Helena. It is easy to see that he is perfectly delighted with her ladyship, for he is constantly talking to her with evident interest and pleasure, or listening to her with pleasure still more evident. He has a broad ribbon across his white waistcoat, and another round his neck, and a glittering star on his black coat. It is his Grace of Ingleborough, Lord Henry Ughtred's noble father. He is a simple, modest little man — both agreeable and, in his way, intelligent; an excellent man of business, as his stewards and agents know too well — and one of the best Greek scholars in England. Habits of real work, in any direction, have a tendency to diminish pride in those gifts of fortune with which work has nothing to do; and if the Duke found a better Greek scholar than himself, or a better man of business, he had that kind of hearty and intelligent respect for him which is yielded only by real workmen to their superiors. Indeed he had true respect for excellence of all kinds, and was incomparably more human, more capable of taking an interest in men and of understanding them, than the supercilious young gentleman his son.

Amongst our acquaintances at this great and brilliant feast are the worthy incumbent of Shayton and his wife, Mr. and Mrs. Prigley. Whilst we were occupied with the graver matters which affected so seriously the history of Philip Stanburne, Lady Helena had been to Shayton and called upon Mrs. Prigley, and after that they had been invited to the great festivities at Wenderholme. It was kind of Lady Helena, when the house was so full that she hardly knew where to lodge more distinguished guests, to give the Prigleys one of her best bedrooms; but she did so, and treated them with perfect tact and delicacy, trying to make them feel like near relations with whom intercourse had never been suspended. Mrs. Prigley was the exact opposite of a woman of the world, having about as much experience of society as a girl of nine years old who is receiving a private education; yet her manners were very good, except so far as she was too deferential, and it was easy to see that she was a lady, though a lady who had led a very retired life. Mrs. Prigley had never travelled more than twenty miles from her two homes, Byfield and Shayton, since she was born; she had read nothing — she had no time for reading — and the wonder is how, under these circumstances, she could be so nice and lady-like as she was, so perfectly free from all taint of vulgarity. The greatest evil which attends ladies like Mrs. Prigley, when they *do* go into society, is, that they sometimes feel obliged to tell white lies, and that these white lies occasionally lead them into embarrassment. Mrs. Prigley never frankly and simply avowed her ignorance when she thought it would not be *comme il faut* to be ignorant. For instance, if you asked her whether she had read some book, or heard some piece of music, she *always* answered with incredible temerity in the affirmative. If your subsequent remarks called for no further display of knowledge it was well — she felt that she had bravely acted her part, and not been behind the age; but if in your innocence or in your malice (for now and then a malicious person found her out and tormented her) you went into detail, asking what she thought, for instance, of Becky Sharp in "Vanity Fair," she might be ultimately compelled to avow that though she had read "Vanity Fair" she didn't remember Becky. Thus she placed herself in most uncomfortable situations, having the courage to run perpetual risks of detection, but not the courage to admit her ignorance of any thing which she imagined that a lady ought to know. When she had once affirmed her former knowledge of any thing, she stuck to it with astonishing hardihood, and accused the imperfection of her memory — one of her worst fibs, for her memory was excellent.

The conversation at a great banquet is never so pleasant as that at a table small enough for everybody to hear everybody else, and the only approach to a general exchange of opinion on any single topic which occurred on the present occasion was about the house in which the entertainment was given. The Duke had never been to Wenderholme before, and during a lull in the conversation his eye wandered over the wainscot opposite to him. It had been painted white, but the carved panels still left their designs clearly visible under the paint.

"What a noble room this is, Lady Helena!" he said; "but it is rather a pity — don't you think so? — that those beautiful panels should have been painted. It was done, no doubt, in the last century."

CHAP. XXV. *Wenderholme in Festivity.*

"Yes, we regret very much that the house should have been modernized. We have some intention of restoring it."

"Glad to hear that — very glad to hear that. I envy you the pleasure of seeing all these beautiful things come to light again. I wish I had a place to restore, Lady Helena; but those delights are over for me, and I can only hope to experience them afresh by taking an interest in the doings of my friends. I had a capital place for restoration formerly — an old Gothic house not much spoiled by the Renaissance, but overlaid by much incongruous modern work. So I determined to restore it, and for nearly four years it was the pleasantest hobby that a man could have. It turned out rather an expensive hobby, though, but I economized in some other directions, and did what seemed to be necessary."

"Does your Grace allude to Varolby Priory?" asked Mr. Prigley, timidly.

"Yes, certainly; yes. Do you know Varolby?"

"I have never been there, but I have seen the beautiful album of illustrations of the architectural details which was engraved by your directions."

Mrs. Prigley was within hearing, and thinking that it would be well not to be behind her husband, said, "Oh yes; what a beautiful book it was!" The Duke turned towards Mrs. Prigley, and made her a slight bow; then he asked in his innocence, and merely to say something, "whether the copy which Mrs. Prigley had seen was a colored one or a plain one?"

"Oh, it was colored," she answered, without hesitation — "beautifully colored!"

This was Mrs. Prigley's way — she waited for the suggestions of her interlocutor, and on hearing a thing which was as new to her as the kernel of a nut just cracked, assented to it with the tone of a person to whom it was already familiar. So clever had she become by practice in this artifice, that she conveyed the impression that nothing *could* be new to her; and the people who talked with her had no idea that it was themselves who supplied, *à mesure*, all the information wherewith she met them, and kept up the conversation. She had never heard of Varolby Priory before — she had never heard of the album of engravings before — and therefore it is superfluous to add that, as to colored copies or plain ones, she was equally unacquainted with either. Mrs. Prigley had however gone a step too far in this instance, for the Duke immediately replied, —

"Ah, then, I know that you are a friend of my old friend, Sir Archibald. You wonder how I guessed it, perhaps? It's because there are only two colored copies of the album in existence — my own copy and his."

Mrs. Prigley tried to put on an agreeable expression of assent, intended to imply that she knew Sir Archibald (though as yet ignorant of Sir Archibald's surname), when her husband interposed. She made him feel anxious and fidgety. He always knew when she was telling her little fibs — he knew it by a certain facile suavity in her tone, which would not have been detected by a stranger.

"The old mural paintings must be very interesting," said the incumbent of Shayton, and by this skilful diversion saved his wife from imminent exposure.

"Most interesting — most interesting: they were found in a wonderful state of preservation under many layers of whitewash in the chapel. And do you know, *apropos* of your carved panels, Lady Helena, we found such glorious old wainscot round a room that had been lined with lath and plaster afterwards, and decorated with an abominably ugly paper. Not one panel was injured — really not one panel! and the designs carved upon them are so very elegant! That was one of the best finds we made."

"I should think it very probable," said Mr. Prigley, "that discoveries would be made at Wenderholme if a thorough restoration were undertaken."

"No doubt, no doubt," said the Duke, "and there is nothing so interesting. Even the workmen come to take an interest in all they bring to light. Our workmen were quite proud when they found any thing, and so careful not to injure what they found. Do induce your husband to restore Wenderholme, Lady Helena; it' would make such a magnificent place!"

This talk about Wenderholme and restoration had gradually reached the other end of the table, and John Stanburne, feeling no doubt rather a richer and greater personage that evening than usual, being surrounded by more than common splendor, announced his positive resolution to restore the Hall thoroughly. "It was lamentable," he said, " perfectly lamentable, that the building should have been so metamorphosed by his grandfather. But it was not altogether past mending; and architects, you know, understand old Elizabethan buildings so much better than they used to do."

It was a delicious evening, soft and calm, without either the chills of earlier spring or the sultriness of the really hot weather. When the ladies had left the room, and the gentlemen had sat long enough to drink the moderate quantity of wine which men consume in these days of sobriety, the Colonel proposed that they should all go and smoke in the garden. There was a very large lawn, and there were a great many garden-chairs about, so the smokers soon formed themselves into a cluster of little groups. The whole lawn was as light as day, for the front of the Hall was illuminated, and hundreds of little glow-worm lamps lay scattered amongst the flowers. The Colonel had managed to organize a regimental band, which, being composed of tolerably good musicians from Shayton and Sootythorn (both musical places, but especially Shayton), had been rapidly brought into working order by an intelligent bandmaster. This band had been stationed somewhere in the garden, and began to fill the woods of Wenderholme with its martial strains.

"Upon my word, Colonel," said the Duke, stirring his cup of coffee, "you do things very admirably; I have seen many houses illuminated, but I think I never saw one illuminated so well as Wenderholme is to-night. Every feature of the building is brought into its due degree of prominence. All that rich central projection over the porch is splendid! A less intelligent illuminator would have sacrificed all those fine deep shadows in the recesses of the sculpture, which add so much to the effect."

"My wife has arranged all about these matters," said John Stanburne; "she has better taste than I have, and more knowledge. I always leave these things to her."

"Devilish clever woman that Lady Helena!" thought his Grace; but he did not say it exactly in that way.

"All these sash-windows must be very recent. Last century, probably — eighteenth century; very sad that eighteenth century — wish it had never existed, only don't see how we should have got into the nineteenth!"

The Colonel laughed. "Very difficult," he said, "to get into a nineteenth century without passing through an eighteenth century of some sort."

"Yes, of course, of course; but I don't mean merely in the sense of numbers, you know — in the arithmetical sense of eighteen and nineteen. I mean, that seeing how very curiously people's minds seem to be generally constituted, it does not seem probable that they could ever have reached the ideas of the nineteenth century without passing through the ideas of the eighteenth. But what a pity it is they were such destructive ideas! The people of the eighteenth century seem to have destroyed for the mere pleasure of destroying. Only fancy the barbarism of my forefathers at Varolby, who actually covered the most admirable old wainscot in the world, full of the most delicate, graceful, and exquisite work, with lath and plaster, and a hideous paper! They preferred the paper, you see, to the wainscot."

"Perhaps paper happened to be more in the fashion, and they did not care about either. My grandfather did not leave the wainscot, however, under the paper. At least, he must have removed a great deal of it. There is an immense lot of old carved work that he removed from the walls and rooms in a lumber-garret at the top of the house."

"Is there though, really?" said the Duke, with much eagerness; then you *must* let me see it to-morrow — you must indeed; nothing would interest me more."

Just then a white stream of ladies issued from the illuminated porch, and flowed down the broad stairs. Their diamonds glittered in the light, flashing visibly to a considerable distance. They came slowly forward to the lawn.

"I think it is time to have the fireworks now," said Lady Helena to the Colonel.

The Colonel called the officers about him, whilst the other gentlemen began to talk to the ladies. "It would prevent confusion," he said, "if we were to muster the men properly to see the fireworks. I should like them to have good places; but there is some chance, you know, that they might damage things in the garden unless they come in military order. There are already great numbers of people in the park, and I think it would be better to keep our men separate from the crowd as much as possible." Horses were brought for the Colonel and other field-officers, and they rode to the camp, the others following on foot. Transparencies had been set up at different parts of the garden, with the numbers of the companies; and the arrangements had been so perfectly made, that in less than twenty minutes every company was at its appointed place.

No private individual in John Stanburne's position could afford a display of pyrotechnics sufficient to astonish such experienced people as his noble guests; but Lady Helena and the pyrotechnician, or "firework-man," as her ladyship more simply called him, had planned something quite sufficiently effective. He and his assistants were on the roof of the Hall, where temporary platforms and railings had been set up in different places for their accommodation; and the floods of fire that soon issued therefrom astonished many of the spectators, especially Mrs. Prigley. And yet when a perfectly novel device was displayed, which the "firework-man" had invented for the occasion, and Lady Helena asked Mrs. Prigley what she thought of it, that lady averred that she had seen it before, in some former state of existence, and had "always thought it very beautiful."

Suddenly these words, "The Fiery Niagara," shone in great burning letters along the front of the house, and then an immense cascade of fire poured over the roof in all directions, and hid Wenderholme Hall as completely as the rock is hidden where the real Niagara thunders into its abyss. At the same time trees of green fire burned on the sides of the flowing river, and their boughs seemed to dip in its rushing gold, as the boughs of the sycamores bend over the swift-flowing water. And behind the edge of the great cascade rose slowly a great round moon.

CHAPTER XXVI.

MORE FIREWORKS.

AFTER the fiery cascade came the bouquet; and the fireworks ended with a prodigious sheaf of rockets, which made the country people think that the stars were falling.

Though the Hall was still illuminated, it looked poorer after the brilliant pyrotechnics; and as this diminution of its effect had been foreseen, arrangements had been made beforehand to cheer the minds of the guests at the critical moment by a compensation. The Venetian lanterns had been reserved till now, and the band had been silent during the fireworks. A large flat space on the lawn had been surrounded by masts with banners, and from mast to mast hung large festoons of greenery, and from the festoons hung the many-colored lanterns. A platform had been erected at one end for the band; and before the last rocket-constellation had burst into momentary splendor, and been extinguished as it fell towards the earth, the lanterns were all burning, and the band playing merrily. Before and during the fireworks the company had been considerably increased by arrivals from neighboring villages and the houses of the smaller gentry, so Lady Helena passed the word that there would be a dance in the space that was enclosed by the lanterns.

It had been part of our friend Philip Stanburne's duty to march to Wenderholme with his company, and to dine with the Colonel in the Hall; but in his present moody and melancholy temper he found it impossible to carry complaisance so far as to whirl about in a waltz with some young lady whom he had never before seen. There was nobody there that he knew; and when Lady Helena kindly offered to introduce him to a partner, his refusal was so very decided that it seemed almost wanting in politeness. The Colonel had not mentioned Philip's love-affair to her ladyship, for reasons which the reader will scarcely need to have explained to him. People who have lived together for some years generally know pretty well what each will think and say about a subject before it has been the subject of open conversation between them; and since Philip Stanburne was now treated as a near relation at Wenderholme, it was clear that her ladyship would be a good deal put out if she heard of his intended misalliance. The Colonel himself was by no means democratic in his aboriginal instincts; but after his experience of married life, the one quality in Lady Helena which he would most willingly have done without was her rank, with its concomitant inconveniences. He did not now feel merely indifferent to rank, he positively disliked it; and with his present views, Alice Stedman's humble origin seemed a guarantee of immunity from many of the perils which were most dangerous to his own domestic peace. But Lady Helena (as he felt instinctively, without needing to give to his thought the consistency of words and phrases) was still in that state of mind which is natural to every one who is born with the advantages of rank — the state of mind which values rank too highly to sacrifice it willingly, or to see any relation sacrifice it without protesting against his folly. Hers would be the natural and rational view of the matter; the common-sense view; the view which in all classes who have rank of any sort to maintain (and what class has not?) has ever been recognized, has ever persisted and prevailed. The Colonel did not go so far as to wish that he had married some other person of humble provincial rank; but he often wished that Lady Helena herself had been the daughter of some small squire, or country clergyman, or cotton-spinner, if he had brought her up as nicely as Alice Stedman had been brought up. It was not to be expected that she could ever share this opinion about herself, or the opinion about Alice Stedman, which was merely a reflection of it.

Owing to Philip Stanburne's exile at Whittlecup, which had continued during the whole of the training, and to his natural shyness and timidity, which the extreme reclusion of his existence had allowed to become the permanent habit of his nature, he had made few acquaintances amongst the officers, and not one friend. There were several men in the regiment to know whom would have done Philip Stanburne a great deal of good, but he missed the opportunities which presented themselves. For instance, on the present occasion, though several of his brother officers, who, like himself, were not dancing, had gathered into a little group, Philip Stanburne avoided the group, and walked away by himself in the direction of the great dark wood. He felt the necessity for a little solitude; he had not been by himself during the whole day, and it was now nearly midnight. A man who is accustomed to be alone will steal out in that way from society to refresh himself in the loneliness which is his natural element — *pour se remettre*, as a Frenchman would express it. So he followed a narrow walk that led into the wood, and soon lost sight of the illuminations, whilst the music became gradually fainter, and at last was confined to such hints of the nature of the melody as could be gathered from the occasional fortissimo of a trumpet or the irregular booming of a drum.

There was, as the reader already knows, a ravine behind Wenderholme Hall, which was a gash in the great hill that divided Wenderholme from Shayton. All this ravine was filled with a thick wood, and a stream came down the middle of it from the moorland above — a little noisy stream that tumbled over a good many small rocks, and made some cascades which the inhabitants of Wenderholme showed to all their visitors, and which lady visitors often more or less successfully sketched. By an outlay of about a hundred pounds, John Stanburne's grandfather had dammed this stream up in one conveniently narrow place, and made a small pond there, and the walk which Philip Stanburne was now following skirted the stream till it came to the pond's edge. It turned round the upper end of the tiny lake, and crossed the stream where it entered by means of a picturesque wooden bridge. From this bridge the Hall might be distinctly seen in the daytime; and Philip, remembering this, or perhaps merely from the habit of looking down towards the Hall when he crossed the bridge, stopped and looked, as if in the darkness of the night he could hope to distinguish any thing at the back of the house, which, of course, was not illuminated.

Not illuminated! Why, the firework-men have applied a more effective device to the back of the house than the elaborate illumination of the front! They have invented a curling luminous cloud, these accomplished pyrotechnicians!

Philip Stanburne began to wonder how it was managed, and to speculate on the probable artifice. Was the smoke produced separately, and then lighted from below, or was it really luminous smoke? However produced, the effect was an admirable one, and Philip admired it accordingly. "But it is odd," he thought, "that I should be left to enjoy it (probably) by myself. It's not likely that they have left their dancing — I'm sure they haven't; I can hear the drum yet, and it's marking the time of a waltz." A gentle breeze came towards him, and rippled the surface of the dark water. It brought the sound of the trumpets and he recognized the air. "They are waltzing still, no doubt."

The luminous smoke still rose and curled. Then a red flash glared in it for an instant. "Those are not fireworks," said Philip Stanburne, aloud; "*Wenderholme Hall is on fire!*"

CHAPTER XXVII.

THE FIRE.

"WHY, Philip," said the Colonel, "I didn't know that you'd been dancing. You've been over-exerting yourself. You look tremendously hot, and very much out of breath."

"Young fellahs will dance, you know, Colonel," said the General with the ladders of clasps — "young fellahs will; I envy them!"

"Where is Edith — your daughter — little Edith?" Philip asked, with a scared and anxious face.

"In bed, of course, at this time of night. You don't want to dance with *her*, a small child like her?" Then fixing his eyes on Philip Stanburne's face, the Colonel exclaimed, grasping his arm so strongly as to cause pain. "Something is wrong, by Jove! out with it, out with it!"

"Where's Edith's room? the house is on fire!"

John Stanburne said nothing, but turned at once with swift steps towards the house. Philip followed him closely: they entered by the great doorway under the porch, and passed rapidly across the hall. It was quiet and empty, lighted by a few lamps suspended from the ceiling by long crimson cords — the portraits of the old fox-hunting Stanburnes looking down with their usual healthy self-possession. The door from the hall to the staircase was closed: when the Colonel opened it, a smell of burning became for the first time perceptible. He took four steps at a time. Edith's rooms were nearly at the top of the house. The nurseries had been up there traditionally, because that situation kept noisy children well out of the way of guests.

Wenderholme was a lofty house, with a long lateral corridor on each story. As they ascended, the smell of burning strongly increased. The lower corridors were lighted — all the guests' rooms were there. But the uppermost corridor, where the servants' rooms and the nurseries were, was not permanently lighted, as the servants took their own bed-candlesticks from below. When the Colonel got there he could not see, and he could not breathe. Volumes of dense smoke rolled along the dark passages. He ran blindly in the direction of Edith's room. Philip tried to follow, but the suffocating atmosphere affected his more delicate organization with tenfold force, and he was compelled to draw back. He stood on the top of the great staircase, agitated by mortal anxiety.

But the Colonel himself, strong as he was, could not breathe that atmosphere for long. He came back out of the darkness, his hands over his face. Even on the staircase the air was stifling, but to him, who had breathed thick fire, it was comparative refreshment. He staggered forward to the banister, and grasped it. This for three or four seconds, then he ran down the stairs without uttering one word.

The two passed swiftly through a complicated set of passages on the ground-floor and reached one of the minor staircases, of which there were five or six at Wenderholme. This one led directly to the nurseries above, and was their most commonly used access. When they came to this, John Stanburne turned round, paused for an instant, and said, "Come with me, Philip; it's our last chance. Poor little Edith! O God, O God!"

In this narrow stair there was no light whatever. The Colonel ran up it, or leaped up it, in a series of wild bounds, like a hunted animal. Philip kept up with him as he could. As they rose higher and higher the temperature quickly increased: the walls were hot — it was the temperature of a heated oven. The Colonel tried to open a door, but the brass handle burnt his hand. Then he burst it open by pushing against it with his shoulder. A gust of air rushed up the staircase, and in an instant the room they were trying to enter was illuminated by a burst of flame. For a second the paper was visible — a pretty, gay paper, with tiny flowers, suitable for a young girl's room — and a few engravings on the walls, and the pink curtains of a little French bed.

Either by one of those unaccountable presentiments which sometimes hold us back at the moment of imminent danger, or else from horror at the probable fate of little Edith, the Colonel paused on the threshold of the burning room. Then the ceiling cracked from end to end, and fiery rafters, with heaps of other burning wood, came crashing down together. The heat was now absolutely intolerable — to remain on the threshold was death, and the two went down the stairs. There was a strong draught in the staircase, which revived them physically, and notwithstanding the extremity of his mental anguish, the Colonel descended with a steady step. When they came into the lighted hall he stood still, and then broke into stifled, passionate sobs. "Edith! little Edith!" he cried, "burnt to death! horrible! horrible!" Then he turned to his companion with such an expression on his white face as the other had never before seen there. "And, Philip, the people were dancing on the lawn!"

Then John Stanburne sat down in one of the chairs against the wall, and set his elbows on his knees, and covered his face with both his hands. So he sat, immovable. The house was burning above him — it might burn. What were all the treasures of Wenderholme to its master, who had lost the one treasure of his heart? What were the parchments and the seals in the charter-room — what were the records of the Stanburnes — what was that waggon-load of massive silver which had shone at the festival that night?

His anguish was not wild — he did not become frantic — and the shock had not produced any benumbing insensibility; for his health was absolutely sound and strong, and his nervous system perfectly whole and unimpaired. But the sound mind in the sound body is still capable of an exquisite intensity of suffering, though it will live through it without either madness or insensibility.

Philip Stanburne felt compelled to respect this bitter agony of his friend; but he was anxious to lose no more time in trying to save the house. So at last he said, "Colonel, the house is burning!"

John Stanburne looked up, and said, "It may burn now — it may burn now." Then suddenly seeming to recollect himself, he added, "God forgive me, Philip, I have not bestowed one thought on the poor girl that was burnt with Edith — Edith's maid! She brought my child to me to say goodnight, just when the fireworks were over, and kiss me " — here his voice faltered — "and kiss me for the last time.' This extension of his sympathy to another did John Stanburne good. "I wonder where her parents are; they must be told — God help them!"

"And the house, Colonel! — the house! can you give some orders?"

"No, Philip; not fit for that — not fit for that yet, you know, dear Philip. Ask Eureton, the Adjutant — ask Eureton."

Then he rose suddenly, and went towards the drawing-room. Some of the older ladies had come in, and were sitting here and there about the room, which was brilliantly lighted. On one of the walls hung a portrait of Edith Stanburne, by Millais — one of his most successful pictures of that class. The Colonel went straight to this picture, but could not politely get at it without begging two old ladies, who were sitting on a *causeuse* under it, to get out of his way.

When a man who has just been brought face to face with

one of the tragical realities of life comes into what is called "society" again, he is always out of tune with it, and it is difficult for him to accept the *légèreté* of its manner without some degree of irritation. He appears brutal to the people in society, and the people in society seem exasperatingly frivolous to him. Thus, when the Colonel came amongst these bediamonded old ladies in the drawing-room, a conversation took place which he was not quite sufficiently master of himself to maintain in its original key.

"Ah, here is Colonel Stanburne! We were just saying how delightful your fireworks were; only they've left quite a strong smell of fire, even in the house itself. Don't you perceive it, Colonel Stanburne?"

"I want to get this picture — excuse me," and he began to put his foot on the white silk damask of the *causeuse*, between the two great ladies. They rose immediately, much astonished, even visibly offended.

"Colonel Stanburne might have waited until we had left the room," said Lady Brabazon, aloud, "if he wished to change the hanging of his pictures."

"The house is on fire! My daughter is burnt to death! I want to save this. You ladies are still in time to save the originals of *your* portraits."

In an instant they were out upon the lawn, running about and calling out "Fire!" They had not time to take care of their dignity now.

Luckily Philip Stanburne was already with the Adjutant, who was giving his orders with perfect calm, and an authority that made itself obeyed. Lady Helena was not to be found.

Fyser had been summoned into the Adjutant's presence. "Fyser," he said, "what are the water supplies here?"

"Pump-water, sir, for drinking, and the stream behind the house for washing."

"No pipes of any sort in the upper rooms?"

"No, sir."

"Sergeant Maxwell, collect all the men who have served in the army. I don't want any others at present." Then, turning to Fyser, "Harness four horses to a carriage, and drive to the nearest station. Telegraph for fire-engines and a special locomotive. Whilst they are coming, collect more horses near the station. When they arrive, leave your carriage there, and harness your team to a fire-engine, and come here as fast as you can. Do you hear? Repeat what I have said to you. Very well."

Then he walked quickly towards the band, and made signs to the band-master to stop. The music ceased abruptly, and Captain Eureton ascended the platform. "I wish to be heard!" he said, in a loud voice. The dancers gave up their dancing, and came towards the orchestra, followed by the other guests.

"Excuse this interruption to your pleasures. You had better not go into the Hall."

At this instant the old ladies (as has just been narrated) came out of the hall-door shrieking, "Fire!" Their cry was taken up immediately, and wildly repeated amongst the crowd.

"Silence!" shouted Eureton, with authority. "Silence! I have something to say to you."

The people crowded round him. "The Colonel wishes me to act for him. Our only chance of saving the house is to set to work systematically. I forbid any one to enter it for the present."

"But my trunks," cried Lady Brabazon; "I will order my people to save my trunks!"

This raised a laugh; but Eureton's answer to it came in the shape of an order. "Sergeant Maxwell," he said, "if any one attempts to enter the house without leave, you will have him arrested."

"Yes, sir."

The sergeant was there with a body of about forty old soldiers.

CHAP. XXVII.   The Fire.

"Captains of numbers one, two, three, four, and five companies!" shouted the Adjutant. They came forward. "You will form a cordon with your men round the front of the house, and prevent any unauthorized person from breaking it. All who enter the cordon will be considered as volunteers, and set to carry water. They will not be allowed to get out of it again, on any pretext."

"Now send me Colonel Stanburne's men-servants."

Several men presented themselves. "Fetch every thing you can lay your hands on in the out-houses that will hold water."

"Pray accept me as a volunteer, Captain Eureton," said the Duke.

"And I'm an old soldier," said the medalled General; "you'll have me, too, I suppose."

The cordon was by this time formed, and a quantity of buckets fetched from the out-houses.

A chain was very soon formed from the brink of the rivulet to the inside of the house, and the Adjutant went in with Philip Stanburne to reconnoitre. When he came out he walked to the middle of the space enclosed by the cordon of militiamen, and cried with a loud voice, "Volunteers for saving the furniture, come forward!"

Such numbers of men presented themselves (including the Colonel's guests), that it was necessary to close the cordon against many of them. Those who were admitted were told off by the Adjutant in parties of a dozen each, and each party placed under the command of a gentleman, with an old soldier for a help. It was Philip Stanburne's duty to guide and distribute the parties in the house — the Adjutant commanding outside. The Colonel, in his kind way, had shown Philip Stanburne over the house on his first visit to Wenderholme, so that he knew and remembered the arrangement of the rooms.

Though the house did not front precisely to the west, it

will best serve our present purposes to speak as if it had done so. Supposing, then, the principal front to be the west front, the back of the edifice, where Philip Stanburne first discovered the fire, was to the east, whilst the south and north fronts looked to the wood on each side the ravine, at the opening of which Wenderholme Hall was situated. The fire had been discovered towards the south-east corner of the edifice, where little Edith's apartments were. The great staircase was in the centre, immediately behind the entrance-hall; but there were five other staircases of much narrower dimensions, two of them winding stairs of stone, the other three modern stairs of deal wood, such as are commonly made for servants.

Acting under Captain Eureton's directions, Philip Stanburne distributed his parties according to the staircases, and other parties were stationed at the doors to receive the things they brought down, and carry them to places already decided upon by the Adjutant. The business of extinguishing or circumscribing the fire was altogether distinct from that of salvage. Two lines of men were stationed from the side of the rivulet to the top of the great staircase. One line passed full buckets from hand to hand, the other passed them down again as soon as they were empty. A special party, consisting of the gardeners belonging to Colonel Stanburne's establishment, a joiner, and one or two other men who were employed at Wenderholme, had been formed by the Adjutant for the purpose of collecting what might serve as buckets, the supply being limited. Various substitutes were found; amongst others, a number of old oyster-barrels, which were rapidly fitted with rope-handles.

Notwithstanding the number of men under his command, and the excellent order which was maintained, it became evident to Captain Eureton that it was beyond his power to save the south wing of the building. Even the northern end of the upper corridor was filled with dense smoke, and towards Edith Stanburne's apartments there was a perfect furnace. By frequently changing places, the men were able to dispute the ground against the fire inch by inch; and the clouds of steam which rose as they deluged the hot walls had the effect of making the atmosphere more supportable. If the fire did not gain on them too rapidly, there seemed to be a fair chance of saving some considerable proportion of the mansion by means of the fire-engines, when they arrived.

Meanwhile the salvage of goods went forward with perfect regularity. The influence of Captain Eureton's coolness and method extended itself to every one, and the things were handed down as quietly as in an ordinary removal. Hardly any thing was broken or even injured; the rooms were emptied one by one, and the contents of each room placed together. Every thing was saved from the charter-room — Philip Stanburne took care to see to that.

What the Duke was most anxious to save was the contents of the lumber-garrets, where lay the dishonored remnants of the old wainscot and carved furniture of Elizabethan Wenderholme. But when he got up there with his party he found that it was not quite possible to breathe. A more serious discovery than the inevitable loss of the old oak was that the fire was rapidly spreading northwards in the garrets.

There was a little ledge round the roof outside, protected by a stone parapet, and broad enough for a man to walk along; so the chain of water-carriers was continued up to this ledge, and a hole was made in the slating through which a tolerably continuous stream was poured amongst the burning lumber inside. The uselessness of this, however, shortly became apparent; the water had little or no effect — it flowed along the floor, and the rafters had already caught fire. The slates were so hot that it was impossible to touch them. It was evident that the lead under the men's feet would soon begin to melt, and the men were withdrawn into the interior.

CHAPTER XXVIII.

FATHER AND DAUGHTER.

WHEN Colonel Stanburne had removed Edith's picture, he carried it away into the darkness. He could not endure the idea of having to explain his action, and instinctively kept out of people's way. Still, he could not leave it out of doors; he dreaded some injury that might happen to it. Where could he put it? In one of the out-houses? A careless groom might injure it in the hurry and excitement of the night. No; it would be safe nowhere but at his mother's, and thither he would carry it.

There were two communications from the Hall to the cottage — a carriage-drive and a little footpath. The drive curved about a little under the old trees in the park, but the footpath was more direct, and went through a dense shrubbery. On his way to the cottage the Colonel met no one, but on his arrival there he met Lady Helena in the entrance. His mother was there too. Late as it was, she had not yet gone to bed.

The sight of the Colonel, bareheaded, and carrying a great oil-picture in his hands, greatly astonished both these ladies.

"What *are* you doing with that picture, John?" said Lady Helena.

"I want it to be safe — it will be safe here;" and he reared it against the wall. Then he said, "No, not here; it will be safer in the drawing-room; open the door. Thank you."

When they got into the drawing-room, the Colonel deliberately took down a portrait of himself and hung Edith's portrait in its place. His manner was very strange, both the ladies thought; his action most strange and eccentric. Lady Helena thought he had drunk too much wine; Mrs. Stanburne dreaded insanity.

With that humoring tone which is often adopted towards persons not in possession of their mental faculties, Mrs. Stanburne said, "Well, John, I shall be glad to take care of Edith's picture for you, if you think that it can be safer here than at the Hall."

"Yes, it will be safer — it will be safer."

This answer, and his strange wild look, confirmed poor old Mrs. Stanburne's fears. She began to tremble visibly. "Helena, Helena," she whispered, "poor John is — has "—

"No, mother, I'm not mad, and I'm not drunk either, Helena, but I've brought this picture here because it's more valuable to me now than it used to be, and — I don't want it to be burnt, you understand."

"No, I don't understand you at all," said her ladyship; "you are unintelligible to-night. Better come home, I think, and not drink any more wine. I never saw you like this before. It is disgraceful."

"Helena!" said the Colonel, in a very deep, hoarse voice, "Wenderholme Hall is on fire, and my daughter Edith is burnt to death!"

Just as he finished speaking, a lurid light filled the sky, and shone through the windows of the cottage. Lady Helena went suddenly to the window, then she left the room, left the house, and went swiftly along by the little path. John Stanburne was left alone with his mother.

She took him by the hand, and looked in his face anxiously. "My dear boy," she said, "it's a pity about the house, you know; but our little Edith " —

"What?"

"Is perfectly safe here, and fast asleep up-stairs in her own little bed!"

John Stanburne did not quite realize this at first. When it became clear to him, he walked about the room in great agitation, not uttering a word. Then he stopped suddenly, and folded his mother in his arms, and kissed her. He kept her hand and knelt down before the sofa; she understood the action, and knelt with him. Edith's picture was hanging just above them, and as his lips moved in inaudible thanksgiving, his eyes rose towards it and contemplated its sweet and innocent beauty. He had had the courage to save it from the burning house, but not the courage to let his eyes dwell upon it thus. Fair hair that hast not been consumed in cruel flame! fair eyes that shall shine in the sunlight of to-morrow! sweet lips whose dear language shall yet be heard in your father's house!—your living beauty shall give him cheerfulness under this calamity!

When they rose, his mother said, "Come and see;" and she took him up to a little dainty room which Edith loved, and there, in a narrow bed curtained with pale blue silk, she lay in perfect peace. The night was warm, and there was a glow on the healthy cheek, and one little hand, frilled with delicate lace, lay trying to cool itself upon the counterpane.

"I'm afraid she's rather too warm," said her grandmother. But John Stanburne thought of the fiery chamber at Wenderholme.

CHAPTER XXIX.

PROGRESS OF THE FIRE.

MRS. STANBURNE'S tender sympathy for her son's grief at the supposed loss of Edith, and participation in his gladness at the recovery of his treasure, had for a time restrained the expression of her anxiety about the fire at the Hall; but now that her son had seen little Edith, Mrs. Stanburne went to the window of the bed-room and looked out. The Hall was not visible from the lower rooms of the cottage, being hidden by the thick shrubbery which bounded the little lawn; but it was clearly visible from the upper windows, which looked in that direction.

No sooner had Mrs. Stanburne opened the curtains and drawn up the blind, than she uttered a cry of alarm. The fire having originated in the garret, the carpentry of the roof had been attacked early, and now a portion of it had given way. A column of sparks, loftier than the Victoria Tower at Westminster, shot up in the dark sky.

Mrs. Stanburne turned round in great agitation. "Let us go, John — let us go to the Hall; it will be burnt down. You will be wanted to give orders."

This recalled the Colonel to himself, and for the present he gave up thinking about his little Edith. "Eureton is in command, and he's a better officer than I am. He will do all that can be done. But come along, mother — come along; let us go there."

As they approached the Hall, it was evident to John Stanburne that the fire had made terrible progress. The whole of the uppermost story was illuminated by the dread light of conflagration. At the south end, which had been burning longest, and where the roof had fallen in, sparks, still rose in immense quantities, and terrible tongues of flame showed their points, darting angrily, above the lofty walls.

Eureton was in the centre of the open space still steadily guarded by the cordon of militia-men. He was looking at his watch, but on lifting his eyes from the dial, saw the Colonel and Mrs. Stanburne, and went to them at once. " I have been anxious to see you for some time, Colonel. Do you wish to take the men under your own orders?"

" My dear fellow, do oblige me by directing every thing just as you have done. You do it ten times better than I should — I know you do."

" I am sorry we have been unable to save the roof. I withdrew the men from it rather early, perhaps, but wished to avoid any sacrifice of life."

" Better let the whole place burn down than risk any of these good fellows' lives. Is there anybody in the house now?"

" Captain Stanburne has eight parties on the first floor removing furniture. He has removed every thing from the upper floors."

" But are they safe?" said Mrs. Stanburne.

"No floors have fallen in yet except part of the garret floor, and one or two in the south wing. We have drenched every room with water, after it was emptied; we have left the carpets on the floors purposely, because being thoroughly wetted, they will help to delay the progress of the fire. We have used all the blankets from the beds in the same way. Every thing else has been removed."

"I hope all the visitors' things will be safe. Some of those old ladies, you know, have wonderful lots of things in their portmanteaus. I believe that in point of mere money's worth, old Lady Brabazon's boxes are more valuable than all Wenderholme and its furniture too, by Jove!"

"I must ask the ladies to sleep at the cottage," said Mrs. Stanburne.

"They are at the summer-house, watching the fire," said the Adjutant. "I believe it amuses them."

"You are uncharitable," said Mrs. Stanburne; "nobody can help watching a fire, you know. A fire always fascinates people."

"I wouldn't let old Lady Brabazon have her boxes, and she's furiously angry with me."

"Well, but why wouldn't you?"

"If I let one, I must let another, and there would be no end to the confusion and breakage that would ensue. I have refused Lady Helena herself, but she took it very nicely and kindly. It's different with Lady Brabazon; she's in a rage."

"I'll go with my mother to the summer-house, and come back to you, Eureton, in ten minutes."

The summer-house in question presented rather a curious picture. It was not strictly a "house" at all, but simply a picturesque shed with a long bench under it, which people could sit down upon at noon, with their backs to the south, well sheltered from the summer sun by a roof and wall of excellent thatch, whilst the stream purled pleasantly at the foot of a steep slope, and seemed to cool the air by its mere sound. The back of the seat was towards the steep wooded hill, and the front of it looked towards the south wing of the house, including a very good view of the front. It was decidedly the best view of Wenderholme which could be had; and when artists drew Wenderholme for those well-known works, "Homes of the Landed Gentry," and "Dwellings of the English Aristocracy," and "Ancient Seats of Yorkshire," here they always rubbed their cakes of sepia and began.

The ladies were not playing the harp or the fiddle, as Nero is said to have done during the burning of Rome; but they were enjoying the spectacle as most people enjoy that which greatly interests and excites. Lady Adisham, John Stanburne's august mother-in-law, was not there; she was in close conference with her daughter, in a part of the grounds yet more private and remote. But Lady Brabazon was there, and some other splendidly adorned dames, who were passing an opera-glass from hand to hand.

As the Colonel and his mother approached, they had the pleasure of overhearing the following fragment of conversation.

"Quite a great fire; really magnificent! Don't you think so? We're safe here, I believe."

"Yes; Captain Eureton said we should be safe here."

"I wonder if Mr. Stanburne has insured his house. They say he's not at all rich. Pity his little daughter was burnt — really great pity; nice little girl!"

"Where are we to sleep to-night, do you think?"

"Really don't know. *À la belle étoile*, I suppose. That horrid man that's ordering the men about won't let us have our boxes. We shall take cold. I have nothing but this shawl."

Just then the Colonel presented himself.

"I am very sorry," he said, with some bitterness, "that my house should be burnt down, if the accident has caused you any inconvenience. Mrs. Stanburne is come to offer you some accommodation at Wenderholme Cottage."

Lady Brabazon was going to make a speech of condolence, but the Colonel prevented it by adding, "Pray excuse me — I ought to be amongst the men;" and bowing very deferentially, he disappeared.

John Stanburne left Eureton in command, and worked himself as a volunteer amongst the water-carriers within the building. The reaction from his despair about Edith made his other misfortunes light, and he worked with a cheerfulness and courage that did good to the men about him.

"This is hot work," he said to one of the volunteers; "have none of the men had any thing to drink?"

"Thank you, sir, we are doing pretty well for that. We take a little water from the buckets now and then."

CHAP. XXIX.   *Progress of the Fire.*   245

" And the other fellows who are removing the furniture ? "
" It must be dry work for them, sir."

On this the Colonel said he could be more useful elsewhere, and went to find out his old butler. This was very easy, since the Adjutant knew where every one was posted.

The Colonel, with a small party of trustworthy sober fellows, went down into the cellar, and returned with some dozens of bottled ale and other liquids. He made it his business to distribute refreshment amongst the men, giving the glass always with his own hand, and never without some kind expression of his personal gratitude for the exertions they had made. He took this office upon himself simply because he "thought the men must be thirsty," as he expressed it ; but the deepest policy could not have suggested a better thing to do. It brought him into personal contact with every volunteer about the place, and in the most graceful way.

Captain Eureton was beginning to be anxious about the fire-engines, and had the road cleared, and kept clear, by a patrol. Fyser had been absent nearly three hours. The distance from Wenderholme to the little station (the same that Lady Helena had arrived at on her return from London) was ten miles. Supposing that Fyser drove at the rate of thirteen miles an hour, or thereabouts (which he would do on such an emergency), he would be at the station in forty-five minutes. He would have to seek the telegraphist in the village, and wake him up, and get him to the station — all that would consume twenty minutes. Then to get the engines from Bradford, over thirty miles of rail, a special locomotive running fifty miles an hour, thirty-six minutes. Time to get the engines in Bradford to the station and to start the train, say thirty minutes — total, a hundred and thirty-one minutes, or two hours and eleven minutes. Then the return to Wenderholme, forty-five minutes — say three hours. " Yes, three hours," said Captain Eureton to himself ; " I believe I should have done better to send for the Sootythorn engines. Fyser would have been there in an hour and a half, and there would have been no delays about the railway."

Just then a sound of furious galloping was heard in the distance, and the welcome exclamation, "The engines, the engines!" passed amongst the crowd. The gates being all open, and the road clear, the engines were soon in the avenue. The drivers galloped into the middle of the space enclosed by the cordon of militia-men, then they trotted a few yards and stopped. The horses were covered with foam and perspiration; the men leaped down from their seats and at once began to arrange the hose.

Captain Eureton went to the captain of the fire-brigade. "You have lost no time; I feared some delay on the railway."

"Railway, sir? there is no railway from Sootythorn to this place."

"But you come from Bradford."

"Beg pardon, sir, we are the Sootythorn brigade — we come from Sootythorn. You telegraphed for us — anyhow, a Mr. Fyser did."

"He did right. What do you think of the fire?"

The fireman looked up. "It's a bad one. Been burning three hours? We may save the first floor, and the ground-floor. Not very likely, though. Where's water?"

"Small stream here;" the Adjutant led the fireman to the rivulet.

"Very good, very good. House burns most at this end, I see."

The hose was soon laid. There were two engines, and the firemen, aided by volunteers, began to pump vigorously. Two powerful jets began to play upon the south wing, and it was a satisfaction to Captain Eureton to see them well at work, though with little immediate effect. There being no sign of Fyser, the Adjutant concluded that he was waiting for the Bradford engines.

The whole remaining mass of roof now fell in with a tremendous crash, and the flames enveloped the gables, issuing from the windows of the uppermost story. The multitude was hushed by the grandeur of the spectacle. All the woods of Wenderholme, all its deep ravine, were lighted by the glare, and even at Shayton the glow of an unnatural dawn might be seen in the sky over the lofty moorland.

And the real dawn was approaching also, the true Aurora, ever fresh and pure, bathed in her silver dews. There are engines hurrying towards Wenderholme, through the beautiful quiet lanes and between the peaceful fields; and the gray early light shows the road to the eager drivers and their galloping steeds, and the breath of the pure morning fans the brows of the men who sit in dark uniforms, helmeted, perilously on those rocking chariots.

But the old house is past any help of theirs! The floors have fallen one after another. All the accumulated wood is burning together on the ground-floor now: in the hall, where Reginald Stanburne's portrait hung; in the dining-room, where, a few hours before, the brilliant guests had been sumptuously entertained; in the drawing-room, where the ladies sat after dinner in splendor of diamonds and fine lace. Every one of these rooms is a focus of ardent heat — a red furnace, terrible, unapproachable. The red embers will blacken in the daylight, under the unceasing streams from the fire-engines, and heaps of hissing charcoal will fill the halls of Wenderholme!

But the walls are standing yet — the brave old walls! Even the carving of the front is not injured. The house exists still, or the shell of it — the ghost of old Wenderholme, its appearance, its eidolon!

I know who laments this grievous misfortune most. It is not John Stanburne: ever since that child of his was known to be in safety, he has been as gay as if this too costly spectacle had been merely a continuation of the fireworks. It is not Lady Helena: she is very busy, has been very busy all night, going this way and that, and plaguing the people with contradictory orders. She is much excited — even irritated — but she is not sad. Wenderholme was not much to her; she never really loved it. If a country house had not been a necessity of station, she would have exchanged Wenderholme for a small house in Belgravia, or a tiny hotel in Paris.

But old Mrs. Stanburne grieved for the dear old house that had been made sacred to her by a thousand interests and associations. There was more to her in the rooms as they had been, than there was either to Lady Helena or to the proprietor himself. She had dreaded in silence the proposed changes and restorations, and this terrible destruction came upon her like the blow of an eternal exclusion and separation. The rooms where her husband had lived with her, the room he died in, she could enter never more! So she sat alone in her sadness, looking on the ruin as it blackened gradually in the morning, and her spirits sank low within her, and the tears ran down her cheeks.

CHAPTER XXX.

UNCLE JACOB'S LOVE AFFAIR.

THE fire at Wenderholme was known all over the country the same morning, so the people who had been asked to the presentation of colors stayed away. The colors were given almost without ceremony, and the men came back to Sootythorn.

Jacob Ogden had got as far as Sootythorn the evening before with the intention of going on to Wenderholme in the morning to see the ceremony, for he had been invited thereto by his brother Isaac. As matters turned out, however, he thought he would go to Whittlecup to fetch his mother back to Milend, for the house seemed to him very uncomfortable without her.

He called at Arkwright Lodge, and spent the day there. The day following, Mr. Anison was to give a small dinner-party composed of some of the leading manufacturers in that neighborhood, so he pressed Jacob Ogden to stay it over.

He stayed three days at Arkwright Lodge — three whole days away from the mill — from the mills, we may now say, for Jacob Ogden was already a pluralist in mills. The new one was rising rapidly out of the green earth, and a smooth, well-kept meadow was now trampled into mud and covered with heaps of stone and timber, and cast-iron columns and girders. And for three days had Jacob Ogden left this delightful, this enchanting scene! What a strong attraction there must have been at Whittlecup, to draw him from his industrial paradise! He felt bound to the unpoetical Shayton, as Hafiz was to his fair Persian valley when he sang —

> "They will not allow me to proceed upon my travels,
> Those gentle gales of Mosellây,
> That limpid stream of Rooknâbâd."

"I've no time for goin' courtin'," thought Jacob to himself as he sat drinking his port wine after dinner. "I've been here three days, and it's as much as I can afford for courtin'. But who's a rare fine lass is Miss Madge, an' I'll write her a bit of a letter."

Before leaving the Lodge, he thought it as well to prepare Mr. Anison's mind for what was to come, so he asked to go and see the works. As they were walking together, Ogden went abruptly into the subject of matrimony.

"Mother's been stoppin' at Whittlecup a good bit, 'long of our Isaac. I felt very lonesome at Milend 'bout th' oud woman, and I thought I s'd be lonesomer and lonesomer if who* 'ere deead."

"No doubt she would be a very great loss to you," said Mr. Anison; "but Mrs. Ogden appears to enjoy excellent health."

Ogden scarcely heard this, and continued, "So I've been thinkin', like, as I 'appen might get wed."

"It would certainly be a good security against loneliness."

"I can afford to keep a wife. You may look at my banker's account whenever you like. I've a good property already in land and houses, and I'm building a new mill."

"There is no necessity for going into detail," Mr. Anison said deprecatingly; "every one knows that you are a rich man."

Ogden laughed, half inwardly. It was a chuckling little laugh, full of the intensest self-satisfaction. "They think they know," he said, "but they don't know — not right.

---

* The reader will please to bear in mind that *who* means *she* in the pure Lancashire dialect.

Nobody knows what I'm worth, and nobody knows what I shall be worth. I'm one o' those as sovereigns sticks to, same as if they'd every one on 'em a bit o' stickin'-plaister to fasten 'em on wi'. If I live ten year, I s'll be covered over wi' gold fourteen inch thick."

"Is there any positive necessity for you to leave us now? Why not remain a little longer?"

"Do you think I've any chance at your house?"

Mr. Anison laughed at the eagerness of Ogden's manner. Then he said, "I see no reason for you to be discouraged. You cannot expect a young lady to accept you before you have asked her."

Ogden hesitated a moment, and then determined to go on to Shayton and write his letter.

CHAPTER XXXI.

UNCLE JACOB IS ACCEPTED.

AND this is the letter Jacob Ogden wrote:—

"MISS MARGARET ANISON.

"MISS,—When I was at your house this afternoon, I meant to say something to you, but could not find a chance, because other people came in just at the time. I wished to ask you to be so kind as to marry me. I believe I shall be a good husband—at any rate, I promise to do all I can to be one. My wife shall have every thing that a lady wants, and I will either build a new house or purchase one, as she may like best. There's a good one on sale near Shayton, but I don't mind building, if you prefer it. I am well able to keep my wife as a lady. I may say that I have always been very steady, and not in the habit of drinking. I never go into an ale-house, and I never spend any foolish money. I shall feel very anxious until I receive your answer, as you will easily understand; for my regard for you is such that I most sincerely wish your answer may be favorable.

"Yours truly, JACOB OGDEN."

Though rather a queer letter, and singularly devoid of the graces of composition and the tenderness of love, its purport, at least, was intelligible. The reply showed that the lover had made himself clearly understood.

CHAP. XXXI. *Uncle Jacob is accepted.*   253

"My dear Sir,—The proposal contained in your letter has rather surprised me, as we have seen so little of each other, but after consulting my parents I may say that I do not refuse, and they desire me to add that there will be a room for you here whenever your business engagements permit you to visit us. Sincerely yours,

"Margaret Anison."

It is to be supposed that Mr. Ogden felt sensations of profound happiness on reading this little perfumed note; but when a man is an old bachelor by nature, he does not become uxorious in a week or two; and we may confess that, after the unpleasantness of the first shock, a positive refusal would have left the lover's mind in a state of far more perfect happiness and calm. His pride was gratified, his passion was fortunate in dreaming of its now certain fruition, and he knew that such a woman as Margaret Anison would add greatly to his position in the world. He knew that she would improve it in one way, but then he felt anxiously apprehensive that she might deteriorate it in another. He would become more of a gentleman in society with a lady by his side, but a wife and family would be a hindrance to his pecuniary ambition. From the hour of his acceptance he saw this a good deal more clearly than he had done since this passion implanted itself in his being. He had seen it clearly enough before he knew Margaret Anison, but the strength of a new passion acting upon a nature by no means subtly self-conscious, had for a time obscured the normal keenness of his sight. After re-reading Margaret's note for the tenth time, Mr. Jacob Ogden said to himself: "She's a fine girl—there isn't a finer lass in all Manchester; but I'm a damned fool—that's what I am. What have I to do goin' courtin'? Howsomever, it's no good skrikin' over spilt milk—we mun manage as well as we can. We've plenty to live on, and she can have four or five servants, if she'll nobbut look well afther 'em." Then he went into the little sitting-room, where his mother sat mending his stockings.

"Mother," he said, abruptly, "there's news for you. Somebody's boun' to be wed."

The stocking was deposited in Mrs. Ogden's lap, and she looked at her son with fixed eyes.

"It's owther our Isaac or me, and it isn't our Isaac."

"Why, then, it's thee, Jacob."

"You're clever at guessin', old woman; you always was a 'cute un."

"What! are you boun' to wed somebody at Whittlecup?"

"She doesn't live a hundred mile off Whittlecup."

Mrs. Ogden rose from her seat and laid down her stocking, and made slowly for the door. She stopped, however, midway, and with a stately gesture pointed to the mended stocking. "Can she darn like that?"

"She 'appen can do, mother."

"Han you seen her do?"

"No."

"Nor nobody else nayther. But what I reckon you think you can do b'out havin' your stockin's mended when you get your fine wife into th' house, and you think servants 'll do every thing. But if you'd forty servants, you'd be badly off without somebody as knew how to look afther 'em all. And if they cannot do for theirselves, they cannot orther other folk — not right."

"Well, but, mother," said Jacob, deprecatingly. He was going to suggest consolatory considerations, founded upon the apparent order and regularity of the housekeeping at Arkwright Lodge, in the midst of which Miss Anison had been educated.

But Mrs. Ogden was not disposed to enter into a discussion which would have involved the necessity of giving her son a hearing, and she cut short his expostulation with a proverb, solemnly enunciated, —

CHAP. XXXI. *Uncle Jacob is accepted.* 255

"As they make their bed, so they must lie," and then she left the room.

"Th' old woman isn't suited," thought Jacob, "but it makes nothing who it had been, she would have been just the same. She used always to reckon she could like me to get wed, but I knew well enough that when it came to the point I could never get wed so as to suit her. Whoever I wedded, she 'd always have said it should have been somebody else." The fact was, that whilst Mrs. Ogden warmly and sincerely approved of marriage as a sort of general proposition, and had even advised her son for many years past to take unto himself a wife, her jealousy only slumbered so long as the said wife remained a vague impersonal idea. Mrs. Ogden had not much imagination, and the mere notion of a possible wife for Jacob was very far from arousing in her breast the lively sensations which were sure to be aroused there by a visible, criticisable young woman, of flesh and blood, with the faults that flesh is heir to. Now she had seen Margaret Anison, and she had thought at Whittlecup, "She might happen do for our Jacob;" but when "our Jacob" announced that he had decided to espouse Margaret Anison, that was quite a different thing.

Matters had been in this condition for a month or two, when Jacob Ogden, whose visits to his beloved one had been made rare by the exigencies of business, became somewhat importunate about the fixing of his wedding-day. It was not that he looked forward thereto with feelings of very eager or earnest anticipation, but he had a business-like preference for "fixtures" and dates over the vague promises of an indefinite *avenir*. Miss Anison, on the contrary, seemed to have a rooted objection to such rigid limitations of liberty; and, like a man in debt whose creditor proposes to draw upon him for an inexorable thirtieth of next month, felt that the vague intention of paying some time was for the present less hard and harassing to the mind. And as the debtor procrastinates, so did Margaret Anison procrastinate. Her heart was not in this marriage, but her interest was; and, so far as she avowed to herself any purpose at all, her purpose was to gain time, and keep Jacob Ogden as a resource, when all chance of Philip Stanburne should be lost finally and for ever.

Miss Anison, in a matter of this kind, was a great deal cleverer than Jacob Ogden, who, though not easily taken in by a man in men's business, had little experience of womankind, and none whatever of polite young ladies and their ways. Margaret Anison had found a capital excuse for delay in the necessity for building a new house, and she set Jacob Ogden to work thereupon with an energy at least equal to that which he lavished on the new mill. He wanted very much to have the house close to the factory, but the young lady preferred the tranquillity of the country, and went to Milend expressly to select a site. She chose a little dell that opened into the Shayton valley; and though of all views in the world the pleasantest for Mr. Ogden would have been a view of his own mills, he was denied this satisfaction, and his windows looked out upon nothing but green fields. "If they'd nobbut been my own fields," Jacob thought, "I wouldn't so much have cared. Not but what a good mill is a prettier sight than the greenest field in Lancashire, but it's no plezur to me to look out upon other folks' property." And the worst of it was, that there was no chance of ever purchasing the said property, for it belonged to an ancient Lancashire family, which had a wise hereditary objection to parting with a single acre of land.

Mrs. Ogden, now that the engagement was a *fait accompli*, expressed the most perfect readiness to quit Milend and go and live in "th' Cream-pot," which, as the reader is already aware, was the expressively rich appellative of the richest of her little farms. But such was the amiable and truly filial consideration displayed by Margaret Anison towards her future mother-in-law, that she would on no account hear of such an arrangement. "Mrs. Ogden," she said, "had always been accustomed to Milend, and it would be quite wrong to turn her out;" indeed she "would not hear of such a thing." So the obedient Jacob hurried on the construction of a mansion worthy of the young lady who had honored him with her affections — a mansion to be replete with all modern comforts and conveniences, such as abounded at Arkwright Lodge.

CHAPTER XXXII.

MR. STEDMAN RELENTS.

PHILIP STANBURNE'S life had not been settled or happy since the date of his visit to Derbyshire. The old tranquil existence at the Peel had become impossible for him now. It was intolerable to him to be cut off from all direct communication with Miss Stedman, and one day he went boldly to Chesnut Hill. He went there, not under cover of the darkness, as cowardly lovers do, but in the broad openness of such daylight as is ever to be seen in Sootythorn. I think, however, that it would have needed still greater courage on his part to present himself there about eight o'clock in the evening; for in the day-time Mr. Stedman was usually at his factory, whereas about eight in the evening a friend might count upon the pleasure of finding him at Chesnut Hill.

The servant-maid who opened the door to Philip showed him at once into the drawing-room. "What name shall I say, sir?" she asked. Philip gave his name, and waited. He had not inquired whether Miss Stedman was at home — he felt a slight embarrassment in inquiring about Miss Stedman — and the servant on her part had simply asked him to walk in.

He had waited about five minutes, when a heavy step became audible in the passage, and the door of the room was opened. The Reverend Abel Blunting stood before him.

"Pray sit down, sir," said the reverend gentleman; "I hope you are quite well. I hope I see you well. Mr. Stedman is not at home — he is down at the mill — but I am expecting him every minute."

Mr. Blunting's bland amiability ought no doubt to have awakened amiable feelings in Mr. Stanburne's breast, but, unfortunately, it had just the opposite effect. "I did not come here to see Mr. Stedman," he replied; "I came to see his daughter."

Now Mr. Blunting was a powerful man, both physically and mentally, and a man by no means disposed to yield when he considered firmness to be a duty. In the present instance he *did* consider it necessary to prevent an interview between Alice and her lover, and he quietly resolved to do so at all costs. "I am sorry," he said, "that you cannot see Miss Stedman."

"Why cannot I see her? Is she not at home?"

"She is under this roof, sir."

"Then I will see her," Philip answered, and rose to his feet.

"Pray sit down, sir — pray sit down," said Mr. Blunting, without stirring from the easy-chair in which he had ensconced himself. He made a gesture with his hand at the same time, which said as plainly as it could, "Calm yourself, young gentleman, and listen to me."

"Pray sit down. Miss Stedman is not very well to-day; indeed she has not been really well, I am sorry to say, for some time past. She does not rise until the afternoon, and of course you cannot go into her bedroom."

"Why not? Come with me if you like. The doctor may go there, I suppose?"

"The doctor goes there professionally, and so does Miss Stedman's spiritual adviser."

"I could do her more good than either of you. How wretchedly lonely she is!"

"My wife comes to sit with Miss Stedman every day."

"What *is* the matter with her? Tell me the plain truth."

"Most willingly — most happy to reassure you, sir. There

is really nothing serious in Miss Stedman's case ; the medical men are agreed upon that. She merely suffers from debility, which has been neglected for some time because she did not complain. Now that the ailment is known, it will be combated in every way. Already there is a decided improvement. But in her present state of weakness, agitation of any kind might be most prejudicial — most prejudicial ; and therefore I hope you will easily see that I dare not accept the responsibility of permitting an interview between you."

"I shall wait here till Mr. Stedman comes, and ask his permission."

"That is a very proper course to pursue, and I highly approve your resolution. But from what we both know of Mr. Stedman's sentiments, it seems scarcely probable that he will grant your request. You will do well, however, to wait and see him. It is always the best, when there are differences of opinion, that the contending parties should meet personally."

Here there was a pause of a minute or two, after which Mr. Blunting resumed, with great politeness of manner, —

"I fear you must need refreshment, sir, if you have come from a distance. Your own residence, as I am informed, is at a considerable distance from this place. In Mr. Stedman's absence, I may take upon myself to offer you something. Would you like a sandwich and a glass of wine ? I cannot offer to drink wine with you, being myself a total abstainer, but as I know that you use it in great moderation, it is not against my conscience to ring for the decanters."

Philip Stanburne had eaten nothing since six in the morning, and willingly accepted the clergyman's proposition. Perhaps he accepted it the more willingly that he felt the need of all his courage for the approaching interview with Mr. Stedman. When the decanters and the sandwich came, the teetotal parson filled a wine-glass with formal courtesy, and young Stanburne could not help feeling a certain liking, and even admiration, for the man. In truth, without being a gentleman, Mr. Blunting had many of the best qualities of a gentleman. He was as brave as a man well could be, more learned than most members of his own learned profession, and he had a feminine softness of manner.

Whilst Philip was engaged with his sandwiches and sherry, he heard the hall-door open, and a manly step on the stone floor. Though by no means a coward, either morally or physically, he had a sensitive constitution, and his pulse was considerably accelerated by the knowledge that Mr. Stedman had entered the house. The heavy steps passed the drawing-room door, and became gradually less and less audible as they ascended the stairs.

"Mr. Stedman is gone to see his daughter," said Mr. Blunting. "He always goes straight to her room when he returns from the mill. He is a most affectionate father."

"Where his prejudices are not concerned," added Philip Stanburne.

"Where his conscience is not involved, you ought to say. His objection to your suit is strictly a conscientious objection. Personally, he likes you, and your position would be an excellent one for Miss Alice; indeed it is beyond what she might have hoped for. But Mr. Stedman—ah! he is coming now."

Philip had somewhat hastily finished his sandwich, and resumed his first seat. Mr. Stedman opened the door slowly, and walked in. He gave no sign of astonishment on seeing Philip (who rose as he entered), but simply bowed. Then turning to Mr. Blunting, he said, quietly, "I think Alice would be glad to see you now," on which Mr. Blunting left the room.

There was an expression of deep sadness on John Stedman's face as he sat down and looked fixedly at the table. His eyes looked in the direction of the decanters, but he evidently did not see them. Suddenly recalling himself to the things about him, he saw the decanters before any thing else, and said, —

"Have you had a glass of wine? Take another. Take one with me."

Astonished at this reception, Philip Stanburne held his glass whilst John Stedman filled it. A tremulous hope rose in his breast. What if this man were relenting? what if the icy barrier were gradually thawing away?

They drank the wine in silence, and Mr. Stedman sat down again. "Sit down," he said, "sit down. You are come to talk to me about my daughter. You are under my roof, and are my guest. I will listen to you patiently, and I will answer you plainly. I can do no more than that, can I?"

Philip urged his suit with all the eloquence at his command. John Stedman listened, as he had promised, patiently; and when his guest's eloquence had exhausted itself, he spoke in this wise : —

"I explained my views to you on a former occasion, in Derbyshire. It is no use going over all that ground again. But since we met then, the position of matters has changed somewhat. My daughter is getting nearer to her majority; at the same time, you and she have made an engagement between yourselves without my sanction, and I have reason to suspect that you have corresponded. Miss Margaret Anison has been here rather too much lately, and I have politely informed Miss Margaret Anison that she had better remain at Arkwright Lodge. But another thing has altered matters still more — that is, my daughter's health. I'm very much grieved to say that I haven't a great deal of confidence in her constitution. She gets weaker every day."

"Mr. Blunting says she is getting stronger again now."

"Stronger? Well, momentarily she may, by the help of tonics and stimulants, but it will not last. She was never really strong, but if I'd not been so much absorbed in business, I might have taken her more out, and given her more exercise. I am ready to give up business now. I'd give up any thing for my Alice. Poor Alice, poor Alice!"

Philip Stanburne became inoculated with Mr. Stedman's openly expressed alarm. "Are you seriously afraid, sir?" he asked, with intense anxiety.

Mr. Stedman looked at him fixedly and seemed absorbed in his own thoughts. "You love my girl, young man, but you don't love her as I do. Ever since I have got this fear into my heart and into my brain I can neither eat nor sleep. I think sometimes I shall go out of my mind. A man loves a daughter, Mr. Stanburne, differently from the way he loves a son. If I'd had a son, I shouldn't have felt so anxious, for it seems that a lad should bear illnesses and run risks; but a tender little girl, Philip Stanburne — a tender little girl, and a great rough fellow like me to take care of her!"

"Is there any change in your feelings towards me, sir?"

"No, none at all. I always liked you very well, and I like you very well still. There isn't a young fellow anywhere who would suit me better, if it weren't for your being such a Papist. I'll tell you what I'll do with you, if you like. You give me an honest promise not to marry my daughter before twelve months are out, and you shall see her every day if you like. And if you can cheer her up and make her get her strength back again, you shall have her and welcome, Papist or no Papist. I'd let her marry the Pope of Rome before I'd see her as sad as she has been during the last two or three months. Stop your dinner, will you? That sandwich is nothing; our dinner-time's one o'clock, and it's just ten minutes to. Alice'll get up when she knows you're here, I'll warrant."

The reader will easily believe that Philip Stanburne heard this speech with a joy that made him forget his anxiety about Alice. He would bring gladness to her, and with gladness, health. How bright the long future seemed for these two, true lovers always, till the end of their lives! O golden hope, fair promise of happy years!

But the doctor, who had been at Chesnut Hill that morning, had heard a little faint sound in his polished black stethoscope, which was as terrible in its import as the noise of the loudest destroyers, as the crack of close thunder, the roar of cannon, the hiss of the hurricane, the explosion of a mine!

CHAPTER XXXIII.

THE SADDEST IN THE BOOK.

LET this part of our story be quickly told, for it is very sad! Let us not dwell upon this sorrow, and analyze it, and anatomize it, and lecture upon it, as if it were merely a study for the intellect, and caused the heart no pain!

It is the middle of winter. The streets of Sootythorn are sloppy with blackened snow, the sky is dreary and gray, and dirtied by the smoke from the factory-chimneys. Sootythorn is dismal, and Manchester is all in a fog. The cotton-spinners' train that goes from Sootythorn to Manchester is running into a cloud that gets ever denser and yellower, and the whistle screams incessantly. The knees of the travellers are covered with "Guardians," and "Couriers," and "Examiners," for there is not light enough to read comfortably. One manufacturer asks his neighbor a question: "Where is John Stedman of Sootythorn? He uses comin' by this train, and I haven't seen him as I cannot tell how long."

The question interests us also. Where is John Stedman?

Not at Chesnut Hill, certainly. There is nobody at Chesnut Hill but the old gardener and his wife. He tends the plants in the hothouse, and keeps them comfortable in this dreary Lancashire winter by the help of Lancashire coal. But the house is all shut up, except on the rare days when a bit of sunshine comes, and the old woman opens the shutters and draws up the blinds to let the bright rays in. Every thing seems ready for Alice, if she would only come. There is her little pretty room upstairs, and there are twenty things of hers in the drawing-room that wait for their absent mistress.

Miss Alice is far away in the south, and her father is with her — and there is a third, who never leaves them.

They had been travelling towards Italy, but when they reached Avignon, Alice became suddenly worse, and they stayed there to give her a long rest. The weather happened to be very pure and clear, and it suited her. The winter weather about Avignon is often very exhilarating and delicious, when the keen frost keeps aloof, and the dangerous winds are at rest.

As for saving Alice now, not one of the three had a vestige of delusive hope. The progress of the malady had been terribly rapid; every week had been a visible advance towards the grave. John Stedman had hoped little from the very beginning, Philip Stanburne had hoped much longer, and Alice herself longest of all. But none of the three hoped any longer now.

When Alice found herself settled at Avignon, she felt a strong indisposition to go farther. The railway tired and agitated her, and the dust made her cough more painful. "Papa," she said one day, as she sat in her easy-chair looking up the Rhone, "I think we cannot do better than just remain where we are. I shall not keep you in this place very long. No climate can save me now, and this weather is as pleasant as any Italian weather could be. I am cowardly about travelling, and it troubles me to think of the journey before us." Mr. Stedman feebly tried to encourage Alice, and talked of the beautiful Italian coast as if they were going to see it; but it soon became tacitly understood that Alice's travels were at an end.

Mr. Stedman, who, since he had left England with his daughter, had never considered expense in any thing in which her comfort was, or seemed to be, involved, sought out a pleasanter lodging than the hotel they had chosen as a tem-

CHAP. XXXIII. *The Saddest in the Book.* 267

porary resting-place. He found a charming villa on the slopes that look towards Mount Ventoux. The view from its front windows included the great windings of the Rhone and the beautiful mountainous distance; whilst from the back there was a very near view of Avignon, strikingly picturesque in composition, crowned by the imposing mass of the Papal palace. Alice preferred the mountains, and chose a delightful little *salon* upstairs as her own sitting-room, whilst her bedroom was close at hand. There was a balcony, and she liked to sit there in the mild air during the warmest and brightest hours.

Mr. Stedman's powerful and active nature suffered from their monotonous life at the villa, and he needed exercise both for the body and the mind. Alice perceived this, and, well knowing that it was impossible for her father to do any thing except in her service, plotted a little scheme by which she hoped to make him take the exercise and the interest in outward things which in these sad days were more than ever necessary to him.

"Papa," she said one day, "I think if I'd a little regular work to do, it would do me good. I wish you would go geologizing for me, and bring me specimens. You might botanize a little, too, notwithstanding the time of the year; it would be amusing to puzzle out some of the rarer plants. It's a very curious country, isn't it, papa? I'm sure, if I were well, we should find a great deal of work to do together here." Then she began to question him about the geology and botany of the district, and made him buy some books which have been written upon these subjects by scientific inhabitants of Avignon. Her little trick succeeded. Mr. Stedman, under the illusion that he was working to please his poor Alice, trudged miles and miles in the country, and extended his explorations to the very slopes of Mount Ventoux itself. In this way he improved the tone of his physical constitution, and Alice saw with satisfaction that it would be better able to endure the impending sorrow.

He had long ceased to treat Philip Stanburne with coldness or distrust. His manner with his young friend was now quite gentle, and even affectionate, tenderly and sadly genial. The one point on which they disagreed was no longer a sore point for either of them. One day, when they were together, they met a religious procession, with splendid sacerdotal costumes and banners, and Philip kneeled as the host was carried by. Their conversation, thus briefly interrupted, was resumed without embarrassment, and Mr. Stedman asked some questions about the especial purpose of the procession, without the slightest perceptible expression of contempt for it. He began to take an interest in the charities of the place, and having visited the hospital, said he thought he should like to give something, and actually left a bank-note for five hundred francs, though the managers of the institution, and the nurses, and the patients, were Romanists without exception. Meanwhile, he read his Bible very diligently every day, and the prayers of the little household, in which Philip willingly joined.

During one of Mr. Stedman's frequent absences on the little scientific missions ordered by his daughter Alice, she and Philip had a conversation which he ever afterwards remembered.

"Philip," she said, "do you ever think much about what *might have been*, if just one circumstance had been otherwise? I have been thinking a great deal lately, almost constantly, about what might have been, for us two, if my health had been strong and good. People say that love such as ours is only an illusion — only a short dream — but I cannot believe that. It might have changed, as our features change, with time, but it would have remained with us all our lives. Do you ever fancy us a quiet respectable old couple, living at the Tower, and coming sometimes to Sootythorn together? I do. I fancy that, and all sorts of things that might have been — and some of them would have been, too — if I had lived. There's one thing vexes me, and that is, that I never saw the Tower. I wish I had just seen it once, so that I might fancy our life there more truly. How glad dear papa would have been to come and stay with us, and botanize and geologize amongst your rocks there! You would have let him come, wouldn't you, dear?—I am sure you would have been very kind to him. You *will* be kind to him, won't you, my love, when he has no longer his poor little Lissy to take care of him? Don't leave him altogether by himself. I am afraid his old age will be very sad and lonely. It grieves me to think of that, for he will be old in a few years now, and his poor little daughter will not be near him to keep him cheerful. Fancy him coming home every evening from the mill, and nobody but servants in the house! Go and stay with him sometimes, dear, at Chesnut Hill, and get him to go to the Tower, and you will sometimes talk together about Alice, and it will do you both good."

Philip had kept up manfully as long as he was able, but the vivid picture that these words suggested of a world without Alice was too much for him to bear, and he burst into passionate tears. As for Alice, she remained perfectly calm, but when she spoke again it was with an ineffable tenderness. She took his hand in hers, and drew him towards her, and kissed him. Again and again she kissed him, smoothing his hair caressingly with her fingers—gentle touches that thrilled through his whole being. "You don't know, my darling," she said, "how much I love you, and how miserable it made me when I thought we must be separated in this world. It isn't so hard to be separated by death; but to live both of us in the same world, seeing the same sun, and moon, and stars, even the same hills, and not to be together, but always living out of sight and hearing of each other, and yet so near—it would have been a trial beyond my strength! And isn't it something, my love, to be together as we are now for the last few weeks and days? You don't know how happy it makes me to see you and papa getting on so nicely as you do. Isn't he nice, now? I don't believe he thinks a bit the worse of you for being a Catholic. We shall all meet again, darling — shall we not? — in the same heaven, and then we shall have the same perfect knowledge, and our errors and differences will be at an end for ever."

She was a good deal exhausted with saying this, and leaned back in her chair, closing her eyes for a while. Philip gradually recovered his usual melancholy tranquillity, and they sat thus without speaking, he holding both her hands in his, and gently chafing and caressing them. He had not courage to speak to Alice — indeed, in all their saddest and most serious conversations, the courage was mainly on her side.

Whilst they were sitting thus, the sky became suddenly overcast, and there came a few pattering drops of rain. Alice started suddenly, and seemed to be agitated by an unknown terror. She grasped Philip's hand in a nervous way, and complained of a strange suffering and foreboding. "I felt so calm and peaceful all the morning," she said; "I wish I could feel so now."

The agitation increased, and it was evident to Philip that a great change had taken place. Alice threw her arms round him, and clasped him to her. "O Philip!" she cried, wildly, "don't leave me now — don't leave me even for a minute! Stay, darling, stay; it is coming, coming!"

The pattering of the rain had ceased. It had been nothing but a few drops — scarcely even a shower — and it had ceased.

But the air was not clearer after the rain. On the contrary, it had been clearer before it than it was now. The snowy summit of Mount Ventoux was hidden in an opaque, thick atmosphere; mist it was not, as we northerns understand mist, but a substantial thickening of the air.

Soon there was the same thickening, the same opacity in the atmosphere of the remote plain that stretched to the

CHAP. XXXIII. *The Saddest in the Book.* 271

mountain's foot. It was invisible now, the Mount Ventoux, the Mountain of the Winds.

And as the plain grew dark the Rhone as suddenly whitened. It whitened and whitened, nearer and nearer Avignon ; then a dull distant roar became audible, steadily increasing. A violent brief squall shook the villa. What! so frightened already? Poor children, it is nothing yet!

Over the terrified plain, over the foaming river, comes the MISTRAL, careering in his strength! Well for you, walls of Avignon, that you were built for the shocks of battle! well for thee, most especially, O palace of the transplanted Papacy, that thy fortress-heights were erected less for pleasure than for resistance!

Louder and louder, nearer and nearer! How the trees bend like fishing-rods! Crash, crash — they break before the tempest. What a clatter against the windows! It is a volley of pebbles that the Mistral carries with it as a torrent does. Bang, bang — the shutters are torn off their iron hinges and pitched nobody knows where — into the court, on the roof-top, it may be, or into the neighbor's garden!

The intensity of the noise made all human voices inaudible. The Mistral likes to make an uproar — it is his amusement, when he comes to Avignon from his mountain. And he whistles at once in a thousand chimneys, as a boy whistles in two steel keys; and he makes such a clatter with destroying things, that the most insured house-property leaves no peace to its possessor. But straight in the midst of his path rise the towers of the fortress-palace, and Peter Obreri, its architect, knows in the world of spirits that they resist the Mistral yet.

But alas for our poor little Alice! This wind does not suit her at all ; this unceasing, this wearisome wind — this agitating, terrible wind! She did not fear death before, in the calm serene weather, when it seemed that her soul might rise in the blue ether, and be borne by floating angels. But to go out into the bleak, stern tempest — to leave *his* encircling arms, and be dashed no one knows whither along the desolate, unfamiliar Provence, with twigs, and dead leaves, and pebbles, and that choking cloud of sand!

"Forgive me these foolish fancies," she prayed, from the depths of this horror. "My soul knows her way to the haven of thy rest, O Lord, my Guide and my Redeemer!"

CHAPTER XXXIV.

JACOB OGDEN FREE AGAIN.

EARLY in the month of February there came a black-edged letter to Arkwright Lodge, with a French stamp upon it. The letter was from Philip Stanburne, and it announced Alice Stedman's death.

Two days after the arrival of that letter another letter arrived at Milend for Jacob Ogden. It bore the Whittlecup post-mark, and had an exact outward resemblance to several other letters which had come from the same place, but its contents were of a new character.

Miss Anison expressed her regret that in consequence of Mr. Jacob Ogden's neglect, of his readiness to postpone his visits on the slightest pretexts, of the rarity and coldness of his letters, she felt compelled, from a due regard to her own happiness, to put an end to the engagement which had existed between them.

The accusations in this letter were perfectly well founded, though it is quite certain that they would never have been made if Philip Stanburne's communication had been edged with silver instead of black. Margaret Anison had remarked with secret satisfaction that Jacob Ogden's behavior as a lover gave her good reasons for retreating from her engagement, whenever she might determine on that decisive step; but in the mean while she had never reproached him with it, had never appeared aware of it when he *did* come, but always received him in the same uniformly gracious way, as if he had been the most assiduous of adorers. She had kept this accusation of negligence to be used against him whenever it might be convenient to throw the blame of a rupture upon *him;* but if she had finally decided to marry him, this and all other faults would have been affectionately overlooked. It had been highly convenient to let him sink deeper and deeper in that sin of negligence, till at last, from mere carelessness and an aversion to all letter-writing that was not upon business, he had actually reached that depth in crime that he no longer observed the common forms of society, and did not even write a line of apology or excuse. Margaret never expected him to be attentive to her as a husband: she intended to spend his money, and, so long as that was forthcoming, cared little about Jacob Ogden's manners. But it was charming to be able to back out of her engagement, now that Alice was dead, and do it in a dignified and honorable manner. For of all sins that a lover can commit, the chief is the sin of neglect; and in this case any competent and just jury would have pronounced the verdict "guilty."

To this letter Jacob Ogden made no reply. His feelings on receiving it were, first, the most unfeigned astonishment (for he thought he had been very attentive, and that "courtin'" had absorbed far too much of his time); next, a paroxysm of indignation, with a sense of injury; and then, when this subsided, a sense of relief so exquisite, so delicious, and so complete, that nobody can have any idea of it unless at some period of his existence a wearing and persistent anxiety has been suddenly removed for ever. The love of Margaret Anison had been one of those masterful passions which sometimes force the most prudent men to folly. He had made his offer in the height of his temporary insanity, but after the engagement had been entered upon, his old self had gradually returned; and though he was fully determined to "go through with it," as a business which had to be done, he by no means looked forward to the conjugal state as an improvement upon his accustomed life. It was like embarking on an unknown and perilous sea, in utter ignorance of the art of navigation, and that sea might be a sea of troubles. The complex details of married life, its endless little duties, were perplexing to a man whose time and thoughts were already taken up by the government of a heavy business, and the care of an increasing estate. And now to escape from these new and unfamiliar troubles — to remain in the old quiet life at Milend — to have full control over his own expenditure, with no female criticism or interference — to see his fortune growing and growing without sons to establish or daughters to dower, or an expensive houseful of servants to eat the bank-notes in his pocket-book like so many nattering mice, — ah! it was sweet to him to think of this in his innermost and sincerest self! He had loved his bachelor life well enough before, but he had never felt the full luxury of its independence as he did now!

Jacob Ogden enjoyed a privilege highly favorable to happiness, but not so favorable to moral or intellectual growth. He lived at peace with himself, and looking back on his life, he approved of its whole course, with the single exception of that hour of folly at Whittlecup. He felt and believed that no man could be wiser or more perfect than he was. When he humbly called his faculties "common-sense," he by no means understood the word as meaning a sense which he had in common with others, but rather a special faculty, to himself vouchsafed by the bounteous gift of nature. He lived in absolute independence of the good opinion of others, because his mind was at peace with itself — because he always manfully did to-day what he was sure to approve to-morrow, or ten years after to-morrow. Am I painting the portrait of a man of pre-eminent virtues? Not exactly, but of a man who would have been pre-eminently virtuous, or pre-eminently learned, if virtue or knowledge had been his ideal. For he had a manly resolution, a steady unflinching determination, to live up to the standard which he fixed for himself. And the inward peace which he enjoyed was due to his obedience to the laws of his own nature, which thus ever remained in harmony with itself in serene strength and efficiency.

This peace had for a while been lost to him, and he had felt a strange change and diminution in the inward satisfactions. His communings with himself had lost their old sweetness, and he no longer masticated the cud of contentment in the fair pastures of reflection and imagination. To go back to those happy pastures once more — to chew that sweet cud again, after months of privation — what a deep, strengthening, cheering, encouraging, replenishing delight it was!

Yet there was one drawback to the plenitude of Ogden's happiness, even though he had escaped the misery of the wedding-day. That new mansion had been begun, he had spent £400 upon it already, and spoilt a pretty meadow, and he had spent some money on presents for Margaret — not very much, for his ideas on the subject of gift-making were not very large ideas, yet still enough to plague and torment him, for the loss of a sovereign would do that. To be jilted did not trouble him much, but to have been cheated into wasting his money! that thought would not let him rest. It followed and harassed him wherever he went, and it was the cause of the following letter, which was received by Mr. Joseph Anison : —

"SIR, — I am instructed by my client, Mr. Jacob Ogden, to lay before you the following statement of facts. Your daughter, Miss Margaret Anison, by a letter bearing date ——, and which is in our possession, accepted his proposal of marriage, and promised marriage ; which promise she now, by a letter bearing date ——, refuses to execute. In consequence of her promise, and in conformity with her desires, our client has been led into considerable expense, especially in the erection of a mansion, of which Miss Anison herself selected the site. The works were immediately stopped when it became known to our client that Miss Anison had determined upon a breach of promise, but a heavy sum had been already expended, which, so far as our client is concerned, is money utterly thrown away. We beg to call your attention to the fact that our client and his mother offered another most commodious and suitable residence to Miss Anison, situated at Milend, and that she declined this, and induced our client to commence the erection of a new and costly mansion on a site which he would never have selected for himself. We therefore claim for our client damages to the amount of one thousand pounds (£1,000), and beg to inform you, that unless this sum is paid before the expiration of one calendar month from this date, we shall institute a suit for breach of promise of marriage, and claim damages on that score to a far heavier amount. The present claim, we desire it to be understood, is not made on the ground of breach of promise, but is merely a claim for compensation on account of outlay which our client has been induced to incur. Our client has no desire to push matters to the extremity of a public exposure, but will not shrink from doing so if his present just claim is refused.

"I am, sir, your obedient servant,

"JONAS HANBY."

"You may decide for yourself, Margaret, said Mr. Anison, "whether you prefer that I should pay this out of your fortune, or stand an action for breach of promise. It is not usual to bring actions of this sort against women, but Ogden is a most determined fellow, and he doesn't care much for what people may say. He will bring his action if we don't send him a cheque, and I don't think such an action would be very pleasant to you. Considering circumstances, too, especially the building of that new house, I am inclined to think that he would get rather heavy damages, certainly at least as much as he is asking for. Such an action would make a tremendous noise, and we should be in all the newspapers. 'We must consider your sisters, too, who wouldn't be much benefited by publicity of this kind. In short, my advice is to send the cheque."

The cheque was accordingly sent to Mr. Hanby, and duly acknowledged. The presents had been returned a few days before. These last had been purchased of a jeweller in St. Ann's Square, Manchester, who took them back in exchange for an excellent gentleman's watch and a big cameo brooch. The watch went into Jacob Ogden's own fob, and the brooch adorned his already sufficiently ornamented mother. All things considered, Jacob Ogden now felt that he could look back upon the whole business with a mind at ease. He had done his duty by himself. After deducting the outlay on the house, and the outlay necessary for restoring the field to its pristine verdure, he found that there remained to him a clear surplus of four hundred and fifteen pounds seven shillings and twopence, which he entered in the column of profits. "It's been rather a good business for once, has this courtin'," said Jacob to himself; "but it's devilish risky, and there's nobody'll catch me at it again. If she'd nobbut stuck to me, she'd 'ave wenly ruined me."

So, when the walls of the mansion that was to have been were levelled with the ground, and the foundations buried under the earth that they might be no more seen, Jacob Ogden buried with them the thought and idea of marriage; and the grass grew on the field that had been so torn, and cut, and burdened, and disturbed by the masons and laborers who had been there.

As the field grew level and green again just as it used to be, so flourished the mind of Jacob Ogden in serene and productive life. But as *beneath* the field — beneath the waving of the rich grass — there still lay the plan of the house that was to have been, traced out in stony foundations, so in the mind of its owner there lay hidden a stony memory of the plans of this strange year ; and though the surface was perfectly restored, there were hard places under his happiness that had not been there before.

CHAPTER XXXV.

LITTLE JACOB'S EDUCATION.

THE rupture between Jacob Ogden and Miss Anison had an immediate effect upon the fortunes of a young friend of ours, who has for a long time been very much in the background. Little Jacob began to occupy a larger and larger place in his uncle's thoughts. For, though Uncle Jacob had formerly always intended, in a general way, to remain a bachelor, this had been nothing more than a sort of intellectual preference for bachelorhood, deduced from his general views of life, and especially from his dominant anxiety to make a fortune. But his objections to matrimony were no longer of this mild kind. Like a wild animal that has once felt the noose of the trapper round its neck, and yet succeeded in freeing itself, he had conceived a horror of the snare which was incomparably more active and intense than the vague alarms of the inexperienced. His former ideas about marriage had been purely negative. He had no intention to marry, and there was the end of his reflections on the matter. But now his preference for celibacy had taken the shape of a passionate and unalterable resolution.

The increase of his fortune, which might henceforth be surely relied on, led him to think a good deal about the little boy at Twistle Farm, who was most probably destined to inherit it; and he determined to use a legitimate influence over his brother Isaac, so that little Jacob might be educated in a manner suitable to his future position.

We have said that Jacob Ogden was perfectly satisfied

with himself, and that knowledge was not his ideal. But although this is true, his views were really larger than the reader may have hitherto suspected. He considered himself perfect in his place; but as little Jacob would probably have a very different place in the world, he would need different perfections. The qualities needed for making a large fortune were, in Jacob Ogden's view, the finest qualities that a human being can possess, and he knew that he possessed them; but then there were certain ornaments and accomplishments which were necessary to a rich gentleman, and which the manufacturer had not had time to acquire. He was not foolish enough to torment himself with regrets that he did not know Latin and Greek; he had none of the silly humilities of weak minds that are perpetually regretting their "deficiencies." Whatever it was necessary for his main purpose that he should know, he always resolutely set himself to· learn, and, by strenuous application, mastered; what was unnecessary for his purpose, he remained contentedly ignorant about. The customary pedantries of the world, its shallow pretension to scholarship, never humiliated *him*. He suspected, perhaps, that genuine classical acquirement was much rarer than the varnish of pseudo-scholarship, and he had not that deferential faith in gentlemen's Latin and Greek which is sometimes found in the uneducated. But, on the other hand, as he had learned every thing that was necessary to a plodding Shayton cotton-spinner, so he was determined that little Jacob should learn every thing necessary to a perfect English gentleman. He had not read the sentence of Emerson, "We like to see every thing do its office after its kind, whether it be a milk-cow or a rattlesnake;" but the sentiment in it was his own. His strong sense perceived that so long as men hold different situations in the world, their preparatory training must be different; and that, as a young pigeon must learn to fly, and a young terrier to catch rats, so the youthful heir of a splendid fortune, and the boy who has his fortune to make, ought to receive respectively a celestial and a terrestrial training.

For Jacob Ogden, himself a terrestrial, knew that there was a heaven above him — the heaven of aristocracy! *There* dwelt superior beings, in golden houses, like gods together, far above the ill-used race of men that cleave the soil and store their yearly dues. There is something ludicrous, if it were not pathetic and painful, in the self-abasement of a man so strong and resolute as Ogden before a heaven whose saints and angels were only titled ladies and gentlemen, mainly occupied in amusing themselves; but to him it was the World of the Ideal. And this religion had one great advantage — it kept him a little humbler than he ever would have been without it. Great was the successful cotton-spinner in his eyes, but there were beings cast by nature in a nobler mould. For Jacob Ogden actually believed, in all sincerity and simplicity, that there was the same natural difference between a lord and a plebeian that there is between a thorough-bred and a cart-horse. This superstition, though founded on a dim sense of the natural differences which do exist, erred in making them the obedient servants of the artificial differences. There are, no doubt, thorough-breds and cart-horses amongst mankind, and the popular phraseology would imply that there are also asses; but these natural differences seem to be independent of title altogether, and dependent even upon fortune only so far as it may help or hinder their development. The superstition that lords, *quâ* lords, are wiser, and better, and braver, and more respectable than other people, was more prevalent in Shayton than it is in places where lords are more frequently seen.

Now, with this deeply rooted Anglican superstition about the heaven of aristocracy and the angels that dwell therein, Uncle Jacob naturally desired that his nephew should be qualified for admission there. And he had a devout belief that the states of probation for a young soul aspiring to celestial bliss were terms of residence at Eton and at Oxford.

Little Jacob had continued his custom of staying at Milend every Sunday, that he might benefit by the services of our friend Mr. Prigley in the pew at Shayton Church. Isaac Ogden, though he had come to church three Sundays in succession after the recovery of little Jacob, and had attended divine service regularly as an officer of militia (being in that character compulsible thereunto by martial law), had, I regret to say, relapsed into his old habits of negligence at Twistle Farm, and spent the Sunday there in following his own devices. It must be admitted, however, that he did little harm, on that day or any other, to himself or anybody else. He remained religiously faithful to his vow of total abstinence, and spent several hours every day in giving a sound elementary education to his son.

"I'll tell you what it is, Isaac," said Uncle Jacob one day when his elder brother had come on one of his rare visits to Milend — "I'll tell you what it is; if you'll just let me have my own way about th' eddication o' th' young un, I'll leave him all my brass, and, what's more, I don't mind payin' for his schoolin' beside. I want nowt nobbut what's reet, but I'll make sich a gentleman on him as there isn't i' o Shayton nor i' o Manchester nother. And to start wi', I reckon nowt of his stoppin' up at Twistle Farm same as he is doin' an' idlin' away auve* his time. Let him live at Milend regular for a twelvemonth, and go to Prigley six hour every day, and then send him to Eton — that's where gentlefolk sends their lads to. And afther that, we'll send him to Hoxford College."

* Half.

CHAPTER XXXVI.

A SHORT CORRESPONDENCE.

NO sooner had Mr. Prigley got into the full swing of work with his young pupil, than he received a letter from our friend Colonel Stanburne of Wenderholme:—

"MY DEAR MR. PRIGLEY,—It would give me great pleasure, and be of great use to me besides, if you could come over here and stay with me for a fortnight or three weeks. We got the house covered in just before the winter, and the works have been going forward since in some parts of the interior, but there are some points about internal fittings, especially in the principal rooms, that I and my architect don't agree about. Now, what I most want is, the advice of a competent unprofessional friend; and as I know that you have studied architecture much more deeply than I have ever done myself, I look to you to help me. It will probably be a long time before the house is finished, but now is the time to decide about the interior arrangements. Helena is at Lord Adisham's, and so I am left alone with the architect. I wish you would come. He seems to want me to adopt a different style for the finishing of the interior to that which was generally prevalent when Wenderholme was built. Now my notion is (*puisque l'occasion se présente*) to make the place as homogeneous as possible.

"Do come. You will stay here at the Cottage. I am living with my mother.

"Very faithfully yours,   JOHN STANBURNE."

A Short Correspondence.

To this letter, which offered to Mr. Prigley's mind the most tempting of all possible baits, for he dearly loved to dabble in architecture and restorations, the reverend gentleman, being bound by his engagement with the Ogdens, could only regretfully answer : —

"MY DEAR COLONEL STANBURNE, — I should have accepted your kind invitation with the greatest pleasure, and the more so that I take a deep interest in the restoration of your noble old mansion, but unfortunately I have a private pupil whom I cannot leave. It is young Jacob Ogden, whose father is one of your militia officers.

"Yours most truly, E. PRIGLEY."

But by return of post Mr. Prigley got the following short reply : —

"MY DEAR MR. PRIGLEY, — The best solution of the difficulty will be, to bring little Jacob with you. I know little Jacob very well, and he knows me. Give my compliments to his father if you have to ask his permission, and tell him we will take good care of his little boy.

"Yours very faithfully, J. STANBURNE."

So the end of it was, that little Jacob found himself suddenly removed to Wenderholme Cottage, where old Mrs. Stanburne lived. The change was highly agreeable to him — not the less agreeable that the companion of his leisure hours was the beautiful little Edith.

CHAPTER XXXVII.

AT WENDERHOLME COTTAGE.

WENDERHOLME Cottage was in fact a very comfortable and commodious house. Its claims to the humble title which it bore, were, first, that its front was all gables, with projecting roofs, and carved or traceried bargeboards; and, secondly, that its rooms were small. But if they were small they were numerous; and when it pleased Mrs. Stanburne to receive visitors — and it often pleased that hospitable lady so to do — it was astonishing how many people the Cottage could be made to hold.

A little kindness soon wins the affections of a child, and little Jacob had not been more than three or four days at Wenderholme before he began to be very fond of Mrs. Stanburne. Hers was just the sort of influence which is necessary to a young gentleman at that age — the influence of a woman of experience, who is at the same time a high-bred gentlewoman. No doubt his old grandmother loved little Jacob more than any thing else in the world; but she was narrow-minded, and despotic, and vulgar in all her ways. Mrs. Ogden, too, had moments of caprice and violence, in which she was dangerous to oppose, and difficult to pacify; in short, she was one of those persons, too common in her class, of whom Matthew Arnold says that they are deficient in sweetness and light. The steady unfailing goodness of Mrs. Stanburne, her uniformly gentle manners, her open intelligent sympathy, produced on her young guest an effect made ten times more powerful by all his early associations. It was like coming out of a chamber where every thing was rough and uncouth, into a pleasant drawing-room, full of light and elegance, where there are flowers, and music, and books. Such a change would not be agreeable to every one: whether it would be agreeable or not depends upon the instinctive preferences. Ladies like Mrs. Stanburne do not put everybody at his ease, and it proves much in little Jacob's favor that he felt happy in her presence. As Jacob Ogden, the elder, had been formed by nature for the rude contest with reluctant fortune, so his nephew had been created for the refinements of an attained civilization. Therefore, henceforth, though he still loved his grandmother, both from gratitude and habit, his young mind saw clearly that neither her precepts nor her example were to be accepted as authoritative, and he looked up to Mrs. Stanburne as his preceptress.

Little Jacob's healthy honest face and simple manners recommended him to the good lady from the first, and he had not been a week under her roof before she took a kind interest in every thing concerning him. The mere facts that he had no mother, no sister, no brother, and that he had lived alone with his father in such a place as Twistle Farm, were of themselves enough to attract attention and awaken curiosity; but the story of his arrival at Wenderholme in the preceding winter was also known to her, and she knew how unendurably miserable his lonely home had been. Mrs. Stanburne talked a good deal with Mr. Prigley about the boy, and learned with pleasure his father's wonderful and (as now might be hoped) permanent reformation.

"He does not seem to have neglected the little boy," she said; "he reads very well. I asked him to read aloud to me yesterday, and was surprised to hear how well he read — I mean, quite as if he understood it, and not in the sing-song way children often acquire."

"He's ten years old now, and he ought to read well," replied Mr. Prigley; "but he knows a great deal for a boy of his age. It's high time to send him to school, though; it's too lonely for him at the farm. I am preparing him for Eton."

Mrs. Stanburne expressed some surprise at this. "Boys in his rank in life don't often go to Eton, do they, Mr. Prigley?"

The clergyman smiled as he answered that little Jacob's rank in life was not yet definitively settled. Mrs. Stanburne replied that she thought it was, since his father was a retired tradesman.

"Yes, but his uncle, Mr. Jacob Ogden of Milend, has not left business; indeed he is greatly extending his business just now, for he has built an immense new factory. And this little boy is to be his heir — his uncle told me so himself three weeks since. This child will be a rich man — nobody can tell how rich. His uncle wishes him to be educated as a gentleman."

It is a great recommendation to a little boy to be heir to a large fortune, and Mrs. Stanburne's natural liking for little Jacob was by no means diminished by a knowledge of that fact. As he was going to Eton, too, she began to look upon him as already in her own rank of life, where boys were sent to Eton, and inherited extensive estates.

During Mr. Prigley's frequent absences with Colonel Stanburne at the Hall, Mrs. Stanburne undertook to hear little Jacob his lessons, and then the idea struck her that Jacob and Edith might both write together from her dictation. In this way the boy and the girl became class-fellows. Edith had a governess usually, but the governess had gone to visit her relations, and Miss Edith's education was for the present under the superintendence of her grandmamma.

So between these two children an intimacy rapidly established itself — an intimacy which affected the course of their whole lives.

One day when they had been left alone together in the

drawing-room, little Jacob asked the young lady some question, and he began by calling her " Miss Edith."

" Miss Edith!" said she, pouting; "why do you call me Miss? The servants may call me Miss, but you mayn't. We're school-fellows now, and you must call me Edith. And I shall call you Jacob. Why haven't you got a prettier name for me to call you by? Jacob isn't pretty at all. Haven't you another name?"

Poor little Jacob was obliged to confess his poverty in names. He had but one, and that one uncouth and unacceptable!

" Only one name. Why, you funny little boy, only to have one name! I've got four. I'm called Edith Maud Charlotte Elizabeth. But I'll tell you what I'll do. As I've got four names and you've only one, I'll give you one of mine. I can't call you Charlotte, you know, because you're not a girl; but I can call you Charley, and I always will do. So now I begin. Charley, come here!"

Little Jacob approached obediently.

" Ha, ha! he answers to his new name already!" she cried in delight, clapping her hands. " What a clever little boy he is! He's a deal cleverer than the pony was when we changed *its* name! But then, to be sure, the pony never properly knew its first name either."

Suddenly she became grave, and put her fingers on the young gentleman's arm. " Charley," she said, "this must be a secret between us two, because if grandmamma found out, she might be angry with me, you know. But you like to be called Charley, don't you? isn't it nice?"

CHAPTER XXXVIII.

ARTISTIC INTOXICATION.

THE London architect who was charged with the restoration of Wenderholme gave advice which could not be followed without a heavy outlay; but in this respect he was surpassed by Colonel Stanburne's amateur adviser, Mr. Prigley, whose imagination revelled in the splendors of an ideal Elizabethan interior, full of carving and tapestry, and all manner of barbaric magnificence. Where the architect would have been content with paper, Mr. Prigley insisted upon wainscot; and where the architect admitted plain panelling, the clergyman would have it carved in fanciful little arches, or imitations of folded napkins, or shields of arms, or large medallion portraits of the kings of England, or bas-reliefs of history or the chase.

Only consider what Mr. Prigley's tastes and circumstances had been, and what a painful contradiction had ever subsisted between them! He had an intense passion for art — not for painting or sculpture in their independent form, for of these he knew little — but Mr. Prigley loved architecture mainly, and then all the other arts as they could help the effect of architecture. With these tastes he lived in a degree of poverty which utterly forbade any practical realization of them, and surrounded by buildings of which it is enough to say that they represented the taste of the inhabitants of Shayton. The ugliest towns in the world are English towns — the ugliest towns in England are in the manufacturing district — the ugliest town in the manufacturing district was the one consigned to Mr. Prigley's spiritual care. Here his artistic tastes dwelt in a state of suppression, like Jack-in-the-box. Colonel Stanburne had imprudently unfastened the lid; it flew open, and Jack sprang up with a suddenness and an energy that was positively startling and alarming.

The fact is, Mr. Prigley lived in a condition of intoxication during the whole time of his stay at Wenderholme Cottage — an intoxication just as real as that which he denounced in Seth Schofield and Jerry Smethurst, and the other patrons of the Red Lion. A man may get tipsy on other things than ale or brandy; and it may be doubted whether any tipsiness is more complete, or more enjoyable whilst it lasts, than that which attends the realization of our ideas and the gratification of our tastes. And it has been kindly ordained that when we are not rich enough to realize our ideas for ourselves, we take nearly as much interest in seeing them realized by somebody else; so that critics who could not afford to build a laborer's cottage, get impassioned about Prince Albert's monument or the future Palace of Justice. How much the more, then, should Mr. Prigley excite himself about Wenderholme, especially seeing that Colonel Stanburne had done him the honor to consult his judgment, and expressed the desire to benefit by his extensive knowledge, his cultivated taste! Was it not a positive duty to interest himself in the matter, and to give the best advice he could? It was a duty, and it was a pleasure.

Mr. Prigley had already half decided the Colonel, when a powerful ally came unexpectedly to his assistance. One morning at breakfast-time, when the Colonel read his letters, he said to Mrs. Stanburne, "Here's a letter from an acquaintance of ours who wants to come and stay here," and he handed her the following note:—

"MY DEAR COLONEL STANBURNE,—Since I had the pleasure of seeing you at Wenderholme, I have often thought about what you are doing there. Having had a good deal of experience with architects, restorations, &c., it has occurred to me that I might be of some use. Would you present my compliments to Mrs. Stanburne, and say that if it occasioned no inconvenience to her, I should very much like to spend a few days at Wenderholme Cottage? I would bring nobody with me except Thompson, my valet; and though our acquaintance is comparatively a recent one, I presume upon it so far as to hope that you will not allow my visit to make any difference — I mean, in asking people to meet me. I should like, on the contrary, to have you all to myself, so that we may talk about the restoration of Wenderholme in detail: it interests me greatly. With kind compliments to Mrs. Stanburne,

"Yours very truly, INGLEBOROUGH."

"Well, dear," said Mrs. Stanburne, when she had read the note, " the Duke must come, of course. I like him very much — he is a very agreeable man. We needn't make any fuss."

So the Duke came; and as Colonel Stanburne had insisted that Mr. Prigley should stay to meet him, he and little Jacob prolonged their visit at the Cottage. "I look upon you, Mr. Prigley, as a necessary shield for my ignorance. Whenever you see that the Duke is puzzling me, you must divert the attack by drawing it on yourself. *You're* a match for him — you know all the technical terms."

His Grace brought with him a heavy box of books, such as made Mr. Prigley's mouth water, and several portfolios of original designs for carvings, which had been executed for an old mansion of his own, contemporary with Wenderholme. He warmly supported Mr. Prigley's views; and in the long conversations which the three held together in the evenings, whilst the Colonel consumed his habitual allowance of tobacco, the books and portfolios were triumphantly appealed to, and it was proved in a conclusive manner that this thing ought to be done, and that this other thing was absolutely indispensable, till poor John Stanburne hardly knew what to think.

"It is an opportunity," said the Duke — "an opportunity such as, we hope, may never occur again; and it rests with you, Colonel Stanburne, whether your noble old mansion is to be restored, in the genuine sense of the word, so that it may have once again the perfect character of an Elizabethan house of the best class — or whether it is to be simply repaired so as to shelter you from the weather, like any other house in the neighborhood. You will never repent a liberal expenditure at the right moment. I say, be liberal now; it is an expense which will not occur twice, either in your lifetime or in that of your descendants for many generations. What are a few thousand pounds more or less in a matter of such importance? Make Wenderholme a perfect mansion of its kind. Restore all the wainscot, and tapestry, and glass; replace all the carved furniture that must have been there in Queen Elizabeth's time" —

"Thanks to Eureton's good management the night of the fire, all our furniture is safe."

The Duke made a little gesture of impatience. "Captain Eureton," he said, "did his duty most creditably on the night of the fire; but as the fire originated in the garrets, where all the old remnants were accumulated, the consequence was, that the most precious things in the house were destroyed, and the less precious were preserved."

"A good deal more useful, though, Duke, if less precious in the eyes of an antiquary."

"Useful? Yes, that is what makes them so dangerous. People admit incongruous things into their houses on the wretched pretext of utility. Do you know, in my opinion, it is a subject of regret that the furniture was saved that night?"

"You worked very hard yourself in saving it."

"Of course, it was my duty to take my share of the work;

but circumstances will sometimes place us in such a position that duty compels us to act against what we believe to be the general interest of mankind. For instance, suppose I were out at sea in my yacht, and that I met with a boatful of Republicans, such as Mazzini, Garibaldi, Louis Blanc, and Ledru Rollin, all so hungry that they were just going to eat each other up, and so thirsty that they were just going to drink salt water and go raving mad, it would be my duty to pick up the rascals, and give them food, and land them on some hospitable shore, and I should do so because to save men from death is an elementary duty; but I should be rendering a far better service to mankind in letting the fellows eat each other, instead of assassinating their betters, and go raving mad out at sea rather than disseminate insane doctrines on the land."

The Colonel could not help laughing at this sally. "Do you mean to compare my furniture with a set of Republicans?"

"What Radicals and Republicans are in an ancient state, common-place and ignoble furniture is in a fine old mansion; and your old remnants in the lumber-room were like men of refined education and ancient descent, who have been thrust out of their natural place in society to make room for vulgar *parvenus.*"

"Well, but what on earth would you have me do with my furniture?"

"'There are many ways of getting it out of Wenderholme. Why not furnish some other house with it? Why don't you have a house in London? you *ought* to have a house in London. The furniture here is quite appropriate in a modern house, though it is incongruous in an old one. Or if you had a modern house anywhere, no matter where, you might furnish it with that furniture, and then Wenderholme would be free to receive things suitable for it."

Amongst other books that the Duke had brought with him was Viollet-le-Duc's valuable and comprehensive "Dictionnaire du Mobilier;" and the three gentlemen were soon as deep in the study of chairs and *bahuts* as they had before been in that of wainscots and stained glass. Colonel Stanburne was not by nature an enthusiast in matters of this kind, and would have lived calmly all his life amidst the incongruities of the Wenderholme of his youth; but nobody knows, until he has been exposed to infection, whether he may not catch some enthusiasm from others which never would have originated in himself. From the very beginning of his stay, Mr. Prigley had begun to indoctrinate John Stanburne in these matters; and after the arrival of the Duke's richly illustrated volumes, the pupil's progress had been remarkable for its rapidity. He now felt thoroughly persuaded that it would be wrong to miss such a rare opportunity, and that economy at such a moment would be unworthy of the owner of Wenderholme. He had a large sum of money in the Funds, entirely under his own control, and he resolved to appropriate a portion of this to the restoration of the mansion, in accordance with the advice of the Duke and Mr. Prigley.

One day at lunch, his Grace was lamenting the loss of the old carvings in the lumber-room, when little Jacob, who dined when his elders lunched, and was usually a model of good behavior, in that he observed a Trappistine silence during the repast, rather astonished the company by saying, "Please, I know where there's plenty of old oak."

The gentlemen took this for one of those remarks, usually so little to the point, which children are in the habit of making. Mrs. Stanburne kindly answered by inquiring "whether there was much old oak at Twistle Farm?"

"Oh no, I don't mean at papa's — I mean here," replied little Jacob, with great vivacity. John Stanburne said, "There used to be plenty, my boy, but it was all burnt in the fire."

"I don't mean that; I never saw that. I mean, what I have seen since I have been here this time, — real old oak. all carved with lions and tigers — at least, I believe they are lions and tigers — and pigs and wolves, too, and all sorts of birds and things."

There was not an atom of old oak in Wenderholme Cottage, and there was not an atom of furniture of any kind in Wenderholme Hall. What could the child mean? Had he been dreaming?

Everybody's attention was drawn to little Jacob, who, becoming very red and excited, reiterated his assertion with considerable boldness and emphasis. When called upon for an explanation, he said that when he had been playing in the great barn, amongst the hay, he had got into a long low garret over the pigsties and the hen-houses, and that it was full of old oak — "quite full of it," he reiterated.

Mrs. Stanburne's face assumed an expression of thought and reflection, as if she were seeking inwardly for something imperfectly remembered.

"It strikes me," she said, "that when my husband's father modernized the house, he must have put part of the old things into other lumber-rooms than those at the top of the house itself. There are places amongst the out-buildings which have not been opened for many years, and I believe we should find something there."

The Duke became eager with anticipation. "The merest fragments of the original furniture would be precious, Mrs. Stanburne. If we only had some specimens, as data, the rest might be reconstructed in the same taste. Let us go and look up whatever may remain. This little boy will be our guide."

Little Jacob, proud and excited, led the way to the great barn. It was fun to him to make the gentlemen follow him up the ladder, and over the hay, to a little narrow doorway that was about three feet above the hay-level. "That's the door," he said, and began to climb up the rough wall. He pushed it open by using all his force in frequent shoulder-thrusts, the rusty hinges gradually yielding. The adult explorers followed, and found themselves in total darkness.

Chap. XXXVIII. *Artistic Intoxication.*

"The old oak isn't here," said little Jacob; "it's a good bit further on."

The garret they were in served as a lumber-room for disused agricultural implements, and both the Duke and Mr. Prigley hurt their shins against those awkward obstacles. At last they came to a blank wall, and then to what seemed to be a sort of cupboard, so far as they could guess by touching.

Behind the cupboard was a small space, into which little Jacob insinuated himself, and afterwards cheerfully sang out, "I'm all right; here's the place!"

The gentlemen pushed the cupboard back a foot or two, and found the doorway behind it by which their guide had passed. They were in a long, low attic, very dimly lighted by a little hole in the wall at its remote extremity. It was full of obstacles, which the Duke's touch recognized at once as carved oak.

"We ought to have had lanterns," he said; "how tantalizing it is not to be able to see!"

"I would rather have a few slates taken off," John Stanburne answered; "that will make us a fine sky-light. I have a dread of fire."

Little Jacob was sent to fetch two or three men, who in half an hour had removed slates enough to throw full daylight on the scene — such daylight as had not penetrated there for many a long year. The old furniture of Wenderholme, gray, almost white, with age, filled the place from end to end in one continuous heap.

"But this is all white," said little Jacob, "and old oak ought to be brown, oughtn't it?"

"A little linseed-oil will restore the color," the Duke replied. Then he exclaimed, "By Jove! Colonel, we have found a treasure — we have indeed! Let us get every thing out into the yard, and then we can examine the things in detail."

The whole of the afternoon was spent in getting the old oak out. The gentlemen worked with the laborers, the Duke himself as energetically as any one. His great anxiety was to prevent injury to the carvings, which were very picturesque and elaborate. When the things were all out of doors, and the garret finally cleared, it was astonishing what a display they made. There were six cabinets, of which four had their entablatures supported by massive griffins or lions, and their panels inlaid with ebony and satin-wood, or carved with bas-reliefs, which, though certainly far from accurate in point of design, produced a very rich effect; whilst even the plainest of the cabinets were interesting for some curious specimen of turner's work or tracery. Then there were portions of three or four state beds, with massive deeply panelled testers and huge columns, constructed with that disdain for mechanical necessity, and that emphatic preference of the picturesque, which marked the taste of the Elizabethan age. Thus, a single bed-post would in one place be scarcely thicker than a man's wrist, and in another thicker than his body; the weight of the whole being enormously out of proportion to its strength. There were a number of chairs of various patterns, but which agreed in uniting weight with fragility, and stateliness with discomfort. There were also innumerable fragments, difficult at first sight to classify, but amongst which might be recognized the legs of tables (constructed on the same principle as the bed-posts), and pieces that had been detached from chairs, and cabinets, and beds. In addition to all these things, there were quantities of old wainscot, some of it carved, or inlaid with various woods.

The men had come to the wainscot at last, for it was reared against the walls of the garret behind the barricade of furniture. As they were removing it, there was a crashing of broken glass. A piece of this glass was brought to the light, and it was found to be stained with the arms of the Stanburnes (or, a bend cottised sa.), simple old bearings like those of most ancient untitled houses. On this other fragments were carefully collected, and they all bore the arms of

Stanburne impaled with those of families with which the Colonel's ancestors had intermarried. Mr. Prigley, who was rather strong in heraldry, and knew the genealogy of his wife's family and all its alliances much better than did John Stanburne himself, recognized the martlets of Tempest, the red lion of Mallory, the green lion of Sherburne, the black lion of Stapleton, the chevron and cinquefoils of Falkingham, the golden lozenges of Plumpton, charged with red scallop-shells, in fess on a field of azure. "This has been a great heraldic window, commemorating the alliances of the family!" cried Mr. Prigley, in ecstasy. "It must be restored, Colonel," said the Duke, "and brought down to the present time — down to you and Lady Helena."

Soon afterwards another discovery was due to the restless curiosity and boyish activity of little Jacob. He had found means to open one of the biggest of the cabinets, and had hauled out what seemed to him an old piece of carpet folded in many folds. He ran to inform the Duke of his discovery; but his Grace, eagerly unfolding the supposed piece of carpet, displayed a rich field of

"Arras green and blue,
Showing a gaudy summer morn,
Where with puffed cheek the belted hunter blew
His wreathéd bugle-horn."

Other pieces of tapestry followed, and the heaviest of the cabinets was found to be nearly full of them. They consisted almost exclusively of hunting scenes and pastorals, with landscapes and foliage, which, though seldom approaching correctness as a representation of nature, must have produced, nevertheless, a superbly decorative effect when hung in the halls of Wenderholme.

The Duke had said very little for nearly an hour, except in ordering the men to arrange the furniture in groups. When this had been accomplished to his satisfaction, he turned to the Colonel, and made him the following little speech: —

"Colonel Stanburne, I congratulate you upon a discovery which would be interesting to any intelligent person, but is so most especially to the representative of the Stanburnes. Here are specimens of the furniture used by your ancestors from the reign of Henry VII. to that of James I. We have here ample data for the complete restoration of Wenderholme, even in the details of wainscot and tapestry and glass. The minutest fragments in these heaps are valuable beyond price. It is getting late now, but to-morrow I will go through every bit of it and ticket every thing, and when I leave I will send you workmen capable of doing every thing that ought to be done."

Here little Jacob whispered to Mr. Prigley, "It was I that found it out, wasn't it, Mr. Prigley?" to which piece of self-assertion his tutor replied by the repressive monosyllable "Hush!"

But his Grace had overheard both of them, and said, "Indeed we are very much obliged to you, my little boy — very much obliged indeed. I should like to make you a little present of some sort for the pleasure you have afforded me this afternoon. You are going to Eton, I hear. Have you got a watch?"

Little Jacob pulled out a silver watch, of the old-fashioned kind popularly known as turnips, from their near approach to the spherical conformation. The Duke smiled as he looked at it, and asked what time it was. Little Jacob's watch was two hours late. "But it ticks yet," he said.

The Duke said no more just then, but when little Jacob was dressed to go down to dessert, his Grace's valet, Thompson, knocked at the door, and brought a gold watch with a short chain, wherewith the young gentleman proudly adorned himself. One of the first things he did was to go to the Duke and thank him; and he did it so nicely that the nobleman was pleased to say that when little Jacob went to Eton he might "show his watch to the fellows, and tell 'em who gave it him."

CHAPTER XXXIX.

GOOD-BYE TO LITTLE JACOB.

LITTLE Jacob was in luck's way, for the day he left Wenderholme Cottage the Colonel tipped him with a five-pound note. He had a private interview, too, with Miss Edith, and there was quite a little scene between the infantine lovers.

"Are you really going away to-day, Charley?" she said, using the name she had given him.

"Yes; Mr. Prigley says he must go back on account of Shayton Church. It will be Sunday to-morrow, you know."

"And when will you come back to us again?"

"I don't know. Perhaps never."

"Perhaps never!" exclaimed Miss Edith; "and aren't you very sorry?"

"Yes, very sorry. I have been very happy here."

"Well, then, you must come again. I wish you would. I like you very much. You are a nice boy," and the frank young lady made him a small present—a little gold pin with a turquoise in it. "Keep that; you must never lose it, you know—it is a keepsake."

When little Jacob left with Mr. Prigley, Mrs. Stanburne was very kind to him, and said he must come again some time. This cheered Edith's heart considerably, but still there was a certain moisture in her eyes as she bade farewell to her boy-friend.

And in the same way I, who write this, feel a sadness coming over me which is not to be resisted. Children *never* live long. When they are not carried away in little coffins, and laid for ever in the silent grave, they become transformed so rapidly that we lose them in another way. The athletic young soldier or Oxonian, the graceful heroine of the ball-room, may make proud the parental heart, but can they quite console it for the eternal loss of the little beings who plagued and enlivened the early years of marriage? A father may sometimes feel a legitimate and reasonable melancholy as he contemplates the most promising of little daughters, full of vivacity and health. How long will the dear child remain to him? She will be altered in six months; in six years she will be succeeded by a totally different creature — a creature new in flesh and blood and bone, thinking other thoughts and speaking another language. There is a sadness even in that change which is increase and progression; for the glory of noon-day has destroyed the sweet delicacy of the dewy Aurora, and the wealth of summer has obliterated the freshness of the spring.

In saying good-bye to little Jacob and his friend Miss Edith, now, I am like some father who, under the fierce sun of India, sends his children away from him, that they may live. He expects to meet them again, yet these children he will never meet. In their place he will see men and women in the vigor of ripened adolescence. And when he quits the deck before the ship sails, and the little arms cling round him for the last time, and for the last time he hears the lisping voices, the dear imperfect words, a great grief comes like ice upon his heart, and he feels a void, and a loss, and a vain longing, only less painful than what we feel at the grave's brink, when the earth clatters down on the coffin, and the clergyman reads his farewell.

PART II.

CHAPTER I.

AFTER LONG YEARS.

IF the reader has ever been absent for many years from some neighborhood where he has once lived — where many faces were familiar to him, and the histories that belonged to the faces — where he once knew the complex relations of the inhabitants towards each other, and was at least in some measure cognizant of the causes which were silently modelling their existence in the future, as masons build houses in which some of us will have to live — if, after knowing the life of a neighborhood so intimately as this, he has left that place for long years, and come back to it again to visit it, that he may renew the old sensations, and revive his half-forgotten ancient self, he has learned a lesson about human life which no other experience can teach. The inhabitants who have never gone away for long, the parson who preaches every Sunday in the church, the attorney who goes to his office every day after breakfast, the shop-keepers who daily see the faces of their customers across the counter, perceive changes, but not change. To them every vicissitude has the air of a particular accident, and it always seems that it might have been avoided. But the great universal change has that in its aspect which tells you that it cannot be avoided; and he who has once seen it face to face knows that all things are moving and flowing, and that the world travels fast in a sense other than the astronomical.

I have endeavored to enlist the reader's interest in a set of persons who lived at Shayton and Sootythorn at the time of the establishment of the militia. The first training of Colonel Stanburne's regiment took place in the month of May, 1853 — to be precise, it met for the first time on the 23d of that month; and the 15th of the month following will long be remembered in the neighborhood on account of the great fire at Wenderholme Hall, which, as the reader is already aware, took place under circumstances of the most exceptional publicity. It is probable that on no occasion, from the times of the Tudors to our own, were so many people collected in the park and garden of Wenderholme as on that memorable night.

It is the misfortune of certain positions that the virtues which are necessary to those who occupy them have to be translated into a money outlay before they can be adequately appreciated. Colonel Stanburne was not an extravagant man by nature; he was simple in all his habits and tastes, liked to live quietly at his own house, hated London, and indulged himself only in an innocent taste for tandem-driving, which certainly did not cost him two hundred a-year. But this was John Stanburne's character in his private capacity; as a leader of men — as the head of a regiment — his nature was very different. Whether his surroundings excited him, and so caused him to lose the mental balance which is necessary to perfect prudence, or whether he acted at first in ignorance of the wonderful accumulativeness of tradesmen's bills, and afterwards went on from the force of established habit, it is certain that from the 23d of May, 1853, when his regiment assembled for the first time, Colonel Stanburne entered upon a new phase of his existence. Hitherto he had lived strictly within his income, whilst from the year 1853 he lived within it no longer.

His whole style of living had been heightened and increased by his position in the militia. The way he drove out was typical of every thing else. Before his colonelcy he had been contented with a tandem, and his tandem was horsed from the four ordinary carriage-horses which were regularly kept at Wenderholme. But since it had seemed convenient — nay, almost indispensably necessary — to have a commodious vehicle of some kind, that he might convey his officers from Sootythorn to Wenderholme every time he asked them to dinner — and since he had naturally selected a drag as the proper thing to have, and the pleasantest thing for himself to drive — there had been an increase in his stable expenses, and a change in his habits, which lasted all the year round. Besides, his natural kindliness and generosity of disposition, which had formerly found a sufficing expression in a general heartiness and good-nature, now began to express themselves in a much more expensive way — namely, by more frequent and more profuse hospitality.

In the year 1865 Colonel Stanburne was still at the head of his regiment of militia, and during the annual trainings the Wenderholme coach has never ceased to run. Wenderholme had become quite a famous place, and tourists knowing in architecture came to see it from distant counties. It is a perfect type now of a great Elizabethan mansion: the exterior, especially the central mass over the porch, is enriched with elaborate sculpture; there are great mullioned windows everywhere, and plenty of those rich mouldings and copings which diversify the fronts of great houses of that age, and crown their lofty walls. There are globes and pinnacles on the completed gables, and at the intersections of the roofing rise fantastic vanes of iron-work, gilded, and glittering in the sunshine against the blue of the summer sky.

The interior has but one defect — it seems to require, in its inhabitants, the costume of Sir Walter Raleigh and the great ladies of his time. It has become like a poem or a dream, and one would hardly be surprised to find Edmund Spenser there reading the "Faëry Queene" to the noble

Surrey, or imagining, in the solitude of one of its magnificent rooms, some canto still to be written.

Let us pause here, and look at the place simply as in a picture, or series of pictures, before the current of events hurries us on till we have no time left to enjoy beautiful things, nor mental tranquillity enough to feel in tune with this perfect peace.

It is noon in summer. Under every oak in the great avenues lies a dark patch of shadow, and on the rich expanse of the open park the sunshine glows and darkens as the thin white clouds sail slowly in the blue aerial ocean. How rich and stately is the rounded foliage — how perfect the fulness of the protected trees! In the midst of them stands the house of Wenderholme, surrounded by soft margins of green lawn and wide borders of gleaming flowers.

It is pleasant this hot day to enter the great cool hall, to walk on its pavement of marble (white marble and black, in lozenges), and rest the eye in the subdued light which reigns there, even at noon.

Under pretext of restoration, Wenderholme had been made a great deal more splendid, and incomparably more comfortable, than it ever was in the time of its pristine magnificence. In the wainscot and the furniture the architect had lavishly used a great variety of strange and beautiful woods, quite unknown to our ancestors; and not contented with the stones and marbles of the British islands, he had brought varieties from Normandy, and Sicily, and Spain, and the Mediterranean shores of Africa. As for the arrangements that regarded comfort and convenience, John Stanburne's architect had learned the extent of a rich Englishman's exigence when he erected the mansions of five or six great cotton-manufacturers, and, strong in this experience, had made Wenderholme a model place for elaborately perfect housekeeping.

What had been done with the modern furniture that had

been saved on the night of the fire? We may learn this, and some other matters also, when the Colonel comes in to lunch.

He crosses his great hall, and goes straight to the dining-room. The twelve years that have passed by have aged him even more than so many dozens of months ought to have done. His hair is getting prematurely gray, and his step, though still firm and manly, has lost a good deal of its elasticity, and something of its grace. The expression on his countenance does not quite correspond with all the glory of the paradise that is his, with the sunshine on the broad green park and vast shade-bestowing trees, with the rich peace of these cool and silent halls. When he is with other people, his face is very much as it used to be; but when he is alone, as he is now, it looks weary and haggard, as if to live were an effort and a care — as if some hateful anxiety haunted him, and wore him hour after hour.

"Tell her ladyship that I have come in to lunch; and stay — you need not wait upon us to-day."

Lady Helena comes with her scarcely audible little step, and quietly takes her place at the table. *She* is not very much changed by the lapse of these last twelve years. She is still rather pretty, and she looks as intelligent as ever, though not perhaps quite so lively. But as for liveliness, she has nothing to encourage her vivacity just now, for the Colonel eats his slice of cold beef in silence, and scarcely even looks in her direction. When he looks up at all, it is at the window, — not that there is any thing particular to be seen there — only the sunny garden with the fountain, fed from the hills behind.

"My dear," said Lady Helena, "as the regiment is disbanded now, I suppose we have no longer any reason to remain at Wenderholme? Suppose we went up to town again for the end of the season? There are several people that you promised to see, and didn't call upon before you came away. There's old Lady Sonachan's ball on the 15th, and I think we ought to do something ourselves in Grosvenor Square — you know we meant to do, if the training of the regiment had not been a fortnight earlier than we expected."

"I think it would be as well to stop quietly at Wenderholme."

"I'm afraid, dear," said Lady Helena, caressingly, "that you're losing your good habits, and going back to the ideas you had many years ago, before the militia began. You've been so very nice for a long time now that it would be a pity to go back again to what you used to be before you were properly civilized. For you know, dear, you were *not* quite civilized then — you were *sauvage*, almost a recluse; and now you like society, and it does you good — doesn't it, dear? Everybody ought to go into society — we all of us need it. *Do* come with me to town, dear, and after that I will go with you wherever you like."

"Helena," the Colonel answered, gravely, "that's the sort of game we have been playing for many years. 'Do indulge me in my fancy, and then I will indulge you in some fancy of your own.' It is time to put a stop to that sort of thing."

"It would be a pity, I think. Have we not been very happy, my love, all these years together?"

"Yes, no doubt, of course. But I'll tell you what it is, Helena — we made a great mistake."

Lady Helena's face flushed, and her eyes filled. "A mistake! I am grieved if you think your marriage was a mistake, John. I never think so of mine."

"It isn't that; I don't mean the marriage. I mean something since the marriage. But it's no use talking about that just now. I say, put your shawl on and take a little walk with me, will you?"

They went in silence by the path that rose towards the moors behind the house. When they came to the pond, the Colonel seemed to pause and hesitate a little; then he said, "No, not here — on the open moor."

They came to the region of the heather, and the park of Wenderholme, with all the estate around it, lay spread like a great map beneath them.

"Sit down here, Helena, and let us talk together quietly. It may be better for both of us." Then came a long pause of silence, and when Lady Helena looked in the Colonel's face, she perceived that his eyes were wandering over the land from one field to another, with a strange expression of lingering and longing and regret. Evidently he had forgotten that she was with him.

"Dear," she said at last, "what was that great mistake you talked about?"

He started and looked round at her suddenly. Then, laying his hand very gently on her shoulder, said with strange tenderness, "You won't be hurt, will you? It was mutual, you know.

"Do you recollect, Helena," he went on, after a little while, "the time when I first began to drive four horses? You didn't approve of it — of course I know you didn't — and there were a good many other things that you didn't approve of either, and your opinion was plain enough in your way with me. Well, then, there were some things that you either did or wanted to do, you know, which didn't quite suit me, and seemed to me as unnecessary as my fancy for driving four horses seemed to you. But I found out that I could keep you in a good temper, and make you indulge me in my fancies, by indulging you in corresponding fancies of your own. So whenever I resolved upon an extravagance, I stopped your criticisms by some bribe; and the biggest bribe of all — the one that kept you indulgent to me year after year — was that house in Grosvenor Square."

"It was your own proposing."

"'That's just what I am saying. I proposed the house in town to keep you quiet — to keep you from criticising me. You had got into a way of criticising me about the time of the fire, and I hated being criticised. So I thought, 'She shall have her own way if she'll only let me have mine;' and it seems you thought something of the same kind, for you became very indulgent with me. That has been our mistake, Helena."

"But *was* it such a mistake after all, darling? Have we not been very happy all these years? I remember we were not so happy just when the militia began. You were not so nice with me as you have been since."

"Perhaps not — and you weren't as nice with me either, Helena; but we were nearer being right then than we ever have been during the last few years. I mean to say that, if we had said plainly to each other then — in a kind sort of way, of course — what each was thinking, we should have spared each other a great deal of suffering."

"We have suffered very little, love; we have been very happy."

"The punishment is yet to come. I've been punished, in my mind, for years past, and said nothing about it to you, because I wanted partly to spare you, and partly to screen myself, for I thought I could bring things round again."

"Do you mean about money?"

"Yes."

"Well, but, dear, you always told me that there had been no diminution in our income. Did you not tell me the truth?"

"All that was perfectly true. The income was not diminished, but the new investments weren't as safe as the old ones. Don't you see, we had less capital to get our income from, and our expenses were even heavier than they used to be. So I invested at higher interest, to make up the difference in our income, and I've been carrying that on to an extent you know nothing about."

Lady Helena began to be alarmed. Nobody knew better than her ladyship that the *prestige* of aristocracy rested ultimately upon wealth, and that she could no more keep up her station without a good income than her strength without food. It had been a capital error of John Stanburne's from the beginning, not to consult his wife on every detail of his money transactions. She had always been perfectly prudent in not letting current expenses go beyond income, although, as they had only one child, there appeared to be no necessity for saving. She would have advised him well if he had invited her to advise him; but though he had always told her, with truth, that their income was four thousand a-year, he had not told her the history of the capital sum from which this income had, in consequence of some devices of his own, been drawn so unfailingly. The restoration of Wenderholme had been a very costly undertaking indeed. The whole outlay upon it John Stanburne had never dared to calculate; but we, who have no reason for that nervous abstinence from terrible totals, know that during the years immediately succeeding the great fire, he did not, in the restoration and adornment of his beautiful home, spend less than twenty-seven thousand pounds. The result, no doubt, was worth even so large an outlay as this; nor was the sum in itself very wildly extravagant, when one reflects that one of the Sootythorn cotton-spinners laid out fully as much on an ugly new house about half a mile beyond Chesnut Hill. But it diminished John Stanburne's funded property by more than one-half, and it therefore became necessary to invest the remainder more productively, to keep his income up to its old level.

Whilst he is telling these things to Lady Helena in his own way, let us narrate them somewhat more succinctly in ours. It had happened, about three years after the fire — that is, in the year 1856 — that a new bank had been established in Sootythorn, called the Sootythorn District Bank, and some of the capitalists both in the immediate locality and in the neighboring country had invested in it rather largely. Amongst these was our acquaintance, Mr. Joseph Anison of Arkwright Lodge, near Whittlecup, who, not having a son to succeed him in his business, did not care to extend it, and sought another investment for his savings which might as nearly as possible approach in productiveness the ample returns of commerce. Mr. Anison was one of the original founders of the new bank, and if the idea had not positively its first source in his own mind, it was he who brought it to a practicable shape, and finally made it a reality. Colonel Stanburne had taken Joseph Anison into his confidence about his money matters — at least so far as to show him the present reduced state of his funded capital; and he added that, with his diminished income, it had become necessary to economize by a determined reduction of expenses, the most obvious means to which would be the resignation of his commission in the militia — which, directly or indirectly, cost him a clear thousand a-year — and the abandonment of the house in town, which had then recently been established for the gratification of Lady Helena, and furnished with the modern furniture saved at the burning of Wenderholme. Mr. Anison, strongly dissuaded the Colonel from both these steps, urging upon him the popularity which he enjoyed both in the regiment and at Sootythorn, and even certain considerations of public duty to which an English gentleman is rarely altogether insensible. The Colonel liked the regiment, he liked his position, and it may even be said, without any exaggeration of his merits, that, independently of the consideration which it procured him, he felt an inward satisfaction in doing something which could be considered useful. To resign his commission, then, would have been difficult for another reason, if not altogether impossible. The regiment, instead of coming to Sootythorn for a month's training in the year, was on permanent garrison duty in Ireland, and he could not gracefully leave it.

The other project — the abandonment of his house in London — might have been agreeable enough to himself personally, but he was one of those husbands who, from weakness or some other cause, find it impossible to deprive a wife of any thing which she greatly cares for. This defect was due in his case, as it is in many others, to an inveterate habit of politeness towards all women, *even* towards his wife; and just as no gentleman would take possession of a chair or a footstool which a lady happened to be using, so John Stanburne could not turn Lady Helena out of that house in town which she liked so much, and which both of them looked upon as peculiarly her own. It is easy for rough and brutal men to do these things, but a gentleman will often get into money embarrassments out of mere delicacy. I don't mean to imply that the Colonel's way of dealing with his wife was the best way. It would have been far better to be frank with her from the beginning; but then a simple nature like John Stanburne's has such a difficulty in uniting the gentleness and the firmness which are equally necessary when one has to carry out measures which are sure to be disagreeable to a lady. The *suaviter in modo*, &c., is, after all, a species of hypocrisy — at least until it has become habitual; and when the Colonel was soft in manner, which he always was with women, he was soft in the matter also. In a word, though no one was better qualified to please a lady, he was utterly incapable of governing one — an incapacity which perhaps he shared with the majority of the sons of Adam.

As retrenchment had appeared impossible, or, at least, too difficult to be undertaken so long as there was the alternative of a change of investments, the Colonel begged Mr. Anison, as an experienced man of business, to look out for something good in that way; and Mr. Anison, who, with his brother capitalists, had just started the Sootythorn District Bank, honestly represented to his friend that a better and a safer investment was not likely to be found anywhere. As he preached not merely by precept but by example, and showed that he had actually staked every thing which he possessed on the soundness of the speculation — he, the father of a family — Colonel Stanburne was easily persuaded, and became one of the largest shareholders. The bank was soon in a very flourishing condition — in fact it was really prosperous, and exceeded the most sanguine hopes of its originators. The manager was both an honorable man and a man of real ability as a financier. The dividends were very large, and *not* paid out of capital.

After five or six years of this prosperity, during which the Colonel's aggregate income had been higher than it ever was during his best days as a fund-holder, he began to conceive the idea of replacing, by economy, the sum of £27,000, which had been withdrawn from his funded capital for the restoration and embellishment of Wenderholme. To do this he prudently began by saving the surplus of his income; but as this did not seem to accumulate fast enough for his desires, he thought that, without permanently alienating his estate, he might mortgage some portion of it, and invest the money so procured at the higher interest received by the shareholders of the Sootythorn District Bank. The mere surplus of interest would of itself redeem the mortgage after a few years, leaving the money borrowed in his own hands as a clear increase of capital.. In this way he mortgaged a great part of the estate of Wenderholme to our friend Mr. Jacob Ogden of Milend.

All these things were done *clam Helenâ* — unknown to her ladyship. She was not supposed to understand business, and probably the Colonel, from the first, had apprehended her womanish fears of the glorious uncertainties of speculation. His conscience, however, was perfectly at ease. At the cost of a degree of risk which he set aside as too trifling to be dwelt upon, he was gradually — nay, even rapidly — replacing the money sunk in Wenderholme; and every day brought him nearer to the time when he might live in his noble mansion without the tormenting thought that it had been paid for out of his inherited capital. At the same time, so far from withdrawing from the world's eyes into the obscurity which is usually one of the most essential conditions of retrenchment, he actually filled a higher place in the county than he had ever occupied before. The taste for society grows, upon us and becomes a habit, so that the man who a year or two since bore solitude with perfect ease, may to-morrow find much companionship a real want, though an acquired one. The more sociable John Stanburne became, the more he felt persuaded that the house in London was a proper thing to keep up, and there came to be quite an admirable harmony between him and Lady Helena. She had always loved him very much, but in the days when he had a fancy for retirement, she had felt just a shade of contempt for the rusticity of his tastes. As this rusticity wore off, her ladyship respected her husband more completely; and the coolness which had existed between them in the year 1853 was succeeded by an affectionate indulgence on both sides, which was entirely satisfactory to Lady Helena, and was only a little less so to the Colonel, because he knew it to be a sacrifice of firmness.

He began to feel this very keenly at the time our story reopens, because some very heavy misfortunes had befallen the Sootythorn District Bank, and the Colonel began to doubt whether, after all, his financial operations (successful as they had hitherto appeared) were quite so prudent as he and Mr. Anison had believed. Mr. Stedman had been against the enterprise from the very first, and had openly attempted to dissuade both Mr. Anison and the Colonel from any participation in it; but then Mr. Stedman, who had neither the expenses of a family nor the drain of a high social position, could afford the utmost extremity of prudence, and could literally have lived in his accustomed manner if his money had been invested at one per cent. However, the Bank had kept up the Colonel's position by giving him an easy income for several years; and by enabling him to put by a surplus, had compensated, by the mental satisfaction which is the reward of those who save, any little anxiety which from time to time may have disturbed the tranquillity of his mind. But now the anxiety was no longer a light one, to be compensated by thinking about savings. A private meeting of the principal shareholders had been held the day before, and it had become clear to them that the position of the Sootythorn Bank (and consequently their own individual position, for their liability was unlimited) was perilous in the extreme. Immense sums had been advanced to cotton firms which were believed to be sound, but which had gone down within the preceding fortnight; and many other loans were believed to be very doubtful. Under these circumstances, the chief shareholders — Colonel Stanburne amongst the number — bound themselves by a mutual promise not to attempt to sell, as any unusual influx of shares upon the market would at once provoke their depreciation, and probably create a panic.

Whilst the Colonel had been telling all these things to Lady Helena, he had not dared to look once upon her face; but when he had come to an end, a silence followed — a silence so painful that he could not bear it, and turned to her that she might speak to him. She was not looking in his direction. She was not looking at Wenderholme, nor on any portion of the fair estate around it; but her eyes were fixed on the uttermost line of the far horizon. She was very pale; her lips were closely compressed, and there was a tragic sternness and severity in her brow that John Stanburne had never before seen.

For a whole minute — for sixty intolerable seconds — not one word escaped her.

"Helena, speak to me!"

She turned slowly towards him, and rose to her feet. Then came words — words that cut and chilled as if they were made of sharp steel that had been sheathed in a scabbard of ice.

"You have been very imprudent and very weak. You are not fit to have the management of your own affairs."

She said no more. She was intensely angry at her husband, but in her strongest irritation she never said any thing not justified by the circumstances — never put herself in the wrong by violence or exaggeration. She had a great contempt for female volubility and scolding; and the effect of her tongue, when she used it, was to the effect of a scold's rattle what the piercing of a rapier is to the cracking of a whip.

John Stanburne dreaded the severity of his wife's judgment more than he would have dreaded the fury of an unreasonable woman. He had not a word to offer in reply. He felt that it was literally and accurately true that he had been "very imprudent and very weak, and was not fit to have the management of his own affairs."

He covered his face with both hands in an agony of self-accusation, and remained so for several minutes. Then he cried out passionately, "Helena, dear Helena!" and again, "Helena! Helena!"

There was no answer. He lifted up his eyes. The place she had occupied was vacant. She had noiselessly departed from his side.

CHAPTER II.

IN THE DINING-ROOM.

ONE of the most strange and painful things about ruin is, that for days, and even weeks, after it has actually come upon a man, his outward life remains in all its details as it was before; so that in the interval between the loss of fortune and the abandonment of his habitual way of living he leads a double life, just as a ghost would do if it were condemned to simulate the earthly existence it led before death amongst the dear familiar scenes. For there are two sorts of separation. You get into a railway train, and take ship, and emigrate to some distant colony or some alien empire, and see no more the land which gave you birth, nor the house which sheltered you, nor the faces of your friends. This separation is full of sadness; but there is another separation which, in its effect upon the mind, is incomparably more to be dreaded, whose pain is incomparably more poignant. I mean, that terrible separation which divides you from the persons with whom you are still living, from the house you have never quitted, from the horses in the stable, from the dog upon the hearth, from the bed you lie in, from the chair you sit upon, from the very plate out of which you eat your daily food! The man who, still in his old house, knows that he has become insolvent, feels this in a thousand subtly various tortures, that succeed each other without intermission. A curse has fallen on every thing that he sees, on every thing that he touches — a wonderful and magical curse, devised by the ingenuity of Plutus, the arch-enchanter! The

wildest fairy tale narrates no deeper sorcery than this. Every
thing shall remain, materially, exactly as it was; but when
you go into your library you shall not be able to read, in your
dining-room the food shall choke you, and you shall toss all
night upon your bed.

And thus did it come to pass that from this hour all the
beauties, and the luxuries, and all the accumulated objects
and devices that made up the splendor of Wenderholme,
became so many several causes of torture to John Stanburne.
And by another effect of the same curse, he was compelled
to torture himself endlessly with these things, as a man when
he is galvanized finds that his fingers contract involuntarily
round the brass cylinders through which flows the current
that shatters all his nerves with agony.

The first bell rings for dinner, and the Colonel, from long
habit, leaves his little den, and is half-way up the grand staircase before he knows that he is moving. That great staircase
had been one of the favorite inventions in new Wenderholme.
It was panelled with rich old yew, and in the wainscot were
inserted a complete series of magnificent Italian tapestries,
in which was set forth the great expedition of the Argonauts.
There was the sowing of the poisoned grain, the consequent
pestilence of Thebes, the flight of Phryxus and Helle on the
winged ram with the golden fleece, the fall of poor Helle in
the dark Hellespont, the sacrifice of the ram at Colchis, the
murder of Phryxus. Above all, there was the glorious embar-
kation in the good ship Argo, when Jason and the Grecian
princes came down to the shore, with a background of the
palaces they left. And in another great tapestry the ship
Argo sailed in the open sea, her great white sail curving
before the wind, and the blue waves dancing before her
prow, whilst the warriors stood quaintly upon the deck, with
all their glittering arms. Then there was the storm on the
coast of Thrace, and the famous ploughing-scene with the
golden-horned bulls, and the sowing of the dragon's teeth.

Dragon's teeth! John Stanburne paused long before that tapestry. Had he not likewise been a sower of dragon's teeth, and were not the armed men rising, terrible, around him?

Who will help him as Medea helped Jason? Who will pass him through all his dangers in a day?

It will not be his wife — it will not be Lady Helena. She is coming up the great staircase too, whilst he is vacantly staring at the tapestry. He does not know that she is there till the rustle of her draperies awakens him. She passes in perfect silence, slowly, in the middle of the broad carpeted space, between the margins of white stone.

They met again that evening at dinner. So long as the men waited they talked about this thing and that. But when the dessert was on the table, and the men were gone, the Colonel handed the following letter to Lady Helena: —

"MY DEAR COLONEL STANBURNE, — As you have been aware for some time of the precarious position of the Bank, the bad news I have to communicate will not find you altogether unprepared. We have been obliged to stop payment, and it will require such a large sum to meet the liabilities of the company that both you and I and many other shareholders must consider ourselves ruined men. God grant us fortitude to bear it! When I advised you to embark in this speculation, God knows I did so honestly, and you have the proof of it in the fact that I am ruined along with you. It will be hard for you to descend from a station you were born for and are accustomed to, and it is hard for me to see the fruits of a life of hard work swept away just as I am beginning to be an old man. Pray think charitably of me, Colonel Stanburne. I did what I believed to be best, and though my heart is heavy, my conscience is clear still. May Heaven give strength to both of us, and to all others who are involved in the same ruin!

"Yours truly,   JOSEPH ANISON."

Lady Helena read the letter from beginning to end, and then returned it to her husband without a word. Her face wore an expression of the most complete indifference.

"Why, Helena!" said John Stanburne, "you haven't a word to say to me. It's far more my misfortune than my fault, and I think you might be kinder, under the circumstances, than you are."

"*Que voulez-vous que je vous dise?*"

CHAPTER III.

IN THE DRAWING-ROOM.

COFFEE having been announced, the Colonel, who had been sitting alone with his burgundy, and perhaps drinking a little more of it than usual, followed her ladyship into the drawing-room. That drawing-room was the most delicately fanciful room in the whole house. It was wainscoted with cedar to the height of eight feet, where the panels terminated in a beautiful little carved arcade running all round the noble room, and following the wall everywhere into its quaint recesses. Heraldic decoration, used so profusely in the great hall and elsewhere, was here limited to John Stanburne's own conjugal shield, in which the arms of Stanburne were impaled with those of Basenthorpe.

If the Colonel could only have drunk his cup of coffee in silence, or made a commonplace remark or two, and then gone straight to bed, or into his own den, it might have been better for them both; but he was stung to the quick by her ladyship's unsympathizing manner, and he had absorbed so much burgundy in the dining-room as to have lost altogether that salutary fear of his wife's keen little observations which usually kept him in restraint. It was a great pity, too, that they were alone together in the drawing-room that evening, and that Miss Stanburne had left Wenderholme two days before on a brief visit to a country house at a distance.

His heart yearned for Helena's sympathy and support, and of this she was perfectly aware; but, with that rashness which is peculiarly feminine, and which makes women play their little game of withholding what men's hearts want, even in moments of the utmost urgency and peril, she determined to give him no help until he had properly and sufficiently humiliated himself and confessed his sins before her. The woman who *could* withhold her tenderness in such an hour as this diminished, in doing so, the value of that tenderness itself; and every minute that passed whilst it was still withheld made such a large deduction from it, that if this coldness lasted for an hour longer, John Stanburne felt that no subsequent kindness could atone for it. As the slow, miserable minutes went by whilst Lady Helena sat yards away from him at a little table in a great oriel window, saying not one word, not even looking once in his direction, John Stanburne's brain, already in a state of intense excitement in consequence of the miseries of the day, began to suffer from an almost insane irritability and impatience on account of the silence and calm that surrounded him. It was a most peaceful and beautiful summer evening, and the sun, as he declined towards the west, sent rich warm rays into the noble room, glowing on the cedar panels, and on the quaintly elegant furniture, with its pervading expression of luxury and ease. This luxury maddened John Stanburne, the soft carpet was hateful to his feet, the easy-chair irritating to his whole body; he hated the great clusters of flowers in the *jardinières*, and the white delicate webs that were the summer curtains. Considering the present temper of his mind, and his horror of everything that had cost him money, the drawing-room was the worst place he could have been in.

If her ladyship would just have left that interesting bit of plain hemming that she was engaged upon (and whereby she was effecting an economy of about twopence a-day), and gone to her husband and said one kind word to him, merely his name even, and given him one caress, one kiss, their fate would have been incomparably easier to endure. They would have supported each other under the pressure of calamity, and the material loss might have been balanced by a moral gain.

But she sat there silently, persistently, doing that farthing's worth of plain needlework.

"Helena!" at last the Colonel broke out, "I say, Helena, I wonder what the devil we are to do?"

"You need not swear at me, sir."

"Swear at you!— who swears at you? I didn't. But if I did swear at you, it wouldn't be without provocation. You are the most provoking woman I ever knew in my life; upon my word you are — you are, by God, Helena!"

"You are losing your temper, Colonel Stanburne. Pray remember whom you are speaking to. I am not to be sworn at like your grooms."

"You never lose *your* temper. Now, I say that as you are such a mistress of yourself under all circumstances, it's your own fault that you don't make yourself more agreeable."

"I regret that you don't think me agreeable, Colonel Stanburne."

"Well, now, *are* you, Helena? Here am I under the blow of a tremendous calamity, and you haven't a word to say to me. If Fyser knew what had happened, he'd be more sorry than you are."

"What would you have me say to you? If I said all you deserve, would you listen to it? You appear to forget that you have as yet expressed no sympathy for me, whom you have ruined by your folly, whereas you are angry because I have said little to you."

"*You* ruined, Helena!". said John Stanburne, with a bitter laugh; "*you* ruined — why, you never had any thing to lose! Your father allows you six hundred a-year, and he'll continue your allowance, I suppose. You never owned a thousand pounds in your life. But it's different with me. I'm losing all I was born to."

The answer to this was too obvious for Lady Helena to

condescend to make it. She remained perfectly silent, which irritated the Colonel more than any imaginable answer could have irritated him.

He certainly was wrong so far as this, that any one who *asks* for sympathy puts himself in a false position. Condolence must be freely given, or it is worthless. And any disposition which her ladyship may have felt towards a more wifely frame of mind was effectually checked by his advancing these claims of his. She was not to be scolded into amiability.

"Hang it, Helena!" he broke out, "I didn't think there was a woman in England that would behave as you are behaving under such circumstances. The thing doesn't seem to make the least impression upon you. There you sit, doing your confounded sewing, just as if nothing had happened, you do. You won't sit there doing your sewing long. The bailiffs will turn you out. They'll be here in a day or two."

"You are becoming very coarse, sir; your language is not fit for a woman to hear."

"It's the plain truth, it is. But women won't hear the plain truth. They don't like it — they never do. But your ladyship must be made to understand that this cannot go on. We cannot stop here, at Wenderholme. The place will be sold, and every thing in it. Now, I should just like to know what your ladyship proposes to do. If my way of asking your ladyship this question isn't polite enough, please do me the favor to instruct me in the necessary forms."

"If you could speak without oaths, that would be something gained."

"Answer me my question, can't you? Where do you mean to go — what do you mean to do?"

"I intend to go to my father's."

"Well, that's plain. Why couldn't you tell me that sooner? You mean to go to old Adisham's. But I'll be hanged if I'll go there, to be patronized as a beggarly relation."

"Very well."

"Very well, is it? It's very well that you are to live in one place, and I in another."

"A distance sufficient to protect me from your rudeness would certainly be an advantage."

"Would it, indeed? You really think so, do you? Well, if you think so, it shall be so."

"Very well."

She spoke with a calmness that was perfectly exasperating, and John Stanburne's brain was too much overwrought by the terrible trial of that day for him to bear things with any patience. He was half insane temporarily; he could not bear to see that calm little woman sitting there, with her jarring self-control.

"I say, Lady Helena, if you mean to go to old Adisham's, the sooner you go the better. All this house is crumbling over our heads as if it were rotten."

Lady Helena rose quietly from her seat, took up her work, and walked towards the door. Just as she was opening it, she turned towards the Colonel, and pronounced with the clearest possible articulation the following sentences:—

"You will please remember, Colonel Stanburne, that it was you who turned me out of your house, and the sort of language you used in doing so. *I* shall always remember it."

Then the door closed quietly upon her — the great heavy door, slowly moving on its smooth hinges.

CHAPTER IV.

ALONE.

IT happened that the hall-door was open, as it usually was in the fine weather, and John Stanburne, without knowing it, went out upon the lawn. The balmy evening air, fragrant from the sweet breath of innumerable flowers, caressed his hot flushed face. He became gradually calmer as he walked in a purposeless way about the garden, and, looking at his mansion from many a different point of view, began to feel a strange, dreamy, independent enjoyment of its beauty, as if he had been some tourist or visitor for whom the name of Wenderholme had no painful associations. Then he passed out into the park, down the rich dark avenues whose massive foliage made a premature night, and wandered farther and farther, till, by pure accident, he came upon the carriage-drive.

A man whose mind is quite absent, and who is wandering without purpose, will, when he comes upon a road, infallibly follow it in one direction or another, not merely because it is plain before the feet; but from a deep instinct in our being which impels us to prefer some human guidance to the wilderness of nature. It happened that the Colonel went in the direction which led him away from the house, perhaps because the road sloped invitingly that way.

Suddenly he heard a noise behind him, and had barely time to get out of the way when a carriage dashed passed him at full speed, with two great glittering lamps. He caught no glimpse of its occupant, but he knew the carriage — Lady Helena's.

For a few seconds he stood immovable. Then, bounding forward, he cried aloud, "Helena! Helena!" and again and again, "Helena!"

Too late! The swift high-spirited horses were already on the public road, hurrying to catch the last train at the little station ten miles off. The sudden impulse of tenderness which drew John Stanburne's heart after her, as she passed, had no magnetism to arrest her fatal course. They had parted now, and for ever.

He would have passed that night more easily if he could have gone at once to the Cottage, and unburdened his wretchedness to his mother, and become, for his hour of weakness, a little child again in her dear presence. But he dreaded to inflict upon her the blow which in any event would only come too soon, and he resolved to leave her whatever hours might yet remain to her of peace.

Somehow he went back to the Hall, and got to his own den. The place was more supportable to him than any other in the house, being absolutely devoid of splendor. A poor man might feel himself at home *there*. He rang the bell.

"Fyser, her ladyship has been obliged to go away this evening for an absence of some days, and I mean to live here. Make up my camp-bed, will you, in that corner?"

It was not the first time that the Colonel had retreated in this manner to his den; for when there were no guests in the house, and her ladyship was away, he found himself happier there than in the great reception-rooms. I think, perhaps, in his place I should have preferred something between the two, and would have allowed myself a couple of tolerably large rooms in a pleasant part of the house; but his mind seems to have needed the reaction from the extreme splendor of new Wenderholme to a simplicity equally extreme. Here, in his den, it must be admitted that he had passed many of his happiest hours, either in making artificial flies, or in reading the sort of literature that suited him; and though the place was so crammed with things that the occupant could hardly stir, and in such a state of apparent disorder that no woman would have stayed in it ten minutes, he here found all he wanted, ready to his hand.

This night, however, not even the little camp-bed that he loved could give him refreshing sleep; and the leathern cylindrical pillow, on which his careless head had passed so many hours of perfect oblivion, became as hard to him morally as it certainly was materially. He found it utterly impossible to get rest; and after rolling and tossing an hour or two, and vainly trying to read, finished by getting up and dressing himself.

It was only one o'clock in the morning, but the Colonel determined to go out. Unfastening a side door, he was soon in the fresh cool air.

He followed the path behind the house that led to the spot where he had made his confession to Lady Helena. A strange attraction drew him to it, and once there, he could not get away. There was no moon, and the details of the scene before him were not visible in the clear starlight, but dark mysterious shades indicated the situation of the Hall and its shrubberies, and the long avenues that led away from it.

And here, in the solitude of the hill, under the silent stars, came upon John Stanburne the hour and crisis of his agony. Until now he had not realized the full extent of his misery, and of the desolation that lay before him. He had *known* it since five o'clock in the afternoon, but he felt it now for the first time. As some terrible bodily disease lays hold of us at first with gentle hands, and causes us little suffering, but afterwards rages in us, and tears us with intolerable anguish, so it had been with this man's affliction.

His brain was in a state of unnatural lucidity, casting an electric light upon every idea that suggested itself. In ordinary life a man of common powers, he possessed for this hour the insight and the intensity of genius. He reviewed his life with Lady Helena,—the twenty years—for it was twenty years!—that they had eaten at the same table, and lived under the same roof. And in all that long space of a thousand weeks of marriage, he could not remember a single instance in which she had been clearly in the wrong. On her side, it now seemed to him, there had always been intelligence and justice; on his side, a want of capacity to understand her, and of justice to recognize her merits. Having now, as I have said, for one hour of excitement, the clear perceptions of genius, it was plain to him where he had erred; and this perception so humbled him that he no longer dared to admit the faults which Lady Helena really had, her constant severity and her lasting *rancune*. Then came the bitterest hour of all, that of remorse for his own folly, for his want of conjugal trust in Lady Helena, for his fatal ambition and pride. How different their life might have been if he had understood her better from the first! how different if he had lived within his means! Had he lived within his means, that great foolish *fête* would never have been given at Wenderholme, the house would not have been burned down, the money lavished on its restoration would still have been in the Funds, and John Stanburne would have kept out of that fatal Sootythorn Bank. All his ruin was clearly traceable to that fatal entertainment, and to his expensive ways as a colonel of militia. He saw now quite clearly that there had never been any real necessity for the profuse manner in which he had thought it obligatory to do the honor of his rank. There were rich colonels and there were colonels not so rich —he might have done things well enough without going beyond his means. "If I alone suffered from it!" he cried aloud; "but Helena, and Edith, and my mother!"

CHAPTER V.

THE TWO JACOBS.

THE twelve years that have passed since we had the pleasure of seeing Mrs. Ogden have not deducted from her charms. The reader has doubtless observed that, notwithstanding the law of change which governs all sublunary persons and things, there are certain persons, as there are certain things, which, relatively at least to the rest of their species, have the enviable privilege of permanence. Mrs. Ogden was like those precious gems that are found in the sarcophagi of ancient kings, and which astonish us by their freshness and brilliance, when all around them bears the impress of death and of decay. One would be tempted to exclaim, "May my old age be like hers!" were it not that advancing years, whilst deducting so little from her physical or mental vigor, have not enriched her mind with a single new idea, or corrected one of her ancient prejudices. However, though intellectual people may think there is little use in living unless life is an intellectual advance, such people as Mrs. Ogden are not at all of that way of thinking, but seem to enjoy life very well in their own stationary way. There are intellectual policemen who are always telling us to "keep moving;" but what if I find a serener satisfaction in standing still? Then, if we stand still, we are to be insulted, and told that we are rusty, or that we are getting the "bluemould." *Et après?* Suppose we *are* getting the blue-mould, what then? So far as may be ascertained by the study of such instances as Mrs. Ogden, the blue-mould is a great comfort and a great safeguard to the system — it is moral flannel. Would she have lasted as she has done without it? I say, it is a solace, amidst the rapid changes of the body politic, and the new-fangled ideas which take possession of the heads of ministers, to feel that there is one personage in these realms who will live on in vigor undiminished, yet never advance one inch. And when the British Constitution shall be finally swept away, and the throne itself no more, it will be something amidst the giddiness of universal experiment to know that in Mrs. Ogden this country will still possess an example that all is not given over to mutability.

"Now, young un," said Uncle Jacob, one day at dinner at Milend, "I reckon you 've been writing no letters to that lass at Wendrum; and if you 've written nout, there 's no 'arm done. It isn't a match for such a young felly as you, as 'll have more brass nor Stanburne iver had in his best days. We 'st 'ave no weddin' wi' bankrupts' dorthers."

"Bankrupts, indeed!" said Mrs. Ogden. "I reckon nout o' bankrupts! Besides, Stanburne had no need to be a bankrupt if he hadn't been such a fool. And foolishness runs i' th' blood. Like father, like dorther. Th' father 's been a wastril with his money, and it 's easy to see 'at the dorther 'ud be none so kerfle."

"Who shalln't have th' chance o' spendin' none o' my brass," said Uncle Jacob. "Do you yer that, young un? Stanburne dorther shall spend none o' *my* brass. If you wed her, yer father 'll 'ave to keep both on ye, an' all yer chilther beside. He 's worth about five hundred a-year, is your father; and I 'm worth — nobody knows what I 'm worth."

Young Jacob knew both his uncle and his grandmother far too intimately to attempt discussion with either of them ; but the news of Colonel Stanburne's bankruptcy, which in their view had put an end to the dream of a possible alliance with his daughter, wore a very different aspect to the young lover. An attachment existed between himself and Edith Stanburne, of which both were perfectly conscious, and yet nothing had been said about it openly on either side. Young Jacob Ogden had felt every year more and more keenly the width of the social gulf which separated them, though his education at Eton and Oxford and his constantly increasing prospects of future riches had already begun to build a bridge across the gulf. Even in his best days Colonel Stanburne had not been what in Lancashire is considered a rich man; in his best days, he had been poorer than the leading manufacturers of Sootythorn; and Jacob Ogden's mill had of itself cost more money than any squire of Wenderholme had ever possessed, whilst Jacob Ogden had property of many kinds besides his mill, and a huge lump of money lying by ready for immediate investment. The superiority in money had therefore for some years been entirely on the side of the Ogdens; but, although aristocracy in England is in reality based on wealth, it has a certain poetic sense which delights also in antiquity and honors. Jacob Ogden and his money might have been agreeable to the matter-of-fact side of English aristocratic feeling, but they were unsatisfying to its poetic sense. Young Jacob was clearly aware of this, and so indeed, in a cruder form, was his uncle. So long therefore as the Colonel was prosperous, or apparently prosperous, the Ogdens knew that the obstacles in the way of a marriage were all but insurmountable, and no proposal had ever been made. The Colonel's ruin changed the relative situation very considerably; and, if young Jacob Ogden could have permitted himself to rejoice in an event so painful to one who had always been kind to him, he would have rejoiced now. He did, indeed, feel a degree of hope about Edith Stanburne to which he had been a stranger for some years.

As young Jacob had said nothing in answer to his uncle and his grandmother, they both gave him credit for a prudent abandonment of his early dream. There existed, however, between him and his father a much closer confidence and friendship; and Isaac Ogden (who, notwithstanding the errors of his earlier life, had the views and feelings of a gentleman, as well as an especial loyalty and attachment to his unfortunate friend, the Colonel) encouraged his son in his fidelity. The materials were thus accumulating for a war in the Ogden family; and whenever that war shall be declared, we may rely upon it that it will be prosecuted with great vigor on both sides, for the Ogdens are wilful people, all of them.

Mr. Isaac has been enjoying excellent health for these last twelve years, thanks to his vow of total abstinence, to which he still courageously adheres. A paternal interest in the education of his son has gradually filled many of the voids in his own education, so that, without being aware of it himself, he has become really a well-informed man. His solitary existence at Twistle Farm has been favorable to the habit of study, and, like all men who have acquired the love of knowledge, he sees that life may have other aims and other satisfactions than the interminable accumulation of wealth. Small as may have been his apparent worldly success, Isaac Ogden has raised himself to a higher stand-point than his brother Jacob is likely ever to attain. Amongst the many expressions of sympathy which reached Colonel Stanburne after his disaster, few pleased him more than the following letter from Twistle Farm:—

"MY DEAR COLONEL STANBURNE, — I am truly grieved to hear that the failure of the Sootythorn Bank has involved you in misfortune. I would have come to Wenderholme to say this personally, but it seemed that, under present circumstances, you might wish to be alone with your family. I hardly know how to say what I wish to say in addition to this. For some years I have spent very little, and, although my income is small, I find there is a considerable balance in my favor with Messrs. ———. If this could be of any use to you, pray do not scruple to draw upon my bankers, who will be forewarned that you may possibly do so. Up to £1,000 you will occasion me no inconvenience, and, though this is not much, it might be of temporary service.

"Yours most faithfully, I. OGDEN."

To this letter the Colonel returned the following reply:—

"MY DEAR OGDEN,—Your kind letter gave me great pleasure. I am greatly obliged by your friendly offer of help, which I accept as one brother officer may from another. If, as is probable, I find myself in urgent need of a little ready money, I will draw upon your bankers, but, of course, not to such an extent as would go beyond a reasonable probability of repayment.

At the last meeting of creditors and shareholders, it appeared that, although we are likely to save nothing from the wreck, the Bank will probably pay nineteen shillings in the pound. This is a great satisfaction.

"Yours most truly, J. STANBURNE."

CHAPTER VI.

THE SALE.

THE Colonel would not expose himself even to the appearance of flight, but remained in the neighborhood manfully, and went personally to Manchester, before the court of bankruptcy, through which he passed very easily. His name then appeared in the Manchester papers, and in the "Sootythorn Gazette," in the list of bankrupts.

Bailiffs were in possession of the house and estate of Wenderholme, and Mr. Jacob Ogden foreclosed his mortgages, by which he became owner of a fair portion of the land.

Finally, Wenderholme Hall and the remainder of the estate, including the Cottage, in which Mrs. Stanburne still resided, were sold by auction in the large room at the Thorn Inn at Sootythorn — the very place which the Colonel's regiment of militia was accustomed to use as a mess-room.

Little had John Stanburne or his officers foreseen, whilst there consuming Mr. Garley's substantial dinners, that the hammer of the auctioneer would one day there transfer Wenderholme from the name of Stanburne to another name — to what name?

The room was crowded. The sale was known all over Lancashire and Yorkshire. Competitors had come even from distant counties. Wenderholme had been a famous place since the fire, and the magnificent restoration which had succeeded to the fire. Drawings of it had appeared in the "Illustrated London News," and, since the failure of the Sootythorn Bank, the creditors had cunningly caused a volume to be made in which the whole place was fully illustrated and described. This volume they had widely circulated.

The sale had been announced for eight o'clock in the evening, and at ten minutes after eight precisely the auctioneer mounted his rostrum. He made a most elaborate speech, in which (with the help of the volume above mentioned) he went over every room in the house, describing, with vulgar magniloquence, all those glories which had cost John Stanburne so dear.

There was one person present to whom the description can hardly have been very agreeable. John Stanburne himself, from anxiety to know the future possesssor, and the amount realized, had quietly entered the room unperceived, for every one was looking at the auctioneer. He had stationed himself near the wall, and there bore the infliction of this torture, his hat over his eyes.

At length all this eloquence had run dry, and the business of the evening began. The place was put up at £30,000, and no bid was to be made of less than £1,000 over its predecessor. The first two or three bids were made by persons with whom this history has no concern, but that for £35,000 was made by our friend Mr. John Stedman. Some one present called out "thirty-six," on which Mr. Stedman replied "thirty-seven," and there he ceased to bid. He knew that this was the value of the remaining estate;* he did not want the house. Philip Stanburne whispered something in his ear, after which he cried "forty-two," the last bid having been forty-one. After that he made no further offer, and Philip Stanburne's countenance fell.

The bidding hitherto had been strictly of the nature of investment, but now the seekers after an eligible investment retired from the field, except one or two dealers in estates who intended to sell the place again, at a profit, by private con-

* The reader will remember that the best part of the estate had been mortgaged to Mr. Jacob Ogden.

tract, and who looked upon its architectural and other beauties as marketable qualities. These men went on to £47,000. The place had now reached what was called a "fancy price."

There was a man of rather short stature, with fair hair, a closely shaven face, a greasy cap on his head, a velveteen jacket on his back, and the rest of his person clothed in old corduroy. Fluffs of cotton were sticking about him, and he presented the general appearance of a rather respectable operative. He stood immediately before Philip Stanburne, who did not see his face, and was rather surprised to hear him call out, " Forty-eight."

" Forty-eight, gentlemen!" cried the auctioneer; "going at forty-eight thousand — forty-nine? Forty-nine — going at forty-nine! Come, who says fifty? — we must round the number, you know, gentlemen — who says fifty? Going, going — forty-nine — only forty-nine, going — going " —

The man in the greasy cap said, " Fifty," and the auctioneer, after the usual delays, hearing no other voice amidst the breathless silence of the room, struck the decisive blow with his little hammer, and Wenderholme was sold.

Then the auctioneer beckoned to him the man in the greasy cap, and said in broad Lancashire, and in a tone of somewhat contemptuous familiarity, " You mun go and tell them as sent you here as they'll have to pay hup one-third as deposit-money. One-third o' fifty thousand pound is sixteen thousand six hundred and sixty-six pound, thirteen and four-pence, and that's what them as sent you here has got to pay hup. You can recklect that. It's all sixes, nobbut the one to start wi' and th' odd shillings."

The man in the greasy cap smiled quietly, and took out an old pocket-book. " You've got a pen and ink?"

" I'll write it down for ye, if ye like. And stop — tell me th' name o' them as sent ye."

" There's no need; you'll know it soon enough." And the man in the greasy cap took out a cheque-book, wrote a cheque, filled it, signed it, crossed it, and handed it to the auctioneer. The name signed was "Jacob Ogden," now owner of Wenderholme.

When the auctioneer perceived his error (for the name of Ogden was now mighty in the land), he was covered with confusion, and profuse in perspiration and apology. Jacob affected to forgive him, but in truth he had little to forgive, for no incident could have been more exquisitely agreeable to his feelings. To stand there in public, and in the dress he usually wore at the mill, to sign a heavy cheque, to buy a fine estate, to feel himself the most important man in the room, to be, in his greasy cap and velveteen jacket, the envied man, the observed of all observers, was for him a triumph sweeter than is the triumph of some fair lady, who, in her diamonds and her lace, and her exquisite cleanliness, shines in some great assembly with the purity of a lily and the splendor of a star.

CHAPTER VII.

A FRUGAL SUPPER.

MRS. OGDEN was sitting up for her son Jacob that night, and she had prepared him a little supper of toasted cheese. She had no positive knowledge of the object of his journey to Sootythorn. She was aware that Wenderholme would be sold by auction one of these days, but she did not know exactly whether her son intended to bid for it. There was not much talk generally between the two about the great financial matters — their money-talk ran chiefly upon minutiæ, such as the wages of a servant or the purchase of a cow.

Notwithstanding the great increase of their riches, the mother and son still lived at Milend in their old simple manner. Mrs. Ogden still made all Jacob's shirts and stockings, and still did a great deal of the cooking. The habits of her life had been formed many years before, and she could not endure to depart from them, even when the departure would have been an increase to her comfort. Thus she continued to keep only one girl as a servant, and did most of the work of the house with her own hands. Her happiness depended upon abundance and regularity of occupation; and she acted much more wisely in keeping up the activity of her habits, even though these habits may have been in themselves somewhat inconsistent with her pecuniary position, than she would have done if she had exposed herself to the certain *ennui* of attempting to play the fine lady.

A Frugal Supper.

The girl was gone to bed when Jacob Ogden came back from Sootythorn, and his mother was seated by the kitchen-fire, darning one of his stockings and superintending the toasted cheese. The kitchen at Milend was a clean and spacious room, with stone floor nicely sanded, and plenty of hams and oatcakes hanging from the ceiling. There was a great clock too in one corner, with shining case, and a rubicund figure above the dial, by which were represented the phases of the moon.

The old lady had laid out a small supper-table in the kitchen, and when Jacob came back she told him he was to have his supper there, "for th' fire 'ad gone out i' th' parlor."

So he sat down to eat his toasted cheese, which was a favorite supper of his, and whilst he was eating, his mother took a little oatmeal-porridge with treacle. She rather feared the effects of toasted cheese, believing porridge to be more easily digested.

Neither one nor the other said any thing about the object of the journey to Sootythorn during supper, and there was nothing in Jacob's face to indicate either extraordinary news or unusual elation. In fact, so accustomed was Jacob Ogden to purchasing estates, that he had little of the feeling of elation which attends the young beginner; and after that momentary triumph at Garley's Hotel, any excitement which he may have felt had subsided, and left in his mind no other feeling than the old spirit of calculation. It was the very first time in his life that he had gone beyond the principle of investment, and paid something over and above for the mere gratification of his fancy or his pride, and his reflections were not of unmixed self-congratulation. "Anyhow," he said to himself, "it'll be Ogden of Wendrum, J.P."

However late Jacob Ogden took his supper, he must necessarily smoke his pipe after it (one pipe), and drink his glass of grog. His mother usually went to bed as soon as the water boiled, but this evening she kept moving about in the kitchen, first finding one little thing to set to rights, and then another. At last she stood still in the middle of the floor, and said, —

"Our Jacob!"

"What, mother?"

"Wherestabeen?"*

"Why, you knoan that weel enough, I reckon. I'n been Sootythorn road."

"And what 'as ta been doin'?"

"Nowt nobbut what's reet." †

"What 'as there been at Sootythorn?"

"There's been a sale."

"'An ‡ they been sellin' a mill?"

"Noah."

"And what 'an they been sellin'?"

"Wendrum 'All."

"And who's bout it?"

"I have."

"And what 'an ye gin for 't?"

"Fifty thousand."

"Why, it's ta mich by th' 'auve!"

"'Appen."

Notwithstanding the laconic form of the conversation, Mrs. Ogden felt a strong desire to talk over the matter rather more fully, and to that end seated herself on the other side the kitchen-fire.

"Jacob," she said, as she looked him steadily in the face, "I never knew thee part wi' thy brass b'out five pussent. How will ta get five pussent out o' Wendrum 'All for the fifty thousand?"

"Why, mother, there's investments for brass, and there's investments for pasition. I dunnot reckon to get so much interest out o' Wendrum, but it 'll be Ogden o' Wendrum, J.P."

"Well, now, Jacob, that's what I call spendin' your money

* Where hast thou been.   † Nothing but what is right.   ‡ Have.

for pride!" Mrs. Ogden said this solemnly, and in as pure English as she could command.

"Why, and what if it is? There's plenty more where that coom from. What signifies?"

"And shall you be going to live at Wendrum 'All, Jacob? *I* willn't go there — indeed I willn't; I'll stop at Milend. Why, you'll require ever so many servants. They tell me there's twenty fires to light! And what will become o' the mill when you're over at Wendrum?"

Mrs. Ogden's face wore an expression of trouble and dissatisfaction. Her eyebrows rose higher than usual, and her forehead displayed more wrinkles. But Jacob knew that this was her way, and that in her inmost soul she was not a little gratified at the idea of being the Lady of Wenderholme. For as an ambitious ecclesiastic, promoted to the episcopal throne, rejoices not openly, but affects a decent unwillingness and an overwhelming sense of the responsibilities of his office, so Mrs. Ogden, at every advance in her fortunes, sang her own little *nolumus episcopari*.

"Why, it's thirty miles off, is Wendrum," she went on, complainingly; "and there's no railway; and you'll never get there and back in a day. One thing's plain, you'll never manage the mill and the estate too."

"All the land between this 'ere mill and Wendrum 'All is mine," said Jacob, with conscious dignity; "and I mean to make a road, mother, across the hill from the mill to Wendrum 'All. It'll be nine mile exactly. And I'll have a telegraph from th' countin'-house to my sittin'-room at Wendrum. And I shall take little Jacob into partnership, and when one Jacob's i' one spot t'other Jacob 'll be i' t'other spot. Recklect there's two Jacobs, mother."

"Well, I reckon you'll do as you like, whatever *I* say. But *I*'ll go non to Wendrum. I'll stop 'ere at Shayton while I live (it 'appen willn't be for long) — I'm a Shayton woman bred and born."

"Nonsense, mother. You'll go to Wendrum, and ride over to Milend in your carriage!"

Mrs. Ogden's face assumed an expression of unfeigned amazement.

"A cayridge! a cayridge! Why, what is th' lad thinkin' about now! I think we shall soon be ridin' into prison. Did ever anybody hear the like?"

There is a curious superstition about carriage-keeping which Mrs. Ogden fully shared. It is thought to be the most extravagant, though the most respectable, way of spending money; and an annual outlay which, if dissipated in eating and drinking, or Continental tours, would excite no remark, is considered extravagance if spent on a comfortable vehicle to drive about in one's own neighborhood. Thus Mrs. Ogden considered her son's proposition as revolutionary — as an act of secession from the simplicity of faith and practice which had been their rule of life and the tradition of their family. In short, it produced much the same effect upon her mind as if the Shayton parson had proposed to buy a gilded dalmatic and chasuble.

"There's folk," said Mrs. Ogden, with the air of an oracle — " there's folk as are foolish when they are young, and grow wiser as they advance in years. But there's other folk that is wise in their youth, to be foolish and extravagant at an age when they ought to know better." She evidently was losing her faith in the prudence of her son Jacob. When they had parted for the night, and Mrs. Ogden got into her bed, the last thing she uttered as she stood with her nightcap on, in her long white night-gown, was the following brief ejaculation : —

"A cayridge! à cayridge! What are we comin' to now!"

But the last thing uncle Jacob thought, as he settled his head on his lonely pillow, was, "It'll be Ogden of Wendrum, J.P."

CHAPTER VIII.

AT CHESNUT HILL.

WE return to Garley's Hotel at the conclusion of the sale.

Philip Stanburne had recognized the Colonel, and gone up to him to shake hands. He had not seen him before since the downfall of the Sootythorn Bank, though he had written a very feeling letter, in which he had begged his friend to make use of Stanithburn Peel so long as he might care to remain in Yorkshire. Indeed the Colonel had received many such letters.

Mr. Stedman, on looking about for Philip, saw him with the Colonel, and joined them.

"Where are you staying, Colonel Stanburne?" asked Mr. Stedman.

"I have been staying with my mother lately at Wenderholme Cottage. I have persuaded her to remain there. It is better, I think, that an old lady should not be obliged to change all her habits. I hope the new owner will allow her to remain. She will have very good neighbors in the Prigleys. I gave the living of Wenderholme to Mr. Prigley when the old vicar died, about three months since. He used to be the incumbent of Shayton."

"It will be a great advance for Mr. Prigley. Shayton was a poor living, but I have heard that Wenderholme is much better."

"Wenderholme is worth seven hundred a-year. The Prigleys have been very poor for many years, with their numerous family and the small income they had at Shayton. I am very glad," the Colonel added, with rather a melancholy smile, "that I was able to do this for them before my own ill-luck overtook me. A few months later I should have missed the chance."

"Do you return to Wenderholme to-night? It is late, is it not?"

"No; I mean to sleep here in the hotel."

"Would you accept a bed at Chesnut Hill, Colonel Stanburne? Philip is staying with me."

The Colonel was only too glad to spend the rest of his evening with two real friends, and they were soon in the comfortable dining-room at Chesnut Hill. The Colonel had often met Mr. Stedman, who had stayed once or twice for a night or two at Wenderholme; and he had dined a few times at Chesnut Hill, and had stayed all night, so that the house was not altogether strange to him; though, since he had repeatedly met with Mr. Stedman at Sootythorn and at Stanithburn Peel (where during the last twelve years he had been a frequent visitor), he knew the owner of the mansion much more intimately than the mansion itself.

Ever since the death of poor Alice, a warm friendship had united her father and Philip Stanburne — a friendship which had been beneficial to them both. Each was still sincerely attached to his own convictions, but the great sorrow which they had suffered in common had drawn them together, and Mr. Stedman considered the younger man as nearly related to him as if the intended marriage had actually taken place. Their loss had been of that kind which time may enable us to accept as an inevitable void in our existence, but which no amount of habit can ever obliterate from the memory. Philip still remembered that conversation with Alice in which she had begged him not to desert her father in his old age; and Mr. Stedman, on his part, felt that every kindness which he could show to the man whom his daughter had loved was a kindness to Alice herself. So there was a paternal and filial tie between these two; and though, after Alice's death, Philip had resumed his solitary existence at Stanithburn, and Mr. Stedman continued his business as a cotton manufacturer (for he felt the need of some binding occupation), they made use of each other's houses, as is done by the nearest relatives; and Mr. Stedman spent many a summer day in botanizing about Stanithburn, whilst his friend, when on duty in the militia, always billeted himself at Chesnut Hill.

"What is the last news about our poor friend Anison?" the Colonel asked, when the three were comfortably seated in Mr. Stedman's easy-chairs.

"It cannot be very good news, but it is as good as can be expected. His works and Arkwright Lodge were sold by auction three days since, at Whittlecup."

"And who bought them?"

"The same man, Colonel Stanburne, who purchased Wenderholme this evening — Jacob Ogden of Shayton."

"They must be rich, those Ogdens. I know his brother Isaac very well, and his nephew is a great friend of mine, but I really know nothing of this Jacob."

"He is the only rich one in the family, but he *is* a rich one. He made a great bargain at Whittlecup. He gave twenty thousand for Anison's works, with every thing in them in working order; and to my certain knowledge, Joseph Anison had a capital of thirteen thousand sunk in copper rollers alone.* He paid four thousand for Arkwright Lodge. It's dirt cheap. The house alone cost more than that, and there's thirty acres of excellent land. I wish I'd bought it myself. I missed it by not going to that sale; but Philip and I wanted to bid for Wenderholme, and we stayed away from Whittlecup so as to keep out of temptation."

* The engraved copper rollers used in calico-printing. The larger printing firms sink immense sums in these rollers, far surpassing the above estimate for Mr. Anison, who was only in a moderate way of business.

"And what do you think Mr. Anison will do?"

"He asked Jacob Ogden to let him remain at Whittlecup and manage the works for a very moderate salary, but Jacob declined; and in doing so he did what I never heard of him doing before — he acted directly against his own interest. He 'l' never get such a manager as Anison would have been, but he refused him out of spite. Twelve years ago Madge Anison jilted Jacob Ogden, just when my daughter died. He made her pay up a thousand for breach of promise. She's an old maid now, or something very like one, for she's over thirty-three; but Jacob Ogden hasn't forgiven her for jiltin' him, and never will. Last news I had of Joseph Anison, he was seeking a situation in Manchester, and his three girls 'll have to seek situations too. It's a bad job there isn't one of 'em married — they were as fine lasses as a man need set his eyes on, and in their father's good time they'd scores of offers, but either they looked too high or else they were very difficult to suit, for they never hooked on, somehow."

Philip Stanburne knew rather more about Madge Anison by this time than Mr. Stedman did, and could have enlightened his friends concerning her had he been so minded. The young lady had thrown Jacob Ogden over, as the reader is already aware, for no other purpose than to leave herself free for Philip Stanburne on his return from the Continent after the death of Alice. When he visited his friends at Arkwright Lodge, Miss Anison had not had the degree of prudence necessary to conceal her designs, and Philip (to his intense disgust, for all his thoughts were with the gentle creature he had so recently lost) perceived that he was the object which Margaret had in view. A young lady can scarcely commit a greater mistake than to make advances to a man so saddened as Philip was then; for in such a condition of mind he has not the buoyancy of spirit necessary for a flirtation, and it is only through a flirtation that he can be led to pay his addresses in earnest. Poor Margaret had fatally under-estimated the duration of Philip Stanburne's sorrow, and also the keenness of his perceptions. For instead of his being less observant and easier to manage than he had been before that episode in his life, it had so wrought upon his intellect and his feelings as to be equivalent to the experience of years. In a word, her project had ended in total failure, and the sense of this failure gave a certain petulance and irritability to her manner, and lent a sharpness of sarcasm to her tongue, which did not induce other gentlemen to aspire to that happiness which Philip had refused. So she was Margaret Anison still, and at the present period of our story was trying, not very successfully, to obtain a situation in Manchester.

It was Mr. Stedman's custom, as in Lancashire it is the custom of his class, to have a little supper about nine or ten o'clock — a pleasant and sociable meal, though not always quite suitable to persons of feeble digestion. Colonel Stanburne, on the other hand, according to the custom of *his* class, dined substantially at seven, and took nothing later except tobacco-smoke. This evening, however, he was in a position to conform to the custom of Chesnut Hill; for though he had dined at Mr. Garley's an hour before the time fixed for the sale, he had felt so melancholy about it, and so anxious to know who would be the future possessor of his home, that he had eaten a very poor dinner indeed. But now that the thing was decided, and that he found himself with two such kind and faithful friends (whose manner to him was exactly the same as it had been in the days of his prosperity), John Stanburne's naturally powerful appetite reasserted itself at the expense of Mr. Stedman's cold roast-beef, which, with plenty of pickles and mashed potatoes, formed the staple of the repast.

The Colonel was already beginning to learn the great art of miserable men — the art which enables them to gain in hours of comparative happiness the energy and elasticity necessary for future times of trial — the art of laying unhappiness aside like a pinching boot, and of putting their weary feet into the soft slippers of a momentary contentment. Wenderholme was sold — it belonged to Mr. Jacob Ogden; why think of Wenderholme any more? The Colonel actually succeeded in dismissing the matter from his thoughts for at least five minutes at a time, till a sort of pang would come upon his heart, and he rapidly asked himself what the pang meant, and then he knew that it meant Wenderholme.

One very curious consequence of the great event of that day was this, that whereas the last time he had been to Chesnut Hill (in the days of his prosperity) the place had seemed to him both vulgar and unenviable, he now appreciated certain qualities about the place which before had been by him altogether imperceptible. For example, when he was rich, mere comfort had never been one of his objects. Having the power to create it wherever he might happen to be, he had often done very well without it, and his rooms in barracks, or his den in his own mansion, had been often very destitute thereof. But now that it had become highly probable that comfort would soon be beyond his reach, he began to awaken to a perception of it. The warm red flock-paper on Mr. Stedman's dining-room wall, the good carpet on the floor, the clean white table-cloth, the comfortable morocco-covered chairs — all these things began to attract his attention in quite a novel and remarkable manner. And yet hitherto he had continued to live like a gentleman, therefore, what will it be, I wonder, when he is reduced a good deal lower in the world?

When they had done supper, and were drinking the inevitable grog, Mr. Stedman said to the Colonel, —

"I hope you will forgive me if I am guilty of any indiscretion, Colonel Stanburne, but you know you are with sincere friends. May I ask what your own plans are?"

Mr. Stedman's age, and his evident good-will, made the

question less an indiscretion than an acceptable proof of kindness, and the Colonel took it in that way. "My dear Mr. Stedman," he said in answer, "you know a position like mine is very embarrassing. I am getting on in life — I mean I am getting oldish; I never had a profession by which money could be earned, you know, though I have been in the army, but that's not a trade to live by. As to the colonelcy of the militia, the lord-lieutenant has my resignation. No, I can't see any thing very clearly just now. The only thing I'm fit for is driving a public coach."

Philip Stanburne said, "Why did you refuse to come and live at the Peel? You would have been very welcome — you would be welcome still." It was already publicly understood that the Colonel and Lady Helena were separated, and that Miss Stanburne would either follow her ladyship to Lord Adisham's, or remain with her old grandmother.

"My dear Philip," the Colonel said, very sadly and affectionately, laying his hand on Philip's hand —" my dear Philip, if I were quite old and done for, I would have no false pride. I would come to the Peel and live with you, and you should buy me a suit of clothes once every two years, and give me a little tobacco, and a sovereign or two for pocket-money. I would take all this from you. But you see, Philip, though I'm not a clever man, and though I really have no profession, still my bodily health and strength are left to me, thank God; and so long as I have these, I think it is my duty to try in some way to earn my living for myself. You know that Helena and I are separated — everybody seems to know it now. Well, I got a letter from her father this morning, in which — but stop, I'll show you the letter itself. Will you read it, Mr. Stedman?"

"DEAR SIR, — My daughter Helena desires me to say to you, that as you shared your means with her in the time of your prosperity, so it is her desire that you should share her income now in your adversity. A sum of three hundred a-year will therefore be paid to your credit at any banker's you may be pleased to name.

"Your obedient servant, ADISHAM."

"Well," said Mr. Stedman, "you may still live very comfortably as a single man on such an income as three hundred a-year. It is a great deal of money."

"I have accepted Lady Helena's offer, but not for myself. I will not touch one penny of Lord Adisham's allowance. I have told the banker to pay it over to my mother, whom I have ruined. She has not a penny in the world. However, you see Helena is provided for, since she is living at Lord Adisham's (a very good house to live in), and my mother is provided for, and between them they will keep Edith till I can do something for her; so my mind is easy about these three ladies, and I've nobody to provide for but myself Any man with a sound constitution ought to be able to earn his bread. You see, Philip, my mind is made up. There is still, notwithstanding my misfortune, a spirit of independence in me which will not permit me to live upon the kindness of my friends. But I am very greatly obliged both to you and others — to you more especially."

"Well, Colonel, haven't I a right to offer you some assistance? Are we not relations?"

The Colonel looked at Philip with tender affection, and gently pressed his hand. Then he said to Mr. Stedman: "This young friend of yours never called me a relation of his when I was prosperous, but now when I am a poor man he claims me. Isn't he an eccentric fellow, to lay claim to a poor relation?"

The next morning at breakfast-time the Colonel did not appear. The servant said he had risen very early, and left a note.

"My dear and kind Friends,—I came to a decision in the middle of the night, but will not just now tell you what it is. The decision having been come to, I am determined to act upon it at once, and leave Chesnut Hill to catch the early train. Pray excuse this, and believe me, with much gratitude for all your kindness,

"Yours most truly,   JOHN STANBURNE."

CHAPTER IX.

OGDEN OF WENDERHOLME.

THE Ogdens did not go to live at Wenderholme for a long time, indeed Mrs. Ogden did not even go to see the place; but her son Jacob went over one day in a gig, and, in the course of his stay of a few hours, settled more points of detail than a country gentleman would have settled in a month. He planted an agent there, and took on several of Colonel Stanburne's outdoor servants, including all his gamekeepers, but for the present did not seem inclined to make any use of Wenderholme as a residence. He had been present at the sale of the furniture, where he had bought every thing belonging to the principal rooms, except a few old cabinets and chairs, and other odd matters, of which the reader may hear more in a future chapter.

It had always been a characteristic of the Ogdens not to be in a hurry to enjoy. They would wait, and wait, for any of the good things of this world — perhaps to prolong the sweet time of anticipation, perhaps simply because the habit of saving, so firmly ingrained in their natures, is itself a habit of waiting and postponing enjoyment in favor of ulterior aims. But in the case of Wenderholme, the habit of postponing a pleasure was greatly helped by an especial kind of pride. Both Jacob Ogden and his mother were proud to a degree which may sometimes have been equalled, but can never have been surpassed, by the proudest chiefs of the aristocracy. Their pride, as I have said, was of a peculiar kind, and consisted far more in an intense satisfaction with themselves and their own ways, than in any ambition to be thought, or to become, different from what they were. Now, it would not have been possible to imagine any thing more exquisitely agreeable to this pride of theirs than that Wenderholme Hall should be *treated as an appendage to Milend*, that the great kitchen-gardens at Wenderholme should supply vegetables, and the hothouse grapes, to the simple table in the little plain house at Shayton.' It was delightful to Mrs. Ogden to be able to say, in a tone of assumed indifference or semi-disapproval, "Since our Jacob bought Wenderholme, he's always been wishin' me to go to see it — and they say it's a very fine place — but I don't want to go to see it; Milend is good enough for me." If the hearer expressed a natural degree of astonishment, Mrs. Ogden was inwardly delighted, but showed no sign of it on her countenance. On the contrary, her eyebrows would go up, and the wrinkles upon her forehead would assume quite a melancholy appearance, and her stony gray eyes would look out drearily into vacancy. In short, the impression which both Jacob Ogden and his mother wished to produce upon all their friends and acquaintances after the purchase of Wenderholme was, that the mansion and estate of the Stanburnes could add nothing to the importance of the family at Milend.

So pleasant was it to Mrs. Ogden to be able to say that she had never been to Wenderholme that, although she burned with curiosity to behold its magnificence, she restrained herself month after month. Meanwhile her son Jacob was getting forward very rapidly with a project he had entertained for twelve years — that is, ever since the idea of purchasing Wenderholme had first shaped itself in his mind — the road from his mills in Shayton to the house at Wenderholme, direct across the moors. He set about this with the energy of a little Napoleon (Emerson tells us that the natural chiefs of our industrial classes are all little Napoleons), and in a few weeks the road existed. Posts were set up on the side of it, and a telegraphic wire connected the counting-house at Ogden's mill with a certain little room in Wenderholme Hall, which he destined for his private use.

Even already, though Jacob Ogden is still quietly living at Milend, he knows incomparably more about the Wenderholme property than John Stanburne ever knew, or any of John Stanburne's ancestors before him. He knows the precise condition of every field, or part of a field, and what is to be done to it. Even in such a matter as gardening, the gardener finds him uncheatable, though how he acquired that knowledge is a mystery, for you can hardly call that a "garden" at Milend.

It follows, from all these valuable qualifications of Mr. Jacob Ogden, that he was likely to be an excellent Mentor for such a youth as his nephew, destined to have to support the cares, and see his way through the perplexities, of property. And he took him seriously in hand about this time, with the consent of the lad's father, who was well aware that without experience in affairs his boy's education could not (in any but the narrow sense of the word, as it is used by pedagogues) be considered to be complete.

Young Jacob had to get up regularly at five in the morning and accompany his uncle to the mill, where he saw the hands enter. After this, his time was divided between the counting-house and overlooking; but his duty at the mill was very frequently broken by orders from his uncle to go and inspect the improvements which were in progress on his various estates, especially, at this particular time, the road from Shayton to Wenderholme. The youth made these journeys on horseback, and, being uncommonly well mounted, accomplished them more rapidly than his uncle Jacob, with all his shrewdness, ever calculated upon. In this way the inspection of the new road permitted very frequent visits to Wenderholme Cottage, where, for the present, Miss Edith resided with her grandmother.

CHAPTER X.

YOUNG JACOB AND EDITH.

THE state of affairs between Edith and young Jacob was this. Nothing had been said of marriage, but their attachment was as perfectly understood between them as if it had been openly expressed. The misfortune of their situation had been, that although many circumstances had been decidedly favorable to them, it had never been possible to unite all the favorable circumstances together at the same time, so as to get themselves formally engaged. In the days of Colonel Stanburne's splendor and prosperity the Milend influence had been openly encouraging, but Lady Helena had warned Edith in such a decided way against allowing herself to form a plebeian attachment, the allusion to young Jacob being (as it was intended to be) as intelligible as if she had named him, that it had been considered prudent by both the lovers to refrain from compromising the future by precipitation, and they had waited in the hope that, by the pressure of constantly increasing riches, her ladyship's opposition might finally be made to give way. If Colonel Stanburne had continued prosperous, the Milend influence was so strongly, even eagerly, in favor of the alliance, that it would have subsidized its candidate very largely ; and as its power of subsidizing increased every day, it was evident that, by simply waiting, his prospects would steadily improve. But the Colonel's ruin, utter and hopeless as it was, had set the Milend influence on the other side ; and nobody who knew the obstinacy of Jacob Ogden in opposition, and the relentless lengths to which he would go to get himself obeyed, or to inflict punishment on those who had opposed him, could doubt that, if his nephew refused compliance in this instance, it would be equivalent to a total renunciation of his prospects.

Edith Stanburne had inherited much of her mother's perspicacity, with the Colonel's frank and genial manner. Some people, Mrs. Prigley amongst the number, disapproved of Edith's manner, and considered her a "bold girl," because she looked people straight in the face, and had not yet learned the necessity for dissimulating her sentiments. But what experienced man of the world would not give half his subtlety for that boldness which comes from the perfect harmony of our nature with its surroundings? Why, that is simply a definition of happiness itself! When we have learned to be careful, it is because we have perceived that between our real selves and the world around us there is so little harmony that they would clash continually, so we invent a false artificial self that may be in harmony with the world, and make it live our outward life for us, talk for us in drawing-rooms and at the dinner-table, and go through the weary round of public pleasures and observances.

It is the worst possible sign of approaching unhappiness when courage begins to give way, and this hour had come for Edith. Young Jacob, relying upon the speed of his horse, had, on one or two occasions, prolonged his visits to Wenderholme Cottage long enough to excite his uncle's suspicions. Jacob Ogden inquired whether Miss Stanburne was with her mother at Lord Adisham's, or with her grandmother at Wenderholme. The young man said he "believed" she was with her grandmother.

"Oh, you 'believe,' do you, young un? Cannot you tell me for certain?"

Young Jacob was no match for his keen-eyed relations at Milend, who saw through the whole matter in a minute.

"That horse o' yours is a fast un, little Jacob, but it isn't quite sharp enough to make up for three hours' courtin' at Wendrum."

The next day young Jacob was sent to look over works in a totally opposite direction; and as he had a good many measurements to take, there was no chance of getting any time to himself. Twenty-four hours later Miss Stanburne received the following letter:—

"MADAM,— I have discovered that my nephew has been idling his time away at Wenderholme Cottage. You may, perhaps, know how he was occupied. Excuse me if I say that, if my nephew idles his time away at Wenderholme Cottage, *he will never be a rich man.*

"Yours truly, JACOB OGDEN."

The note was very intelligible, and the consequence of it was, that Edith resolved to sacrifice herself. "I love him too much," she said, "to ruin him."

The reader may remember one Jerry Smethurst whom Isaac Ogden met at Whittlecup when on duty in the militia, and with whom he got drunk for the last time. It is twelve years since then, a long interval in any place, but an especially long interval in Shayton, where *delirium tremens* carries off the mature males with a rapidity elsewhere unknown. There had been hundreds of deaths from drinking in that township since 1853; and of all the jolly companions who used to meet at the Red Lion, the only one remaining was the proprietor of Twistle Farm. James Hardcastle, the innkeeper, was dead; Seth Schofield was in Shayton churchyard, and so was Jerry Smethurst. A new generation was drinking itself to death in that parlor, served by another landlord.

Most of these worthies had ruined themselves in fortune as in health. Men cannot spend their time in public-houses without their business feeling the effects of it; and they cannot fuddle their intellects with beer and brandy and preserve their clearness for arithmetic. So, as the prosperity of a society is the prosperity of the individuals composing it, Shayton was not a very prosperous locality, and, in comparison with Sootythorn, lagged wofully behindhand in the race. A few men, however, managed somehow to reconcile business and the brandy-bottle, and the most successful conciliator of pleasure and affairs had been the notable Jerry Smethurst. He managed it by never drinking any thing before the mill was closed; drink, to him, was the reward of the labors of the day, and not their accompaniment. His constitution had been strong enough to resist this double strain of laborious days and convivial evenings for a much longer time than Dr. Bardly ever expected; and when the end came, which it did by a single attack of *delirium tremens*, succeeded by a fit of apoplexy (the patient had always apprehended apoplexy), Mr. Smethurst's affairs were found to be in admirable order, and his only daughter, then a fine girl of fourteen, became heiress to an extensive mill and a quantity of building land, as well as many shops and tenements in the interior of the town which would infallibly increase in value. In a word, Sarah Smethurst was worth forty thousand now, and would be worth a hundred thousand in twenty years; so that, as the charms of her youth faded, the man fortunate enough to win her might count upon a progressive compensation in the increase of her estate.

Jacob Ogden, senior, was very accurately acquainted with Miss Smethurst's property, and could calculate its future value to a nicety. He had the best opportunities for knowing these matters, being one of Jerry Smethurst's trustees. When Colonel Stanburne was a rich man, Jacob Ogden would have preferred Miss Stanburne for his nephew to any girl in Sally Smethurst's position; for though nobody could love and appreciate money more than Jacob did, he wished to see his nephew take a higher place in society than money of itself would be able to procure for him. As in mixing a glass of grog the time comes when we want no more spirit, but turn our attention to the sugar-basin, although there can be no doubt that the spirit is the main thing (since without it the glass would be nothing but *eau sucrée*), so, when we want to make that composite of perfections, a gentleman, there is a time when money is no longer needed, though that is the main element of his strength, and we turn our attention to the sugar-basin of the *comme il faut*. When Jacob Ogden, senior, was favorable to the Wenderholme match, it was not so much on account of Miss Stanburne's money as on account of her decided position as a young lady of the aristocracy; and when the Colonel was ruined, he did not disapprove of the match because Miss Stanburne would have no fortune, but because her position as member of a county family had been upset by her father's bankruptcy.

Well, if the lad could not marry like a gentleman, he should marry like a prince among cotton-spinners, and contract alliance with a princess of his own order. Sally Smethurst was such a princess. Therefore it was decided that young Jacob should espouse Sally Smethurst.

And a very nice lass she was, too — a nice fat lass, with cheeks like a milkmaid, that anybody might have been glad to kiss. Mrs. Ogden invited her to stop at Milend, and young Jacob saw her every day. But the effect of this acquaintance was precisely contrary to uncle Jacob's plans and intentions. Sally had never been out of Shayton in her life, except to a school at Lytham, and she had not a word to say. Neither was her deportment graceful. A good lass enough, and well to do, but not the woman with whom an intelligent man would be anxious to pass his existence.

The image of Miss Stanburne, already somewhat idealized by absence, was elevated to the divine by this contrast. There is no surer way of making a noble youth worship some noble maiden, than by presenting to him a virgin typical of the commonplace, and ordering him to marry her. Edith became henceforth the object of young Jacob's ardent and chivalrous adoration. Two fortunes — his uncle's and Sally Smethurst's — making in the aggregate a prodigious heap of money, were offered to him as the reward of infidelity, and the higher the bribe rose, the higher rose his spirit of resistance.

Sally had come to Milend on a Wednesday. She was to stay Sunday over, and go to Shayton Church with the Ogdens. On Saturday night, at tea-time, young Jacob declared his intention of going to Twistle Farm.

"Why, and willn't ye stop Sunday with us and Miss Smethurst, and go to Shayton Church?"

"I haven't seen my father for a fortnight."

"Then, all that I've got to say," observed Mrs. Ogden, "is, that it's your father's own wickedness that's the cause of it. If he came regularly to church, as he ought to do, you'd be sure to see him to-morrow, and every Sunday as well, and you'd have no need to go up to Twistle Farm. I could like to drag him to Shayton Church by the hair of his head, that I could!" Here Mrs. Ogden paused and sipped her tea — then she resumed, —

"I declare I *will not have* you goin' up to Twistle Farm and missin' church in that way. It's awful to think of! You miss church many a Sunday to go and stop with your father, who should know better, and set you a better example."

The lad drank his scalding tea, and rose from the table. He was not a boor, however; and, offering his hand to Miss Smethurst, he said, very courteously, "I am sorry, Miss Smethurst, not to have the pleasure of going to church with you to-morrow; it looks rude of me, but many things trouble me just now, and I must talk them over, both with my father and somebody else." And with that, and a simple good-night to the elder people, he left the room.

The owner of Twistle Farm had become a great recluse since he gave up drinking, except during his weeks of active duty in the militia, and occasional visits to his brother officers.

In fact, a Shayton man, not in business, must either be a drunkard or a recluse; and Ogden, by his own experience, had learned to prefer the latter. Young Jacob, however, had a friend in Shayton who did not lead quite such a retired life, and whose opinion on the present crisis it might be worth while to ask for. Need I say that this friend was the worthy doctor, Mr. Bardly?

So, when the young gentleman rode through the town on his way to Twistle Farm, he turned into the Doctor's yard.

The twelve years that have passed since we saw the Doctor have rather aged him, but they have certainly deducted nothing from the vigor of his mind. He received his young friend with his old heartiness of manner, and made him promise to stop supper with him. "You'll ride up to Twistle Farm after supper; your father willn't be gone to bed — he sits up reading till one o'clock in the morning. I wish he wouldn't. I'm sure he's injuring his eyes."

Young Jacob laid the perplexities of his case before his experienced friend. The Doctor heard him for nearly an hour with scarcely a word of comment. Then he began:—

"I'll tell you what it is, little Jacob; you're not independent, because you haven't got a profession, don't you see? You've had a fine education, but it's worth nothing to live by, unless you turn schoolmaster; and in England, education is altogether in the hands o' them parsons. Your father isn't rich enough to keep a fine gentleman like you, never talk o' keepin' a fine wife. That's how it is as you're dependent on them at Milend, and they know it well enough. You'll always be same as a childt for your uncle and your grandmother, and you'll 'ave to do just as they bid you. As long as your uncle lives you'll be a minor. I know him well enough. He governs everybody he can lay his hands on, and your grandmother's exactly one o' th' same sort; she's a governin' woman, is your grandmother — a governin' woman. There's a certain proportion of women as is made to rule folk, and she's one on 'em."

" Well, but, Doctor, what would you advise me to do?"

" I 'm comin' to that, lad. There 's two courses before you, and you mun choose one on 'em, and follow it out. You mun either just make up your mind to submit to them at Milend "—

" And desert Edith?"

" Yes, to be sure, and wed Sally Smethurst beside, and be manager of Ogden's mills, and collect his cottage-rents, and dun poor folk, and be cowed for thirty years by your uncle, and have to render 'count to him of every hour of every day — for he 'll live thirty years, will your uncle; or else you mun learn a profession, and be independent on him."

" Independence would be a fine thing certainly, but it is not every profession that would suit the aristocratic prejudices of Lady Helena. I think it very likely the Colonel would give his consent, for he has always treated me very kindly, and he must have seen that I was thinking of Edith, but with Lady Helena the case is different. She was never encouraging. She might give way before a large fortune like my uncle's, and the prospect of reinstating Edith at Wenderholme, but if I were a poor man in a profession all her aristocratic prejudices would be active against me. Besides, there are only two professions which the aristocracy really recognizes, the army and the church. The army is not a trade to live by, and the church "—

" Nay, never turn parson, lad, never be a parson!"

Young Jacob smiled at the Doctor's sudden earnestness, and soon reassured him. " I have no vocation for the church," he said quietly but decidedly, " and shall certainly never take orders." Then he went on, half talking to himself and half addressing the Doctor. " There is no other profession by which an income may be earned that Lady Helena would be likely to tolerate. People like her look down upon attorneys and — and "—

" And Doctors!" added Bardly, laughing, " except when they think there 's summat wrong i' their insides, and then they 're as civil as civil."

"I cannot see my way at all, for if I please my uncle I am not to think of Edith, and if I displease him I am to have no money, so that it will be no use thinking about Edith."

"Are you sure of the young woman herself? D' ye think she would have you if you had just a decent little income from a profession such as doctorin'? It strikes me 'at if th' lass herself is o' your side, who 'll bring her feyther to her way o' thinkin', an' her feyther 'll find ways o' makin' his wife listen to him."

Young Jacob's eyes sparkled, and his heart beat. "I believe she would, Doctor, I do really believe she would."

"Tell her then as you 'll be Shayton doctor. It 's worth £500 a-year to me; and you might increase it, an active young fellow like you. Come and learn doctorin' wi' me. I 'll allow you £250 a-year to start wi', if you get wed to Miss Stanburne; your father will do as much, — that 'll be £500; and you may live on that, if you live quietly. And then when there 's chilther, there 'll be more brass."

Young Jacob's eyes moistened. "I 'd take help from you, sir, sooner than from anybody else, but I cannot accept half your income."

"Half my income, young man! Do you know who you are speaking to? You 're speaking to one of the Shayton capitalists, sir. I 've never been much of a spender, and have had neither wife nor child to spend for me. I can live well enough on the interest of my railway shares, young gentleman, and yet I 've other investments. I can say like your Uncle Jacob that nobody knows what I 'm worth. How can they know, if I never told 'em?"

Here the Doctor gave a very knowing wink and a grin, and shook young Jacob very heartily by the hand.

CHAPTER XI.

EDITH'S DECISION.

SUCH was young Jacob's piety, that rather than remain all the Sunday at Twistle Farm with that heterodox father of his, he rode over to Wenderholme in order to attend divine service there.

He got to church in very good time; and when he took his seat in Mrs. Stanburne's pew, the ladies had not yet arrived. Indeed, even the Prigleys had not taken their places, so that young Jacob had something to interest him in watching the gradual arrival of the members of the congregation.

The reader may remember that Mrs. Stanburne had a small pew of her own appertaining to the Cottage, whereas there was a large pew appertaining to the Hall. Mrs. Stanburne still remained faithful to her little pew, and the great comfortable enclosure (a sort of drawing-room without ceiling, and with walls only four feet high) had been empty since the departure of the Colonel and Lady Helena.

The congregation gradually constituted itself; the Prigleys soon filled the pew belonging to the vicarage; the principal farmers on the Wenderholme estate penned themselves like sheep (Mr. Prigley's sheep) in their narrow wooden partitions; and lastly came Mrs. Stanburne and Edith. When people meet in a pew at church, their greetings are considerably abridged; and if Edith's face was more than usually sad, her lover might, if he liked, attribute the expression to religious seriousness.

Young Jacob kneeled whilst Mr. Prigley read the general

confession, and when he got up again his eyes wandered over the pews before him, before they settled again upon his prayer-book.

He gave a start of astonishment. In the great Wenderholme pew, quietly in one corner of it, sat the present owner of the estate!

Young Jacob's heart beat. He knew that the plot was thickening, and that a great struggle was at hand. But he was in a better position to meet his uncle to-day than he had been yesterday. Yesterday he had been undecided, and though inwardly rebellious, had had no plans; to-day he was resolved, and *had* plans. The conversation with the Doctor had been succeeded by another conversation with his father, and the consequence was that young Jacob was resolved that, rather than give up Edith, he would go to the length of a rupture with the authorities at Milend.

Mr. Prigley preached one of his best sermons that day, but neither of the two Jacob Ogdens paid very much attention to it, I am afraid. They were polishing their weapons for the combat. Each was taking the gravest resolutions, each was resolving upon the sacrifice of long-cherished hopes; for, notwithstanding the hardness of the manufacturer's nature, he had still rather tender feelings about "little Jacob," as he still habitually called him, and it was painful to think that a youth in all respects so perfectly the gentleman should not succeed to a splendid position for which he had been expressly and elaborately prepared. On the other hand, the manufacturer could not endure that anybody should thwart his will and not be sufficiently punished for it; and if little Jacob persisted in marrying in opposition to the authorities at Milend, the only punishment adequate to an offence so heinous was the extreme one of disinheritance.

Both the hostile parties were made aware that the service was at an end by the general movement of the congregation. Jacob Ogden left his pew before anybody else, and walked straight to that of Mrs. Stanburne. He bowed slightly to the ladies, and beckoned to young Jacob, who came to the pew-door. Then he whispered in his ear, —

"Come and have your dinner with me at Wendrum 'All."

"I cannot, uncle. I've promised to lunch at the Cottage."

"You'd better have your dinner with me. If you stop at the Cottage, it'll be worse for you and it'll be worse for 'er."

"Do what you like, sir; my mind is made up."

"Very well; you'll rue it."

And the owner of Wenderholme walked alone across the park, and dined alone in the great dining-room. During dinner (an extravagance very rare at all times with him, and in solitude unprecedented), he ordered a bottle of champagne.

Meanwhile young Jacob lunched with the two ladies at the Cottage. Mrs. Stanburne saw that there was something wrong, some cause of trouble and anxiety, so she did her best to remove the burden which seemed to oppress the minds of the young people. Old Mrs. Stanburne had great powers of conversation, and *made* young Jacob talk. She made him talk about Oxford, and then she made him talk about his present occupations, and of the transition from one to the other. Finally she asked him how he liked the life of a cotton-manufacturer.

"Not much, Mrs. Stanburne. But it signifies very little whether I liked it or not, for I have left it."

"Left it! Well, but is not that very imprudent? When gentlemen have a great deal of property in factories, they ought to know all about it, and I have always heard that the only way to do that is to pass a year or two in the trade."

"Very true. But then I shall never have any property in factories, so there is no occasion for me to learn the trade."

Mrs. Stanburne was much astonished, but her good-breeding

struggled against curiosity. Edith did not seem to be paying any attention to what was going forward; she looked out of the window, and it was evident that she was mentally absent.

"Edith," Mrs. Stanburne said at last, "do you hear what Jacob says? He says he has left business. I think it is very imprudent; and when I say so, he tells me that he will never have any factories."

Edith lent the most languid attention to her grandmother's piece of information. Her whole conduct was just the reverse of her usual way of behaving. Formerly she had taken the liveliest interest in every thing that concerned her lover, so, to *make* her listen, he blurted out the truth suddenly in one sentence.

"My uncle has disinherited me. I am going to be a doctor. I am going to learn the profession with Mr. Bardly in Shayton."

Mrs. Stanburne was more surprised by this news than Edith was. "But *why?*" she asked, emphatically; "*why* has he disinherited you? I thought you were on the best possible terms. He spoke to you to-day as he was going out of church."

Young Jacob was silent for a minute. Mrs. Stanburne came back to the charge. "But *why*, I say — *why?*"

"My uncle wants me to marry a girl of his own choosing, called Sally Smethurst."

Here young Jacob paused, then he took courage and added, — "and I, Mrs. Stanburne, have ventured for some years past to indulge dreams and hopes which may never be realized. You know what my dreams have been. I had hoped that perhaps my plain common name might have been forgotten, and that as you and Colonel Stanburne had always been very kind to me, and Miss Edith had never wounded me by any haughtiness or coldness, I had hoped that perhaps some day any difficulties which existed might be overcome, and that she would accept me with the consent of her parents."

Edith Stanburne rose from her seat and quietly left the room. There was no agitation visible in her face, but it was very pale.

"My dear Jacob," Mrs. Stanburne said decidedly, "we like you very much — we have always liked you very much, and you have always behaved honorably, and as a gentleman. But I am sure that Edith would not sacrifice your prospects. Every thing forbids it; our esteem for yourself forbids it, and our pride forbids it. Besides, I have not authority to allow you two young people to engage yourselves without the consent of the Colonel and Lady Helena."

"May I not speak to Miss Stanburne?"

"It would be better that you should not speak to her in private, but you may speak to her if you like in my presence."

"I should be glad to know what she herself really thinks."

Mrs. Stanburne left the room, and after ten minutes had elapsed, which seemed to young Jacob like a century, she returned, accompanied by her grand-daughter.

Edith was still pale, but she had a look of great self-possession. What was going on in her mind just then may be best expressed by the following little soliloquy: —

"Poor, dear Jacob, how I do love him! What a paradise it would be, that simple, quiet life with him — at Shayton, anywhere in the world! But I love him too much to ruin him, so I must be hard now." And then she acted her part.

Looking at her lover coldly, she was the first to speak. "Mr. Ogden," she said, "I may sink a good deal in your esteem by what I am going to say to you, but my own future must be considered as well as yours. We should be sorry to sacrifice your prospects, but I am thinking of myself also. I do not think that I could live contentedly as a surgeon's wife at Shayton."

Young Jacob was astounded. This from Edith! The very last thing he had ever anticipated was an objection of the selfish kind from her. He had counted upon all obstacles but this; and all other obstacles were surmountable, but this was insurmountable. He saw at once that it would be madness to marry a young lady who despised his life, and the labors which he went through for her sake.

If he could only have known! She, poor thing, was new in this game of cruelty with a kind intention, and she played it with even more than necessary hardness. Perhaps she felt that without this overstrung hardness she could not deceive him at all; that the least approach to tenderness would be fatal to her purpose. She had imagination enough to conceive and act a part utterly foreign to her character, but not imagination enough to act a part only just sufficiently foreign to herself to serve her immediate end. So there was a harsh excess in what she did.

"Miss Stanburne," he said at last, "this gives me great pain."

The poor girl writhed inwardly, but she maintained a serene countenance, and, looking young Jacob full in the face, said, with a well-imitated sneer, —

"I may say with truth that it has latterly been agreeable to me to think that the daughter of Colonel Stanburne would one day live at Wenderholme. — But I confess I have not the sort of heroism which would consent to be a surgeon's wife in such a place as Shayton."

"If these are your reasons, Miss Stanburne, I have done. A man would be a fool to sacrifice his prospects, and slave at a profession all his life, for a woman who paid him with contempt. And I think I may say that you dismiss me with uncommon coolness. I've loved you these twelve years — I've loved you ever since I was a child. I never loved any other woman; and the reward of this devotion is, that I am sent away when my prospects are clouded, without a sign of emotion or a syllable to express regret. I think you might say you are sorry, at any rate."

"Very well, I will say that. I am sorry."

By a supreme effort of acting, Edith put an expression into her face which conveyed the idea that she considered emotion ridiculous, and young Jacob's own conduct as verging slightly upon the absurd. This stung him to the quick.

"Miss Stanburne," he said, after a pause, "this conversation is leading to no good. It is useless to prolong it."

"I quite agree with you."

And he was gone.

If he could have seen what passed after his departure, he would have gone back to Shayton in a very different frame of mind. Edith had acted her part and held out bravely to the last, but when Jacob was once fairly out of the house, the faithful heart could endure its self-inflicted torture no longer, and she ran upstairs to her bed-room and locked the door, and burst into bitter tears. "How good and brave he is, and how he loves me! It is hard, it is *very* hard, to have to throw away a heart like his. But I will not be his ruin — I never will be his ruin!" Then a thousand tender recollections came into her memory — recollections of the long years of his faithful love and service. It had begun in their childhood, when first she called him "Charley," giving him one of her own names; it had continued year after year until this very day, when he would have sacrificed all for her, and she had treated him with coldness and cruelty — *she* who so loved him! And to think that he would *never know the truth* — that the long dreary future would wear itself gradually out until both of them were in their graves, and that he would never know how her heart yearned to him, and remained faithful to him always! That thought was the hardest and bitterest of them all, *that he would never know*; that all his life he would retain that misconception about her which she herself had so carefully created! It is easy to bear the bad opinion of people we care nothing about, but when those we most love disapprove, how eagerly we desire their absolution!

Edith was not quite so strong as she herself believed. The

late events had tried her courage to the utmost, and outwardly she seemed to have borne them well; but they had strained her nervous system a good deal, and this last trial of her fortitude had been too much, even for her. Her agony rapidly passed from mental grief into an uncontrollable crisis of the nerves. She went through this alone, lying upon her bed, sobbing and moaning, her face on the pillow, her hands convulsively agitated. Then came utter vacancy, and after the vacancy a slow, painful awakening to the new sadness of her life.

CHAPTER XII.

JACOB OGDEN'S TRIUMPH.

AT length the great day arrived, towards the end of October, when the new road from Shayton to Wenderholme was to be solemnly inaugurated.

Mr. Jacob Ogden had made all his arrangements with that administrative ability which distinguished him. He had gone into every detail just as closely as if the work of this great day had been the earning of money instead of its expenditure. The main features of the programme were: 1. A procession from Shayton to Wenderholme by the new route. 2. A grand dinner at Wenderholme. 3. A ball.

The procession was to leave Shayton at noon precisely; and about half-past eleven, a magnificent new carriage, ornamented with massive silver, and drawn by two superb gray horses, whose new harness glittered in the sunshine, rolled up to Mrs. Ogden's door. On the box sat a fine coachman in livery, and a footman jumped down from behind to knock at the Milend front door.

Just at the same moment Mr. Jacob Ogden walked quietly up the drive, and when the door opened he walked in. The splendid servants respectfully saluted him.

The Shayton tailor had surpassed himself for this occasion, and Mr. Jacob looked so well dressed that anybody would have thought his clothes had been made at Sootythorn. He wore kid gloves also.

But however well dressed a man may be, his splendor can never be comparable to a lady's, especially such a lady as

Mrs Ogden, who had a fearlessness in the use of colors like that which distinguished our younger painters twenty years ago. She always managed to adorn herself so that every thing about her looked bright, except her complexion and her eyes. Behold her as the door opens ! The Queen in all her glory is not so fine as the mistress of Milend ! What shining splendor ! What dazzling effulgence ! A blind man said that he imagined scarlet to be as the sound of a trumpet ; but the vision of Mrs. Ogden was equal to a whole brass band.

"Why, and whose cayridge is this 'ere, Jacob?"

"Cayridge, mother? It's nobbut a two-horse fly, fro' Manchester, new painted."

The fact was, it was Mrs. Ogden's own carriage, purchased by her son without her knowledge or consent ; but, to avoid a scene before his new domestics, he preferred the above amiable little fiction. So Mrs. Ogden stepped for the first time into her carriage without being aware that she had attained that great object of the *nouveau riche.* There was no danger that she would recognize the armorial bearings which decorated the panels and the harness. Jacob himself had not known them a month before, but he had sent "name and county" to a heraldic establishment in Lincoln's Inn Fields ; and, as his letter had been duly accompanied by a post-office order, three days afterwards he had received a very neat drawing of his coat of arms, emblazoned in azure and gold. It was cheaper than going to the College of Arms, and did just as well.

There was nobody in the new carriage except Mrs. Ogden and her son. Miss Smethurst was invited, but she had a carriage and pair of her own, which she used to do honor to the occasion. Many other friends of the Ogdens (friends or business acquaintances) also came in their carriages, for the tradesmen of those parts had generally adopted the custom of carriage-keeping during the last few years. Even our friend the Doctor now kept a comfortable brougham, in which he joined the procession. Mr. Isaac Ogden of Twistle Farm, and Mr. Jacob Ogden, Jr., his son, joined the procession on horseback, riding very fine animals indeed. A pack of harriers was kept a short distance from Shayton, and it had been agreed that all the gentlemen of the hunt who had invitations should be asked to come as equestrians.

Jacob Ogden had contrived to give a public character to his triumph by his gift of the new road to the township. The magistrates for the time being were to be the trustees of it, hence the magistrates (including one or two country gentlemen of some standing) found themselves compelled to take part in the triumph. All men were that day compelled to acknowledge Jacob Ogden's greatness, and to do him homage.

The telegraph was already established, and when the Shayton procession started on its way, the fact was known instantaneously at Wenderholme. At the same moment a counter-procession left Wenderholme on horseback to meet the one coming from Shayton. The Yorkshire procession consisted chiefly of the tenants of the estate on horseback, headed by the agent. Most of them were in any thing but a congratulatory frame of mind, but as they dreaded the anger of their landlord, they rode forth to meet him to a man.

A holiday had been given at the mill, and all the mill hands were to accompany the Shayton procession for two miles upon the road, after which they were to return to Shayton, and there make merry at Mr. Ogden's expense. Most of the hands belonged to benefit clubs such as the Odd Fellows, the Druids, the Robin Hood, and so on; and they borrowed for the occasion the banners used in the solemnities of these societies, and their picturesque and fanciful costumes. These added immensely to the effect, and gave the procession a richness and a variety which it would otherwise have lacked.

The departure of the *cortège* had been timed at the dinner-hour, when all the mills were loosed, so that the whole Shayton population might witness it. As it moved slowly along the streets, the crowd was as dense as if Royalty itself had made a progress through the town. Mrs. Ogden repeatedly recognized acquaintances in the crowd, and bowed and smiled most graciously from her carriage-window — indeed a queen could hardly have looked more radiant or more gracious. Seeing her good-humor, Jacob ventured to inform her that she was "sitting in her own carriage."

" Sitting in my own cayridge! Well, then, stop th' horses, for I s'll get out."

"Nay, nay, mother, you munnut do so — you munnut do so. You 'll stop o' th' procession. There's no stoppin' now. It's too latt for stoppin'."

" Well, if I'd known I'd never a coom! What is th' folk sayin', thinken ye? Why, they're o' sayin,' one to another, ' There's Mistress Ogden in her new cayridge, an' who's as fain * as fain.' "

" Well, mother, and what if they do say so? What means it?"

" Draw them there blinds down."

" Nay, but I willn't. We aren't goin' to a funeral."

After a while Mrs. Ogden began to look at the nice blue lining of her carriage somewhat more approvingly. At last she said, " Jacob, I'n never thanked thee. Thank ye, Jacob — thank ye. I shalln't live to use it for long, but it 'll do for little Jacob wife at afther."

When Mrs. Ogden had made this little speech, her son knew that the carriage difficulty was at an end, and indeed she never afterwards evinced any repugnance to entering that very handsome and comfortable vehicle.

The procession moved at a walking pace for the first two miles, on account of the people on foot. When these, however, had returned in the direction of Shayton, the speed was somewhat increased, though, as the road steadily ascended till it reached the Yorkshire border, the horses could not go

---

* Fain is a combination of happy and proud. It answers very nearly to a certain sense of the French word "content."

very fast. The road, too, being quite new, the macadam was rather rough, though Jacob Ogden had sent a heavy iron roller, drawn by fourteen powerful horses, from one end to the other.

The weather could not possibly have been more favorable, and it would be difficult to imagine a more cheerful and exhilarating route. There had been a slight frost during the night, and the air of the high moorland was deliciously fresh and pure. The startled grouse frequently whirred over the heads of the horsemen, and made not a few of them regret the absence of their fowling-pieces, and the present necessity for marching in military order. The view became gradually more and more extensive, till at length, on approaching the border, a splendid prospect was visible on both sides, stretching in Lancashire far beyond Shayton to the level land near Manchester — and in Yorkshire, beyond Wenderholme and Rigton to the hills near Stanithburn Peel. A landmark had been erected on the border, and as the Shayton procession approached it, the body of horsemen from Wenderholme were seen approaching it from the other side. It had been arranged that they should meet at the stone.

When both processions had stopped, the Wenderholme agent came and presented an address to Mrs. Ogden, which he read in a loud voice, and then handed to her in the carriage. She was graciously pleased to say a few words in reply, which were not audible to the people about. This ceremony being over, the combined procession formed itself in order of march, and began to descend the long slope towards Wenderholme.

The road entered the village, and therefore did not go quite directly to the Hall. As it had been Jacob Ogden's intention from the first to play the part of Public Benefactor in this matter, he guarded the privacy of his mansion.

At the entrance of the village there was a triumphal arch made of heather and evergreens, and decorated with festoons of colored calico. Here the procession paused a second time, whilst the villagers came to make their little offering to Mrs. Ogden.

The lord of Wenderholme was both surprised and offended by the absence of Mr. Prigley. "I'll make him pay for't," he thought, "if he wants out * doin' at his church, or any subscriptions, or the like o' that." Indeed, the absence of Mr. Prigley was the more surprising that it was contrary to the traditions of his caste, usually sufficiently ready to do honor to the powers that be.

Also, Jacob Ogden thought that the church bells might have rung for him. But they didn't ring. A hostile Prigley or Stanburne influence was apparent there also. It was irritating to have the great triumph marred by this pitiful ecclesiastical opposition. "He shall rue it," said Jacob, inwardly—"he shall rue it!"

A table had been set in the middle of Wenderholme green, and on this table was a large and massive silver inkstand, and in the inkstand a gold pen with a jewelled penholder. Here Jacob Ogden descended from his carriage, and, surrounded by all the chief personages in the procession, sat down under a spreading oak, and signed the deed of gift by which the road from Shayton to Wenderholme was transferred in trust to the Shayton magistrates and their successors for ever and ever.

The inkstand bore an inscription, and was formally presented to Mr. Ogden. And a great shout rose—all John Stanburne's former tenants distinguishing themselves in the "hip, hip," &c.

After that the procession entered Wenderholme Park, and Mrs. Ogden descended at the grand entrance, and moved across the hall, and up the tapestried staircase.

* Any thing.

CHAPTER XIII.

THE "BLOW-OUT."

THE reader is not to suppose, from the parsimony which marked the habitual life of Jacob Ogden and his mother, that when they had made up their minds to what they called a "blow-out," there would be any meanness or littleness in their proceedings. Under all circumstances they acted with clear minds, knowing what they were doing; and when they resolved to be extravagant, they *were* extravagant. The fine principle of that grand and really moral motto, "*Pecca fortiter*," was thoroughly understood and consistently acted upon by the man who had won Wenderholme by his industry and thrift. When he sinned, there was no weak compromise with conscience — he did it manfully and boldly, and no mistake. He never "muddled away" a sovereign, but his triumph cost him many a hundred sovereigns, and he knew beforehand precisely what he was going to spend. When it was all over he would pay the piper, and lock up his cash-box again, and return to his old careful ways.

The Ogdens did not receive many visitors at Milend, and yet they had rather an extensive acquaintance amongst people of their own class — rich people belonging to trade, and living in the great manufacturing towns. And to this festivity they had invited everybody they knew. The house of Wenderholme, large as it was, was filled with Jacob Ogden's guests, and his mother did the honors with a homely but genuine hospitality, which made everybody feel kindly disposed to her; and though they could not help laughing a little at her now and then, they did it without malice. The reader will remember that, from a sort of pride which distinguished her, she had refrained from visiting Wenderholme until the completion of the new road; and as the chariot of the Olympic victor entered his city by a breach in the wall, so Mrs. Ogden's carriage came to Wenderholme by a route which no carriage had ever before traversed. It would have been better, however, in some respects, if the good lady had familiarized herself a little with the splendors of Wenderholme before she undertook to receive so many guests therein, for it was quite foreign to the frankness of her nature to act the *nil admirari*. Thus, on entering the magnificent drawing-room, where many guests were already assembled, she behaved exactly as she had done when, during a visit to Buxton, some friends had taken her to see Chatsworth.

"Well!" she exclaimed, lifting up both her hands, "this *is* a grand room!" Nor was she contented with this simple exclamation, but she went on examining and exclaiming, and walked all round, and lifted up the curtains, and the heavy tassels of their cords, and touched the tapestry on the chairs, and, in a word, quite forgot her dignity of hostess in the novelty of the things about her.

"Those curtains must have cost thirty shillings a-yard!" she said, appealing to the judgment of the elder ladies present, "and the stuff's narrow beside."

Impressions of splendor depend very much upon contrast, so that Wenderholme seemed very astonishing to a person coming directly from Milend. But such impressions are soon obliterated by habit, and in a week Mrs. Ogden will have lost the "fresh eye," to which she owes her present sense of enchantment. How long would it take to get accustomed to Blenheim, or Castle Howard, or Compiègne? Would it take a fortnight? However, Mrs. Ogden had the advantage of a far fresher eye than *nous autres*, who are so accustomed to gilding and glitter in public *cafés* and picture-galleries, that we are all, as it were, princes, insensible to impressions of splendor.

All that Mrs. Ogden said upon that memorable day it would be tedious to relate. She thought aloud, and the burden of her thoughts, their ever-recurring refrain, was her sense of the grandeur that surrounded her. Jacob Ogden had bought a good deal of Colonel Stanburne's fine old silver plate, and this formed the main subject of Mrs. Ogden's conversation during dinner. "I think our Jacob's gone fair mad with pride," she said to all the company, and in the hearing of the attentive servants, "for we'd plenty of silver at Milend — quite plenty for any one; we've all my uncle Adam's silver spoons, and my aunt Alice's, and plenty of silver candlesticks, and a tea-service — and I cannot tell what our Jacob would be at." Then she added, with serene complacency, "However, it's all paid for."

She had not the art of avoiding a topic likely to be disagreeable either to herself or anybody else, but would make other folks uncomfortable, and torture her own mind by dwelling upon their sores and her own. I don't think that in this she was altogether wrong, or that the most delicate people are altogether right in doing exactly the contrary, for it is as well to grasp nettles with a certain hardihood; but she carried a respectable sort of courage to a very unnecessary excess. Thus, when she had done about the silver and the general extravagance of "our Jacob," the next topic she found to talk about was the absence of Mr. and Mrs. Prigley. She launched forth into a catalogue of all the benefits wherewith she had overwhelmed Mrs. Prigley in the days of her poverty at Shayton, and represented that lady as a monster of ingratitude. "Why, they were so poor," Mrs. Ogden said, "that they couldn't even afford carpets to their floors; but now that they're better off in the world, they turn their backs on those that helped them. We were always helping them, and making them presents." Every one saw that the Ogdens were dreadfully sore about the absence of the vicar and his wife, and it was not very good policy on Mrs. Ogden's part to draw attention to it in that way; for a parson, though ornamental, is not absolutely indispensable to a good dinner, and they might have got on very well without one.

The dinner was served in the great hall at five o'clock, and few of the guests, as they sat at the feast, could help lifting their eyes to the wainscot, and the frescoes, and the great armorial ceiling — few could help thinking of the Colonel. No one present, however, was in such a conflicting and contradictory state of mind as young Jacob, nor was any one so thoroughly miserable. The whole triumph had disgusted him from beginning to end, and he was not in a humor to be either charitable or indulgent, or to see things on their amusing side. Ever since that last interview with Edith, he had been moody and misanthropical, accepting the position his uncle had made for him, but accepting it without one ray of pleasure. Such a condition of mind, if prolonged for several years, would end by making a man horribly cynical and sour, and probably drive him to take refuge in the lowest pleasures and the lowest aims. When the bark of love is wrecked, and the noble ambition of work and independence lies feeble and half dead, and we allow others to arrange all our life for us, what is the use of being young? what is the use of having health and riches, and all sorts of fine prospects and advantages?

When the banquet was over, the company returned to the drawing-room, and young Jacob began to think that Sally Smethurst was the nicest-looking young person there. His uncle was pleased to observe his polite attentions to the young lady, and, taking him aside, said, "That's reet, lad — that's reet; ax 'er to dance, and when you've been dancin' a good bit, ax her summat elz. You'll never have such another chance. She's quite fresh to this place, and she never saw out like Wendrum 'All; she's just been tellin' my mother what a rare fine place it is."

"Well," thought young Jacob to himself, "as I cannot have Edith, why not please my uncle and my grandmother? Sally Smethurst is a nice honest-looking young woman, and I daresay she 'd make a very good sort of wife." The male nature is so constituted that, when not firmly anchored in some strong attachment, it easily drifts away on the *fleuve du tendre*, and this poor youth had been cut away from his moorings. What wonder, then, if he drifted?

Sally thought him very nice, and handsome, and kind, and she promised to dance with him most willingly. The dining-room had been prepared for dancing, and it answered the purpose all the better as there was a dais at one end of the room which afforded at once a safe retreat and a convenient position for spectators, whilst at the other was a gallery for musicians, now occupied by an excellent band of stringed instruments from Manchester. In short, the dining-room at Wenderholme had been arranged strictly on the principle of the old baronial hall. The gallery was supported by fantastic pillars of carved oak, and decorated with gigantic antlers which had been given to Colonel Stanburne by a friend of his, a mighty hunter in South Africa.

The ball went on with great spirit till after midnight, when supper was served in the long gallery. Even Mrs. Ogden, old as she was, had danced, and danced well too, to the astonishment of the spectators. The host himself had performed, though his proficiency might be questioned.

What with the dancing, and the negus, and the champagne, and the splendors of the noble house, and the flattery of so many guests, and the obsequious service of so many attendants, and the sense of their own greatness and success, not only Jacob Ogden, senior, but all the Ogdens, were a little elevated that night. Young Jacob did not escape this infection — at his age, how could he? — and having taken Miss Smethurst up the grand staircase to supper, rapidly approached that point which his uncle desired him to attain.

The Blow-Out.

Amidst the noise of the talk around him, the lad went further and further. He talked about Wenderholme already almost as if it were his own, and forgot, for the time, his old friend the Colonel and his misfortunes in an exulting sense of his own highly promising position. "He intended to live at Wenderholme a good deal," he said, and then asked Miss Smethurst whether *she* would like to live at Wenderholme.

But he did not hear her answer. A figure like a ghost, with pale, sad, resolute face, approached silently, moving from the darker end of the long gallery into the blaze of light about the supper-table.

It was Mr. Prigley.

The master of the house saw him, too, and as he approached said aloud, and not very politely,—

"Better late than never, parson ; come and sit down next to my mother and get your supper."

But Mr. Prigley still remained standing. However, he approached the table. Still he would not sit down.

Every one looked at him, and no one who had looked once took his eyes off Mr. Prigley again. There was that in his face which fixed attention irresistibly. The roar of the conversation was suddenly hushed, and a silence succeeded in which you might have heard the breaking of a piece of bread.

Mr. Prigley went straight to Mrs. Ogden, not noticing anybody else. He spoke to her, not loudly, but audibly enough for every one to hear him.

"I have come to tell you, Mrs. Ogden, that Mrs. Stanburne, mother of Colonel Stanburne of Wenderholme, is now lying in a dying state at the vicarage."

Mrs. Ogden did not answer at once. When she had collected her ideas, she said, "I thought Mrs. Stanburne had been in her own house and well in health. If I 'd known she was dyin', you may be sure, Mr. Prigley, as there should 'ave been no dancin' i' this house, though she 's not a relation of ours. We're only plain people, but we know what's fittin' and seemly."

"Then you cannot be aware, Mrs. Ogden, of what has happened at Wenderholme Cottage. Mrs. Stanburne's illness has been brought on by the suddenness with which the present owner of Wenderholme ordered her to quit her cottage on this estate. She was an old lady, in feeble health, and the trouble of a sudden eviction has proved too much for her. If there is any surgeon here, let him follow me."

This said, Mr. Prigley quitted the table without bowing to anybody, and his gaunt figure and pale grave face passed along the gallery to the great staircase. Dr. Bardly left his place at the supper-table, and followed him.

Miss Smethurst's young partner made no more soft speeches to her that night. A great pang smote him in his breast. Had he forgotten those dear friends who had been so good to him in the time of their prosperity? And what was this horrible story of an eviction? Mrs. Stanburne turned out of Wenderholme Cottage! Could it be possible that his uncle had gone to such a length as that?

The boy was down the staircase in an instant, and overtook the Doctor and Mr. Prigley as they were crossing the great hall. They walked swiftly and silently to the vicarage.

"You'd better wait here, little Jacob," said Dr. Bardly; "I'll go upstairs." And he put Jacob into a small sitting-room, which was empty.

The lad had been there five minutes when the door opened, and Edith came in. She looked very ill and miserable.

All the old tenderness came back into Jacob's heart as he felt for her in this trial. "Miss Stanburne," he said, "dear Miss Stanburne, what does he say?" Weak and shattered as she was by the trials of these last days, that word of tenderness made any farther acting impossible. She went to him, took both his hands in hers, and the tears came.

"There's no hope; she's dying. Come upstairs — she wants to see you."

Mrs. Stanburne was lying in a state of extreme exhaustion, with occasional intervals of consciousness, in which the mind was clear. When Jacob entered the sick-room, she was in one of her better moments.

"Go quite near to her," said Mr. Prigley; "she can only speak in a whisper."

There had always existed a great friendship between the youth and the old lady now lying on the brink of the grave. He bent down over her, and tenderly kissed her forehead.

"God bless you!" she whispered, "it is very kind of you to come."

Then she said, in answer to his enquiries, —

"I shall not live long, but I shall live rather longer than they think. I shan't die to-night. I want my son — my son!"

After this supervened a syncope, which Jacob and Edith believed to be death. But the Doctor, with his larger experience, reassured them for the present. "She will live several hours," he said.

Jacob told them that she had asked for Colonel Stanburne, and added, "I have not the slightest idea where he is."

Then Edith made a sign to him to follow her, and led him downstairs again to the little sitting-room. "Papa is a long way off; he is in France. He must be telegraphed for." And she took a writing-case and wrote an address.

Now, although there was a telegraph from Wenderholme to Ogden's Mill at Shayton, there was none from Shayton to Sootythorn, which was the nearest town of importance. So the best way appeared to be for Jacob to ride off at once with the despatch to the station, which was ten miles off.

"And you must telegraph for mamma at the same time." And Edith wrote Lady Helena's address.

A little delay occurred now, because Jacob's horse had to be sent for to Wenderholme Hall. Edith went upstairs, and soon came down again with rather favorable news. The syncope had not lasted long, and the patient seemed to rally from it somewhat more easily than she had done from the preceding ones.

"Miss Stanburne!" said Jacob, "will you give me a word of explanation? You were hard and unkind the last time we spoke to each other."

"I did very wrong. I thought I was sacrificing myself for your good. I told you nothing but lies."

Half an hour since Miss Smethurst was within a hair's-breadth of being lady of Wenderholme; but her chances are over now, and she will not bring her fortune to this place — her coals to this Newcastle. As her late partner in the dance rides galloping, galloping through the wooded lanes to the telegraph station, his brain is full of other hopes, and of a far higher, though less brilliant, ambition. He will free himself from the Milend slavery, and work for independence — and for Edith!

CHAPTER XIV.

MRS. OGDEN'S AUTHORITY.

AFTER the apparition of Mr. Prigley, the supper in the long gallery changed its character completely. Until he came it had been one of the merriest of festivals; after he went away, it became one of the dullest. A sense of uncomfortableness and embarrassment oppressed everybody present, and though many attempts were made to give the conversation something of its old liveliness, the guests soon became aware that for that time it was frozen beyond hope of recovery. It had been intended to resume the dancing after supper, but the dancing was not resumed, and the guests who intended to return to Shayton that night became suddenly impressed with so strong a sense of the distance of that place from Wenderholme, that all the pressing hospitality of the Ogdens availed not to retain them.

Notwithstanding the Philistinism of Mrs. Ogden's character, and the external hardness which she had in common with most of her contemporaries in Shayton, she was not without heart; and when she heard that her son had turned old Mrs. Stanburne out of the Cottage, she both felt disapproval and expressed it. "Jacob," she said, "you shouldn't 'ave done so." And she repeated many a time to other people in the room, "Our Jacob shouldn't 'ave done so."

And when the carriages had departed, although there were still many people in the house, Mrs. Ogden put her bonnet on, and had herself conducted to the vicarage.

The situation there might have been embarrassing for some

people, but Mrs. Ogden was a woman who did not feel embarrassment under any circumstances. She did what was right, or she did what was wrong, in a simple and resolute way, and her very immunity from nervous reflectiveness often enabled her to do the right thing when a self-conscious person would hardly have ventured to do it. So she knocked at Mrs. Prigley's door.

It happened that the person nearest the door at that moment was Edith, who was crossing the passage from one room to another. So Edith opened the door.

Mrs. Ogden walked in at once, and asked very kindly after Mrs. Stanburne. Edith was pleased with the genuine interest in her manner, and showed her into the little sitting-room.

The news was rather more favorable than might have been hoped for. Mrs. Stanburne had had no return of unconsciousness; and though the Doctor still thought she was gradually sinking, he began to be of opinion that her illness might be much longer than was at first anticipated, and thought that she would live to see the Colonel.

"You don't know me," said Mrs. Ogden; "but as you speak of Mrs. Stanburne as your grandmamma, I know who you are. You're Miss Edith. I'm little Jacob's grandmamma — Mrs. Ogden of Milend, whom no doubt you've heard speak of."

Edith bowed slightly, and then there was rather an awkward pause.

"My son Jacob did very wrong about your grandmother in turning her out of her house. I wish we could make amends."

Edith tried to say something polite in acknowledgment of Mrs. Ogden's advance, but it ended in tears. "I'm afraid it is too late," she said, finally.

The young lady's evident love for her grandmother won the heart of Mrs. Ogden, who was herself a grandmother. "Tell me what has been done, my dear. I know nothing about it; I only heard about it to-night. Has Mrs. Stanburne removed her furniture?"

"Not quite all yet. Most of it is here, in Mr. Prigley's out-houses. It was the hurry of the removal that brought on grandmamma's illness."

"Well, my dear," said the old lady, laying her hand upon Edith's, "let us pray to God that she may live. And we'll have all the furniture put back into the Cottage."

"I don't think grandmamma would consent to that."

"But I'll make my son come and beg her pardon. I'll make him come!"

Edith could not resist Mrs. Ogden's earnestness. "I will try to bring grandmamma round, if she lives. You are very kind, Mrs. Ogden."

"Now, if you'd like me to sit up with Mrs. Stanburne, if you and Mrs. Prigley was tired, you know? I'm an old woman, but I'm a strong one, and I can sit up well enough. I've been used to nursing. I nursed our Isaac wife all through her last illness."

"Mrs. Prigley and I can do very well for to-night; but to-morrow, in the day-time, we shall need a little rest, and if you would come we should be much obliged."

"And if there was any thing I could send from the great 'ouse — any jellies or blomonge?"

"Thank you; if we want any thing we will send for it to the Hall."

Mrs. Ogden rose to take her leave, which she did very affectionately. "I am very sorry for you, my dear," she said, "and I am angry at our Jacob. He shouldn't 'ave done so — he shouldn't 'ave done so."

She had no notion of abdicating parental authority — no idea that, because a lad happened to be twenty-one, or thirty-one, or forty-one, he was to be free to do exactly as he liked. And when she got back to the Hall, and the guests were in bed, she treated "our Jacob" *en petit garçon*, just as if he had been fifteen. She informed him that Mrs. Stanburne's furniture would be reinstated in Wenderholme Cottage immediately, and that if she recovered he would have to go there and eat humble-pie. "An' if who doesn't get better, it'll be thee as has murdered her; and thou'll desarve to be hanged for 't, same as Bill o' great John's * as shot old Nanny Suthers wi' a pistil."

* A common form of sobriquet in Lancashire.

CHAPTER XV.

LADY HELENA RETURNS.

MRS. OGDEN returned to the vicarage the next day, and found Mrs. Stanburne in the same condition of extreme exhaustion. The Rigton doctor had arrived in the interval, and relieved Dr. Bardly, who returned to Shayton. The two medical men had expressed the same opinion — namely, that the old lady was gradually, but quite surely, sinking.

Mrs. Ogden took her place by the bedside, and relieved Mrs. Prigley and Edith. The patient being perfectly conscious, and in possession of all her mental faculties, Edith had told her about Mrs. Ogden's first visit; and when she came near the bedside, Mrs. Stanburne held out her hand, or rather attempted to do so — for she had not strength to lift it — and it fell upon the counterpane. Then she whispered a few words of thanks and welcome. "My son Jacob shouldn't have done so — he shouldn't have done so," said Mrs. Ogden; and in reply there came faint syllables of forgiveness. Then Mrs. Ogden asked Mrs. Stanburne if she would prove her forgiveness by going back to Wenderholme Cottage.

"If I live, I will."

"Live! why you're sure to live. You're quite a young woman. Look at me, how strong I am, and I'm older than you are. It's nothing but the hurry and worry of leaving your 'ouse that you was accustomed to that's brought you down in this way. You'll get well again — I'm sure you will; only, we must take care of you. Now we've had enough talking for the present, and I'll get my sewing; and if you want any thing, I'll fetch it for you."

Then the strong old woman sat down by the bedside of the weaker one, and from that time forth established herself as one of her recognized nurses, and by no means the least efficient. In one essential point she was superior both to Edith and Mrs. Prigley — she was less melancholy and more encouraging. The others could not help crying, and the patient saw that they had been crying, which made her feel as if she were assisting at her own funeral; whereas Mrs. Ogden kept a cheerful countenance, and, though as gentle as a woman could be, had nevertheless a fine firmness and courage which made Mrs. Stanburne feel that she could rely upon her. Another immense advantage was, that in the presence of this hale and active example of a vigorous old age, Mrs. Stanburne altogether ceased to feel the burden of her years, and began to consider herself simply as a sick person in a state of temporary exhaustion, instead of an old woman whose thread of life had come to its inevitable end. Indeed, Mrs. Ogden had not been long with the invalid before both of them had given up the theory that she was gradually sinking, and replaced it by more hopeful views.

Young Jacob's interest in Mrs. Stanburne's health proved to be so strong that he could hardly absent himself from the vicarage; yet though Mrs. Ogden must have been perfectly well aware that he passed a good deal of his time there with Miss Edith, she showed no sign of displeasure, but when she found them together, seemed to consider it perfectly natural, and spoke to Edith always affectionately, calling her "my dear," and putting an unaccustomed tenderness even into the very tones of her voice. The lord of Wenderholme and his remaining guests left for Shayton in the course of the afternoon, but Mrs. Ogden declared her intention of remaining until her patient was out of danger; and though her son had suggested that young Jacob was not absolutely necessary as a nurse, Mrs. Ogden asserted that it was "a great comfort" to her to have him near her, and that he should go back to Milend with his grandmother at such times as she might see fit to return thither. Jacob Ogden was a wilful and a mighty man; but either from habit or some genuine filial sentiment, or perhaps because no man can be really happy unless he is governed by a woman of some sort — either a wife, or a mother, or a maiden aunt — this hard and terrible master-spirit submitted to "the old woman" without question, and whatever *she* willed was done.

In saying that all Jacob Ogden's guests went back with him to Shayton, an exception must be made in the case of his elder brother. Captain Ogden, as he was now generally called (for the people had gradually got into the habit of giving militia officers their titles), remained at Wenderholme, for reasons of his own. He knew that Colonel Stanburne had been telegraphed for, and wished to see him. Perhaps, too, he thought it might be agreeable to John Stanburne to find a sincere friend in his old place, and that he might be able in some degree to mitigate the painfulness of an unavoidable return to scenes which could not be revisited without awakening many regretful associations.

As all the Prigley children were at school except Conny, now a young lady who was supposed to have "come out," though in fact no such ceremony had taken place, from the want of any society to come out in, the vicarage was able to accommodate a good many guests, and the Prigleys were only too happy to place it at the disposal of the family to whom they owed their recent advancement in the world. It was a pleasant and spacious, though not a very elegant, house; and there was a large garden, and an orchard, and a glebe of two or three fields, with sufficient stabling and out-houses. They had set up a small pony-carriage, or rather continued that which belonged to the late vicar, which they had purchased at the sale, with pony and harness complete, for the moderate sum of nine guineas ; and Conny Prigley set off in this machine to await the train by which Lady Helena was expected to arrive. This arrangement was made without Mrs. Ogden's knowledge, and when she came to be aware of it, she exclaimed, " Well, now, I wish I 'd known — I do indeed, I *wish* I 'd known — for there 's my cayridge at the 'All, which is quite at your service. Our Jacob's gone back with Miss Smethurst, and he's left me my cayridge, which you would have been quite welcome to." But the Prigleys had tact enough to know, that although her ladyship rather liked to be magnificent, she might not particularly care for it to be Mrs. Ogden's magnificence ; and that the little green pony-carriage, driven by Conny Prigley, was a more suitable vehicle to bring her ladyship to the vicarage than the sumptuous chariot in which Mrs. Ogden had triumphed the day before.

Lady Helena duly arrived. It did not require much explanation from Edith to make the whole situation quite clear to her perspicuous mind. She went upstairs to see Mrs. Stanburne, who was grateful to her for coming so soon, and the first person she saw in the room was Mrs. Ogden.

There was a little stiffness at first, but it did not last long. Lady Helena and Mrs. Ogden got into conversation about the state of the patient, and then about other matters connected with what might be called the diocese of the Lady of Wenderholme. Had Mrs. Ogden been one of the examples, so numerous in these days, of amazingly refined ladyhood in the middle classes, Lady Helena might have been jealous of her ; but how was it possible for her ladyship to feel jealous of a simple old woman like Mrs. Ogden, who spoke broad Lancashire, and in every movement of her body, and every utterance of her lips, proclaimed the humility of her birth? Lady Helena, moreover, had a keen sense of humor, and it was impossible not to feel interested and amused, as soon as the first anxiety about Mrs. Stanburne was at least temporarily tranquillized, by Mrs. Ogden's quaint turns of expression, and her wonderful reliance on her own wisdom and experience. Even Mrs. Stanburne, ill as she was, could not help smiling, as she lay in her bed of sickness, when Mrs. Ogden came out with some of those sayings which were peculiarly her own.

The condition of the invalid had become less distressing and less alarming, though the Doctor still held out no hopes of a recovery. Mrs. Ogden, however, had succeeded in making the patient believe that she would get better because she believed it herself, and she believed it herself because the idea of a person dying of mere weakness at the early age of seventy-two was not admissible to her patriarchal mind. It was a great thing for Mrs. Stanburne to have somebody near her who did not consider that she was used up, and she began to regard Mrs. Ogden with the partiality which human nature always feels for those who preach comfortable doctrine.

As there were so many ladies to nurse Mrs. Stanburne, and as the invalid now gave comparatively little immediate anxiety, Edith easily got Lady Helena to herself for half an hour.

The young lady was firmly resolved upon one thing—namely, that this opportunity for a reconciliation between her father and mother should not be lost through any pusillanimity of hers.

"Mamma," she said boldly, "why did you leave papa when he was ruined?"

"Because he ordered me to leave him; because he turned me out of the house."

"But why did he do so? It is quite contrary to his character to turn anybody out. When he dismissed the servants, he did it very kindly, and only because he could not afford to keep them."

Lady Helena remained silent.

"Do tell me, mamma, why he behaved so. It isn't like him; you know it isn't like him."

"There are people, Edith," said her ladyship, "who commit great follies; and then, when the misfortunes come which they themselves have caused, they cannot endure to hear one word of blame. They must be pitied and sympathized with, and then they are very nice and amiable; but if you express the least censure, they fly into a passion and insult you."

"You mean that you censured papa for his imprudence, and that he got angry."

"I said very little to him. I said a few words which were strictly true. I never scold."

"No, mamma, you never scold; but scolding would be easier to bear than your blame. I see how it all was; you blamed papa in two or three terribly just and severe words, and then, after that, you said nothing to console him in his misery, and he became irritable, and said something hasty."

Lady Helena said nothing to this, but she did not look displeased; and she showed no inclination either to leave the room or to change the subject.

"Dear mamma, I don't think you did wrong in blaming papa's imprudence; but if you had given him one word of kindness afterwards, you would never have lost him."

"Is not this rather"—

"Impertinent from a daughter, you mean to say. You know I don't want to be impertinent, mamma; but I'm old enough to be of some use, and I mean to be, too, whether your ladyship is quite satisfied or not. Are you aware that papa will be here to-morrow?"

"It is natural that he should come here, as his mother is ill."

"And when he comes, we must do what we can to help him to bear his afflictions, I suppose."

"Certainly."

"Well, we won't pass any more votes of censure, mamma, will we? And we shall forgive him his trespasses, shall we not?"

To this Lady Helena made no reply; but her face wore

a new and a softer expression. This encouraged Edith, who continued:—

"He has suffered enough. He has been living all by himself in a miserable little French town on the Loire. I have a whole heap of his letters. He told me every thing about his situation. Grandpapa has been allowing him three hundred a-year—he has never touched a penny of it; it is paid regularly to grandmamma Stanburne, who does not know that she is ruined, and who fancies that papa has an allowance, and lives abroad for his pleasure. His letters to her are all about amusements, but he writes to me sincerely, and *I* know what his life has been. He has got a post as English master in a school, and they pay him twenty-five francs a-week, but he gives lessons in the town, and gets two francs a lesson, only he has not many of these. He is *en pension* in an inn. It is a miserably lonely life. I would have gone to him, but I could not leave grandmamma."

Lady Helena's eyes glistened in the firelight. They were brimming with tears. "You should have told me this sooner, Edith," she said, at last.

"Would you have gone to him? Would you have gone to live with him there, in his lodgings, and cheer him after his day's work?"

"I have been less happy, Edith, during these last months, than I should have been with him, wherever he is, however poor he is."

After this avowal of her ladyship, the chances are great, I think, that the Colonel will be agreeably received at the vicarage. Miss Edith communicated as much to the worthy vicar himself, who, though with Anglican discretion he would have avoided intruding in the character of peacemaker, thought it a duty to encourage Lady Helena in the path of charity and forgiveness.

"Forgive him heartily and entirely any thing you may have to forgive. Go to him at once when he comes. All your days will be blessed for this."

CHAPTER XVI.

THE COLONEL COMES.

IN the evening came a telegram from the Colonel, dated from Dover, and announcing his arrival for the following morning. "What a pity it is," said Lady Helena, "that he did not give us a London address! we might have spared him a whole night of anxiety." She was thinking about him just as she used to think about him in their happiest years.

On reference to the time-table, it appeared that the Colonel would arrive at the station at about eight o'clock in the morning. When Captain Ogden heard of this, he said he would go to meet him, and so did young Jacob; and Mrs. Ogden offered her carriage, and, in short, there was a general fuss, to which Lady Helena suddenly put an end by declaring her intention of going to meet him herself in the little pony-carriage that belonged to the vicarage. Mr. Prigley smiled approbation, and assured her ladyship that he would lend her that humble equipage with great pleasure, meaning a great deal more than he said.

So Lady Helena drove off in the little green carriage at six o'clock in the morning; for the station, as the reader may remember, was ten miles from Wenderholme, and it was necessary to bait the pony before he came back. It was a rude little equipage altogether, not very well hung, and by no means elegant in its proportions. The pony, too, in anticipation of winter, was beginning to put on his rough coat, and his harness had long since lost any brilliance it might have once possessed. The morning was cold and raw, and a chilly gray dawn was in the east — an aurora of the least encouraging kind, which one always feels disposed to be angry at for coming and disturbing the more cheerful darkness. Some people at the vicarage were astonished that Mr. Prigley should allow her ladyship to drive off alone in this dreary way at six o'clock in the morning; but then these people did not know all that Mr. Prigley knew. When Lady Helena got into the carriage, the vicar shook hands with her in an uncommonly affectionate manner, just as if she had been leaving him for a very long time, and then he said something to her in a very low tone. " Dear Lady Helena," he said, " God bless you ! " and it is my firm belief that if Mrs. Prigley had not been within sight, that vicar would have given Lady Helena a kiss.

Away went the pony through the darkling lanes, with the rattling machine after him. Poor pony ! he had often done that long journey to the station, and done it with reasonable celerity, but he had never trotted so fast as he trotted now. Can it be the early morning air that so exhilarates her ladyship? Her face is so bright and cheerful that it conquers the dreariness of the hour, and brings a better sunshine than the gray October dawn. How little we know under what circumstances we shall enjoy the purest and sweetest felicity ! This little woman had been in lordly equipages, in all sorts of splendid pleasures and stately ceremonies; she had been drawn by magnificent horses, with a powdered coachman on the box, and a cluster of lacqueys behind ; she had gone in diamonds and feathers to St. James's ; better still, she had driven through the fairest scenery under cloudless skies, when all nature rejoiced around her. All the luxury that skilled craftsmen can produce in combination had been hers ; carriages hung so delicately, and cushioned so softly, that they seemed to float on air ; harness that seemed as if its only purpose were to enhance the beauty of the horses which it adorned ; liveries, varnish, silver, and the rest of it. And yet, of all the drives that Lady Helena had ever taken in her whole life, *this* was the most delightful, this drive in the dreary dawn of an October morning in a rattling little carriage with stiff springs, painted like a park paling, and drawn by a shaggy pony at the rate of six miles an hour!

She reached the station half an hour before the train came, and sat a little in the waiting-room, and walked about on the platform, in a state of nervous fidgetiness and anxiety. At length the bell rang, and the engine came round a curve, and grew bigger and bigger, and her heart beat faster and faster. "There he is, poor John, getting out of a third-class carriage!" Lady Helena had been seeking him amongst the well-to-do first-class passengers.

She ran to him, and took his hand in both hers, and said, "She's better, love — a good deal better since yesterday." And the tears ran down her cheeks.

The Colonel looked at her for a moment, and took both her hands, and would have said something, or perhaps gone so far as to give her just one little kiss on the forehead — which is a wonderful thing for an Englishman to achieve in a railway station — but these good intentions were frustrated by the guard, who, in rather a peremptory way, demanded to know whether he had any luggage.

John Stanburne felt like a man in a dream. Going back to Wenderholme, no longer his, with Helena, his own Helena once more! It was not in his nature to cherish the least vindictive feeling, and that one word of his wife had wiped away every evil recollection. When they got into the little pony-carriage, and were out of hearing of the hostler, the Colonel turned to her ladyship, and said, —

"I owe you a great many apologies, dear. I behaved very badly the last time we were together, but I was upset, you know. You are a good woman to come and meet me in this way, and forgive me. I have meant to write to you many a time and say how sorry I was, but I put it off because — because" —

The Colonel comes.

It is well that the pony was quiet, and knew its own way to Wenderholme, for when they got into an uncommonly retired lane, with very high hedges, her ladyship, who was driving, threw the reins down, and embraced the gentleman by her side in an extraordinary manner. Then came passionate tears, and after that she grew calmer.

"What geese we were to fancy we could live separately!" she said.

And then they talked incessantly the whole way. She asked him a thousand questions about his life abroad, — how he passed his evenings, whether he had found any society, and so on. As the Colonel told her about his humble, lonely life, she listened with perfect sympathy; and when he said that some people had been kind to him, and got him pupils, she wanted to know all about them. "I'm getting on famously," said the Colonel. "I'm earning nearly sixty francs a-week, and I pronounce French better than I used to do."

CHAPTER XVII.

A MORNING CALL.

SINCE we are obliged to leave the vicarage now, the reader must be told the exact truth about Mrs. Stanburne's condition. It continued to give great anxiety for several weeks, and all her friends, even including the doctors, gave her up over and over again, believing that she had not more than an hour or two to live; yet she always passed through these times of danger, and gradually, very gradually, began to feel rather stronger in the month of December. The season of the year was not favorable to her, but Dr. Bardly hoped that if she could be sustained till the return of spring, she would regain her strength, at least in a great measure, and probably have several years of life still before her. She bore the winter better than had been expected, though without quitting her room at the vicarage, and in the month of April entered upon a convalescence which astonished all around her.

The old lady's illness led to very important consequences. Since the period of her danger was protracted, her friends remained near her day after day, and week after week, always believing that they were performing the last duty by a deathbed. A great sadness reigned in the vicarage during all this season of watching, but it was sadness of the kind which is most favorable to sympathy and good feeling. The vicar and his good wife, so far from feeling the presence of the invalid and their other guests a burden, were glad that it was in their power to do any thing for her and for them;

and whilst the old lady lay upon her bed of sickness she was producing happier and more important results, simply by throwing certain persons together by invisible bonds of mutual approval and a common anxiety, than she could ever have achieved by an active ingerence in their affairs. Everybody who loved old Mrs. Stanburne was grateful to everybody who gave proof of a real interest in her condition; and the majestic approach of death, whose shadow lay on the vicarage so long, subdued all its inhabitants into a more perfect spiritual harmony than they would ever have attained to amongst the distractions of gayer, though not happier, days. Lady Helena was admirable. There was a tenderness and a simplicity in her manner which pleased the Colonel greatly, and won the warm approval of the vicar. She devoted herself mainly to the care of Mrs. Stanburne, but, saying that exercise was necessary to enable her to do her duty as a nurse, made the Colonel walk out with her every day. These walks were delightful to both of them — for even though the scenery about the village of Wenderholme was full of painful associations, their sense of loss was more than balanced by the sense of a yet larger gain; and the future, though it could not have the external brilliance of the past, promised a deeper and more firm felicity. Sadness and unhappiness are two very different conditions of the mind, and it does not follow that because we are saddened we are incapable of being very happy in a certain quiet and not unenviable way. Indeed, it might even be asserted, that as

"Our sweetest songs are those which tell of saddest thought" —

so it is with life itself, as well as poetry, and that our sweetest hours are far from being our gayest.

It had become tacitly understood that neither Lady Helena nor Mrs. Ogden would offer any opposition to the marriage between Jacob and Edith. Whatever Mrs. Ogden determined to do, she did in a thorough and effectual manner; and as she had resolved that amends ought to be made to the Stanburnes for her son's conduct to the old lady, she considered that the best way to do this would be to receive Edith kindly into her family. In this resolution she was greatly helped by a genuine approval of the young lady herself. " There 's some girls as brings fortunes," she said to young Jacob, "and there 's other girls as *is* a fortune themselves, and I think Miss Stanburne will be as good as a fortune to any one who may marry her." Nor had this opinion been lightly arrived at, for during her frequent visits to the vicarage, Mrs. Ogden had studied Edith, much in the same way as an entomologist studies an insect under a microscope.

One day, when the weather became a little warmer, Lady Helena said to the Colonel, " Don't you think, dear, that we ought to go and call upon that old Mrs. Ogden at the Hall? She has been exceedingly kind in coming to sit with mamma. I would have suggested it sooner, but I was afraid it might be painful for you, dear, to go to the old house again."

So they set out and walked to the Hall together, both of them feeling very strange feelings, indeed, as they passed up the familiar avenue. When they came at last in sight of the great house, John Stanburne paused and gazed upon it for a long time without speaking. It stood just as he had left it — none of the carved Stanburne shields had been removed. " I 'm glad they 've altered nothing, Helena," he said.

Then they met their old gardener, who spoke to them with the tears in his eyes. " It 's different for us to what it used to be, my lady," he said; "not but what Mrs. Ogden is a good woman, but her son is a hard master."

"We were coming to see Mrs. Ogden," said Lady Helena; " do you know if she is at home ? "

" You won't find her in the house, my lady ; but if you will come this way, I 'll take you to where she is."

Nature always puts some element of comedy into the most touching circumstances, and saves us from morbid feelings by glimpses of the ludicrous side of life. Thus, although the gardener had had tears in his eyes when he saw the Colonel and Lady Helena, there was a smile upon his face as he led them in the direction of the stables.

"Your ladyship will find Mrs. Ogden in that carriage," he said, pointing to the magnificent Ogden chariot, which stood, as if to air itself, without horses, in the middle of the yard. When he had said this, the gardener made his bow and disappeared, smiling with keen satisfaction at what he had just done.

The visitors were much surprised, but, as the gardener well knew, curiosity alone was strong enough to make them go up to the carriage and see whether there was anybody inside it. The Colonel peeped in at the window, and saw Mrs. Ogden sitting in the vehicle, apparently in quite a settled and permanent way, for she had her knitting.

"Eh, well, it's the Colonel and her ladyship, I declare!" cried Mrs. Ogden, opening the carriage-door. "Come and get in — do get in — it's very comfortable. I often come and sit here a bit of an afternoon with my knitting. But what perhaps you'd rather go and sit a bit i' th' 'ouse?"

They got inside the carriage with the old lady, and their amusement at this circumstance quite relieved those feelings of melancholy which had naturally taken possession of them on revisiting Wenderholme. The conversation was quite agreeable and animated, and half an hour passed very rapidly. After that, the callers proposed to depart.

"Nay," said Mrs. Ogden, "you willn't be going away so soon, will you? Come into th' 'ouse, now — *do* come and have a glass of wine."

Lady Helena promised that they would come to the house another day, but said that she wished to go back to Mrs. Stanburne. On this Mrs. Ogden said, "Well, then, if you *will* go back, sit you still." And she let down the glass and called out in a loud voice for the horses.

The horses were put to the carriage, and the visitors shortly found themselves in motion towards the vicarage, which proves the advantage of receiving friends in a small drawing-room on four wheels. The incident created a great deal of amusement, and even old Mrs. Stanburne laughed at it very heartily. Very trifling and absurd things are often of great use in putting people in a good temper, and chasing melancholy ideas; and Mrs. Ogden's fancy for sitting in her carriage developed a wonderful amount of kindly humor at the vicarage. Nothing does people more good than laughing at their neighbors, and they love their neighbors all the better for having laughed at them; so Mrs. Ogden's popularity at the vicarage was increased by this incident, and I dare say it accelerated Mrs. Stanburne's recovery in an appreciable, though not ascertainable, degree.

CHAPTER XVIII.

MONEY ON THE BRAIN.

IMMEDIATELY after the Colonel's return from France, Captain Ogden went back to his solitude at Twistle Farm, but his son spent a good deal of his time with old Mrs. Ogden at Wenderholme. Jacob Ogden, senior, came to Wenderholme frequently to look after the work-people on the estate, but did not mark his disapproval of his nephew's proceedings otherwise than by quietly excluding him from all participation in his affairs. Although the young man passed a great deal more time at Wenderholme than his uncle did, he was never requested, and he never offered, to do any of the duties of an overlooker, and his uncle treated him strictly upon the footing of a visitor — a visitor, not to himself, but to his mother. There is so much firmness in the character of the typical Lancashire man, that he can assume, and maintain for an indefinite length of time, an attitude towards a friend or relation which would be impossible for more mobile temperaments; and young Jacob knew his uncle well enough to be aware that having once decided upon his line of conduct, there was every probability that he would follow it without deviation. Therefore, although young Jacob could have made himself of the greatest use at Wenderholme without interfering either with his amusement of shooting or his dutiful attendance upon Miss Edith, he paid no more attention to the work-people than if they had been employed by some proprietor entirely unknown to him. It is unnecessary to add, that when at Twistle Farm, where he spent about one week out of three, he never went near his uncle's factories.

And yet, notwithstanding the apparent indifference with which Jacob Ogden dispensed with his nephew's services, they were more than ever necessary to him. The great factories at Shayton were enough of themselves to absorb the whole time of a very active master; but, in addition to these, Jacob Ogden was now working the calico-printing establishment at Whittlecup, which had formerly belonged to Mr. Joseph Anison, and carrying out extensive improvements, not only upon the Wenderholme estate, but upon many other properties of his, scattered over the neighboring parishes, and often at a considerable distance from his headquarters at Milend. Though his constitution was a strong one, he had always taxed its strength to the utmost; and his powers were not what they had been, nor what he still believed them to be. He might have gone on for many years in the old routine that he had been accustomed to — for a hard-worked man will endure labor that seems beyond his present strength if he merely continues the habits of his better time. But a man already in the decline of life cannot *add* to his labor without danger, if it is already excessive, and especially if the new labors require thought and study before they can be fully mastered. The improvements at Wenderholme, to an experienced land-owner like Jacob Ogden, required no new apprenticeship; but that was not the case with the calico-printing business at Whittlecup. It was a new trade that had to be learned, and not a very easy trade — not nearly so simple as cotton-spinning. He applied himself to it with that indomitable will and resolution which had hitherto overcome every obstacle in his career, and he rapidly acquired the new knowledge that he needed. But this effort, in addition to the enormous burden of his daily work — the daily work of a rich man who could not endure to be robbed, and would trust nothing to his agents — began to tell upon his cerebral system in a peculiar manner; and these effects were the more dangerous that Jacob Ogden had no conception of the terrible nature of the enemy that was invading him, but believed this enemy might be conquered by his will and perseverance, as every other obstacle had been. If he had frankly consulted Dr. Bardly on the appearance of the first symptoms, and followed the advice which Dr. Bardly would have given, the evil would have been checked in time ; but he felt a certain hostility to the Doctor, which disinclined him to communications which he did not feel to be immediately necessary ; and even if this could have been laid aside, a man so wilful as Jacob Ogden, and so accustomed to look after his own affairs, would scarcely have consented under present circumstances to give up the management of his business to his nephew, and retire to a premature and inglorious repose.

Hitherto he had gone through his work with great energy, in combination with perfect calm. The energy still remained, it even increased ; but the calm did not remain — it was succeeded by a perpetual hurry and fever. In a short time after these symptoms first developed themselves, Jacob Ogden could not add up a column of figures without excitement; when he came to the totals his heart beat violently, and he began to make mistakes, which he perceived, and was afterwards nervously anxious to avoid. As his malady increased, he could not open a letter without emotion, or sign a cheque without a strong effort of self-control ; in a word, the nervous system was rapidly giving way. And instead of taking rest, which could alone have restored him to health — rest at Wenderholme amongst his own fair fields in the beautiful months of spring — he persisted and persisted, and would not allow himself to be beaten.

The people about him did not know any thing of his condition. He was more irritable, he pushed everybody faster than he had formerly done, and he was constantly moving from one place to another; but his determination to control himself was so strong, and his power of *appearing* well still so considerable, that such people as Mrs. Ogden and young Jacob (unaccustomed as they both were to that kind of suffering, and incapable of imagining it) had not the most distant suspicion that he had become unfit for work. Indeed, although an experienced London physician, who had made brain disease his particular study, would no doubt have seen at a glance that this was a case which needed the most watchful care, it may be doubted whether a country practitioner (even so clever, naturally, as Dr. Bardly) would have warned Jacob Ogden in time.

The overtasked brain translated its own dangerous condition by *anxiety*, and the anxiety was not about health, but, as often happens in such instances, about that subject which had most occupied the patient's mind before the approaches of disease — namely, money. With all his riches, Jacob Ogden grew more nervously anxious about money matters than the poorest laborer on his estate. His mind ran incessantly upon possible causes of loss; and as in the best-regulated property such causes are always infinitely numerous, he found them only too easily. The thousands of details which, when in health, he had carried in his head as lightly as we carry the words of a thoroughly mastered language, began to torment him with the apprehension that they might escape his memory; and whereas, in his better days, no fact troubled him except just at the moment when he wanted it, they now importunately intruded upon his mind when they could only disturb and confuse it.

At length, as his disease advanced towards its sure and terrible development, the ANXIETY, which was the form it had taken, and the mental hurry and worry which accompanied it, arrived at such a pitch that the least delicate and acute observers remarked it in Jacob Ogden's face. His mother earnestly entreated him not to torment himself so much about his affairs, but to take a partner, and allow himself more rest. The advice came too late. The tender cells of the cerebrum were in a state of fevered disturbance, which must now inevitably lead to one of the forms of madness.

It broke out one night at Wenderholme. He toiled till three o'clock in the morning, alone, at his accounts. There was nothing in them which he would not have mastered quite easily when in health, but the condition of his brain had led to many errors, and the attempt to correct these had only increased and multiplied them. He toiled and toiled till his brain could no longer stand the confusion, and he went mad.

First there came a sense of strangeness to every thing about him, and then a wild alarm — a *terror* such as he had never known! For a few minutes Reason fiercely struggled to keep her seat, and would not be dispossessed. Those minutes were the most fearful the man had ever passed through. He sprang from his place, and paced the room from wall to wall in violent agitation. "I'm very ill," he thought; "I cannot tell what's the matter with me. I believe I'm going to have a fit. No, it isn't that — it isn't that; I know what it is — I know now — *I'm going mad!*"

No visible external foe can ever be so terrible as the mysterious internal avengers. They come upon us we know not when nor where. They come when the doors are locked, the mansion guarded, and all the household sleeps. They come in their terrible invisibility, like devils taking possession. The strokes of mortal disease are dealt mysteriously *within;* and who would not rather meet a body of armed savages than invisible apoplexy or paralysis?

For five minutes Ogden wrestled with his invisible enemy. "I *will* not go mad," he cried aloud — " I *will* not!"

And a minute afterwards the struggle ceased, and he was another being, mad beyond hope of recovery.

A strange smile came over his face, and he pressed his hand upon his forehead. "I'll dodge them yet," he said;

"they aren't as sharp as I am. I'm sharper than the best of them!"

He began to count the money in his purse. It was not much — five pounds eighteen exactly. He counted the sum quite correctly, over and over again; then he looked anxiously about for a place to hide it in. Whilst he was doing this, his mother, who had felt anxious about him all night, and had been unable to sleep, came to his room-door and listened. She heard him walking about and muttering to himself. Then she opened the door and went in.

He concealed his purse cunningly, and placed himself between the intruder and its hiding-place.

"Jacob," she said, "you ought to be in bed; why are you up like that? It's three o'clock in the morning."

He began to talk very rapidly. He knew his mother perfectly well. "Mother," he said, "when bailiffs comes you willn't tell 'em where I have hid my brass; see, I've hidden it here, but you willn't tell 'em, mother?" And then he lifted up a corner of the carpet and showed his little purse.

Mrs. Ogden trembled from head to foot. "Our Jacob's crazed," she said to herself — "our Jacob's gone crazed!"

She felt too weak to remain standing, and sat down, never taking her eyes off him. He put the purse back, and covered it again with great care. Then he took his memorandum-book, and seemed to be making an entry.

"Let me look at that book," Mrs. Ogden said.

It was as she had feared. The entry was a hopelessly illegible jumble of unmeaning lines and figures.

"Hadn't you better go to bed?"

"Go to bed, mother — not if I know it!" He said this with a smile of intense cunning, and then added, confidentially, "The bailiffs are comin' to-morrow, and Baron Rothschild has bought all my property, a large price, a million sterling — a million sterling; it's Baron Rothschild that bought it, mother, for a million sterling!"

The poor old woman burst into tears. "O Jacob!" she said, "I wish you wouldn't talk so!"

"Why, mother," he replied, with an injured air, and a look of intense penetration, "you know well enough what I failed for. I never should have failed if it hadn't been for that Sootythorn Bank; but they came to borrow money of me at Milend, and I took up shares for a hundred thousand, and then the smash came, and I failed. But never you mind, mother. Baron Rothschild bought my estates for a million sterling. That shows I was a millionnaire. Doesn't it, mother? for if I hadn't been worth a million, Baron Rothschild wouldn't have given a million for my property. He willn't give more for property than what it's worth."

"O Jacob! you do make me miserable with talking so."

She did not know what to do with him. Young Jacob and her son Isaac were both at Twistle Farm. At last she thought of Colonel Stanburne, who was staying at Wenderholme Cottage. She left her son for a few minutes, and sent a messenger for the Colonel. On returning to Jacob's room, she found him busy counting his money over again. He had taken the purse from its hiding-place.

The strength of her own nervous system was such that she bore even this appalling event with firmness. She was grieved beyond power of expression, but she was not overcome.

Happily there was no violence in Jacob Ogden's madness; he was not in the least dangerous. He simply kept repeating that story about his supposed failure, which he always attributed to the Sootythorn Bank, and the purchase of his property by Baron Rothschild. When the Colonel came, he told him the same story in the same words.

"You are mistaken on one point," the Colonel said. "It was I, Colonel Stanburne, who was ruined by the failure of the Sootythorn Bank, not you. You were never ruined. You purchased Wenderholme."

Mr. Ogden looked at him with the air of a professional man when a layman has advanced something which he knows to be absurd. Then he shook his head, and repeated the story about Baron Rothschild.

The Colonel kindly remained with him till morning, and bravely watched him through the dreary hours. A messenger had been despatched on horseback to Twistle Farm and to Dr. Bardly. Isaac Ogden and his son were at Wenderholme by breakfast-time, and the Doctor's brougham drove up very shortly afterwards.

Dr. Bardly tried to be encouraging. "He has been working too much," he said, "and made himself too anxious; he may get round again with rest and care. Give him good roast-meat and plenty of physical work."

But about ten o'clock Jacob Ogden became anxious to quit Wenderholme, being full of apprehension about the bailiffs. "Better let him have his own way," said the Doctor; so he was taken to Milend.

At Milend, however, there were other causes of anxiety. The bailiffs tormented him at Wenderholme; the idea of Baron Rothschild haunted him at Milend.

The experiment was tried of showing him the factory and the counting-house, but with most discouraging results. The factory produced a degree of excitement which, if continued, would probably lead to madness of an aggravated and far more dangerous kind.

Specialists were telegraphed for from Manchester and from London, and a consultation was held. They agreed that the patient must be kept out of the way of every thing that might remind him of his former career, recommending extreme tranquillity, good but simple diet, and as much physical exercise as the patient could be induced to take.

These might be had conveniently in Mrs. Ogden's favorite little farm, the Cream-pot. It was situated in a glen or clough, out of sight of the Shayton factory-chimneys.

So the old lady went there to live with her afflicted son. She could manage him better than anybody else, and he was never dangerous.

After a time, a happy discovery was made. He counted the money in his purse several times a-day, and Mrs. Ogden told him that if he would dig their little garden, she would pay him wages. He seized upon this idea with great joy and eagerness, and she paid him a sovereign on the Saturday night. The week following he worked very hard, and counted the days, and spoke of his anticipated earnings with delight. So his mother paid him another sovereign, and ever afterwards this became the rule, and she employed him at a pound a-week.

He kept all the sovereigns in his purse, and they were his joy and treasure. His physical health became excellent, and though his intellect gave no hope of restoration, his days passed not unhappily. His mother tended him with the most touching devotion, and a self-sacrifice so absolute that she ceased to visit her friends, and abandoned all the little amusements and varieties of her life.

CHAPTER XIX.

THE COLONEL AT STANITHBURN.

THE long illness and slow convalescence of Mrs. Stanburne, and the deplorable mental affliction which fell upon Jacob Ogden, and threw a cloud of lasting sadness over the whole Ogden family, produced long delays in the projects of young Jacob and Edith, and were the cause of much indecision on the part of the Colonel and Lady Helena. Mrs. Stanburne returned to Wenderholme Cottage in the earliest days of spring, but the Colonel and his wife had already stayed there for many weeks, being anxious not to abuse the kind hospitality of the vicarage. The vicar's sentiments when they left him were of a mixed kind. He was glad, and he was sorry. In his gladness there was no selfish calculation — the Stanburnes were welcome to every thing he could offer them; but in his warm approval of Lady Helena's conduct towards the Colonel, he had been a little too demonstrative to be quite agreeable to Mrs. Prigley, and therefore Mrs. Prigley had thought it incumbent upon her, as a British matron of unspotted virtue, to make his life as miserable as she could. Mrs. Ogden, too, had inflamed Mrs. Prigley's jealousy in another way by coming and nursing Mrs. Stanburne. What right had one of those "nasty Ogdens" to come and nurse Mrs. Stanburne? Mrs. Prigley looked upon the invalid as exclusively her own property. Edith, being young and insignificant, might sit a little with her grandmother — but Mrs. Ogden!

If Lady Helena had not come just in time to take upon

herself a good deal of this now inflamed and awakened jealousy, the consequence would have been that poor Mr. Prigley would have incurred grave suspicions of an amorous intrigue with the old lady of Milend ; but as Lady Helena was younger than Mrs. Prigley, and Mrs. Ogden a good deal her senior, the vicaress paid her husband the compliment of believing that he had placed his sinful affections on the more eligible of the two ladies. So soon, therefore, as she had ascertained to her own satisfaction the culpability of the guilty pair (and when the commonest politeness was evidence, proofs were not far to seek), the vicaress treated her ladyship with the haughty coldness which is the proper behavior of a virtuous and injured woman towards her sinful rival, and she treated her husband as his abominable wickedness deserved. In a word, she made life utterly insupportable for Mr. Prigley.

Lady Helena saw the true situation of affairs before the parson did (for he in his masculine simplicity attributed his wife's behavior to any cause but the right one), and she migrated at once to the Cottage with the Colonel. When Mrs. Stanburne was well enough to bear the removal, she was brought back to her old house, and continued steadily to improve. Still her health was far from being strong enough to make the idea of leaving her an admissible one, so the Colonel and Lady Helena remained at Wenderholme a long time. Young Jacob came frequently to see Edith, but the marriage, though now agreed upon by all parties, was indefinitely postponed.

Whilst matters were in this state of suspension, the relation between Mr. Jacob Ogden and his family had to be legally settled. His brother Isaac received the factories and estates, in trust, conjointly with his mother, with the usufruct thereof, £500 a-year being set aside for the patient's maintenance. On account of the urgency of the situation, but much against the grain of his now acquired habits, Mr. Isaac Ogden quitted his solitude at Twistle Farm, and resumed, at Milend, the life of a cotton-manufacturer, in partnership with his son.

Meanwhile Colonel Stanburne's position was, from the financial point of view, any thing but brilliant. He had no income, after paying the allowance to his mother, except a share in the £300 a-year remaining to his wife. He was anxious to return to France and resume the humble profession which he had found for himself there. Lady Helena said that wherever he went she would go too, and nothing but the slowness of Mrs. Stanburne's recovery prevented them from leaving England.

They were in this state — being, as things in life often are, in a sort of temporary but indefinite lull and calm — when an event occurred which produced the most important changes.

Mr. John Stedman being on a visit to his friend at Stanithburn Peel, took one of his customary long walks amongst the wild rocky hills in that neighborhood, and was caught — not for the first time — in a sudden storm of rain. By the time the storm was over he was wet through, but being interested in the search for a plant, went on wandering till rather late in the evening. If he had kept constantly in movement it is probable that no harm would have resulted from this little imprudence, but unfortunately he found the plant he was in search of, and this led him to do a little botanical anatomy with a microscope which he carried in his pocket. Absorbed in this occupation, he sat down on the bare rock, and forgot the minutes as they passed. He spent more than an hour in this way, and rose from his task with a feeling of chill, and a slight shiver, which, however, disappeared when his pedestrian exercise was resumed. On returning to the Peel he thought no more of the matter, and ate a hearty dinner, sitting rather late afterwards with Philip Stanburne, and drinking more than his usual allowance of brandy-and-water. The next day he did not go out, and towards evening complained of a slight pain or embarrassment in the chest. The symptoms gradually became alarming, a doctor was sent for, and Mr. Stedman's illness was discovered to be a congestion of both lungs.

Of this malady he died. In his will, after various legacies, liberal but not excessive, to all the poor people who were his relations, and the relations of his deceased wife, he named "his dear friend and son, Philip Stanburne," residuary legatee, "both in token of his own friendship and gratitude towards the said Philip Stanburne, and also because in making this bequest the testator believes that he is best fulfilling the wishes of his beloved daughter, Alice."

But, notwithstanding John Stedman's affectionate friendship for the man whom Alice had loved, there still remained in him much of the resolution of a stalwart enemy of Rome, and the resolution dictated a certain codicil written not long before his death. In this codicil he provided that, "in case the said Philip Stanburne should enter any order of the Church of Rome, whether secular or ecclesiastical, or endow the said Church of Rome with any portion of his wealth, then the foregoing will and testament should be void, and of none effect. And further, that the said Philip Stanburne should solemnly promise never to give or bequeath to the Church of Rome any portion of this bequest, and in case of his refusal to make such promise," the money should be disposed of as we will now explain.

The testator proceeded to affirm that it was still his desire to leave part of his property in such a manner as to testify his gratitude to Philip Stanburne ; and therefore, if the latter took orders in the Church of Rome, Mr. Stedman's bequest should still pass to a person of the name of Stanburne, but professing the Protestant religion — namely, to John Stanburne, formerly of Wenderholme. In this case, however, a large deduction would be made from the legacy in favor of an intimate friend of the testator, Joseph Anison, formerly of Arkwright Lodge, near Whittlecup. All this was set forth with that minute and tedious detail which is necessary, or is supposed to be necessary, in every legal document.

Now for several years past Philip Stanburne had been firmly resolved, on the death of Mr. Stedman (which would release him from his promise to Alice), to enter a monastic order remarkable for industry and simplicity of life, founded by the celebrated Father Muard, but since affiliated to the Benedictines; and it was a suspicion of this resolve, or perhaps more than a suspicion, which had dictated Mr. Stedman's codicil. The will made no difference in Philip Stanburne's plans, and he was delighted that the Colonel should inherit what would probably turn out to be a fortune. When the question was formally put to him, he affirmed his intention of being a monk of *La Pierre qui Vire.*

In consequence of this declaration, the codicil took effect. The factory in Sootythorn, the house at Chesnut Hill, and a capital sum of £20,000, went to Mr. Joseph Anison; but even after all the legacies to poor relations, there still remained a residue of £35,000, which passed directly to the Colonel. Mr. Stedman had been much richer than any one believed, and his fortune, already considerable in the lifetime of his daughter, had doubled since her death.

Philip Stanburne, who had been occasionally to Wenderholme since the Colonel's return, to inquire after Mrs. Stanburne, and pass an hour or two with an old friend, now proposed to sell him Stanithburn Peel. "It would make me miserable," he said, "to sell it to anybody else, but to you it's different. Buy it, and go to live there."

But he did not really sell the Peel itself. He sold the land, and gave the strong old tower. The place was valued by friends, mutually appointed, who received a hint from Philip that they were not to count the Peel. The Colonel knew nothing about this, but gave £20,000 for the estate, and invested the remainder of his capital in something better than the Sootythorn Bank.

CHAP. XIX. *The Colonel at Stanithburn.* 423

As Mrs. Stanburne was now well enough to be left, the Colonel and Lady Helena set off one fine day for Stanithburn. The Peel had been admirably restored, though with great moderation, in Philip Stanburne's quiet and persevering way, and all its incongruities and anachronisms had been removed. When they came to the front door, who should open it but — Fyser!

"Please, sir," he said, "would you be so kind as to take me on again?"

The Colonel said not a word in answer, but he gave honest Fyser's hand such a shake that it was perfectly natural the tears should come into his eyes. The tears would come into anybody's eyes if his hand was squeezed like that.

Whilst her ladyship went to take her things off, Fyser said, "Would you like to step this way, sir?" The Colonel followed obediently.

"This will be your den, I suppose, sir, unless you would like to have it in another part of the 'ouse."

John Stanburne felt like a man in a dream. There was every scrap of his old den-furniture in the place. Philip Stanburne had bought it all at the Wenderholme sale — every atom of it, even to his old boot-jack. And as Mr. Fyser had had the arrangement of it, you may be sure that it was in the old convenient and accustomed order.

But the Colonel and Lady Helena were still more surprised to find in the principal rooms of the house various cabinets and other things of value which had formerly been at Wenderholme, and especially a museum of family relics which had occupied the centre of the great hall. In these cabinets and cases little plates of silver were discovered, on examination, to be inlaid, and each of these little plates was engraved with the inscription, "Presented to Colonel Stanburne by the Officers of the Twentieth Royal Lancashire Militia."

The regiment happened to be just then up for its annual training under a major-commanding, no new colonel having as yet been appointed. And one day there came rather a solemn deputation of officers to Stanithburn Peel, all in full uniform.

The spokesman of the deputation was our old acquaintance, Captain Eureton. He began by informing Colonel Stanburne that, although the lieutenant-colonelcy had been offered to the senior major, he had begged the lord-lieutenant to permit him to remain at the head of the regiment as major-commanding ; and that now he and all the officers unanimously joined in entreating Colonel Stanburne to withdraw his resignation, and resume his old position amongst them. There was no mistaking the earnestness and sincerity of this petition, and John Stanburne consented. He was received at Sootythorn at a great banquet given by the officers just before the disbanding of the regiment ; and at the review which concluded the training, it was John Stanburne who commanded.

CHAPTER XX.

A SIMPLE WEDDING.

"I COULD so like to go to little Jacob weddin'," said Mrs. Ogden one day in her little home at the Cream-pot, " but I 'm like as if I were 'feard to leave our Jacob for one single day. He 's just same as a childt, an' to-morrow 's his pay-day, an' I couldn't like anybody else to pay him his week's wage. But what I suppose they 'll be just as well wed as if I 'd been there, for that matter."

It seems to us quite a pity that Mrs. Ogden could not contrive to be at Wenderholme church on the wedding-day, for she would have been well received by Mrs. Stanburne at the breakfast given by that lady at Wenderholme Cottage, but ever since "our Jacob misfortin'" no power on earth could get her away from the Cream-pot, and all reasoning on the subject was trouble thrown away. Little Jacob's weddingday passed like all other monotonous days for Mrs. Ogden, so far as action or variety was concerned, but she thought of him from morning till night. As for the elder Jacob, he tranquilly pursued his digging in the garden, looking forward with eager anticipation to the payment of his week's wages on the same evening, for he had some consciousness of the lapse of time, especially towards the close of the week. On Thursdays he began to ask if it were not Saturday, on Fridays the question became frequent, and on Saturday itself his mother had to promise a hundred times that she would pay his wages at six o'clock. His old habits of energy and perseverance were still visible in his daily work. He labored conscientiously to make the garden produce as much as spade labor could do for it, he carefully economized every inch of ground, and did all that mere physical labor could for its advantage. On the other hand, wherever the intelligence of a gardener was necessary, his shattered intellect was constantly at fault, and he committed the wildest havoc. He rooted up the garden-flowers as weeds, and could only recognize one or two of the most familiar and most productive plants. He knew the carrot, for example, and the potato, and these he cultivated in his own strange way. His mother sacrificed the little Cream-pot garden to him entirely, and got the vegetables for house use from Milend, and the fruit from Wenderholme, so that he could destroy or cultivate at his own absolute will and pleasure, and this he did with the cunning and self-satisfaction of the insane.

The evening of that day when little Jacob was married, his grandmother had a new idea about her afflicted son. "Jacob," she said to him when the time for payment came, and his eyes were glistening as he clutched the golden coin, "Jacob, thou shouldn't let thy money lie by same as that without gettin' interest for it. There's twenty pound in thy purse by this. Lend me thy twenty pound, an' I'll give thee five per cent, that'll make a pound a-year interest for thee."

When the magical word "interest" sounded in his ear for the first time since the break-down of his mental faculties, uncle Jacob's face assumed a look of intelligence which startled his mother and gave her a gleam of hope. "Interest, interest!" he said, and paused as if lost in thought; then he added, "Compound interest! doubles up, compound interest, doubles up fast!" These words, however, must have been mere reminiscences of his former state, for he proved utterly incapable of understanding the nature of even simple interest as a weekly payment. Mrs. Ogden offered him sixpence as a week's interest for his money, but he asked for a sovereign, being accustomed to weekly payments of one pound, and he seemed troubled and irritated when it was not given to him. He understood the pound a week for his digging, but he could not grasp any more complicated idea. His constant secret occupation, when not at work, was to handle his accumulating sovereigns. In this way, notwithstanding his insanity and his incapability of imagining the great fortune he had heaped up when in health, he enjoyed money as much as ever, for the mere quantity has really very little to do with the delight of the passion of avarice. It is the *increase* which gives delight, not the quantity, and Jacob Ogden's private store was incessantly increasing, so much indeed that his mother had to give him a money-box. When the weekly sovereigns became numerous, he was incapable of counting them, but he had a certain sense of quantity and a keen satisfaction in the evident increase of his store.

Little Jacob's marriage was strangely simple, considering the wealth of one of the two families and the station of the other; but the elder Jacob's condition, and recent events in the life of Colonel Stanburne, had so sobered everybody that there was not the slightest desire on either side for any demonstration or display. As it concerned Lady Helena, this simplicity was not displeasing to her, for reasons of her own. She was glad, in her own mind, that Mrs. Ogden did not come, for she keenly dreaded the old lady's strange sayings on a semi-public occasion like the present, and the privacy of the marriage was a good excuse for not inviting many of her own noble friends. The bridesmaids were the Prigley girls and a young sister of Lady Helena. Mr. Prigley performed the ceremony, and there was not a stranger in the little Wenderholme church, except a reporter for the "Sootythorn Gazette," who furnished a brilliant account of this "marriage in high life," which we have no disposition to quote.

If Mrs. Ogden had chosen to bring to bear upon poor Edith all the weight of her terrible critical power as a supreme judge of housekeeping accomplishments, I am afraid that the young lady would have come out of the ordeal ignominiously for she could neither darn a stocking properly nor make a potato-pie, but criticism is often mollified by personal favor and partiality; and the old lady never goes farther in the severity of censure than to say, "Little Jacob wife is not much of a housekeeper, but she was never brought up to it you know; and they'll have plenty to live upon, so it willn't matter so much as it would 'ave done if they'd been poorer people."

Poverty is certainly not the evil which the young couple need apprehend, for the condition of Jacob Ogden the elder being considered permanent, a judicial decision transferred his income to his brother Isaac, after deducting £1,000 a year for his maintenance, which was paid to his mother; an entirely superfluous formality, as she accumulated the whole of it for her grandson, and kept Jacob Ogden well supplied with all that he needed, or had intelligence to desire, out of her own little independent fortune. Isaac Ogden was now charged with the management of the business and estates. It then became apparent how splendidly successful the life of the cotton-manufacturer had been. At the time of the opening of this history, he was already earning, or rather *netting*, since the operatives earned it for him, an income larger than the salary of a Prime Minister, and successive years raised him to a pecuniary equality with the Lord Chancellor, the Archbishop of Canterbury, and the Governor-General of India. At the time of his cerebral catastrophe, he was at the height of his success; and his numerous rills and rivers of income, flowing from properties of all kinds, from shares, from the print-works at Whittlecup, and from his enormous mill at Shayton, made, when added together, an aggregate far surpassing the national allowance to princes of royal blood. In a word, at the time of what Mrs. Ogden always called "our Jacob's misfortin'," "our Jacob" had just got past £50,000 a year, and was beginning to encourage the not improbable anticipation that his income would get up to the hundred thousand before he died. Such as it was already, it exceeded by exactly one thousand times the pittance for which, as the slave of his own disordered imagination, he was now toiling from morning till night.

Nothing is more difficult than to get rid of a great business. Such mills as Jacob Ogden's are very difficult to let, and to close them entirely would be to throw a whole neighborhood out of work and diminish the value of property within a considerable radius. There was nothing for it, therefore, but to keep the business going, so Mr. Isaac Ogden threw aside his habits of leisure at Twistle Farm and came to live at Milend. He managed the work for some time with considerable energy; but he had been so long unused to the employment, that this business life, with its incessant claims upon time and attention, required a constant effort of the will, and he felt himself incapable of continuing it indefinitely. Young Jacob helped him energetically; but the vast concern which his uncle had established, with the addition of the print-works at Whittlecup, required more looking after than even he was equal to; so in order that Isaac Ogden might have some leisure at Twistle Farm, and be able to join the militia at the annual training, the calico business at Whittlecup had to be given up. It could not be sold during old Jacob Ogden's life; but it was let, together with Arkwright Lodge, to Mr. Joseph Anison, on terms exceedingly advantageous to the latter, who will be able, after all, to give handsome dowries to his younger daughters, and to leave Miss Margaret the richest old maid in Whittlecup.

Young Jacob and his wife established themselves at Wenderholme, but she soon complained that he was too much away on business, and declared her intention of accompanying him on his journeys to Milend, which she has ever since been in the habit of doing. When at Milend (which has been much beautified and improved), they go a great deal to the

Cream-pot, where old Mrs. Ogden still devotes herself to the care of her unfortunate son. "I'm thankful to God," she says, "that our Jacob is so 'appy with his misfortin'. Every time I give him his sovereign of a Saturday night he's as 'appy and proud as a little lad ten year old. And he's as well in 'ealth as anybody could wish for." Young Jacob and Edith are both very attentive to him, but it is thought better not to bring him to Wenderholme again, nor even to Milend. This makes it a great tie for poor Mrs. Ogden, but she fulfils her duty with a noble self-abnegation, and tends "our Jacob" with the most minute and unrelaxing care. As for her fine carriage, she made a wedding-present of it to Edith, and has never been in it since, not even to do a little knitting. Her life is the simple old life that she was accustomed to in her youth, and it suits her health so well, that if all old women that one hears of did not finish some day by dying, one might almost expect her to prolong her sojourn permanently upon the earth, in the green "Cream-pot" fields. But the recent death of old Sarah at Twistle Farm has been a serious warning, and the new Shayton clergyman is a frequent visitor at the Cream-pot. Dr. Bardly is not so much in request, on account of his heterodox views, and because Mrs. Ogden's physical condition is still excellent, whatever may be her spiritual state.

CHAPTER XXI.

THE MONK.

THE Colonel and Lady Helena made a tour on the continent in the autumn, and visited the little French city where he had earned his living as a teacher of English.

Young Jacob and Edith accompanied them as far as Geneva, and on their way from Paris it was decided that they should stop at Auxerre, and go thence to Avallon, which was not very far from the monastery of *La Pierre qui Vire.* The Colonel desired to see Philip Stanburne once again.

Through narrow and rocky valleys, indescribably picturesque, and full of a deep melancholy poetry of their own, they journeyed a whole day, and came at last to the confines of the monastery, in a wild stony desert amongst the hills, through which flowed a rapid stream. The ladies could not enter, but young Jacob and the Colonel passed through the simple gateway. A monk received them in silence, and, in answer to a question of the Colonel, put his finger upon his lips. He then went to ask permission to speak from his superior.

The monk promised to lead the Colonel to Philip Stanburne. They passed along wild paths cut in the rock and the forest, with rudely carved bas-reliefs of the chief scenes of the Passion erected at stated distances. They saw many monks engaged in the most laborious manual occupations: some were washing linen in the clear river; others were road-making, with picks and wheel-barrows; others were hard at work as masons, building the walls of some future portion of the monastery, or the enclosures of its fields. All worked and were silent, not even looking at the strangers as they passed. At length the three came to a little wood, and, having passed through the wood, to a small field on the steep slope of a hill. In the field two monks were ploughing in their monastic dress, with a pair of white oxen.

Suddenly the Angelus rang from the belfry of the monastery, and its clear tones filled the quiet valley where these monks had made their home. All the monks heard it, and all who heard it fell instantaneously on their knees in the midst of their labor, wherever they might happen to be. The masons dropped their stones and trowels, the washermen prayed with the wet linen still in their grasp, the ploughman knelt between the handles of his plough, and the driver with the goad in his right hand. The Colonel's guide dropped upon the ploughed earth, and prayed. All in the valley prayed.

When this was over, the two Englishmen were led forward towards the oxen, and before the slow animals had resumed their toil, the Colonel had recognized their driver. So this was the life he had chosen — a life of rudest labor, with the simplest food and the severest discipline — a life of toil and silence. He knew the Colonel at once, but dared not speak to him, and placed his fingers on his lips, and goaded his oxen forward, and resumed his weary march.

A special permission having been procured, the monk talked with John Stanburne freely, saying that he loved his new life and the hardships of it, dwelling with quiet enthusiasm on the beautiful discipline of his order, and leading him over the rude and picturesque lands which had been reclaimed by the industry of his brethren.

But when they parted, there came a great pang of regret in Philip Stanburne's heart for the free English life that he had lost — a pang of regret for Stanithburn, and that Alice should not be mistress there instead of Lady Helena.

And after the service in the humble chapel of the monastery — a service singularly devoid of the splendors of the Catholic worship — a monk lay prostrate across the threshold, doing penance. And all his brethren passed over him, one by one.

MR. HAMERTON'S WORKS.

The style of this writer is a truly admirable one, light and picturesque, without being shallow, and dealing with all subjects in a charming way. Whenever our readers see or hear of one of Mr. Hamerton's books, we advise them to read it." — SPRINGFIELD REPUBLICAN.

THE INTELLECTUAL LIFE. Square 12mo. Price $2.00.

"Not every day do we take hold of a book that we would fain have always near us, a book that we read only to want to read again and again, that is so vitalized with truth, so helpful in its relation to humanity, that we would almost sooner buy it for our friend than spare him our copy to read. Such a book is 'The Intellectual Life,' by Philip Gilbert Hamerton, itself one of the rarest and noblest fruits of that life of which it treats. (Here we must beg the pardon of our younger readers, since what we have to say about this book is not for them, but for their parents, and older brothers and sisters, though we can have no better wish for them than that they may soon be wise and thoughtful enough to enjoy it too.)

"Just how much this book would be worth to each individual reader it would be quite impossible to say, but we can hardly conceive of any human mind, born with the irresistible instincts toward the intellectual life, that would not find in it not only ample food for deep reflection, but also living waters of the sweetest consolation and encouragement.

"We wonder how many readers of this noble volume, under a sense of personal gratitude, have stopped to exclaim with its author, in a similar position, 'Now the only Crœsus that I envy is he who is reading a better book than this.'" — *From the Children's Friend.*

THOUGHTS ABOUT ART. New Edition, Revised, with Notes and an Introduction. "*Fortunate is he who at an early age knows what art is.*" — GOETHE. Square 12mo. Price $2.00.

"The whole volume is adapted to give a wholesome stimulus to the taste for art, and to place it in an intelligent and wise direction. With a knowledge of the principles, which it sets forth in a style of peculiar fascination, the reader is prepared to enjoy the wonders of ancient and modern art, with a fresh sense of their beauty, and a critical recognition of the sources of their power." — *New York Tribune.*

"Beginning with a recommendation to capable artists to write on art, and illustrating his arguments on this point by some forcible illustrations, Mr. Hamerton proceeds to discuss the different styles of painting, defines the place of landscape among the fine arts, treats of the relation between photography and painting, makes some curious comparisons between word-painting and color-painting, speaks of the painter in his relation to society, and finally offers some practical and valuable suggestions concerning picture-buying and the choice of furniture of artistic patterns for our houses. All these subdivisions of the general subject are touched airily and pleasantly, but not flippantly, and the book is delightful from beginning to end." — *New York Commercial Advertiser.*

A PAINTER'S CAMP. A new edition, in 1 vol. 16mo.
Price $1.50. Square 12mo. Price $2.00.

"We are not addicted to enthusiasm, but the little work before us is really so full of good points that we grow so admiring as to appear almost fulsome in its praise. . . . It has been many a day since we have been called upon to review a work which gave us such real pleasure" — *Philadelphia Evening Telegraph.*

"If any reader whose eye chances to meet this article has read 'The Painter's Camp,' by Mr. Philip Gilbert Hamerton, he will need but little stimulus to feel assured that the same author's work, entitled 'Thoughts about Art,' is worth his attention. The former, I confess, was so unique that no author should be expected to repeat the sensation produced by it. Like the 'Adventures of Robinson Crusoe,' or the 'Swiss Family Robinson,' it brought to maturer minds, as those do to all, the flavor of breezy out-of-door experiences, — an aroma of poetry and adventure combined. It was full of art, and art-discussions too; and yet it needed no mere technical knowledge to understand and enjoy it." — *Joel Benton.*

"They ('A Painter's Camp' and 'Thoughts about Art') are the most useful books that could be placed in the hands of the American art public. If we were asked where the most intelligent, the most trustworthy, the most practical, and the most interesting exposition of modern art and cognate subjects is to be found, we should point to Hamerton's writings." — *The Atlantic Monthly.*

THE UNKNOWN RIVER: An Etcher's Voyage of Discovery. With an original Preface for the American edition, and thirty-seven plates etched by the author. One elegant 8vo volume, bound in cloth, extra, gilt, and gilt edges. Price $6.00. (A cheaper edition now ready.)

"Wordsworth might like to come back to earth for a summer, and voyage with Philip Gilbert Hamerton down some 'Unknown River"! If this supposition seem extravagant to any man, let him buy and read 'The Unknown River, an Etcher's Voyage of Discovery,' by P. G. Hamerton. It is not easy to write soberly about this book while fresh from its presence. The subtle charm of the very title is indescribable; it lays hold in the outset on the deepest romance in every heart; it is the very voyage we are all yearning for. When, later on, we are told that this 'Unknown River' is the Arroux, in the eastern highlands of France, that it empties into the Loire, and has on its shores ancient towns of historic interest, we do not quite believe it. Mr. Hamerton has flung a stronger spell by his first word than he knew.

"It is not too much to say that this book is artistically perfect, perfectly artistic, and a poem from beginning to end; the phrasing of its story is as exquisite as the etching of its pictures; each heightens the other; each corroborates the other; and both together blend in harmonious and beautiful witness to what must have been one of the most delicious journeys ever made by a solitary traveller. The word solitary, however, has no meaning when applied to Hamerton, poet, painter, adventurous man, all in one, and with a heart for a dog! There is no empty or barren spot on earth for such as he. The book cannot be analyzed nor described in any way which will give strangers to it any idea of its beauty." — *Scribner's Monthly.*

CHAPTERS ON ANIMALS. With Twenty Illustrations by J. VEYRASSAT and KARL BODMER. Square 12mo. Price $2.00.

"This is a choice book. No trainer of animals, no whipper-in of a kennel, no master of fox-hounds, no equine parson, could have written this book. Only such a man as Hamerton could have written it, who, by virtue of his great love of art, has been a quick and keen observer of nature, who has lived with and loved animal nature, and made friends and companions of the dog and horse and bird. And of such, how few there are! We like to amuse ourselves for an idle moment with any live thing that has grace and color and strength. We like to show our wealth in fine equipages; to be followed by a fond dog at our heel, to hunt foxes and bag birds, but we like all this merely in the way of ostentation or personal pleasure. But as for caring really for animals, so as to study their happiness, to make them, knowing us, love us, so as to adapt ourselves to themselves, is quite another thing. Mr. Hamerton has observed to much purpose, for he has a curious sympathy with the 'painful mystery of brute

www.ingramcontent.com/pod-product-compliance
Lightning Source LLC
Chambersburg PA
CBHW032010300426
44117CB00008B/968